Complexity Theory and the Philosophy of Education

Lea....
Services

D1346805

Complexity Theory and the Philosophy of Education

Edited by
Mark Mason

WILEY-BLACKWELL

A John Wiley & Sons, Ltd., Publication

This edition first published 2008
Chapters © 2008 the Authors
Book Compilation © 2008 Philosophy of Education Society of Australasia
First published as a special issue of *Educational Philosophy and Theory* (volume 40, issue 1)

Blackwell Publishing was acquired by John Wiley & Sons in February 2007. Blackwell's publishing program has been merged with Wiley's global Scientific, Technical, and Medical business to form Wiley-Blackwell.

Registered Office
John Wiley & Sons Ltd, The Atrium, Southern Gate, Chichester, West Sussex, PO19 8SQ, United Kingdom

Editorial Offices
350 Main Street, Malden, MA 02148-5020, USA
9600 Garsington Road, Oxford, OX4 2DQ, UK
The Atrium, Southern Gate, Chichester, West Sussex, PO19 8SQ, UK

For details of our global editorial offices, for customer services, and for information about how to apply for permission to reuse the copyright material in this book please see our website at www.wiley.com/wiley-blackwell.

The right of Mark Mason to be identified as the author of the editorial material in this work has been asserted in accordance with the Copyright, Designs and Patents Act 1988.

All rights reserved. No part of this publication may be reproduced, stored in a retrieval system, or transmitted, in any form or by any means, electronic, mechanical, photocopying, recording or otherwise, except as permitted by the UK Copyright, Designs and Patents Act 1988, without the prior permission of the publisher.

Wiley also publishes its books in a variety of electronic formats. Some content that appears in print may not be available in electronic books.

Designations used by companies to distinguish their products are often claimed as trademarks. All brand names and product names used in this book are trade names, service marks, trademarks or registered trademarks of their respective owners. The publisher is not associated with any product or vendor mentioned in this book. This publication is designed to provide accurate and authoritative information in regard to the subject matter covered. It is sold on the understanding that the publisher is not engaged in rendering professional services. If professional advice or other expert assistance is required, the services of a competent professional should be sought.

Library of Congress Cataloging-in-Publication Data

Complexity theory and the philosophy of education / edited by Mark Mason.
    p. cm.
Includes bibliographical references and index.
ISBN 978-1-4051-8042-9 (pbk. : alk. paper) 1. Education–Philosophy. 2. Computational complexity. I. Mason, Mark, 1959-
LB14.7.C652 2008
370.1–dc22
                2008027427

A catalogue record for this book is available from the British Library.

Set in 10pt Plantin by Graphicraft Limited, Hong Kong
Printed in Singapore by Fabulous Printers Pte Ltd

01 2008

Contents

NORWICH CITY COLLEGE

Stock No.	237 355	
Class	370·1	MAS
Cat.	SSA	Proc	3wL

Notes on Contributors

Michel Alhadeff-Jones is currently Instructor at Teachers College, Columbia University, in the Department of Organization and Leadership. He is also associated with the Interuniversity Research Centre EXPERICE (Experience, Cultural Resources and Education, Universities of Paris 8 and Paris 13). He studied psychology and taught in the Department of Adult Education at the University of Geneva before completing his PhD in educational sciences at the University of Paris 8. Based on Edgar Morin's philosophy, his doctoral dissertation developed an epistemological and methodological framework to design a multi-referential approach to *critique* as a complex phenomenon. His teaching and research interests are in critical and complexity theories, French and English-language philosophies of education, adult learning, biographical approaches, trans-disciplinarity, and science studies. He has published several papers and chapters related to these issues.

Gert Biesta is Professor of Education at the Institute of Education, University of Stirling in Scotland, and Visiting Professor for Education and Democratic Citizenship at Örebro University and Mälardalen University, Sweden. He is Editor-in-Chief of *Studies in Philosophy and Education*. His research focuses on the relationships between education and democracy, the philosophy and methodology of educational research, and lifelong learning in formal and non-formal settings. He takes inspiration from pragmatism (Dewey, Mead) and poststructuralism (Derrida, Levinas, Foucault). Recent books include *Derrida and Education* (co-edited with Denise Egéa-Kuehne, Routledge, 2001), *Pragmatism and Educational Research* (co-authored with Nicholas Burbules, Rowman & Littlefield, 2003), *Beyond Learning: Democratic education for a human future* (Paradigm Publishers, 2006), and *Improving Learning Cultures in Further Education* (with David James, Routledge, 2008).

Paul Cilliers is Professor of Philosophy at the University of Stellenbosch in South Africa. He teaches Cultural Philosophy, Deconstruction and Philosophy of Science. He also has a degree in Electronic Engineering and worked professionally as an engineer for many years. His research is focused on the philosophical and ethical implications of complexity theory and he has published widely in the field. He is the author of *Complexity and Postmodernism* (Routledge, 1998). He also has a lively interest in literature and music.

Brent Davis is Professor and David Robitaille Chair in Mathematics, Science, and Technology Education in the Faculty of Education at the University of British Columbia. His research is developed around the educational relevance of recent developments in the cognitive and complexity sciences. He is a founding co-editor of *Complicity: An International Journal of Complexity and Education* and current editor of *For the Learning of Mathematics*. He has published books and articles in the areas of mathematics learning and teaching, curriculum theory, teacher education, epistemology, and action research.

William Doll is the V. F. and J. R. Eagles Emeritus Professor of Curriculum at Louisiana State University. In his 53 years of teaching he has taught all grades and most subjects. He has done administration at the school, college, and university level. He has also served on the Fulton, NY Board of Education. Professor Doll holds degrees from Cornell University, Boston University, and The Johns Hopkins University. He has taught at SUNY-Oswego, the University of Redlands, and now LSU, where he formerly directed the Holmes Elementary Education program and co-directed the Curriculum Theory Project. His books are *A Post-Modern Perspective on Curriculum, Curriculum Visions* (co-edited), and *Chaos, Complexity, Curriculum and Culture* (co-edited). He also contributed to *The Internationalization of Curriculum Studies* (edited by his wife, Donna Trueit). William Doll is a Fulbright Senior Scholar, and in 2005 was awarded the American Educational Research Association's Division B Lifetime Achievement Award. Interests in international education take Professor Doll regularly to Finland and China. His website is at www.lsu.edu/faculty/wdoll.

Tamsin Haggis is Lecturer in Lifelong Learning at the Institute of Education at the University of Stirling. Her research focuses on the different ways that learning is defined, researched and theorised, particularly within the field of Higher Education. More generally she is exploring the possibilities of complexity and dynamic systems theories in relation to theory, epistemology and method in educational research. She is a co-investigator in the EPSRC-funded project 'Emerging Sustainability', a cross-disciplinary project focussed on the theme of Emergence, which is in turn connected to three other projects: The Emergence of Culture in Robot Societies; Biological Metaphors and Crisis: Building Self-Healing, Emergence and Resilience into Critical Infrastructures; and Defying the Rules: How Self-regulatory Social Systems Work.

James Horn is Assistant Professor of Educational Foundations at Monmouth University, where he teaches courses in educational theory and practice, educational philosophy and history, and research. His scholarly interests include the social and cultural effects of educational policy implementation, the understanding of autonomous learning systems, and the development of educational thinking consistent with the new sciences of complexity.

Tammy Iftody is a doctoral student in the Department of Curriculum Studies at the University of British Columbia. Her research interests bring a complexivist orientation to understandings of popular culture, curriculum, computer-mediated communication, and studies in consciousness.

Lesley Kuhn is a Senior Lecturer in the College of Business at the University of Western Sydney in Australia. Dr. Kuhn's academic interests are in applied philosophy. Her research and teaching are concerned with exploring and promoting human agency and epistemic awareness, flexibility and humility. She holds degrees in music, education, environmental science and philosophy, with her doctoral work focussing on the nature of epistemology and belief. Over the past ten years Dr. Kuhn has been active in leading the development of complexity informed ethnographic research approaches. She is the author of more than 40 book chapters and published articles, and has led more than 30 research projects. Most recently she edited a special issue of *World Futures: The Journal of General Evolution*, show-casing the work of UWS academics in bringing complexity informed approaches to social inquiry. Her book, *Adventures for Organisations near the Edge of Chaos*, is due for completion in 2008.

Jay L. Lemke is Professor of Educational Studies at the University of Michigan and Co-editor of the journal *Critical Discourse Studies*. He took his PhD at the University of Chicago in theoretical physics and is the author of *Talking Science* (1990), *Textual Politics* (1995), and numerous contributions to the theory and applications of functional linguistics, social semiotics and multimedia semiotics in education and sociocultural studies. His current research interests include analysis of meaning-making and experience across multiple timescales and issues of institutional and organizational change.

Rebecca Luce-Kapler is Professor of Language and Literacy in the Faculty of Education at Queen's University in Kingston, Ontario, Canada. Her research focuses on writing processes and technologies. Her book, *Writing With, Through and Beyond the Text: An ecology of language*, brings together her work with women writers and her understanding of learning, writing, and teaching. She has been a fiction writer and poet for over 25 years, and is the author of a collection of poetry, *The Gardens Where She Dreams*.

Mark Mason is Associate Professor in Philosophy and Educational Studies in the Faculty of Education at the University of Hong Kong, where he is also Director of the Comparative Education Research Centre (CERC). With research interests in philosophy, educational studies, comparative education and educational development, he is Regional Editor (Asia & The Pacific) of the *International Journal of Educational Development*, Editor of the *CERC Studies in Comparative Education Series* (co-published by Springer), and President of the Comparative Education Society of Hong Kong. He has published some fifty articles, chapters and books in these research areas. His philosophical research interest in complexity theory and education led to the invitation from the Editor of *Educational Philosophy and Theory* to edit this book.

Keith Morrison taught in schools in the UK for many years before moving into higher education. He has worked in higher education for over twenty-five years, in the UK and Macau, formerly at the University of Durham, UK, and currently as Professor, Vice-Rector and Dean at the Macau Inter-University Institute. He is the author of twelve books, including *Research Methods in Education (6th edition)*, *School Leadership and Complexity Theory*, and *A Guide to Teaching Practice (5th edition)*, and around one hundred articles in his areas of interest. He is the editor of the journal *Evaluation and Research in Education*. His current fields of research include research methodology and evaluation, critical theory and policy scholarship, complexity theory and management, curriculum and assessment development, management and leadership, and the sociology of the curriculum.

Mark Olssen is Professor of Political Theory and Education Policy in the Department of Political, International and Policy Studies at the University of Surrey. His most recent book is *Michel Foucault: Materialism and education*, published by Paradigm Press in 2006. He has also published recently a book with John Codd and Anne-Marie O'Neill, titled *Education Policy: Globalisation, citizenship, democracy* (Sage, 2004); an edited volume, *Culture and Learning: Access and opportunity in the classroom* (IAP Press); with Michael Peters and Colin Lankshear, *Critical Theory and the Human Condition: Founders and praxis*; and *Futures of Critical Theory: Dreams of difference*, also with Peters and Lankshear (Rowman & Littlefield). He has published extensively in leading academic journals in Britain, North America and Australasia.

Deborah Osberg is a lecturer in Education in the School of Education and Lifelong Learning at the University of Exeter in England. Her work is inspired by Prigoginean complexity and Derridean deconstruction, and she uses the closely associated notions of 'dynamic relationality' and 'emergence' to rethink aspects of educational theory and practice. She is Editor-in-Chief of *Complicity: An International Journal of Complexity and Education*.

Mike Radford is based in the Canterbury Christ Church University (UK) Faculty of Education and is Programme Director for the Doctorate in Education programme. His PhD on philosophical and psychological issues in relation to the concept of intelligence was completed at Leeds, and he has substantial teaching experience in schools and universities across the UK. His research interests include aesthetic, religious and spiritual education as well as issues in social and educational research. He has published papers on complexity and educational research in leading international journals.

Nora H. Sabelli is Senior Science Advisor at the Center for Technology in Learning, at SRI International. She earned her PhD in theoretical chemistry at the University of Buenos Aires, Argentina, for research undertaken at the University of Chicago. Her research interests are in the use of new scientific metrologies in science education, including complexity, visualization, and other applications of modern technologies.

Inna Semetsky joined the Research Institute of Advanced Study for Humanity at the University of Newcastle in Australia after a two-year (2005–2007) Postdoctoral Research Fellowship in the Faculty of Education at Monash University. Her book, *Deleuze, Education and Becoming*, was published by Sense Publishers in 2006 in their series, 'Educational Futures: Rethinking Theory and Practice'. In 2004 and 2005 she guest-edited two special issues of *Educational Philosophy and Theory*, 'Peirce and Education', and 'Deleuze and Education'. In 2007 she was guest editor of a special issue, 'Semiotics and Education', of *Studies in Philosophy and Education*, published by Springer.

Dennis Sumara is Professor of Curriculum Studies and Department Head in the Faculty of Education at the University of British Columbia, Vancouver, Canada. His research focuses on phenomenological studies of imaginative engagement, with an emphasis on how these create opportunities for tactical interventions into normalizing discourses of identity and identification. His most recent book, *Why Reading Literature in School Still Matters: Imagination, interpretation, insight*, was awarded the National Reading Association Ed Fry Book Award.

Foreword: Complexity and knowledge systems

MICHAEL A. PETERS

University of Illinois at Urbana-Champaign

Mark Mason has done us great service in assembling these chapters from a distinguished group of international scholars who are well known or who have devoted space in their thinking and writing to complexity theory and its relation to education. This collection brings together a total of fifteen chapters: an introductory set of five chapters; two chapters that address the issue of complexity theory and philosophy of education; five chapters that pick up on the theme of complexity theory and educational research; and, finally, three chapters that address complexity theory and the curriculum. The final effect is a comprehensive and significant introduction to complexity theory in educational theory and philosophy.

Given that Mark Mason, the editor of this book, has already addressed the contents of the book and that there are no less than five introductory chapters, I will not repeat the points raised or confine myself to issues that have been raised or attempt to summarize arguments or interpretations. This also obviates the need for much of a Foreword on my part. John Urry (2005) introducing a special issue of *Theory Culture and Society* commented that the social and cultural sciences over the last few decades have experienced a number of incursions including Marxism of the 1970s, the linguistic and postmodern turns of the 1980s, and the body, performative and global culture turns of the 1990s. Without commenting on the simple metaknowledge schema he introduces he then goes on to introduce the latest turn—'complexity'—which he describes as follows:

> This turn derives from developments over the past two decades or so within physics, biology, mathematics, ecology, chemistry and economics, from the revival of neo-vitalism in social thought (Fraser *et al.*, 2005), and from the emergence of a more general 'complex structure of feeling' that challenges some everyday notions of social order (Maasen and Weingart, 2000; Thrift, 1999).

> Within these scientific disciplines, an array of transformations took place, loosely known as chaos, complexity, non-linearity and dynamical systems analysis. There is a shift from reductionist analyses to those that involve the study of complex adaptive ('vital') matter that shows ordering but which remains on 'the edge of chaos'. Self-assembly at the nanoscale is a current example of new kinds of matter seen as involving emergent

complex adaptive systems. At the nanoscale the laws of physics operate in different ways, especially in the way that molecules stick together and through self-assembly can form complex nanoscale structures that could be the basis of whole new products, industries and forms of 'life' (Jones, 2004) (Urry, 2005: 1).

It is, he says, in the 1990s that the social sciences 'go complex' which he dates from the 1996 Gulbenkian Commission on the Restructuring of the Social Sciences, chaired by Wallerstein and including non-linear scientist Prigogine, who together wanted to break down some of the divisions between the social and natural sciences. Complexity thought he dates from the 1990s and also the global spread of 'complexity practices' and its popularizations, including applications to the social and cultural sciences.

The historiography of these successive turns does not attract Urry's attention although to me it demands more of an explication and one that in a very real sense bears on the complexification of the social sciences and philosophies of practice like philosophy of education. An analogy and related phenomenon is the history of the *avant garde* in twentieth century modernism and its uneven geographical spread across cultural capitals of the world—Paris and Impressionism, Moscow and formalist linguistics and poetics, Vienna and Dadism, Paris and Cubism, New York and Abstract Expressionism etc., and the dissipation of the *avant garde* as a series of successive paradigms, each critique-ing the other, as it traveled to the west coast and finally gave up the struggle and died among the eclecticism of a postmodernism in arts and architecture that admitted strands of diverse and multicultural thought and experience, as well as a total consumerism that incorporated art.

We could also tell a similar story of disciplinary reception of new formalist techniques and developments in mathematics and physics and their penetration into the social and cultural sciences, and indeed into philosophy (although this, it might be argued, had a different trajectory especially with developments in logic and philosophy of time, from Kant onwards), especially after Minowski's elegant equations gave mathematical expression to Einstein's theories of relativity in the early twentieth century. The subsequent mathematicization of 'space-time' and its vectorization in the social and cultural sciences, as much a series of flows and influences from the arts, indicated that epistemologically speaking scientific communities exhibited an increasing complexity in their influence and formation, and in the development of formalist methodologies and techniques adopted from developments in mathematics.

What is interesting to me here and is part of the kernel of investigating knowledge systems is that complexity as non-lineal, emergent, self-organizing and dynamic systems, with the advent of computers, with Claude Shannon's 1948 'Mathematical Theory of Communication', with the development of cybernetics and the Macy group (von Neumann, Shannon, Bateson, Mead etc.) after the war, and with the development of the Internet as the preferred academic mode of scholarly communication, the epistemological complexity of knowledge systems per se and their interdisciplinization was set in motion as an irreversible development of global systems. These developments in mathematics and in physics, evidenced in topology, in forms of spatial analysis, in cybernetics and systems theory, in relativity, thermodynamics, and chaos theory, as well as in the growth of techniques in military surveillance, coding and decoding of military intelligence, soon spread to allied disciplines and fields in the physical sciences that were open to quantification and required the processing of very large numbers, and also to emergent sciences like biology, ecology and other studies of living and social systems that seemed to accompany the first awarenesses of globalization and socio-epidemiological studies. The globalization of system analyses within and across the disciplines demands a complexity approach, but more importantly, it demonstrates that these complex systems operate at the level of infrastructure, code and content to enable certain freedoms while controlling others.

Complexity as an approach to knowledge and knowledge systems now recognizes both the growth of global systems architectures in (tele)communications and information with the development of *open knowledge production systems* that increasingly rest not only on the establishment of new and better platforms (sometimes called Web 2.0), the semantic web, new search algorithms and processes of digitization but also social processes and policies that foster *openness* as an overriding value as evidenced in the growth of open source, open access and open education and their convergences that characterize global knowledge communities that transcend borders of the nation-state. This seems to intimate new orders of global knowledge systems and cultures that portend a set of political and ethical values such as universal accessibility, rights to knowledge, and international knowledge rights to research results especially in the biosciences and other areas that have great potential to alleviate human suffering, disease and high infant mortality. Openness seems also to suggest political transparency and the norms of open inquiry, indeed, even *democracy* itself as both the basis of the logic of inquiry and the dissemination of its results.

References

Fraser, M., Kember, S. & Lury, C. (eds) (2005) *Inventive Life: Approaches to the New Vitalism.* Special Issue of *Theory Culture & Society* 22(1): 1–14.

Jones, R. (2004) *Soft Machines: Nanotechnology and Life.* Oxford: Oxford University Press.

Law, J. & Urry, J. (2004) 'Enacting the social', *Economy and Society*, 33(3) August: 390–410.

Maasen, S. & Weingart, P. (2000) *Metaphors and the Dynamics of Knowledge.* London: Routledge.

Nowotny, H. (2005) 'The Increase of Complexity and its Reduction Emergent Interfaces between the Natural Sciences, Humanities and Social Sciences', *Theory, Culture & Society*, 22(5): 15–31.

Urry, J. (2005) 'The Complexity Turn', *Theory, Culture & Society* 22(5): 1–14.

1
Complexity Theory and the Philosophy of Education

MARK MASON

University of Hong Kong

It's probably a good idea to begin an introduction to complexity theory and the philosophical study of education on a sceptical note, by taking note of the comments of the physicist, Philip Ball (2004, p. 5):

> We have been here before. In the 1970s, the catastrophe theory of René Thom seemed to promise an understanding of how sudden changes in society might be provoked by small effects. This initiative atrophied rather quickly, since Thom's phenomenological and qualitative theory did not really offer fundamental explanations and mechanisms for the processes it described. Chaos theory, which matured in the 1980s, has so far proved rather more robust, supplying insights into how complicated and ever-changing ('dynamical') systems rapidly cease to be precisely predictable even if their initial states are known in great detail. Chaos theory has been advocated as a model for market economics, ... [b]ut this theory has not delivered anything remotely resembling a science of society.

> The current vogue is for the third of the three C's: complexity. The buzzwords here are *emergence* and *self-organization*, as complexity theory seeks to understand how order and stability arise from the interactions of many components according to a few simple rules ... . But very often what passes today for 'complexity science' is really something much older, dressed in fashionable apparel. The main themes in complexity theory have been studied for more than a hundred years by physicists who evolved a tool kit of concepts and techniques to which complexity studies have added barely a handful of new items.

Nevertheless, having pointed out that '[a]t the root of this sort of physics is a phenomenon that immediately explains why the discipline may have something to say about society: it is a science of *collective behaviour*' (ibid., p. 5), Ball goes on to suggest (ibid., p. 6) that

> ... even with our woeful ignorance of why humans behave the way they do, it is possible to make some predictions about how they behave collectively. That is to say, we can make predictions about society even in the face of individual free will.

The physics might then not be new, but the substantial development of and rapidly increasing interest in complexity theory in the social sciences certainly is. As Mason indicates in the third chapter in this collection, complexity theory offers some useful insights into the nature of continuity and change, and is thus of considerable interest in both the philosophical and practical understanding of educational and institutional change. Complexity theory's notion of *emergence* implies that, given a significant degree of complexity in a particular environment, or *critical mass*, new properties and behaviours emerge that are not contained in the essence of the constituent elements, or able to be predicted from a knowledge of initial conditions. These concepts of *emergent phenomena* from a critical mass, associated with notions of *lock-in*, *path dependence*, and *inertial momentum*, contribute to an understanding of continuity and change that has not hitherto been readily available in other theories of or perspectives on change.

Developed principally in the fields of physics, biology, chemistry and economics, complexity theory arises in some senses out of chaos theory, and before that, catastrophe theory, in that it shares chaos theory's focus on the sensitivity of phenomena to initial conditions that may result in unexpected and apparently random subsequent properties and behaviours. Chaos theory suggests that even a very slight degree of uncertainty about initial conditions can grow inexorably and cause substantial fluctuations in the behaviour of a particular phenomenon. Perhaps more importantly, complexity theory shares chaos theory's concern with wholes, with larger systems or environments and the relationships among their constituent elements or agents, as opposed to the often reductionist concerns of mainstream science with the essence of the 'ultimate particle'. While it was pioneered in economics (Holland, 1987; Arthur, 1989, 1990), complexity theory is otherwise a relative stranger to the social sciences. It is, as Morrison (2002, p. 6) puts it, 'a theory of survival, evolution, development and adaptation'. It concerns itself with environments, organisations, or systems that are complex in the sense that very large numbers of constituent elements or agents are connected to and interacting with each other in many different ways.

Many authors in this collection offer an introduction to complexity theory in their particular chapters—this on top of the fact that some of the earlier chapters (see especially Morrison, Mason, Davis and Alhadeff-Jones) are dedicated substantially to introducing the field. Individual authors have not been asked to remove these introductions in their chapters for two main reasons: first, leaving them in the chapters enables readers who are not familiar with the field to read just one or a small selection of chapters, because they will find in that or those chapters a brief introduction to complexity theory; and second, the introductions offered by this volume's various authors offer different entries to and perspectives on the field—together they thus enhance the experience of the reader who studies the whole volume. In particular, the first two chapters that follow this introduction to the collection are best read in conjunction with each other, in that each is concerned with providing an accessible introduction to complexity theory, with Morrison raising ten challenges to complexity theory for the philosophy of education, and Mason considering some of the implications of complexity theory for educational change.

In his chapter, 'Educational Philosophy and the Challenge of Complexity Theory', Keith Morrison introduces some core tenets and features of complexity theory in a manner helpful to readers entirely new to the field. While Morrison does indicate some of the insights offered by complexity theory for educational philosophy, and its attractiveness, not least because of its critique of positivism, its affinity to Dewey and Habermas, and its arguments for openness, diversity, and the importance of relationships, agency and creativity, he is rather less sanguine about its use in and for education. There are many questions still to be answered. While complexity theory challenges educational philosophy to reconsider accepted paradigms of teaching, learning and educational research, the theory is not without its difficulties. These, as Morrison elucidates in the chapter, lie in complexity theory's nature, status, methodology, utility and contribution to the philosophy of education, in that it is a descriptive theory that is easily misunderstood as a prescriptive theory, that it is silent on key issues of values and ethics that educational philosophy should embrace, that it is of questionable internal consistency, and that it currently adds limited further value to educational philosophy. Morrison nevertheless raises some interesting and difficult questions for education—principally with regard to schools, the curriculum, learning and teaching—and educational research in the light of the insights of complexity theory. With respect to educational research, he concludes that complexity theory suggests the need for case study methodology, qualitative research and participatory, multi-perspectival and collaborative (self-organised), partnership-based forms of research, premised on interactionist, qualitative and interpretive accounts. In this, complexity theory points to methodological, paradigmatic and theoretical pluralism.

As the title of his chapter suggests, Mark Mason asks 'What Is Complexity Theory, and What Are Its Implications for Educational Change?' Mason considers questions of continuity and change in education from the perspective of complexity theory, introducing the field to educationists who might not be familiar with it. Given a significant degree of complexity in a particular environment (or 'dynamical system'), new properties and behaviours, which are not necessarily contained in the essence of the constituent elements or able to be predicted from a knowledge of initial conditions, will emerge. These concepts of emergent phenomena from a critical mass, associated with notions of lock-in, path dependence, and inertial momentum, suggest that it is in the dynamic interactions and adaptive orientation of a system that new phenomena, new properties and behaviours, emerge. The focus thus shifts from a concern with decontextualised and universalised essence to contextualised and contingent complex wholes. This is where complexity theory seeks the levers of history. Mason takes the notion of *inertial momentum* from physics and posits it as the conceptual link between the principle of emergent phenomena as developed principally in the natural sciences and the notion of socio-historical change in human society. He argues that educational and institutional change is less a consequence of effecting change in one particular factor or variable, and more a case of generating momentum in a new direction by attention to as many factors as possible. Complexity theory suggests, in other words, that what it might take to change a school's inertial momentum from an ethos of failure is massive and sustained intervention at every possible level until the phenomenon of learning excellence emerges from this new set of interactions among these new factors, and sustains itself autocatalytically.

In 'Complexity and Education: Vital Simultaneities', Brent Davis considers how complexity theory might be appropriate to the concerns of educators and educational researchers. He addresses this question by exploring several 'simultaneities' offered by complexity thinking. Using the term to refer to events or phenomena that exist or operate at the same time, he sets it down as a deliberate contrast to the modern and Western tendency to think in terms of discontinuities around such matters as theory and practice, knowers and knowledge, self and other, mind and body, art and science, and child and curriculum. In the context of popular debate, he reminds us, the terms of these sorts of dyads tend to be understood as necessarily distinct, opposed, and unconnected, even though they seem always to occur at the same time. In other words, such simultaneities tend to be seen as coincidental, but not co-implicated. Thinking in the perspectives of complexity theory challenges these modes of interpretation and, in the process, offers useful insights into the projects of education and educational research. The simultaneities that Davis addresses include:

- 'knower and knowledge', where complexity theory, by considering both simultaneously, aims to move beyond the common distinction between teachers' representing the established and objective knowledge of the curriculum while pedagogically fostering subjective knowing in learners;
- 'transphenomenality', where complexity theory offers insights that can be had only by the simultaneous consideration of factors normally associated with apparently quite different phenomenal levels of explanation;
- 'transdisciplinarity', where, similarly, complexity theory offers insights that can be had only by the simultaneous consideration of factors normally associated with apparently quite different disciplinary perspectives;
- 'interdiscursivity', where, similarly, complexity theory offers insights that can be had only by the simultaneous consideration of factors normally associated with apparently quite different discursive perspectives;
- 'descriptive and pragmatic insights', where Davis asserts that the emphasis in complexity research has recently moved beyond careful descriptive accounts of complex phenomena toward deliberate attempts to prompt the emergence and affect the character of such phenomena, an emphasis well suited to the pragmatic concerns of educationists;
- 'representation and presentation', where Davis aligns himself with Derrida in pointing out how the representation (say, in an academic paper) of a phenomenon is inexorably complicit in presenting that phenomenon: our representations 'contribute to the shape of possibility', being 'partial rather than comprehensive, active rather than inert, implicated rather than benign';
- 'affect and effect', in the terms of which Davis argues that educators and educational researchers are uniquely positioned to contribute to complexity thinking, most obviously because of the transphenomenal nature of the educational project, the transdisciplinary character of educational research, and the interdiscursive nature of educational thought; and

- 'education and research', where Davis suggests that educational research and educational practice might be considered aspects of the same project—namely, 'expanding the space of human possibility by exploring the space of the existing possible'.

Michel Alhadeff-Jones provides in 'Three Generations of Complexity Theories' a historical survey of the development of complexity theory. What is particularly interesting about his chapter is that it offers to English-speaking readers a history that includes contributions by French and other Latin scholars, which might not otherwise be readily accessible in English. Because it functions in some ways as a historical introduction to the field, Alhadeff-Jones's chapter has been placed in the introductory section of this collection, but readers might prefer to consider it after sampling some of the other chapters that follow it, when its history might be better placed in context. Alhadeff-Jones points out that the term 'complexity' is frequently used in a manner which suggests that it is a unified concept, which may contribute to a neglect of the range of different theories that deal with the implications of complexity. He suggests a more nuanced use of the term, which would avoid simplification of the concept to some of its dominant expressions only. He explores the etymology of 'complexity' and offers a chronological presentation of three generations of theories that have shaped its uses, introducing also the epistemic and socio-cultural origins of these theories. From an epistemological point of view, his chapter sheds light on some competing interpretations underlying what is considered complex; and from an anthropological perspective, it considers both the emancipatory and the potentially alienating dimensions of complexity. Alhadeff-Jones suggests in conclusion that contributions grounded in contemporary theories related to complexity, as well as critical appraisals of their epistemological and ethical legitimacy, ought to follow the recursive feedback loops and dynamics that they themselves constitute. In doing so, researchers and practitioners in education would consider their own practices as a learning process that does not reduce the dichotomies and the similarities that shape its own complexity.

Complexity Theory and the Philosophy of Education

In 'On the Creative Logic of Education', Inna Semetsky 're-read(s) Dewey through the lens of complexity science', finding depths of association between Dewey's thought and some of the central ideas and metaphors of complexity theory that will astonish many readers. Her chapter is yet another indication of the prescience of one of the greatest thinkers in philosophy of education. Semetsky considers some of Dewey's key philosophical concepts in relation to some of the ideas associated with founders of dynamical systems theory such as Ludwig von Bertalanffy, Ervin Laszlo, and Erich Jantsch. Her chapter introduces some elements of non-linear dynamics, relating them to the problematic of learning and the transformation of what Dewey referred to as habits. She also considers Dewey's concepts of growth and transaction in the light of complexity theory, but what comes through most strongly is an almost astonishing degree of coherence between Dewey's very philosophical orientation and that of complexity theory. One might be tempted to suggest that there are striking similarities in the core or essence of each, but such metaphors would do violence to both. She concludes by considering the balance between novelty and confirmation in a self-organised system, positing it as an issue of pedagogical significance.

Considering Dewey and Foucault in successive paragraphs with respect to the same subject might strike some as remarkable, but it is true that complexity theory has much in common with both. Complexity theory echoes also Foucault's emphasis on 'polymorphous correlations in place of simple or complex causality' (cited in Harvey, 1990, p. 9). Mark Olssen expands on this notion at some length in his chapter, 'Foucault as Complexity Theorist'. Drawing on Heidegger, Olssen begins by exploring parallels between Foucault's Nietzschean view of history and that implied by complexity theory. He suggests that Foucault's rejection of structuralism and Marxism is a consequence of his radical ontology, where the conception of the totality or whole 'is reconfigured as an always open, relatively borderless system of infinite interconnections, possibilities and developments'. Olssen goes on to highlight further ways in which Foucault's approach parallels those of complexity theory: Foucault emphasises, for example, notions such as self-organisation, time as an irreversible dimension, and a world of infinite possibility because it is characterised by the principles of openness, indeterminism, unpredictability and uncertainty. Olssen then considers the implications of Foucault's approach with respect to identity, creativity, and the uniqueness of the person. He suggests that the insights of complexity theory might enable old conundrums, such as those concerning determinism and creativity, social constructionism and uniqueness, to be overcome.

Complexity Theory and Educational Research

Jay Lemke and Nora Sabelli consider some key questions that need to be asked in research from a complexity perspective on educational change, beginning by asking how we might usefully apply concepts and procedures derived from the study of other complex dynamical systems to analyzing systemic change in education. They describe a number of the important concepts and research issues that have to do with the application of complex systems approaches to education. Included in their discussion is a review of key issues identified by groups of researchers in the field regarding defining the system under study, structural analysis of the system, relationships among subsystems and levels, the drivers for change, and modelling methods. These new conceptual approaches to the study of complex systems, developed in the last two decades by mathematicians, physicists, chemists, biologists and computer scientists, are being applied and extended by economists, psychologists, organisational scientists and researchers in many disciplines whose insights, suggest Lemke and Sabelli, are being scaffolded not only by new quantitative techniques, but by new qualitative conceptions of phenomena common to many different complex systems. These concepts include multi-scale hierarchical organisation, emergent patterning, agent-based modelling, dynamical attractors and repellors, information flows and constraints, system-environment interaction, developmental trajectories, selectional ratchets, fitness landscapes, interaction across timescales, and varieties of self-organisation. They are fast becoming key tools for qualitative reasoning about complex socio-natural systems as well as for quantitative modelling and simulation.

Similarly to Mason's view about the implications of complexity theory for educational change, Lemke and Sabelli remind us that in this perspective there are no independent interventions: proposed changes at the classroom level, for example, have implications at school and district levels (for example, for teacher development, parental expectations, school resources, accountability, and so on) and need to be supported by related interventions across multiple levels. Most important, they conclude, is a change in the paradigms of our thinking about research on education: away from input–output 'black-box' causal models to modelling the specific, local linkages that actually interconnect actors, practices, and events across multiple levels of organisation; and away from single interventions and simplistic solutions to the recognition of the need for coordinated changes throughout the system and to its constraining and enabling contexts and resources.

In his chapter, 'Human Research and Complexity Theory', James Horn suggests that the language, concepts and principles of complexity are central to the development of 'a new science of qualities' to complement 'the science of quantities' that has shaped our understanding of the physical and social worlds. Researchers working in this domain would aspire to a hermeneutic social science that would contribute to description and explanation of the emergence, sustenance and change of social systems understood primarily in terms of information and communication. Horn draws on Murray Gell-Mann, Nobel Laureate and Distinguished Fellow of the Santa Fe Institute: complexity focuses necessarily on 'coarse-grained' (Gell-Mann, 1994, pp. 29–30) descriptions and explanations of systems whose self-organising intra- and inter-actions render them too complex to be encapsulated by the standard repertoire of educational research tools, unless the complexity of the phenomena is abstracted and reduced to a workable level of statistical generalisation. Complexity offers a theoretical framework for acknowledging and helping to sustain the self-organising capacity of fully embodied systems that are realised through the intra- and inter-actions of agents within the boundary that those activities help to generate and sustain. It follows, Horn reminds us, that a certain amount of uncertainty must be sustained.

The translation or extrapolation of these findings into research theory and practice is then a possibility, particularly if optimal and adjustable parameters can be established in self-organising learning communities where longitudinal, observational, and experimental methods can be applied. Here Horn cites Ralph Stacey's setting down of the three all-important control parameters that drive complex adaptive systems: 'the rate of information flow through the system, the richness of connectivity between agents in the system, and the level of diversity within and between the schemas of the agents' (1996, p. 99). Although a daunting prospect, there is a growing body of theory and research that provides some directions to pursue.

Daunting indeed: Paul Cilliers (2005) has noted that the sheer scope of the variables within complex systems makes modelling them a tricky, if not impossible, task. Such models would have to be as complex as the original, since the distributed, non-linear features of complex systems do not allow for the compression of data. This creates the need to observe complex human systems as comprised of fully embodied interactive agents, which then highlights the importance of viewing the researching of such systems from an ethical perspective. Horn suggests that it will be the interactive and reflexive research practice based upon this recognition that instantiates the ethical ideal, which would yield a research practice in which humans are not subjected to research but, rather, are acknowledged as participants engaged in the ongoing elaboration of the communicative behaviours that include researchers as well.

How then, asks Horn in conclusion, do such possibilities fit with the reality of schools and the needs of teachers and students? He suggests that every teacher needs to understand that she is working within a sensitive learning ecology whose directions can be altered by small changes in the boundary conditions and interaction patterns of the classroom. Understanding the consequences of complexity, while helping educators to keep in perspective that classrooms and individual schools are linked within larger institutional systems, places teachers and students, suggests Horn, closer to the locus of control in terms of classroom learning.

Mike Radford considers in 'Complexity and Truth in Educational Research' the impact of complexity theory on the way in which we understand propositions corresponding to the reality that they describe, and our concept of truth in that context. He argues that complexity theory, with its emphasis on non-linear and dynamic interactions between multiple variables, within indeterminate and transient systems, supports the case for connectionist and holistic analyses. From this perspective, theories are more likely to be under-determined by evidence and open to interpretation, with the potential for 'certainties' weakened. If educational situations are complex, it follows, suggests Radford, that the drive towards specific and focused research findings that will support policy and practice, and the associated notion of control, is illusory. Rather than providing evidence for prescription, research should be understood as descriptive and explanatory, within a range of interpretive possibilities. Our actions in education accordingly take place within necessarily incomplete and constantly changing situations, and are more appropriately understood in terms of survival than control. In this regard Radford is less optimistic than Horn about the efficacy of complexity theory for 'managing' education.

How then, asks Radford, does research relate to policy and practice in the context of complexity theory? Complexity theory, he suggests, inclines us to extreme caution in relation to our explanations, and similarly to the degree of control that we have over the complex social technology of schooling. Research cannot deliver the kinds of clear and simplistic lines between evidence and practice or policy that is all too frequently demanded—a point that has often been made before, but which is emphasised all the more in the light of complexity theory. The complexity of the social reality that is being researched and the explanatory frameworks within which new explanations are generated mean that these are invariably fragile and open to layers of interpretation and reinterpretation. The social technology of schooling is, suggests Radford, like a work of art, rich in interpretive possibilities: the role of research is to offer tentative identification and critical analysis of these interpretations. Radford's conclusion echoes that of other authors in this collection: the success of educational interventions in the interests of one objective or another is unpredictable. There are simply too many variables, and the relative significance of each (even if we could identify them all) is generally too difficult to assess from a knowledge of initial conditions, to predict clear lines of effect between intervention and result.

In her chapter that justifies why 'Knowledge Must Be Contextual', Tamsin Haggis employs complexity theory to draw attention to some conceptual limitations of the epistemologies that underpin much qualitative research. She finds these epistemologies problematic in relation to their conceptualisation of difference, context, processes through time, multi-factor causality, and the specificity of situations. In contrast, she argues, complexity's concept of open, dynamic systems, embedded within and partly constituting each other, while at the same time maintaining their own coherence, allows for different ways of thinking about context, and provides a rationale for the investigation of individuals, difference and specificity. By focusing on interactions, rather than on static categories, complexity theory also makes it possible to consider different aspects of process. It does this, she suggests, not only in the general sense of providing a language with which to consider dynamic interactions, but also specifically in relation to the importance of histories of interactions through time. She shows additionally that complexity theory articulates a notion of causality that is multi-factorial: it is impossible to isolate 'key' factors, because all 'factors' work together. The causality implied by complexity theory, she continues, is also de-centred, in the sense that there is no 'pacemaker cell' (Johnson, 2001), no gene-type entity in a dynamic system that could be said to 'cause' a particular effect or set of effects. Causation is too multi-dimensional, too fast, and in some senses too unpredictable to occupy the full focus of our attention. Complexity therefore suggests a shift from our preoccupation with causes to a focus on effects. The combination of multi-factor causality, occurring through time, in the absence of a central, generative force, results in emergence, and requires a reconsideration of the concept of 'structure'. From a complexity perspective, things emerge at particular points in the history of a set of multiple interactions through time, simply as a result of the interactions among constituent elements, rather than as the result of 'deep', generative causal structures. This is partly, Haggis suggests, what makes emergence, to some extent at least, unpredictable: what emerges will depend upon what interacts, which is at least partly determined by chance encounters and changes in environments. Emergence, however, though unpredictable, is, she reminds us, nonetheless also constrained: by features which are both internal (in terms of initial conditions and interaction histories) and external (in the sense that the system is partly made up of the interactions of larger systems, and also in the more conventional sense of physical, 'environmental' factors) to the system under study. She concludes with the reminder that complexity theory does not provide, in her analysis, a way of talking about random or intuitive phenomena. While the causalities involved in the interactions may not be able to be tracked, what emerges from them is not 'mysterious': it is consistent with the nature and histories of the interactions involved.

Concluding the section on Complexity Theory and Educational Research, Lesley Kuhn offers in her chapter a critical reflection on educational research in the paradigm of complexity theory. She directs her critique at the appropriateness *per se* of complexity theory in educational research; and at the ways in which complexity is engaged in the educational domain. With respect to the first, she argues that complexity and education may indeed be brought together in research endeavour because in the language of complexity, such human cultural settings, productions and institutions as educational endeavour are complex and dynamic. Individual human beings (learners, educators and administrators), various associations of individuals (classes, schools, universities, educational associations) and human endeavour (such as educational research) are multi-dimensional, non-linear, interconnected, far from equilibrium and unpredictable. Rather than seek, she points out, to undertake inquiry that simplifies through reducing this complexity to that which can be measured objectively, a complexity approach begins by acknowledging that human settings and activities are necessarily complex. A complexity approach, after all, acknowledges that all levels of focus, whether on the individual, class, school, or national or international associations, reveal humans and human endeavour as complex, and that focussing on one level will not reduce the multi-dimensionality, non-linearity, interconnectedness, or unpredictability encountered.

Also with respect to the first, Kuhn considers and rebuts two frequent objections to the use of complexity in educational research: that complexity draws inappropriately on images and metaphors from mathematics and science; and that many discourses outside of science and mathematics, in domains such as philosophy, arts, humanities, social sciences, relating to constructivist, postmodernist, poststructuralist or critical perspectives, provide adequate, equivalent or superior means of addressing similar ideas to insights claimed by complexity. This view positions complexity as redundant.

Having addressed each objection, Kuhn concludes by addressing the second main focus of her critique: the ways in which complexity is engaged in the educational domain. Here she offers a number of caveats to educational researchers working in the framework of complexity, perhaps the most interesting of which is her reminder that while complexity theory is descriptive, education is a normative activity. While complexity offers organisational principles for describing how the world and humans function, education is oriented towards the achievement of particular purposes and goals, not least among them normative aims. Engaging complexity in educational research thus involves researchers in a complex process of meshing the perspectives of complexity with a range of normative commitments. It means recognising that while complexity does not itself have ethical intent, education is essentially and pervasively normative, and all research is in some respects normative. The careful researcher in this paradigm will be aware of this, and will tread with appropriate caution.

Complexity Theory and the Curriculum

William Doll's chapter, 'Complexity and the Culture of Curriculum', has two main foci: the history of curriculum design; and implications from the new sciences of chaos and complexity for the development of new thinking in curriculum design. With respect to the first focus, Doll sketches similarities between the well known 16th century curriculum design of Ramus and the 20th century curriculum principles of Tyler, tracing genealogical strands from Ramus to Comenius to the Puritans to colonial New England to Horace Mann to Tyler. What unites these strands, Doll suggests, is the concept of Method, the metanarrative that informs Tyler's *Basic*

Principles of curriculum design—those starting with set goals and concluding with measured assessment.

Turning to the chapter's second focus, Doll then provides a useful sketch of some of the main ideas and authors in chaos and complexity, with a view to disrupting Tyler's rationale by developing a different sense of curriculum and teaching— 'open, dynamic, relational, creative, and systems oriented'. For Doll, this implies at university level 'a caution in using too rigid a syllabus—instead using one which is rich in problematics ... . Students—individually or in groups—[might, for example,] work on various texts which web together into a frame that combines closure with openness, *a modest rigidity with a structured flexibility*'. Embracing complexity, the aim, says Doll, is 'a process of cross-fertilization, pollination, catalyzation of ideas':

> Over time ... a network of connections and interconnections becomes more and more webbed. Learning now occurs, not through direct transmission from expert to novice, ... but in a non-linear manner through all in a class exploring a problem together ... . In other words, the curriculum (with its expression in a syllabus) is now an emerging one within an ongoing process that actually catalyzes itself via interactions within the system or network.

In their chapter, 'From Representation to Emergence', Deborah Osberg, Gert Biesta and Paul Cilliers consider some challenges to the epistemology of schooling that are raised by complexity theory. They argue that much schooling is organised around a 'representational epistemology: one which holds that knowledge is an accurate representation of something that is separate from knowledge itself'. They refer to this also as a 'spatial epistemology', since the object of knowledge is assumed to exist separately from the knowledge itself. They show in their chapter how ideas from complexity have challenged this spatial epistemology of representation, partly through the problem of incompressibility (open, complex systems cannot be modelled by a process of compression that excludes some apparently less salient factors), and partly by showing the problem of attempting to represent open systems (reality) by closed systems (representations, models, theories). They then explore some possibilities for an alternative, 'temporal' understanding of knowledge in its relationship to reality, drawing also on Dewey's 'transactional realism' and on Derrida's deconstruction. They suggest that 'knowledge' and 'reality' should not be understood as separate systems, but as part of the same emerging complex system, a move which introduces, crucially from a complexity perspective, *time* into our understanding of the relationship between knowledge and reality.

This understanding of knowledge suggests that the acquisition of curricular content should not be considered an end in itself. They conclude that this 'epistemology of emergence' therefore calls for a shift in curricular thinking, away from questions about presentation and representation and towards questions about engagement and response:

> When we consider the purpose of schooling in terms of an emergentist understanding of knowledge *and* reality, we begin to imagine schooling as a practice which makes possible a dynamic, self-renewing and creative

engagement with 'content' or 'curriculum' by means of which school-goers are able to respond, and hence bring forth new worlds. With this conception of knowledge, the purpose of the curriculum is no longer to facilitate the *acquisition* of knowledge *about* reality ... . This means questions about what to present in the curriculum and whether these things should be directly presented or should be represented ... are no longer relevant as curricular questions. While content is important, the curriculum is less concerned with *what* content is presented and how, and more with the idea that content *is* engaged with and responded to.

'With this conception of knowledge and the world', they conclude, 'the curriculum becomes a tool for the emergence of new worlds, rather than a tool for stabilization and replication'.

Dennis Sumara, Rebecca Luce-Kapler and Tammy Iftody conclude the section on complexity theory and the curriculum with some insights from complexity theory into, as their chapter is entitled, 'Educating Consciousness through Literary Experiences'. They understand and describe human consciousness as an embodied experience that emerges from a complex relationship of the biological and the phenomenological. Following arguments made by Lodge (2002) and Donald (2001), they argue that one primary way that human beings develop self-awareness of their own minds is by becoming aware of other minds. These mind-reading abilities are of course fundamental to the continual adaptations that human beings need to make in their daily lives. They conclude their exposition of a complexity-informed understanding of consciousness with the key observation that consciousness is an emergent phenomenon, 'an emergent property of an information-seeking human biology in complicity with a complex socio-cultural environment'.

Sumara, Luce-Kapler and Iftody then offer descriptions of two literary texts (one print-based and one electronic) to illustrate how these texts participate with other forms of culture and with human biology to produce experiences of self-consciousness awareness. They argue that if consciousness is understood as an emergent property of biology and culture, and if human beings develop self-awareness of their own minds by becoming cognisant of other minds, then it follows that literary experiences create productive mind-reading practices that contribute to the ongoing development and emergence of consciousness and, as such, are important for education. They conclude that extended opportunities to inquire into readers' imagined identifications with characters and their situations can support the development of empathic understanding of others:

> For educators, complexity science points to structural conditions that one can implement to help students become aware of how self-consciousness does not precede or follow pedagogical encounters: instead, consciousness emerges from the complex nested intertwinings of memory, imagination, and sensation. Like all complex forms, the experience of consciousness is the product of simple processes, ones that teachers can notice and nurture in the context of the classroom.

Concluding, and Simultaneously Introductory, Remarks

What I hope has come through in this brief introduction to complexity theory and to the chapters in this collection is a range of perspectives that do not simply advocate the wholehearted embrace of complexity in all aspects of educational research, practice and philosophical study. Complexity theory offers in my view the most cogent understanding of the nature of continuity and change, and its theories of critical mass, phase transition, emergence and auto-catalysis offer most insightful perspectives on questions as difficult as those to do with the origins of life and of consciousness, with the evolution of species. Yet the theories and sciences of complexity are in some respects still young and their associated phenomena far from well understood. Nobody in the social sciences has been able to describe, let alone predict, what degree of mass is sufficient to be critical, when a phase transition will occur, what will be the characteristics—described in more than just general terms—of the emergent phenomena. These would be useful things to know, but even to ask after them is in some ways to misunderstand complexity. Some might be sceptical of the possibility of any practical import of complexity if all of these questions cannot be asked. They could also point out that the phenomena associated with complexity really only begin to, well, emerge when open dynamical systems are of incredible scale—scales far greater than are evident in classrooms or schools, for example. But complexity theory's defenders would suggest that such a view misses, by looking only at the classroom level, or only at the level of the school, the scale of the complexity at other levels of the environment or system: the conscious (and the complexity associated with just that) human learners in the classroom, or the school as constituted by and reflective of a myriad factors in the wider society, for example.

What this introduction to the concerns of this volume has also shown is that complexity theory offers some interesting insights and challenges for the philosophical study and practice of education, but that educational theory has much still to ask of complexity theory. As mentioned earlier in this chapter, and as indicated by Horn, researchers working in the paradigm, and it might indeed be called that, or with the perspectives, of complexity theory would understand it as a hermeneutic social science that contributes to the description and explanation of the emergence, sustenance and change of social systems understood not least in terms of information and communication, with the latter's corollaries of feedback, adaptation, self-organisation and evolution. Complexity theory, it bears repeating here, with its emphasis on non-linear and dynamic interactions between multiple variables, within indeterminate and transient, open and dynamic systems of incredible scale, supports the case for connectionist and holistic analyses. Such analyses depend on interpretive perspectives that are transphenomenal in character, since complexity theory offers insights that can be had only by the simultaneous consideration of factors normally associated with apparently quite different phenomenal levels of explanation. Such analyses depend also, as was mentioned earlier, and as Davis explains in his chapter, on interpretive approaches that apprehend and engage with the perspectives of multiple disciplines and of multiple discourses simultaneously.

Philosophers of education will have been struck, even in the few introductory remarks offered above on Semetsky's chapter, by the degree of coherence between Dewey's philosophical orientation and that of complexity theory. For me, as I mentioned, this is a further indication of the prescience of one of the greatest thinkers in philosophy of education. Educational philosophers will also have been struck by the extent to which Foucault might be read as a complexity theorist, but this should come as no surprise when reading Olssen's chapter in the light of complexity theory's similar emphasis on what Harvey describes, as mentioned earlier, as Foucault's preference for understanding change in the light of 'polymorphous correlations in place of simple or complex causality' (cited in Harvey, 1990, p. 9).

Much has also been made in this introduction, and is made in the pages of this collection, of the implications of complexity theory for educational research: how educational research informed by complexity theory might ask different questions with different analytical perspectives—connectionist, holistic, non-linear, rather than input–output 'black-box' causal modelling, for example. And much has been and is made of how curriculum, teaching, the epistemology of schooling, and the 'education of consciousness'—understood as an emergent phenomenon—might be different when viewed from the perspective of complexity theory. But with respect to these two important domains of educational practice—research, and curriculum—it is worth repeating in conclusion the challenge raised by Morrison and elaborated by Kuhn: while complexity theory is descriptive, education is a normative activity. While complexity offers organisational principles for describing how the world and humans function, education is oriented towards the achievement of particular purposes and goals, not least among them normative aims. Engaging complexity in educational research and practice thus involves educational philosophers, practitioners and researchers in a complex process of meshing the perspectives of complexity with a range of normative commitments. On those commitments and on their integration into research and theorising in this paradigm, complexity theory has been largely silent.

References

Arthur, W. B. (1989) Competing Technologies, Increasing Returns, and Lock-in by Historical Events, *The Economic Journal*, 99, pp. 106–131.

Arthur, W. B., et al. *Emergent Structures: A Newsletter of the Economic Research Programme*, March 1989 and August 1990 (Sante Fe, The Santa Fe Institute).

Arthur, W. B. (1990) Positive Feedbacks in the Economy, *Scientific American*, 262, pp. 92–99.

Ball, P. (2003) *Critical Mass: How One Thing Leads to Another* (New York, Farrar, Straus and Giroux).

Cilliers, P. (2005) Knowing Complex Systems, in: K. Richardson (ed.), *Managing the Complex, Volume One: Philosophy, Theory and Application* (Greenwich, CT, Information Age Publishers).

Donald, M. (2001) *A Mind So Rare: The Evolution of Human Consciousness* (New York and London, W.W. Norton and Co.).

Gell-Mann, M. (1994) *The Quark and the Jaguar: Adventures in the Simple and the Complex* (New York, W.H. Freeman).

Harvey, D. (1990) *The Condition of Postmodernity* (Oxford, Blackwell).

Holland, J. H. (1987) The Global Economy as an Adaptive Process, in: P. W. Anderson, K. J. Arrow & D. Pines (eds), *The Economy as an Evolving Complex System*, Santa Fe Institute Studies in the Sciences of Complexity, Vol. 5 (Redwood City, Addison-Wesley).

Johnson, S. (2001) *Emergence* (London, Penguin).

Lodge, D. (2002) *Consciousness and the Novel* (London, Penguin).

Morrison, K. (2002) *School Leadership and Complexity Theory* (London and New York, Routledge/Falmer).

Stacey, R. (1996) *Complexity and Creativity in Organizations* (San Francisco, Berrett Koehler).

2
Educational Philosophy and the Challenge of Complexity Theory

KEITH MORRISON

Macau Inter-University Institute

What is Complexity Theory?

For Newton, the universe was rationalistic, deterministic and of clockwork order; effects were functions of causes, small causes (minimal initial conditions) produced small effects (minimal and predictable) and large causes produced large effects. Predictability, causality, patterning, control, universality, linearity, continuity, stability, objectivity, all contributed to the view of the universe as an ordered mechanism in an albeit complicated equilibrium, a rational, closed, controllable and deterministic system susceptible to comparatively straightforward scientific discovery and laws. This view has been increasingly challenged by complexity theory, which suggests alternative ways of conceiving the world and, thereby, of researching it. This chapter introduces complexity theory through seminal texts, and then raises questions about the application of complexity theory to education.

Change is ubiquitous, and stability and certainty are rare. Complexity theory is a theory of change, evolution, adaptation and development for survival. It breaks with simple successionist cause-and-effect models, linear predictability, and a reductionist approach to understanding phenomena, replacing them with organic, non-linear and holistic approaches respectively (Santonus, 1998, p. 3), in which relations within interconnected networks are the order of the day (Youngblood, 1997, p. 27; Wheatley, 1999, p. 10).

Prigogine and Stengers (1985, pp. 156–9) provide a fascinating example of a central tenet of complexity in the self-organization of the lowly slime-mould: the *Acrasiales* amoebas. If the environment of the slime-mould becomes depleted in the essential nutrients needed to sustain life, the amoebas discover this through chemical sensors and cease to reproduce. They collect together and form a 'foot' containing about a third of the aggregated cells and spores. These migrate in search of a new environment that is suitable to sustain life, forming a new colony of amoebas.

What has happened here? The organism is responding to the environment by reconfiguring itself and metamorphosing in order to survive: it is an open system responding to its environment. The process involves self-organization, and the slime mould, reinvigorated, is capable of survival; the whole process is dynamic. The slime mould demonstrates *autocatalysis*, a central feature of self-organization: the ability of a system to evolve itself, from within. In this process local circumstances dictate the nature of the emerging self-organization: it is a 'bottom-up' process (Marion, 1999, p. 31). This is a very simplified example of a central pillar of complexity theory: self-organization. It contains several features: *adaptability, open systems, learning, feedback, communication* and *emergence*. Closed systems in equilibrium die; systems *need* disequilibrium in order to survive. Stable systems fail (Stacey, 1992, p. 40). Change, disequilibrium and unpredictability are *requirements* for survival: a butterfly that flies only in a straight line is soon eaten. The caterpillar must become a butterfly for the species to survive.

A self-organizing system is both autocatalytic and demonstrates *autopoiesis*. Each living system possesses its own unique characteristics and identity (Kelly & Allison, 1999, p. 28), which enable the system to perpetuate and renew itself over time— it creates the conditions for its own survival. Autopoiesis as self-production (Wheatley, 1999, p. 20) takes place through engagement with others in a system. The system is self-regenerating (able to sustain its identity even though aspects of the system may change, for example, staff turnover in a school), and self-perpetuating. Schools need to create their own identity in their local context and community (Wheatley, 1999, p. 11). When an organization such as a business corporation is clear about its identity, it can respond intelligently to its environment, finding its survival niche by being different from others.

Through feedback, recursion, perturbance, autocatalysis, connectedness and self-organization, higher levels of complexity and new, differentiated forms of life, behaviour and systems arise from lower levels of complexity and existing forms. These complex forms derive from often comparatively simple sets of rules—local rules and behaviours generating emergent complex global order and diversity (Waldrop, 1992, pp. 16–17; Lewin, 1993, p. 38). General laws of emergent order can govern adaptive, dynamical processes (Waldrop, 1992, p. 86; Kauffman, 1995, p. 27).

The interaction of individuals feeds into the wider environment, which, in turn, influences the individual units of the network; they co-evolve, shaping each other (Stewart, 2001). This co-evolution requires connection, cooperation and competition: competition to force development, and cooperation for mutual survival. The behaviour of a complex system as a whole, formed from its several elements, is greater than the sum of the parts (Bar-Yam, 1997; Goodwin, 2000).

Feedback must occur between the interacting elements of the system. Negative feedback is regulatory (Marion, 1999, p. 75). Positive feedback brings increasing returns and uses information to change, grow and develop (Wheatley, 1999, p. 78); it amplifies small changes (Stacey, 1992, p. 53; Youngblood, 1997, p. 54). Once a child has begun to read she is gripped by reading; she reads more and learns at an exponential rate.

Connectedness, a key feature of complexity theory, exists everywhere. In a rainforest ants eat leaves, birds eat ants and leave droppings, which fertilize the soil for growing trees and leaves for the ants (Lewin, 1993, p. 86). As April *et al.* (2000, p. 34) remark, nature possesses many features that organizations crave: flexibility, diversity, adaptability, complexity, and connectedness. In schools, children are linked to families, teachers, peers, societies and groups; teachers are linked to other teachers, support agencies (e.g. psychological and social services), policy-making bodies, funding bodies, the state legislature, and so on. The child (indeed the school) is not an island, but is connected externally and internally in several ways. Disturb one element and the species or system must adapt or possibly die; the message is ruthless. Connectedness requires a *distributed knowledge* system, in which knowledge is not centrally located in a command and control centre. Rather, it is dispersed, shared and circulated throughout the system: communication and collaboration are key elements of complexity theory (Cilliers, 1998).

Emergence is the partner of *self-organization*. Systems possess the ability for self-organization, which is not according to an *a priori* grand design—a cosmological argument—nor a teleological argument. Complexity is neither. Further, self-organization emerges, it is internally generated; it is the antithesis of external control. As Kauffman (1995) suggests, order comes for free and replaces control. The self-organized order emerges of itself as the result of the interaction between the organism and its environment, and new structures emerge that could not have been predicted from a knowledge of initial conditions; that emerged system is, itself, complex and cannot be reduced to those parts that gave rise to the system. As Davis and Sumara (2005, p. 313) write, 'phenomena have to be studied at their level of emergence, i.e. not in terms of their lower level activities but at their new—emerged—level'.

The movement towards greater degrees of complexity, change and adaptability for survival in changing environments is a movement towards 'self-organized criticality' (Bak & Chen, 1991; Bak, 1996), in which systems evolve, through self-organization, towards the 'edge of chaos' (Kauffman, 1995). Take, for example, a pile of sand (Bak, 1996). If one drops one grain of sand at a time a pyramid of sand appears. Continue to drop another piece of sand and a small cascade of sand runs down the pyramid; continue further and the sand pile builds up again in a slightly different shape; continue further and the whole pyramid falls down like a house of cards. This is chaos, and complexity resides at the edge of chaos, at the point just before the pyramid of sand collapses, between mechanistic predictability and complete unpredictability (Bak, 1996):

Linear systems → Complexity → Chaos

Stacey (2000, p. 395) suggests that a system can evolve, and evolve spontaneously, only where there is diversity and deviance (ibid., p. 399)—a salutary message for command-and-control teachers who exact compliance from their pupils. The movement, reconfiguration and subsequent destruction of the sand pile are largely unpredictable. At the point of 'self-organized criticality', the tipping point, the effects of a single event are likely to be very large, breaking the linearity of Newtonian reasoning wherein small causes produce small effects; the addition of a single grain of sand contributes massively to the destruction the pyramid. Change implies, then, a move towards self-organized criticality, and such self-organized criticality evolves 'without interference from any outside agent' (Bak, 1996, p. 31). Order is not imposed; it emerges. In this way it differs from control. Bak (1996) suggests that the sand pile would be nothing if the grains did not relate to each other and hold each other together, i.e. connectedness and mutual support are essential. The closer one moves towards the edge of chaos, the more creative, open-ended, imaginative, diverse, and rich are the behaviours, ideas and practices of individuals and systems, and the greater is the connectivity, networking and information sharing (content and rate of flow) between participants (Stacey *et al.*, 2000, p. 146).

'Complex adaptive systems' (Waldrop, 1992, pp. 294–9) scan and sense the external environment and then make internal adjustments and developments in order to meet the demands of the changing external environment. This is the 'law of requisite variety' (Ashby, 1964), which states that internal systems, flexibility, change and capability must be as powerful as those in the external environment. Closed systems, as Prigogine and Stengers (1985) remind us, run down and decay into entropy unless they import energy from outside. Change or die.

Complexity Theory and Education

Schools exhibit many features of complex adaptive systems, being dynamical and unpredictable, non-linear organizations operating in unpredictable and changing external environments. Indeed schools both shape and adapt to macro- and micro-societal change, organizing themselves, responding to, and shaping their communities and society (i.e. all parties co-evolve).

Complexity theory, as a theory of change, development and evolution through relationships, raises an interesting agenda for the philosophy of education. As Fullan (1989) remarks, change equals learning; learning is a central element in both complexity theory and education. All complex phenomena and systems have to learn, adapt and change in order to survive. Learning and educational research are here considered as two instances of complexity theory's possible influence on education. Research concerns finding out, an essential feature that feeds into complexity theory's need for learning and for intelligence about internal and external environments.

Complexity theory poses a major question: What do the following mean for the philosophy of education: emergence and self-organization; connectedness; order without control; diversity and redundancy; unpredictability and non-linearity; co-evolution; communication and feedback; open, complex adaptive systems; and distributed control?

Several consequent questions are raised; indeed, in an unknowable future, the essence of complexity is to raise questions rather than to provide answers. With regard to *aims and values*, questions arise such as: Should the elements of complexity be addressed in education and schools, and, if so, how? What should be, and how mutable are, the aims and values of the school in a climate of uncertainty, change and unpredictability? Whose aims and values should prevail in a networked and connected school? How can the school decide how to decide its aims and values? What and whose identity should the school pursue? What does school positioning actually mean? How can perpetual instability be sustained? How can theoretical and value pluralism be addressed in schools and education? What constitutes 'progress' in complex educational systems and practices? How do we identify and value order rather than control?

With regard to *curricula*, questions arise such as: What does it mean to 'know' in a climate of uncertainty? How can an anarchistic theory of knowledge (such as that underpinned by complexity theory) be handled in school? How do logical relations (e.g. inclusion, exclusion) apply in an uncertain, web-based, boundlessly interconnected world? Who are the learners? How can, and should, diversity, autonomy, creativity and unpredictability thrive in prescribed circumstances (e.g. nationally mandated curricula)? How can freedom, diversity, autonomy and choice be exercised within centrally-prescribed curricula? What are the risks and benefits in moving from imposed control to emergent order in education? How can, and how should, risk-taking be promoted in education? What constitutes a web of learning rather than a programmed sequence of learning? How can and should assessment, which is overwhelmingly of an individual's performance, catch interactivity, connectedness and collective knowledge? What kind of feedback promotes emergence, self-organization and connectedness in education? What should we do as a result of feedback? What constitutes openness in education? What are the necessary and sufficient conditions for the state of being complex, for emergence and self-organization? What are the differences among ideas, ideology and theory in deciding 'what works' in education if unpredictability, change and diversity reign? On what criteria are some methods, curricula, pedagogies, assessments to be judged preferable to others if their outcomes are, in principle, uncertain? Why try to measure performance when, by definition in complexity, even if it were measurable, the measures may add little of significance to our understanding?

With regard to *connectedness*, questions arise such as: How can the educational environment both shape and be shaped by individuals and groups? How can self-organization and emergence be fostered in a climate of externally regulated education? Who should decide what and how to teach? How can conformity for system integration and a necessary critical mass of diversity for emergent change in education be balanced? Should schools seek to change the outside world? Should schools bow to external pressure for change and, if so, to which pressures, and how should they react? What constitutes 'standards' in a climate of uncertainty and non-linearity? What does connectedness mean in practice? How can connectedness yet diversity be developed simultaneously? How, and why, should schools be developed as complex adaptive systems? What is a connected, shared and collective mind?

With regard to *pedagogy*, questions are raised such as: What is the relationship between cooperation and competition in education (survival requires both in complexity theory)? How can diversity be amplified while building sufficient commonality for interaction? How can, and should, emergence and self-organization be promoted in education and through interaction? What kind of emergent forms are preferred over others, and how can these be justified? How far should redundancy and trial-and-error be tolerable and tolerated in the widespread pressure-cooker systems of high-stakes education? How can teachers educate for uncertainty? How can autonomy, creativity, and cooperative and collaborative learning be promoted in learners? What are acceptable limits to all of this, if there are no clear boundaries to webs? What is the nature and status of expertise in teachers-as-learners and teachers-as-facilitators? How can order without control be promoted in classrooms? How can non-linearity be promoted and recognized, whilst still ensuring high quality educational outcomes and avoiding a low-level, caprice-driven curriculum? How can teachers (who may know more than their students) participate as equal, rather than dominating, partners in the collaborative search for truth? How can 'structure' in learning be theorised in non-linear systems? How can 'increasing returns' be maximised in learning?

Of course, most of these questions are not new. Complexity theory affords the opportunity for a re-awakening of such topics which have lain dormant in climates of increased control of education, heavy prescription and mandated content, reinforced by high-stakes assessment systems and constant surveillance of an individual's performance against predicted targets. Complexity theory redefines 'the basics' of education, away from a controlled and controlling discipline-based education and towards a discovered, inter-disciplinary, emergent curriculum, and a reassertion of freedom as a *sine qua non* of education. Complexity theory takes us in a direction opposite to the neatly stated, over-determined, tidy, traditional, externally mandated and regulated prescriptions of governments for the aims, content, pedagogy and assessment of learning and education.

Additionally, complexity theory suggests a movement towards bottom-up development and change, local and institutional decision-making, a re-assertion of child-centeredness and experiential, exploratory learning, a rejection of tight prescription and linear programming of teaching and learning, and a move towards non-linear learning, anarchistic epistemologies and their curricular correlates. Complexity theory emphasises the process rather than the content of learning, as the constituents of relevant and enduring curriculum content are uncertain. Disciplinary boundaries dissolve as connections among areas of knowledge are permeable, fluid and hypertext-linked; curricula are differentiated and different rather than Procrustean. The ethical, epistemological and ontological implications of complexity theory are, in other words, key areas for the philosophy of education.

In a climate of uncertainty it is unclear what values a school should espouse, yet that same climate requires schools to have their own identity, values and autopoeisis in order to survive. How can schools live in this situation—caught between the Scylla of constant change and the Charybdis of having to remain resolute and holding fast to their values? It is an echo of the postmodernist's dilemma of proscribing fixity and firmness yet holding such proscriptions fixedly and firmly.

Complexity Theory, Learning and Teaching

Within complexity theory, learning is a process of emergence and co-evolution of the individual, the social group and the wider society. Emphasis is placed on the *relationship* between elements, rather than the elements themselves, and the human mind is regarded as a complex adaptive system. This argues against the 'empty vessel' theory of learning; rather, knowledge is emergent and the mind is emergent and developing. Our minds are not static; each new event is met and learned by a new mind—it is not the same mind as it was moments before.

The mind is also a shared, collective and distributed property. Kelly's (1994) 'hive mind' is a collective consciousness wherein the whole transcends the sum of the parts and in which there is no single locus of control; the swarm of bees is more than the activity of the single bee multiplied thousands of times. Knowledge is a cultural and shared good. No individual is possessed of complete knowledge; individuals are fallible and knowledge resides within communities. Redefining the mind as a collective mind with a collective consciousness poses significant questions of epistemology, curriculum planning and assessment in education, for example, how can an individual 'know' when knowledge, by definition here, is collective? The mind is a composite of the biological brain and the cultural and symbolic environment in which each constantly influences and adapts to the other. Individuals and their environments (however defined, whether cognitive, cultural, communitarian, social, emotional, physical) shape each other emergently and agentically. Knowledge is simultaneously socially, culturally, temporally and locally contextualised, situated, learned and shaped.

The complexity-based curriculum would be dynamic, emergent, rich, relational, autocatalytic, self-organized, open, existentially realized by the participants, connected and recursive (e.g. Doll, 1993), with the teacher moving from the role as an expert and transmitter to a facilitator, co-learner and co-constructer of meaning, enabling learners to connect new knowledge to existing knowledge. Learners, for their part, have to be prepared to exercise autonomy, responsibility, ownership, self-direction and reflection.

Complexity theory stresses people's connections with others and with both cognitive and affective aspects of the individual persona. The curriculum and learning bind cool reflection with passion and humanity. As Forster (1910) remarks in *Howards End* (chapter 22), 'Only connect the prose and the passion, and both will be exalted … . Live in fragments no longer. Only connect, and the beast and the monk, robbed of the isolation that is life to either, will die'. The natural consequence of this view of learning is an emphasis on the *conditions* to promote emergence, including motivation, enjoyment, passion, cooperative and collaborative activity. Here knowledge is perpetually being constructed and reconstructed (the mind and the brain being complex adaptive systems) through the assimilation and accommodation of new knowledge to existing knowledge (connectionist models—'joined-up thinking'), thereby changing both the existing and new knowledge, rather than either being fixed and finite. As Zull (2004, p. 68) remarks: 'learning changes the brain, and the young child's brain is plastic'.

The young child's brain deliberately seeks out—proactively—information from the environment in order to learn. Cohen and Stewart (1995, p. 348) point out that there are more neural connections *from* the brain to the ear than from the ear *to* the brain, and that some 10% of the fibres in the optic nerve go 'the wrong way'. Sense organs do not passively receive information—in their words, 'they go fishing for it': learning is an active search. Interactions among elements of knowledge, learners and teachers are vital, with teachers as facilitators and co-learners and with learning changing both the learner and the teacher in a process of co-evolution.

Learning is dynamic, active, experiential and participatory, open-ended, unpredictable and uncertain, and cognition requires interaction, decentralized control, diversity and redundancy (Davis & Sumara, 2005). In the hive there are multitudes of individuals, and small failures are lost in the crowd; creativity and novelty through trial and error can be developed through redundancy and critical mass. Emergence and self-organization require room for development; tightly prescribed, programmed and controlled curricula and formats for teaching and learning, and standardised rates of progression are anathema to complexity theory. It breaks a lock-step curriculum.

Discussion-based inquiry is significant here, as is autonomous, experiential and flexible learning that embodies the weak classification and framing of permeable subject boundaries: free and freed thinking. Negotiated learning and higher-order, existential, interrogative and evaluative approaches to curriculum content feature highly, and problem-solving activities and a challenging stance towards received knowledge are advocated, with teachers acting as transformative facilitators (complexity theory is after all a theory of transformation for survival). Learning in the internally- and externally-connected brain unites creativity, emotion and cognition; they are hard-wired into apparently cool cognition and higher faculties (Zohar, 1997, p. 31). Meaning, value and feelings precede cool logic and the austere beauty of calm, disinterested rationality. As Bruner (1986) suggests, actual minds are a precursor to possible worlds, and it is good to listen to voices speaking to us from possible worlds about values, excitements, arguments and visions. This is neo-Deweyism and child-centeredness from Montessori with a contemporary ring.

In complexity theory, learning becomes a joint voyage of exploration, not simply of recycling given knowledge. For learning to be promoted, rich and positive feedback between learners and teachers is essential. Cognition is dialogic and high quality verbal interaction is essential. The teacher is vital, intervening judiciously to scaffold and create the conditions for learning-through-self-organization and the child's emergent knowledge. Cognition is not simply the acquisition of new knowledge: it engages motivation, personalities, learning styles, dispositions and preferences, the whole person. Teaching and learning take place at the intersection of the individual and society, and the outcomes are unpredictable. This is a difficult model for those managers to entertain who seek certainty, control, predictability and narrow accountability. Learning is an ongoing, emergently choreographed dance between partners and agents (co-evolution through relationships and connections); the partners both create, and are in, their dance. All parties come together as co-evolving, co-adaptive and fluid communities of practice.

The web of learning transcends its metaphorical status and becomes actual: learning is complexly inter-related in a myriad ways, breaking the simple linearity of positivism and behaviourism. The learning web has an ecology of its own, and each learner inhabits several webs (communities) of learning simultaneously. Ecological validity takes on additional meaning as that learning which is determined and valued collectively by the group. Indeed, teachers have to become 'eco-technicians' (Kelly & Allison, 1999, pp. 201–214), understanding the webs of learning that learners inhabit, the fitness landscapes of each, how to promote them holistically, and how to comprehend and work with fuzzy and infinitely receding boundaries to webs of learning. Learning and knowledge are not external, with the realist learner inhabiting a pre-existing, external world; rather, the constructivist learner produces and reproduces knowledge evolutionarily and actively. Students and teachers together create, share and shape their own and each other's meanings. The self is a constitution of a network of inter-connected and inter-related systems, as Zohar (1997, p. 110) writes: 'I am defined by my relationships ... the boundaries of my own identity are quite ambiguous and contextual'. The person emerges from the dynamic interactions of the elements of the webs that he/she inhabits. The individual, the group, the class, the school, the community are all inter-related and affect each other; they are neither isolated nor independent.

   Pedagogy is not transmissive or delivery-based—that is for assembly lines—but cast in a language and practice of 'possibility', of openness, freedom, autonomy and exploration. To have it otherwise is intellectually totalitarian, controlled and closed, and complexity theory proscribes closure, control, conformity and uniformity. A complexity-informed pedagogy *requires* communication. That locates it firmly within Habermas's advocacy of communicative action and the *ideal speech situation* including, *inter alia* (Habermas, 1979):

- Freedom to enter a discourse, check questionable claims, evaluate explanations and justifications;
- Freedom to modify a given conceptual framework and alter norms;
- Mutual understanding between participants;
- Equal opportunity for dialogue that abides by the validity claims of truth, legitimacy, sincerity and comprehensibility, and recognises the legitimacy of each subject to participate in the dialogue as an autonomous and equal partner;
- Equal opportunity for discussion, and the achieved—negotiated—consensus resulting from discussion deriving from the force of the better argument alone, and not from the positional power of the participants;
- Exclusion of all motives except for the cooperative search for truth.

Habermas's 'unforced force of the better argument', dialogue and discussion are part of this complex, cooperative search for truth in teaching and learning. One cannot, of course, press the Habermasian connection too far, as complexity theory is concerned more with strategic than communicative action.

Complexity Theory and Educational Research

Learning implies researching. In the field of educational research, complexity theory challenges the value of experimental and positivist research in education. It argues against the linear, deterministic, predictable, positivist, universalizable, stable, atomized, objective, mechanistic, controlled, measurable, closed systems of law-like behaviour and simple causality. Complexity theory replaces these with an emphasis on networks, linkages, holism, feedback, relationships and interactivity in context (Cohen & Stewart, 1995), emergence, dynamical systems, self-organization and an open system (rather than the closed world of the experimental laboratory). Even if we could conduct an experiment, its applicability to ongoing, emerging, interactive, relational, open situations, in practice, is limited (Morrison, 2001).

It is misconceived to hold variables constant in a dynamical, evolving, fluid, open situation. What is measured is already history.

Complexity theory challenges randomised controlled trials—the 'gold standard' of research. Classical experimental methods, abiding by the need for replicability and predictability, may not be particularly fruitful since, in complex phenomena, results are never clearly replicable or predictable: As Heraclitus noted, we never step into the same river twice. Complexity theory suggests that educational research should concern itself with: (a) how multivalency and non-linearity enter into education; (b) how voluntarism and determinism, intentionality, agency and structure, lifeworld and system, divergence and convergence interact in learning (Morrison, 2002; 2005); (c) how to both use, but transcend, simple causality in understanding the processes of education; and (d) how viewing a system holistically, as having its own ecology of multiply-interacting elements, is more powerful than an atomized approach. To atomize phenomena into measurable variables and then to focus only on certain of these is to miss synergies and the significance of the whole. Measurement, however acute, may tell us little of value about a phenomenon: I can measure every observable variable of a person to an infinitesimal degree, but his/her nature, what makes him/her who he or she is, eludes atomization and measurement. *Pace* Wittgenstein (1961, p. 56), the limits of our consciousness mark the limits of our world: we may be prisoners of our present consciousness in seeking to explain or understand complexity. We need new holistic tools and a new consciousness to understand and research complexity.

Complexity theory suggests that the conventional units of analysis in educational research (e.g. individuals, institutions, communities and systems) should merge, so that the unit of analysis becomes a web or ecosystem (Capra, 1996, p. 301), focused on, and arising from, a specific topic or centre of interest (a 'strange attractor'). Individuals, families, students, classes, schools, communities and societies exist in symbiosis; complexity theory tells us that their relationships are necessary, not contingent, and analytic, not synthetic. Complexity theory offers considerable leverage in understanding societal, individual, and institutional change; it provides the nexus between macro- and micro-research.

In addressing holism, complexity theory suggests the need for case study methodology, qualitative research and participatory, multi-perspectival and collaborative (self-organized), partnership-based forms of research, premised on interactionist, qualitative and interpretive accounts (e.g. Lewin & Regine, 2000). Heterogeneity is the watchword. Complexity theory suggests both a substantive agenda and also a set of methodologies, arguing for methodological, paradigmatic and theoretical pluralism.

Ten Challenges to Complexity Theory for the Philosophy of Education

First, complexity theory is caught in a double bind. Though it offers an explanation for change and evolution in particular instances and circumstances, it is essentially a *post hoc* explanation; one can see the hidden hand of complexity theory—the ghost in the machine—working in the present and past only; this limits its *prospective* utility. However, it can be, and has been, used *prospectively*, to prescribe actions and situations that promote change and development: for example, one can promote a climate for emergence-through-self-organization by nurturing creativity, openness, redundancy, diversity, networking, relationships, order without control, co-evolution, feedback, distributed power and risk taking.

However this immediately raises a difficulty for complexity theory: it is essentially a descriptive theory, and to move from a descriptive to a prescriptive theory is to commit a category mistake, to mix fact and value, to derive an 'ought' from an 'is', to commit the naturalistic fallacy. How easily one can slip from an 'is' to an 'ought' is evidenced in the discussion of learning above. Davis and Sumara (2005, p. 318) state that 'complexity science will not tell educators or educational researchers what to do in any prescriptive sense ... but it can provide direct advice on how to focus efforts when preparing for teaching'. This is a leap from an 'ought' to an 'is', however benignly intended. Whilst it is still possible to be prescriptive for an indeterminate future, the two being not mutually exclusive, in the very notion of unavoidable unpredictability, complexity theory undermines its own power to guide behaviour with any certain future in mind. It is a theory for the here and now, locked into the youthfulness of perpetual contemporaneity. For educationists this is to recognize that, whilst complexity theory may offer suggestions for practice, it gives no guarantees; it is a theory without responsibility or accountability. Certainty is elusive. As a descriptive theory, complexity theory may help only short-term planning, and that, too, may not turn out as intended. As the Hawthorne effect showed, experiments may work in the short term but not in the long term.

Second, a related issue is that complexity theory is amoral, it only describes—and maybe explains—what happens and has happened. Complexity theory alone cannot provide a sufficient account of education, as education is a moral enterprise requiring moral debate and moral choices. Complexity theory does not rule out discussions of good or bad, desirable and undesirable; it simply regards them as irrelevant. As such it offers an incomplete reading of education. Though many theorists in the field have moved quickly from description to prescription of practice, perhaps in an effort to ensure a sympathy between *observed* principles of complex change and *desired* practices of development, complexity theory cannot tell us how we should act. Education, learning and teaching are, at their core, normative activities, but complexity theory is silent on justifying values; it reports evolution, it analyses—and suggests how to analyse—phenomena, but it does not speak to morals. It describes the amoral law of the jungle.

Like Darwin's theory of evolution through natural selection, complexity theory may not help us to plan for the moral activity of education. Whilst avoiding the putative 'anything goes' criticism of relativism, one can recall Wittgenstein's (1961, pp. 73–4) famous remark that 'when all possible scientific questions have been answered, the problems of life remain completely untouched ... . What we cannot speak about we must pass over in silence'. Education cannot afford such silence. Complexity theory can suggest what to do if one wishes to promote development, but it does not tell us if those actions are desirable. Indeed, one has to consider whether bringing complexity theory into education is a covert form of scientism.

This is not to wish to abandon complexity theory, only to recognize its limits for a philosophy of education or to recognize that we do not yet have the appropriate conceptual tools to understand it. Complexity theory is a new way of thinking; it requires new constructs, rather than seeking to explain phenomena using existing constructs. One sees this in the need for a new mathematics to explain Kauffman's (1995) fitness landscapes. We may not yet have the appropriate tools to understand the phenomena in front of our eyes.

Third, complexity theory regards knowledge as a social construct, created by participants at a particular socio-historical-geographical conjuncture. Complexity theory is highly pragmatic and suggests that what is right at any moment is what works at that time to ensure survival. The charge of relativism is one which complexity theory cannot shake off easily, though, of course, relativism has many hues and degrees. It is no accident, perhaps, that complexity theory should have come to the fore at this moment in history, and in the west; it would be difficult to imagine it coming earlier or elsewhere. As Mackenzie (2003, p. 1) writes:

> ... the movement of complexity attests to a structure of feeling rooted in a long-standing European-American time-sense ... which could be called 'possibilization' ... . Complexity metaphors are particularly temporally significant because they attest to a sense, a 'structure of feeling', of openness and possibility concerning the future. What we are tracking is an expansion of the older Euro-American mind-set, not its extinction, as the future becomes a space for possibility for subjects who believe that anything is possible, given means.

One could not see several key elements of complexity theory (e.g. distributed control, self-organization, order without control, open systems, unpredictability) emerging in totalitarian regimes or in pre-modernist or modernist times. Though its *explanandum* has always been with us, the theory—the *explanans*—is a child of a postmodern world.

The question of whether complexity theory's potential relativism predicts its own ultimate demise or undermines its own status is one which, on the one hand, complexity theory has difficulty answering, yet which, on the other hand, suggests that the relativism/absolutism debate is trying to judge a new understanding and new reality with old conceptual tools. It is easy to dismiss any theory of dynamical systems as relativist, but that only becomes problematic if relativism and absolutism are seen to be appropriate criteria; indeed, one could ask, what is not relativist? Even the cool world of mathematics has changed itself over time. Relativism is an easy charge to level; the more important question is whether, if complexity theory is relativist, that actually matters.

The issue runs deeper. Complexity theory is anti-positivist and anti-predictability, yet, *post hoc*, it generates laws and regularities, for example, of emergence, self-organization, self-organized criticality, co-evolution, the regularity or inescapability of indeterminacy and nonlinearity. In emphasising a few simple rules that govern change, is complexity theory reaffirming a neo-structuralist and neo-reductionist reading of the world? Behind the backs of agentic players there is a hidden hand of emergence, conditioned choices and determinist laws of development and survival. Using conventional analysis, the question against complexity theory is harsh: either it undermines its own status, being relativist, or it is incoherent, being absolutist and determinist in its observed laws of development whilst purporting to celebrate indeterminism, unpredictability, relativism and temporality. As such, it is a slippery construct with which to approach the philosophy of education: should educationists use a theory that is so uncertain of its own status?

Fourth, many of the concepts of complexity theory are the everyday stuff of educational discourse, for example, control; self-organization and emergence; communication and networking; creativity and openness; unpredictability and non-linearity; relationships and dynamical systems; feedback and learning for development; redundancy and diversity; collectivity and connectedness; co-evolution, continuous development and adaptation; agency and structure; the social construction of knowledge. Whilst complexity theory has the attraction of drawing these together into a coherent framework, one has to ask what 'added value' complexity theory brings to an analysis of education which dealing with each of these concepts directly and without complexity theory does not bring. It raises the question of how far education and practice *need* complexity theory. What we have in the application of complexity theory is a set of exhortations backed up by descriptive report, and these can stand alone, i.e. they do not need to be shoehorned into complexity theory for their allure.

Fifth, though complexity theory provides a sharp and timely critique of positivism, one cannot overlook the contribution that positivism makes to many improvements in everyday life. Though positivism risks the scientization of society, it is too soon to write its epitaph; it continues to deliver many benefits. Whilst complexity theory raises significant challenges to positivism, this is not to mark the total demise of positivism, only its possible boundaries. Indeed one could ask about the nature of explanation if causal connections are no longer acceptable.

Sixth, the capability of participants for, and indeed their will to exercise, diversity, autocatalysis, emergence, self-organization, and their willingness to live in an open, unpredictable and non-linear world should not be assumed. People may prefer equilibrium and certainty in their lives. To this the answer from complexity theory is unforgiving and inhumane: adapt or die. Further, the discourses of complexity may over-emphasize unpredictability, difference, diversity, openness, change, freedom and emergence, and under-emphasize similarity, sameness, the value of homogeneity, predictability and control. Perpetual novelty, agency and autonomy are not characteristics of many people's lives, and many people would not wish even to possess them: the existentialist's description of the classic fear of freedom. Of course, emergent order may be marked by homogeneity; systems are often more similar than dissimilar. Take, for example, the persistence of bureaucracies: decades after Weber they are still with us because they *emerge* as a practical outcome of self-organization.

Seventh, complexity theory under-theorises power, or its lack, regarding it as the momentum of the moment; though this may capture the spirit of complexity, it does little to address powerlessness in society. Its comments on autocatalysis and self-organization fit poorly to systems of schooling whose hidden curricula, reaffirming

Jackson's celebrated *Life in Classrooms* (1968), comprise obedience, compliance, passivity and conformity, unequal power, delay, denial, rules, rituals and routines.

Eighth, the issues of unpredictably and connectedness raise difficult issues of responsibility. If I cannot predict the consequences of my actions, in what sense can I be held responsible for what happens after my actions? What is the nature of responsibility if the same behaviour does not produce the same results twice? Where does responsibility lie in a shared ethical, epistemological, and ontological web? Is my intention to act to bring about such-and-such a consequence a sufficient, though necessary, justification for my actions? Maybe it is the best that we can do. Further, unpredictability questions the criteria for rationality: in what senses can behaviour be said to be rational if its outcomes are unknowable? What constitutes collective and dispersed rationality in a collective mind? What constitutes acceptable (and necessary) deviance in an individual or group?

Ninth, complexity theory needs to clarify whether it is a theory of survival in an unfriendly world, or simply a call to development. If it is the former then whether this is an apt model for education is questionable. Education should be touched by humanity, rather than being red in tooth and claw.

Finally, though complexity theory discusses 'systems', it is difficult to discern the boundaries of systems. In advocating holism, what constitutes the 'whole' is problematic. What is the whole realm of a class, and of an individual? These are boundless, seamless, unmeasurable, and susceptible to infinite regress.

Conclusion

This chapter suggests that, whilst complexity theory informs many branches of philosophy, there are significant areas of philosophy that it does not touch—perhaps most significantly, ethics and values, and these are the very areas which the philosophy of education should address.

If one takes philosophy to be, *inter alia*, a process of analysis, problem-posing, understanding and raising questions, then complexity theory raises important questions and can help us, but the justifications for its prescriptions need resolution. Complexity theory is alluring; once we are aware of it we see it happening everywhere. This should not obscure the very real questions that have to be answered about its nature, status, methodology, utility and contribution to the philosophy of education.

Complexity theory, with its challenges to conventional epistemology, cognition, simple and reductive certainties, linear causality, coupled with its advocacy of holism, autonomy and creativity, raises intriguing questions for the philosophy of education. As a true science, it sounds a call constantly to create new knowledge; it forces creativity, rather than recycling the old and familiar; it is a theory of perpetual novelty, disequilibrium and creativity; and it is a restatement of the need for humility and humanity in admitting that our knowledge, though only partial and incomplete, may be the best that we can do. Our minds limit us. Epistemological and ontological shock at the realization of our own fallibility are to be expected. As Feyerabend (1975, p. 17) writes: 'theoretical anarchism is more humanitarian and more likely to encourage progress than its law-and-order alternatives'.

In an interview about her work with one of the founding fathers of complexity theory—Ilya Prigogine—the philosopher Isabelle Stengers (2004, p. 97) notes that she often had to tell his visitors that his complexity-driven physics did not offer a universal key, that 'nothing can take the place of the process of creation of relevant questions in each field', that 'there are no good answers if the question is not the relevant one', and that 'feeling matters in science also'. Humanity supersedes technocracy. These are both salutary and courageous principles for complexity theory and the philosophy of education.

References

April, K. A., Macdonald, R. & Vriesendorp, S. (2000) *Rethinking Leadership* (Cape Town, University of Cape Town Press).

Ashby, W. R. (1964) *Introduction to Cybernetics* (London, Methuen).

Bak, P. (1996) *How Nature Works* (New York, Copernicus).

Bak, P. & Chen, K. (1991) Self-Organized Criticality, *Scientific American*, January, pp. 46–53.

Bar-Yam, Y. (1997) *Dynamics of Complex Systems* (New York, Perseus Press).

Bruner, J. S. (1986) *Actual Minds: Possible worlds* (Cambridge, MA, Harvard University Press).

Capra, F. (1996) *The Web of Life* (New York, Anchor Books).

Cilliers, P. (1998) *Complexity and Postmodernism* (London, Routledge).

Cohen, J. & Stewart, I. (1995) *The Collapse of Chaos* (Harmondsworth, Penguin).

Davis, B. & Sumara, D. J. (2005) Challenging Images of Knowing: Complexity science and educational research, *International Journal of Qualitative Studies in Education*, 18:3, pp. 305–321.

Doll, W. (1993) *A Postmodern Perspective on Curriculum* (New York, Teachers College Press).

Feyerabend, P. (1975) *Against Method: Outline of an anarchistic theory of knowledge* (London, New Left Books).

Forster, E. M. (1910) *Howards End* (New York, Bantam Books).

Fullan, (1989) Managing Curriculum Change, in: M. Preedy (ed.), *Approaches to Curriculum Management* (Milton Keynes, Open University Press), pp. 144–149.

Goodwin, B. (2000) Out of Control into Participation, *Emergence*, 2:4, pp. 40–49.

Habermas, J. (1979) *Communication and the Evolution of Society*, T. McCarthy, trans. (London, Heinemann).

Jackson, P. (1968) *Life in Classrooms* (Eastbourne, Holt, Rinehart and Winston).

Kauffman, S. A. (1995) *At Home in the Universe: The search for the laws of self-organization and complexity* (Harmondsworth, Penguin).

Kelly, K. (1994) *Out of Control* (Cambridge, MA, Perseus Books).

Kelly, S. & Allison, M. A. (1999) *The Complexity Advantage: How the science of complexity can help your business achieve peak performance* (New York, McGraw-Hill).

Lewin, R. (1993) *Complexity: Life on the edge* (London, Phoenix).

Lewin, R. & Regine, B. (2000) *The Soul at Work: Listen, respond, let go: Embracing complexity science for business success* (New York, Simon and Shuster).

Mackenzie, A. (2003) The Practice of Complexity. Unpublished paper, Institute for Cultural Research, University of Lancaster.

Marion, R. (1999) *The Edge of Organization: Chaos and Complexity Theories of Formal Social Systems* (London, Sage Publications Ltd.).

Morrison, K. R. B. (2001) Randomised Controlled Trials for Evidence-Based Education: Some problems in judging 'what works', *Evaluation and Research in Education*, 15:2, pp. 69–83.

Morrison, K. R. B. (2002) *School Leadership and Complexity Theory* (London, RoutledgeFalmer).

Morrison, K. R. B. (2005) Structuration, Habitus and Complexity Theory: elective affinities or new wine in old bottles?, *British Journal of Sociology of Education*, 26:3, pp. 311–326.

Prigogine, L. & Stengers, I. (1985) *Order Out of Chaos* (London, Flamingo).

Santonus, M. (1998) *Simple, Yet Complex*. Available at: <http://www.cio.com/archive/enterprise/ 041598_qanda_content.html> Retrieved 4 May, 2001.

Stacey, R. D. (1992) *Managing the Unknowable* (San Francisco, Jossey-Bass).

Stacey, R. D. (2000) *Strategic Management and Organizational Dynamics*, 3rd edn. (Harlow, UK, Pearson Education Limited).

Stacey, R. D., Griffin, D. & Shaw, P. (2000) *Complexity and Management: Fad or radical challenge to systems thinking?* (London, Routledge).

Stengers, I. (2004) The Challenge of Complexity: Unfolding the ethics of science. In memoriam Ilya Prigogine, *Emergence: Complexity and Organization*, 6:1–2, pp. 92–99.

Stewart, M. (2001) *The Co-Evolving Organization* (Rutland, UK, Decomplexity Associates Ltd.). <http://www.decomplexity.com/Coevolving%20Organization%20VU.pdf> Retrieved 27 August, 2001.

Waldrop, M. M. (1992) *Complexity: The emerging science at the edge of order and chaos* (Harmondsworth, Penguin).

Wheatley, M. (1999) *Leadership and the New Science: Discovering order in a chaotic world*, 2nd edn. (San Francisco, Berrett-Koehler Publishers).

Wittgenstein, L. (1961) *Tractatus Logico-Philosophicus* (London, Routledge and Kegan Paul).

Youngblood, M. (1997) *Life at the Edge of Chaos* (Dallas, TX, Perceval Publishing).

Zohar, D. (1997) *Rewiring the Corporate Brain* (San Francisco, Berrett-Koechler Publishers Inc.).

Zull, J. E. (2004) The Art of Changing the Brain, *Educational Leadership*, 62:1, 68–72.

3

What Is Complexity Theory and What Are Its Implications for Educational Change?

Mark Mason
University of Hong Kong

Introduction

> The issue is that in the social world, and in much of reality ... , causation is complex. Outcomes are determined not by single causes but by multiple causes, and these causes may, and usually do, interact in a non-additive fashion. In other words the combined effect is not necessarily the sum of the separate effects. It may be greater or less, because factors can reinforce or cancel out each other in non-linear ways. (Byrne, 1998, p. 20)

This is an obvious point, but it bears repeating to establish an uncontroversial premise for what follows in this chapter, which seeks to understand better the forces of continuity and change by considering problems of educational change from the perspective of complexity theory. Complexity theory's notion of emergence implies that, given a significant degree of complexity in a particular environment, or critical mass, new properties and behaviours emerge that are not contained in the essence of the constituent elements, nor can be predicted from a knowledge of initial conditions. These concepts of emergent phenomena from a critical mass, associated with notions of lock-in, path dependence, and inertial momentum, contribute to an understanding of continuity and change that sheds more than just an interesting light on educational change, both organisational and institutional (to use the distinction drawn by Waks, 2007).

Complexity Theory

Developed principally in the fields of physics, biology, chemistry, and economics, complexity theory arises in some senses out of chaos theory in that it shares chaos theory's focus on the sensitivity of phenomena to initial conditions that may result in unexpected and apparently random subsequent properties and behaviours. Chaos theory suggests that even a very slight degree of uncertainty about initial conditions can grow inexorably and cause substantial fluctuations in the behaviour of a particular phenomenon. Perhaps more importantly, complexity theory shares chaos theory's concern with wholes, with larger systems or environments and the relationships among their constituent elements or agents, as opposed to the often reductionist concerns of mainstream science with the essence of the 'ultimate particle'. While in the social sciences it was pioneered in economics (Holland, 1987; Arthur, 1989, 1990), complexity theory was otherwise as little as ten years ago a relative stranger to the social sciences.

Complexity theory is, as Morrison (2002, p. 6) puts it, 'a theory of survival, evolution, development and adaptation'. It concerns itself with environments, organisations, or systems that are complex in the sense that very large numbers of constituent elements or agents are connected to and interacting with each other in many different ways. These constituent elements or agents might be atoms, molecules, neurons, human agents, institutions, corporations, *etc.* Whatever the nature of these constituents, the system is characterised by a continual organisation and re-organisation of and by these constituents

> into larger structures through the clash of mutual accommodation and mutual rivalry. Thus, molecules would form cells, neurons would form brains, species would form ecosystems, consumers and corporations would form economies, and so on. At each level, new emergent structures would form and engage in new emergent behaviours. Complexity, in other words, [is] really a science of emergence. (Waldrop, 1993, p. 88)

Complexity is of course inherently systemic in nature. But the connotations in the commonly associated term, 'dynamical systems theory', should already indicate to the reader that it will not be susceptible to accusations of a-historical, static, de-contextualised, functionalist—and, by implication, conservative—analytic perspectives. As Byrne (1998, p. 51) reminds us, 'What is crucially important about [complexity] is that it is systemic without being conservative. On the contrary, the dynamics of complex systems are inherently dynamic and transformational'.

One of the most important insights of complexity theory is this notion of emergence which implies that, given a sufficient degree of complexity in a particular environment, new (and to some extent unexpected) properties and behaviours emerge in that environment. The whole becomes, in a very real sense, more than the sum of its parts in that the emergent properties and behaviours are not contained in or able to be predicted from the essence of the constituent elements or agents. A central concern of complexity theory is thus with the relationships among the elements or agents that constitute a particular and sufficiently complex environment or system. Once a system reaches a certain critical level of complexity, otherwise known as critical mass, a phase transition takes place which makes possible the emergence of new properties and behaviours and a momentum whose inertia is significantly increased. A certain critical level of diversity and complexity must be reached for a system to achieve a sustainable autocatalytic state—that is, for it to maintain its own momentum in a particular direction. This model posits the phase transition as a fundamental law of increasing complexity, but the specific details of this phase transition—when and how it occurs, what properties and behaviours emerge—are contingent on specific contextual factors and are probably unique to that particular context. Johnson (2001, p. 18) describes the emergence of these concepts of self-organisation and emergence as follows:

> [s]ome of the great minds of the last few centuries—Adam Smith, Friedrich Engels, Charles Darwin, Alan Turing—contributed to the unknown science of self-organization, ... [but] didn't even themselves realise that they were struggling to understand the laws of emergence. They were wrestling with local issues, in clearly defined fields: how ant colonies learn to forage and build nests; why industrial neighbourhoods form along class lines; how our minds learn to recognise faces ... . Keller and Segel saw [patterns of self-organization] in slime mould assemblages; Jane Jacobs saw it in the formation of city neighbourhoods; Marvin Minsky in the distributed networks of the human brain ... .
>
> In the simplest terms, [these systems] solve problems by drawing on masses of relatively stupid elements, rather than a single, intelligent, 'executive branch'. They are bottom-up systems, not top-down ... . [T]hey are complex adaptive systems that display emergent behaviour. In these systems, agents residing on one scale start producing behaviour that lies one scale above them: ants create colonies; urbanites create neighbourhoods; simple pattern-recognition software learns how to recommend new books. The movement from low-level rules to higher-level sophistication is what we call emergence.

As Morrison (2002, p. 10) puts it,

> [t]hrough feedback, recursion, perturbance, autocatalysis, connectedness and self-organization, higher and greater levels of complexity and differentiated, new forms of life, behaviour, systems and organizations arise from lower levels of complexity and existing forms. These complex forms derive from often comparatively simple sets of rules—local rules and behaviours generating complex global order and diversity.

As Kuhn (1962) recognised in *The Structure of Scientific Revolutions*, phenomena that are not predictable and do not display uniformity within the constraints of a particular theoretical paradigm tend to be marginalised by the theories within that paradigm—until these marginal cases gather sufficient momentum to generate a paradigmatic shift, that is. Complexity theory, however, makes no claim to predict what is essential and what can be marginalised in the search for the levers of history. Unlike the rigid—as intimated by Kuhn—paradigms of scientific endeavour to date, complexity theory makes space for individuality, for the apparently marginal, for the seemingly trivial accidents of history. As a research paradigm, complexity theory cautions us not to marginalise or dispense with what is apparently trivial or inexplicable. What may appear to be marginal may well be part of the complexity of a system, and may be constituent of the critical level above which emergent properties and behaviours become possible.

The predominantly reductionist approach of Newtonian physics has resulted in a quest for the ultimate particle, from molecules to atoms to nuclei to quarks, an approach which focuses more on discrete and static building blocks than on the dynamics of the interactions among them. However, as the Nobel laureate physicist Philip Anderson pointed out in his article, 'More is Different', in *Science* (1972), cited by Waldrop (1993, p. 81),

> ... the ability to reduce everything to simple fundamental laws does not imply the ability to start from those laws and reconstruct the universe. In fact, the more the elementary particle physicists tell us about the nature of the fundamental laws, the less relevance they seem to have to the very real problems of the rest of science, much less society.

Where complexity theory differs from other theories that may exhibit reductionist tendencies in research rationale and methodology, is that it suggests that it is in the dynamic interactions and adaptive orientation of a system that new phenomena, new properties and behaviours, emerge, that new patterns are developed and old ones change. Complexity theory seeks the levers of history, the sources and reasons for change, in the dynamic complexity of interactions among elements or agents that constitute a particular environment. It is in this sense that seemingly trivial accidents of history may increase dramatically in significance when their interactions with other apparently minute events combine to produce significant redirections in the course of history, significant shifts in its prevailing balance of power.

A theory oriented towards reduction in search of the ultimate particle, the essential generative element or concept that gives rise to all other phenomena in the field, is certainly useful where such a primary generative source exists. But complexity theory draws attention beyond this. It accepts the existence of certain essential generative elements in a particular field, but suggests that the field as a whole is much more than merely predictably determined by the primary generative element. While this may be a trigger, and indeed only one of many triggers, of subsequent phenomenal (in the literal and figurative sense) developments, complexity theory suggests that it is the manifold interactions among constitutive elements or agents, whether essential or not, that are responsible for the phenomena, the patterns, properties, and behaviours that characterise a particular field.

The addition of new elements or agents to a particular system multiplies exponentially the number of connections or potential interactions among those elements or agents, and hence the number of possible outcomes. This is an important attribute of complexity theory. While one element or agent in a particular field cannot interact with any other if it exists in isolation, between two elements or agents, one connection is made; among three, three; among four, six; among five, ten; among six, fifteen; among seven, twenty one, and so on. The number of connections (y_n), between any two elements, associated with a given number of elements or agents (n) is given by the following formula which, because it is quadratic, illustrates the dramatic rate of increase of the number of connections in a curve that gets increasingly steep:

$$y_n = {}^1/_2(n^2 - n)$$

The importance of this observation is that the connections among individual agents or elements assume an importance that is critical to complexity theory's assertions about emergent properties. This emergence becomes possible by virtue of the exponential relationship between the elements or agents and the connections among them. The essence of the individual elements or agents that constitute a particular system does not alone provide the key to understanding that system. Complexity theory draws attention to the emergent properties and behaviours that result not only from the essence of constituent elements, but more importantly, from the connections among them. But it's not only the exponential relationship between the elements or agents and the connections among them; and it's also not just the 'essence' of the constitutive elements or agents. Ralph Stacey has set down three vitally important parameters that drive complex adaptive systems: 'the rate of information flow through the system, the richness of connectivity between agents in the system, and the level of diversity within and between the schemas of the agents' (1996, p. 99). So, apart from rich, exponentially generated connectivity among constituent elements, it's also about the diversity of those constituent elements, and the rate of information flow—and feedback—through the system across time.

An obvious but critical difference between the human and the natural sciences is that the former need to take account of conscious agents, and hence of the notions of strategy and expectations. And when one is dealing with intelligent agents (who can reflect and formulate strategies) in the social sciences, this means taking account of an individual's conscious intentionality as it is constrained and enabled by the environment, which in turn is constituted *inter alia* by other conscious individuals, who thus are said to co-evolve. The focus thus shifts from a concern with decontextualised and universalised essence to a concern with contextualised and contingent complex wholes. Complexity theory echoes Foucault's emphasis on 'polymorphous correlations in place of simple or complex causality' (cited in Harvey, 1990, p. 9). Admittedly, complexity theory does suggest that new properties and behaviours will emerge out of these 'polymorphous correlations', but the point is that there can be little or no teleologically imputed causal relationship between known initial conditions and these emergent phenomena.

The notions of scale and complexity are what underlie the principle of emergent phenomena. New properties or behaviours emerge when sufficient numbers and varieties of constituent elements or agents cluster together to form a sufficiently complex arrangement of incredible scale. The principle of emergent phenomena on account of increasingly complex networks among constituent elements has been used by the theoretical biologist Stuart Kauffman (1992) to explain the origins of life. Life, and indeed consciousness, are emergent phenomena: the brain is after all a complex arrangement of billions of neurons functioning according to the laws of cell biology, but the phenomenon of mind emerges as much more than a biological agglomeration of nerve cells. As Anderson (1972), cited by Waldrop (1993, p. 82) argues,

> At each level of complexity, entirely new properties appear. [And] at each stage, entirely new laws, concepts, and generalisations are necessary, requiring inspiration and creativity to just as great a degree as in the previous one. Psychology is not applied biology, nor is biology applied chemistry.

I would define *power*, in the light of complexity theory, as the directional course of the phenomenon that enjoys the dominant inertial momentum over other competing phenomena. The prevailing power structure will sustain and indeed increase its dominance by virtue of what can be simply and analogously understood as the snowball effect. Individual and apparently trivial incidents in the purview of the dominant power structure's momentum will be gathered up in its path and those outside of its purview will remain marginal and ineffective unless and until sufficient momentum in a different direction is sustained by sufficient complexity of these originally trivial events. How radical the power shift is will depend on the degree of difference in strength and direction (as in velocity or in vector analysis, but rather more amorphously) between the existing and the emerging power structures. The term path-dependence (allied to the notion of lock-in) illuminates this idea by suggesting that the inertial momentum of a particular phenomenon will sustain its direction and speed (i.e. its velocity) along a particular path, that a phenomenon is describable in terms of the direction of its path, and that it will continue in that path unless and until sufficient inertial momentum of a competing phenomenon results in a redirection of that path. Thus, good educational institutions will sustain and probably increase their own momentum, and weaker educational institutions will likewise compound the failure of their students, thereby further weakening themselves in an endless and vicious cycle.

This notion of inertial momentum, referring to the snowball effect, or the ever-increasing probability of the development and sustenance of correlated possibilities on account of recently developed phenomena, provides the conceptual link between the principle of emergent phenomena as developed principally in the natural sciences and the notion of socio-historical change in human society. Inertial momentum is inextricably related to the phenomenon of power. The power of an existing dispensation or social arrangement to sustain itself and to increase its purview of influence or control is directly related to its inertial momentum, to the aggregate weight of the phenomena of which it is constituted. And this aggregate is the result of the number and scale of the elements and agents that constitute the social arrangement, and of the degree of complexity of the interactions among them.

This snowball effect can be understood in terms of what the economist Brian Arthur (1989) calls 'the economics of increasing returns'. Examples are the siting of increasing numbers of high-tech companies in Silicon Valley (because it was already the location of a number of older high-tech companies), or the conquering of the video market by the VHS system—which was held to be marginally inferior to its former competitor, the Beta system (because steadily increasing VHS sales produced lock-in for its product), or the astounding dominance of the QWERTY typewriter keyboard. When mechanical typewriters were developed, touch-typists had to be slowed down by inefficient keyboard layouts because their increasing dexterity would continually jam the mechanically slow machines. One of the most inefficient designs (by Christopher Scholes in 1873) was the QWERTY layout, which was adopted and mass-produced by Remington. More typists accordingly learned on the QWERTY layout, more companies therefore adopted the same layout, and a virtually unbreakable lock-in of the QWERTY keyboard resulted.

Other far more efficient keyboard layouts have been designed, but the probability of their breaking the locked-in monopoly of the QWERTY keyboard, particularly now, given the proliferation of computer keyboards in the information technology revolution (and ironically, when we no longer have to worry about the mechanical jamming of the keyboard), is almost zero.

A fundamental tenet of free-market economics is that the market will winnow out inferior competitors and naturally produce the most efficient product. The QWERTY keyboard is a dramatic example of the economics of increasing returns, or of the phenomenon of lock-in as described by complexity theory, which challenges this tenet. This and other examples of lock-in of a technically inferior product illustrate an important feature of complexity theory: it does not exist at the meta-level of idealism or abstracted theoretical models, but is immersed in the way things are. Complexity theory is pragmatic in its philosophical orientation. Certainly perfect capital markets or the perfectly planned command economy would produce the perfect product, but this would be in an abstract, ideal world. Complexity theory suggests that we cannot discount the importance of apparently trivial accidents of history: much more cognisance is taken here of externalities, of the unintended consequences of actions. Outcomes occur as a result of sufficient levels of complexity at lower levels of the system. Consequently, the predictions that can be made with some degree of certainty from an idealised theoretical model are not possible in the paradigm of complexity theory. Newtonian physics may have made possible a fair amount of prediction and control, but complexity theory's orientation is more towards the humbler domain of comprehension and explanation, and less in the direction of prediction.

This phenomenon of lock-in is associated with the 'spontaneous self-organisation' of systems identified by the Belgian Nobel Laureate physicist Ilya Prigogine (1980) in his research on the origins of order and structure at all levels of the universe. The spontaneous dynamics of living systems result from the positive feedback to or self-reinforcement of phenomena, a process which is characterised by the increased incidence and significance of initially apparently trivial events under the random (at first anyway) conduciveness of circumstances. While the circumstances in which the positive feedback eventually occurs may have been initially random, the self-reinforcement leading to lock-in of a particular phenomenon reflects an autocatalytic chain of events in the field. The direct implication is of a self-sustaining phenomenon which, while the statistical chances of its appearance may have been negligible at first, emerges adaptively, locks itself in, and sustains its inertial momentum autocatalytically. To complexity theorists, 'positive feedback seem[s] to be the *sine qua non* of change, of surprise, of life itself' (Waldrop, 1993, p. 34). Any young and idealistic teacher, no matter how energetic, who has gone into a weak school with the intention of turning it around, will tell you that fighting its momentum is like shouting into the wind. She may touch the lives of two or three students, but that is probably it. At the risk of stating the obvious, it takes more than the efforts of one energetic teacher to affect the inertial momentum of a weak school that sustains its weakness autocatalytically.

A salient feature of a theory of increasing returns is that there are multiple possible outcomes. Which possible outcome is realised in the social sciences is a question of intervention at as many levels as possible: at the macro-structural level, at the intentional human agency level, so that sufficient momentum is generated in a particular direction to displace the inertial momentum of the current dispensation and to create a dominant inertial momentum for the desired policy. The dominant status of a particular social policy is as much a function of that policy's inertial momentum as the legislation that supports it. It is worth noting that complexity theory renders largely irrelevant the agency–structure debate about which of the two is more important in effecting change. Both are, and much else is too.

As the economist Brian Arthur argues, 'in the real world, outcomes don't just happen. They build up gradually as small chance events become magnified by positive feedbacks' (cited in Waldrop, 1993, p. 45). Working in probability theory, Arthur and others have constructed mathematical models by which it is possible to follow the process of the emergence of one historical outcome, to 'see mathematically how different sets of historical accidents could cause radically different outcomes to emerge' (ibid., p. 46). What this means for successful policy implementation is that positive feedbacks shaped towards a particular outcome need to be created through conscious interventions, so that new patterns are established. Once sufficient momentum is generated in the new (and desired) direction, the positive feedback becomes incorporated into the system autocatalytically, and new phenomena predominantly typical of the desired policy's characteristics, emerge. This is key to successful policy implementation and institutional management and leadership. Changing education systems to rid them of their inequities and inefficiencies will, in other words, require massive interventions at all levels.

The phenomenon of increasingly rapid technology change in late twentieth and early twenty first century society provides a good example of the notion of emergent phenomena which is central to complexity theory. It hardly needs mentioning that the rate of technology development in contemporary society is accelerating dramatically. Economic theory used to hold that new technological inventions were exogenous to the system: they reflected random flashes of insight in the minds of the odd genius here and there who had enjoyed the good fortune of a visit from the technological muse. More recent theory held that technological development was endogenous to the economic system: it was a direct result of increased investment in research and development. Complexity theory's concept of emergent phenomena suggests that the ever-accelerating pace of technological development occurs as a result of new inventions becoming possible because of networks of existing technological developments. The cellular telephone, for example, becomes possible because of satellite technology (which depends on rocket technology), computer technology, telephone technology, electrical technology, and so on. The list is virtually endless. The point is that new phenomena become more and more possible on account of networks of existing phenomena. To revert to our familiar metaphor, the process snowballs, and new possibilities become increasingly probable.

Lock-in of these emergent phenomena becomes all the more likely because each new technology creates a niche for related service and technology providers, each of whom has a stake in the continued dominant inertial momentum of the newly developed technology, and each of whose activity contributes to the web of phenomena (or, again, to the metaphorical snowball) associated with the new technology. The direction of history thus changes in accordance with these emergent phenomena. Of course this implies the extinction of outmoded technologies and related service and technology providers unless they are able to adapt to the new direction. This is what underlies the concept of adaptive institutions: those that are most able to adapt to new conditions are those most likely to survive. This process of the emergence of new phenomena and the extinction or adaptation of existing arrangements explains the 'adaptive' and 'spontaneous self-organisation' (Waldrop, 1993, p. 11) of a system, the 'incessant urge of complex systems to organise themselves into patterns' (ibid., p. 118). Darwin and complexity theory are, in other words, complementary in their explanation of evolution, in their explanation of the nature of change.

Understanding the market economy as a complex adaptive system, the Santa Fe Institute's John Holland (1987) reminds us that control in such an environment is considerably dispersed. It is not centralised direction that furnishes the system with any level of coherence, but the competition and co-operation among the economy's constituent agents. The properties and behaviours associated with the economy are best understood not merely by reference to government regulations, but in terms of their emergence and autocatalytic sustenance by virtue of the complexity and consequent inertial momentum of the system. Such a complex adaptive system is constituted by successive levels of organisation, from each of which, if sufficiently stable and coherent, emerge new phenomena on which subsequent emergent properties and behaviours are predicated. The emergence of phenomena stimulates the creation of multiple niches, each of which is exploited by agents providing goods and services, which sustain the newly emergent levels and in turn create new niches. Thus emergent phenomena are locked in and an economy of increasing returns is developed. Successfully adaptive institutions will continually rearrange their constituent networks according to the future that is anticipated by internal modelling based on prediction and environmental feedback. The operative principle is of course induction from empirical experience to general principle, rather than deduction.

Within these networks the optimisation of utility by individual agents is always a never-ending process and not a perfectly optimal state, first, because imperfectly intelligent agents can never perfectly comprehend their environment on account of its infinite range of possibilities, and second, because the environment is always changing by virtue of the adaptive orientation of other agents, and hence is unknowable. The essence of an element or agent or institution does not thus reflect its potential. This notion of an almost infinite possibility, not limited by the substance or essence of a particular agent or element or institution, is a result of the principle of emergence. The choices an individual makes in the face of her environment will emerge from this complex web of constraining and enabling elements.

Complexity Theory and Educational Change

It has been my intention through this short exposition to understand better the forces of continuity and the levers of change (although, of course, 'lever' is now an inappropriate metaphor). In the complexity of the educational environment, the plethora of relevant agencies and structures includes teachers, students, parents and other community leaders, the state and its education departments, economic structures and business organisations, and so on. Intervention to differing but sufficient extents in each of these areas is what would probably be necessary to shift a prevailing ethos in education. In other words, change in education, at whatever level, is not so much a consequence of effecting change in one particular factor or variable, no matter how powerful the influence of that factor. It is more a case of generating momentum in a new direction by attention to as many factors as possible.

Take the case of a school where the prevailing ethos is one of failure, where students are, for any number and combination of reasons, not learning. The agency–structure debate, to which I alluded earlier, invites us to consider whether change can be effected through human agency, or whether deeper and more powerful structural forces are at work. Structuralists who find the levers of history in economic factors might suggest that there is little we can do about this as human agents, because the despair that pervades the school is primarily a consequence of its poverty-stricken context and the jobless future that awaits school leavers, whether certificated or not. The ethos of the school will not change until the structure and nature of the economy change in such a way as to provide meaningful and worthwhile employment for certificated school leavers. Culturalists on the agency side of the debate might point to the importance of an excellent school leader, or of a committed corps of teachers. Complexity theorists would suggest that it is probably both—the structural factors and the influence of human agents—and far more. But because we can never know exactly what it is that is causing the school's failure, or exactly what it is that will turn the place around, our best chance of success lies in hitting the problem from as many angles, levels and perspectives as possible. It's more than that we cannot quantify the salience of any individual factor: we probably cannot even isolate any individual factor's influence in order to assess its salience. This is of course because various factors compound each other's effects in ways that both increase and diminish their aggregate influence.

The exercise of trying to isolate the influence of a particular factor is about as facile as attempts in the popular media to report which particular gene is responsible for, say, aggression, or agoraphobia, or a penchant for chocolate. Geneticists know enough about this emerging field to know that it is a combination of genes working in tandem and in tension with each other that leads to the attributes that mark each of us as individuals. And far more than just our genetic inheritance, psychologists and other social scientists have known for a long time that these attributes are an outcome of the complex interactions of factors associated with both 'nature' and 'nurture'. My point here is that trying to isolate and quantify the salience of any particular factor is not only impossible, but also wrongheaded. Isolate, even hypothetically, any one factor, and not only is the whole complex web of connections among the constituent factors altered—so is the influence of (probably) every other factor too.

To change the ethos of the school, then, requires intervention at every possible level. These levels would include factors associated with the state and its education and economic policies, and possibly factors beyond even the grasp of the state—those that are associated with the forces and consequences of globalisation, for example. They would include factors associated with the school's leaders and with its teachers, with the students themselves, with their parents, with the curriculum, with the school's organisation, with the local community—the list is probably endless. But, given that I indicated earlier that complexity theory enables little or no causal relationship to be teleologically imputed between known initial conditions and emergent phenomena, how can we know what to do about each of these factors? If it's both impossible and wrongheaded to try to isolate and assess the importance of any one factor, how can we even know in which direction we should try to push any factor? Fortunately, what we know from research in education gives us quite a few clues. The fact that complexity theory has little predictive utility does not negate education's research findings. This is because we're talking about two different spheres with very different levels of complexity. We know, for example, that feedback provided to learners on the appropriateness of their constructions has an immensely powerful effect on learning. We can predict with substantial confidence that learners who receive feedback on the soundness of the inferences they have drawn in the process of learning will learn more effectively than those who don't. Complexity theory's lack of predictive utility doesn't undermine our confidence in predicting this outcome, because this is not in itself, at this isolated level, a particularly complex phenomenon. Complexity theory's caveats do not apply here (at least not at the level at which we're discussing the phenomenon). Complexity theory has to do with complex systems, and it's at this level that it lacks predictive utility.

We know that feedback from teachers powerfully enhances learning. We know that parental involvement in their children's learning enhances learning; that good school leaders create effective learning environments through good management practices; that relevant and appropriately pitched curricular activities enhance learning more effectively than those that are not; that poor children provided with a school lunch learn more effectively than students who do not benefit from such a policy; that students who are likely to find employment learn more effectively than those who perceive little likelihood of work. If we know all this, and can predict with a reasonable degree of confidence an improvement in learning outcomes in each of these domains, then surely we can predict that change in the direction of enhanced learning outcomes in each of these domains is more likely to aggregate, in a complex adaptive system constituted by all of these factors (and more), to enhanced learning than to decreases in learning outcomes across the school?

Complexity theory tells us, in other words, that what it might take to change a school's inertial momentum from an ethos of failure to learning excellence is massive and sustained intervention at every possible level (including even those factors that, from a knowledge of initial conditions, appear trivial) until the phenomenon of learning excellence emerges from this new set of interactions among these new factors and sustains itself autocatalytically. And despite complexity theory's relative inability to predict the direction or nature of change, by implementing at each constituent level changes whose outcome we can predict with reasonable confidence, we are at least influencing change in the appropriate direction and surely stand a good chance of effecting the desired changes across the complex system as a whole.

Massive and sustained intervention at every possible level demands, unfortunately, very substantial resources. If there are many failing schools in a state's education system, choices might have to be made about where resources should be targeted. Trying to spread whatever resources are available across all failing schools may well result in the effects of the investment simply being dissipated. In each school, in other words, the intervention will have been too meagre to make any impact on the prevailing inertial momentum. Each school will in all likelihood revert to its ethos of failure, with the resources wasted. It may therefore be necessary to target the available resources at only a few selected schools for maximum impact—which is what it will probably take in terms of the arguments I have presented here. This will of course increase the level of inequity in the education system, a consequence that is morally questionable. But as yet I can see almost no way around this.

One might in response to this conundrum select the target schools based on a criterion that may reduce levels of inequity: for example, one might select, say, the thousand worst performing schools, or those schools that are attended predominantly by students from the poorest homes. Or one could select schools that are attended predominantly by students from minority groups (if those minority groups are indeed the least well off or in other ways excluded). The additional challenge in these cases is, of course, that these schools are going to be the hardest to turn around, and will demand substantial additional resources. The question then arises as to how policy makers might be able to predict which schools are more likely to change under the impact of massive and sustained investment of resources. Some writers have pointed to the efficacy of crises in this regard: it is when a school, or an education system, or a society, faces a crisis that it is probably more amenable to change. A good example here is the case of the USA's response to the Soviet Union's launch of Sputnik: the former country perceived this as a crisis in the so-called 'space race', and resolved that a key strategy to gain the initiative in the race was massive investment in mathematics and science education.

Conclusion: The 'Conditions of Emergence'

In one of the most interesting chapters of their book, *Complexity and Education*, Davis and Sumara (2006) consider the 'conditions of emergence' (pp. 129–52). If education is about fostering the emergence of learning, of creativity, of imaginative and critical perspectives, then educators would be fair in asking of complexity theory how we might set about establishing, or at least contributing to the establishment of, the conditions, insofar as it is possible to influence those conditions, for emergence to occur. Davis and Sumara list the following factors or conditions, many of which have been considered above, but which more than bear repeating by way of conclusion (the first six of which are probably more open to manipulation by educators and researchers):

1) The extent of *internal diversity* of the elements or agents that constitute the system, since 'internal diversity defines the range and contours of possible responses: ...

one cannot specify in advance what sorts of variation will be necessary for appropriately intelligent action—hence the need to ensure and maintain diversity in the
current system' (ibid., p. 138).

2) The extent of *internal redundancy* among the elements or agents that constitute the
system, understood not in terms of their being unnecessary or contributing to
'inefficiency', but as a complement to internal diversity and in terms of what is
common among at least some of those constituents. By virtue of these shared
characteristics, redundancy 'enables interactions among agents ... [and] makes it
possible for agents to compensate for others' failings' (ibid., p. 139).

3) The extent of *neighbour interactions* among constituents: in education, 'the neigh-
bours that must interact with one another are ideas, hunches, queries ... [and]
teachers must [accordingly] make provision for the representation and interaction
of ideas' (ibid., pp. 142, 143).

4) The extent to which control is distributed: the *decentralisation of control* refers to
'emergent conceptual possibilities, ... [to] interpretive possibilities' (ibid., p. 144),
and not at all to a *laissez faire* classroom environment. Greater degrees of decentralised
control are associated with enhanced neighbour interactions.

5) The extent of *randomness*, or sources of disruption, in the system and its environment
(remembering that its environment is not conceptually or materially distinct from
the system), which 'compel the collective to constantly adjust and adapt' (ibid.,
p. 147).

6) The extent of *coherence* in the system, which allows 'a collective to maintain a focus
of purpose/identity (ibid., p. 147). Davis and Sumara introduce the notion of
'enabling constraints' (ibid.) to refer to the structural conditions that help to create
a balance between coherence and randomness.

7) 'Negative feedback loops (... to keep systems in check)' (ibid., p. 151).

8) 'Positive feedback loops (... to amplify specific qualities or dynamics)' (ibid.).

9) 'The possibility of dying (... the departure of an agent presents the possibility of
cascading failure and catastrophic collapse of the system)' (ibid.). This is probably
not a possibility to be entertained by teachers *vis-à-vis* their students.

10) Sufficient 'means to preserve information' since 'complex entities embody their
histories and identities' (ibid.).

11) In this regard, other researchers, including, elsewhere, Davis and Sumara, have
also identified the rate of flow of information through the system as critical (see,
for example, Stacey, 1996).

12) 'Stability under perturbations' (Davis & Sumara, 2006, p. 151.).

13) 'Reproductive instability (there must be room for 'error'—that is, for the emergence
of variations on relatively stable patterns—if a system is going to be adaptable)' (ibid.).
Darwin's theory of the evolution of species famously depends on this, of course.

And, although not explicitly included in this particular list by Davis and Sumara,
but which is implicit throughout their work and that of other theorists in the field:

14) The 'richness of connectivity between agents in the system' (Stacey, 1996, p. 99).

15) The scale of the system. Complexity itself emerges only in systems of sufficient scale.

To conclude by way of a restatement of what I see as the most important insight of complexity theory with regard to educational change: it is that new properties and behaviours emerge not only from the elements that constitute a system, but from the myriad connections among them. The linear addition of new elements multiplies exponentially the number of connections among the constituent elements. It is in this shift from linear to exponential orders of magnitude, but of course only in systems of incredible scale, that the power of complexity lies.

References

Arthur, W. B. (1989) Competing Technologies, Increasing Returns, and Lock-in by Historical Events, *The Economic Journal*, 99, pp. 106–131.

Arthur, W. B., *et al. Emergent Structures: A Newsletter of the Economic Research Programme*, March 1989 and August 1990 (Sante Fe, The Santa Fe Institute).

Arthur, W. B. (1990) Positive Feedbacks in the Economy, *Scientific American*, 262, pp. 92–99.

Byrne, D. (1998) *Complexity Theory and the Social Sciences* (London and New York, Routledge).

Davis, B. & Sumara, D. (2006) *Complexity and Education: Inquiries into Learning, Teaching, and Research* (Mahwah, NJ and London, Lawrence Erlbaum Associates).

Harvey, D. (1990) *The Condition of Postmodernity* (Oxford, Blackwell).

Holland, J. H. (1987) The Global Economy as an Adaptive Process, in: P. W. Anderson, K. J. Arrow & D. Pines (eds), *The Economy as an Evolving Complex System*, Santa Fe Institute Studies in the Sciences of Complexity, Vol. 5 (Redwood City, Addison-Wesley).

Holland, J. H., Holyoak, K. J., Nisbett, R. E. & Thagard, P. R. (1986) *Induction: Processes of Inference, Learning, and Discovery* (Cambridge, MA, MIT Press).

Johnson, S. (2001) *Emergence* (London, Penguin).

Kauffman, S. A. (1992) *Origins of Order: Self-Organisation and Selection in Evolution* (Oxford, Oxford University Press).

Kuhn, T. (1962) *The Structure of Scientific Revolutions* (Chicago, Chicago University Press).

Morrison, K. (2002) *School Leadership and Complexity Theory* (London and New York, Routledge/ Falmer).

Prigogine, I. (1980) *From Being to Becoming* (San Francisco, W. H. Freeman).

Stacey, R. (1996) *Complexity and Creativity in Organizations* (San Francisco, Berrett-Koehler Publishers).

Waks, L. J. (2007) The Concept of Fundamental Educational Change, *Educational Theory*, 57:3, pp. 277–295.

Waldrop, M. (1993) *Complexity: The Emerging Science at the Edge of Order and Chaos* (London, Viking).

4
Complexity and Education: Vital simultaneities

BRENT DAVIS
University of British Columbia

In this chapter, I argue that complexity science can and should be embraced by educators and educational researchers. Indeed, I put forward a case for thinking of complexity science as a properly 'educational' discourse.

Such a project is rendered problematic at the outset by education's chequered history of borrowing from other domains. Educational research and practice have been net importers of methods, theories, and discourses. Their histories have been ones of adopting (and sometimes, but certainly not always, adapting) interpretive frames from other disciplines, often with dubious results. For example, one need only consider the consequences of the pervasive embrace of behaviourist psychology in the middle of the 20th century. Positivist psychology's refusal to consider phenomena that were not readily measured, and its consequent reduction of learning to changes in a learner's actions that are due to the environment, impacted not only educational research but also many aspects of the educational process. Curricula were redefined and pedagogies rethought, even though behaviourists openly acknowledged that the narrow focus on overt personal actions might be insufficient for making sense of formal education (e.g. Skinner, 1964). Thought, interpersonal dynamics, collective activity, social context, and biological constitution were among the topics with obvious relevance that were bracketed out by this *science* of behavioural change.

That moment in the history of modern education might be brushed off as a curious and unfortunate anomaly, were it not for the fact that similar importations happened prior and since. At the moment, for example, there is an exponential growth of published academic papers on constructivism in education—a growth that is paralleled in the professional literature. Although I am much more sympathetic to the principles and insights of this theoretical frame (at least, those versions rooted in the work of Jean Piaget), I join with many others in the concern that constructivism may be no better suited for the wide-ranging concerns of educators than behaviourism (cf. Davis & Sumara, 2002; 2006).

In what sense, then, might complexity science be understood as appropriate to the concerns of educators and educational researchers? I address this issue in this chapter by exploring several simultaneities offered by complexity thinking. The word *simultaneity* refers to events or phenomena that exist or operate at the same time. It is used here as a contrast to the modern and Western habit of thinking in terms of *discontinuities* around such matters as theory and practice, knowers and knowledge, self and other, mind and body, art and science, and child and curriculum. In the context of popular debate, the terms of these sorts of dyads tend to be understood as necessarily distinct, opposed, and unconnected, even though they always seem to occur at the same time. In other words, such simultaneities tend to be seen as coincidental, but not co-implicated. Complexity thinking troubles this habit of interpretation and, in the process, offers important advice on the projects of education and educational research.

The simultaneities addressed in this chapter include the following:

- Knower and Knowledge,
- Transphenomenality,
- Transdisciplinarity,
- Interdiscursivity.
- Descriptive and Pragmatic Insights,
- Representation and Presentation,
- Affect and Effect, and
- Education and Research.

This list is hardly exhaustive. In fact, it is highly selective. As I delve more deeply into complexity thinking, I have found that new responses to old paradoxes arise regularly. And so, while I am eager to avoid the suggestion that complexity thinking might hold the answers to all our educational questions (I do not believe that it does), at the same time, I feel it offers a means of helping educationists to get past many of the this-or-that debates that have frustrated efforts to understand what it is we are doing when we claim to be educating.

Simultaneity 1—Knower and Knowledge

Through most of the history of Western thought, it has been assumed that knowers and knowledge are discontinuous. They have most often been cast in terms of two separate phenomena that must somehow be bridged.

The knowledge/knower dichotomy has been institutionalized in the commonplace distinction between *curriculum* (generally used in reference to the educator's responsibilities toward established knowledge) and *pedagogy* (used in reference to the teacher's responsibilities toward knowers). Educators are assumed to straddle the two phenomena, and their role is typically described in terms of the dual responsibility of representing objective knowledge while fostering subjective knowing. Most often, these responsibilities are understood to exist in tension.

Not surprisingly, in efforts to cope, many researchers and teachers have downplayed or ignored the particularities of either knowledge or knowers, arguing that effective pedagogy is mainly a matter of either strong subject matter knowledge or effective teaching skills. Alternatively, knowledge and knowers have sometimes been conflated or collapsed. Or, more recently, attempts have been made to erase one category by arguing that it can be understood as determined by or subsumed within the other.

Knowing agents, for example, might be argued to comprise knowledge domains; conversely, knowledge domains might be argued to specify the range of possibilities for knowing agents. Complexity thinking provides a contrast to these sorts of interpretations, and it does so by looking neither upward from knowers to knowledge, nor downward from knowledge to knowers, but simultaneously at the phenomena in their own rights. For complexivists, *knowledge-producing systems* (knowers) and *systems of knowledge produced* (knowledge) are simultaneous, but non-collapsible.

Knowledge-producing systems—that is, knowers—are among the phenomena that are studied by those interested in *systems theory*, one of the major tributaries to complexity thinking. Systems theorists focus in large part on living systems, seeking to understand the manners in which *physical* systems self-organize and evolve. These systems include brains, individuals, social collectives, and cultures (among many others, such as beehives and slime moulds). This area of inquiry also has risen to a certain prominence among educational researchers, particularly those who have investigated the relational dynamics of students in classroom groupings (Burton, 1999; Davis & Simmt, 2003; Senge *et al.*, 2000).

Unfortunately, in broader discussions of the sociology of knowledge, there has been some confusion around the relationships between knowledge-producing systems and the systems of knowledge they produce. For example, studies of the tools, symbols, and interactive strategies of scientists have not always been undertaken alongside critical interrogations of the nature of science—or, if they have been simultaneously addressed, the knowledge-producing system (in this case, scientists) has often been conflated with the system of knowledge produced (science). This latter sort of system is among the core interests within cybernetics, which, like systems theory, is a major tributary to complexity thinking. However, in contrast to systems theory, cybernetics is more concerned with *ideational* systems than physical systems. Particular attention is paid to the networked structures of ideas/concepts/information that, in a sense, 'pass through' knowledge-producing systems.

Studies of ideational systems reach across many different levels of social organization. For example, personal knowledge tends to remain highly stable even though the physical system supporting it completely regenerates itself many times through a typical lifespan. Similarly, disciplinary knowledge can maintain its coherence through many generations of the thinkers and researchers.

I have attempted to portray some aspects of the dynamic and reflexive relationships between knowing systems and knowledge systems in Figure 1. To reiterate the simultaneity, a knower is a physical system that might be described as a stable pattern in a stream of matter; a body of knowledge is an ideational system and might be understood in terms of stabilized but mutable patterns of acting that are manifest by a knower. In offering these descriptions, I in no way mean to gesture toward the body/mind or material/ideal dichotomies of ancient Western (esp. Greek) metaphysics. Quite the contrary, my point is that the ideational is insepar-able from the material, but that their inseparability does not mean they are the same thing. Phrased somewhat differently, I am offering a complexivist reading of an ancient intuition. A system of ideas is indeed transcendent of a material system; hence, knowers and knowledges can be considered separately, even if they cannot

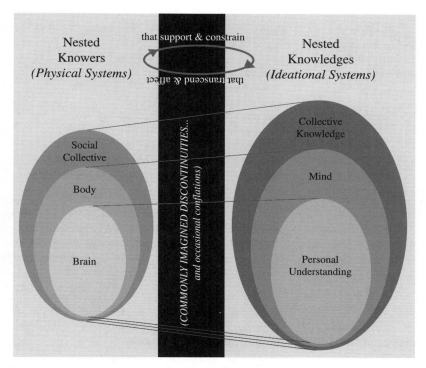

Figure 1: A small sampling of some knowers (knowledge-producing systems) and the knowledges (systems of knowledge) that they support

be considered separate. One cannot exist without the other; they are enfolded in and unfold from one another.

One might use the word *learning* to refer to ongoing transformations of both knowledge-producing systems and systems of knowledge produced. That usage could be refined by noting that learning can be understood more explicitly in terms of the continuous processes through which knower and knowledge are simultaneously redefined in relation to one another. Education, with its fundamental interest in matters of learning, then, is always already dealing with the knower-knowledge simultaneity. Of course, this suggestion is hardly new. As Dewey (1902/1956) urged:

> Abandon the notion of subject-matter as something fixed and ready-made in itself, outside the child's experience; ... see [the child's experience] as something fluent, embryonic, vital; and we realize that the child and the curriculum are simply two limits which define a single process. (p. 11)

Simultaneities 2, 3, and 4—Transphenomenality, Transdisciplinarity, and Interdiscursivity

One of my favourite 'research' activities is to listen to how practising teachers use the word *they* in their staffroom conversations. The labile term might be in reference to individual students, or to clusters of neurons, or to classrooms, or to the world

Some roots of a personal understanding of multiplication:	Specific contributions
Innate capacities	– distinction-making ability – pattern-noticing ability – rudimentary quantity sense
Pre-school (recursive) elaborations	– experiences of collecting, ordering, sharing, etc. – refinement of object/quantity permanence – learning of counting systems – preliminary development of number sense – preliminary development of binary operations (esp. addition)
Early grades (recursive) elaborations	– physical action-based metaphors for binary operations – mastery of a symbol system for numbers and operations – grouping, repeated addition, and skip counting
Middle grades (recursive) elaborations	– Introduction to range of images and applications – In particular, shift from discrete to continuous contexts – Conceptual blending of old and new metaphors, including ... grouping processes ... sequential folds ... many-layered ... scaling ... ratios and rates ... grid-generating ... dimension-changing ... number-line-stretching or -compressing ... rotating ...
Senior grades (recursive) elaborations	– broader range of applications – algebraic and graphical representations – distinguishing arithmetic, geometric, and exponential growth – severing of ties to concrete realm

Table 1: A summary of the origins of personal understandings of multiplication, as understood by a collective of K–12 mathematics teachers

of adolescents, or to society, or any of a number of coherent collectives that are of relevance to the educational project. It would seem that, to cope with the task of educating, one must be able to jump fluidly among and across these levels of coherence.

In a more formal attempt to study such *transphenomenal* hopping, colleagues and I recently posed the question, 'Where does a learner's understanding of multiplication come from?' to a group of practising teachers during a research seminar (see Davis & Simmt, 2006, for an elaborated discussion). Their collective response, generated and organized over the course of an hour, is presented in Table 1.

As the entries in the table illustrate, these teachers are well aware that an individual's understanding of multiplication (and every other concept) makes sense only when considered in transphenomenal terms, as:

- rooted in biological structure (genetic predisposition),
- framed by bodily activity (personal experience),
- elaborated within social interactions (symbolic tools),
- enabled by cultural tools (societal usages), and
- part of an ever-unfolding conversation of humans and the biosphere.

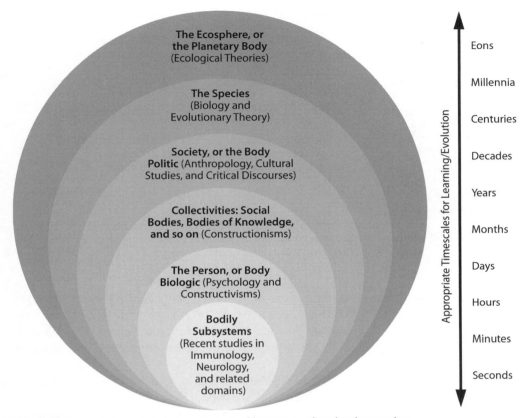

Figure 2: Some of the nested systems that are of interest to educational researchers

Unfortunately, in the main, the education literature simply does not treat such topics in this manner. Rather, investigations of issues such as personal understandings of multiplication tend to be oriented by an assumption that a single level of analysis (e.g. the neurological, or the personal-experiential, or the symbolic-linguistic) is sufficient for making sense of the matter.

An interesting aspect of the piece of research mentioned above is that the teacher-participants did not seem to be aware that they were jumping among different levels of phenomena during the discussion. I surmise that a reason for this unconscious but fluid level-hopping is that the relevant phenomena evolve at radically different paces (see Figure 2)—a realization that demands simultaneous attendance to many categories of expertise and diverse methodologies if the overarching phenomenon is to be studied in detail. In other words, a phenomenon as 'simple' as personal understanding of multiplication demands a *transdisciplinary* approach.

Just as transphenomenality entails a sort of level-jumping, transdisciplinarity compels a sort of border-crossing—a need to step outside the limiting frames and methods of phenomenon-specific disciplines. I attempt to illustrate this point in the second column of Table 2, in which I list a few of the disciplines that are of immediate relevance to the issue of personal understanding of multiplication. Such

Transphenomenality *Personal understandings of multiplication are:*	*Transdisciplinarity* *Relevant disciplines* *include:*	*Interdiscursivity* *Relevant discourses include:*
• rooted in **genetic** structure (biological predisposition),	Neurology	Analytic Science
• framed by **bodily** activity (personal experience),	Psychology	Phenomenology
• elaborated within **social** interactions (symbolic tools),	Sociology	Post-structuralism
• enabled by **cultural** tools (societal usages), and	Anthropology	Cultural Studies
• part of an ever-unfolding conversation of humans and the biosphere.	Ecology	Ecosophy

Table 2: One illustration of the levels of phenomena, intersections of disciplines, and interlacings of discourses that arise in the study of educational issues

a listing presents a powerful refutation of the early 20th century assertion that education is an 'applied psychology', or the more recent contention that teaching should be construed as an 'applied science of the brain' (see Zull, 2002). Clearly, such formulations engender profound ignorance of the complexity of the phenomenon at hand.

The third column of Table 2 is likely the one that would be most troubling to researchers. The discourses that support and are supported by the various disciplines are commonly seen as incompatible, if not flatly contradictory. Complexity thinking provides a means around this apparent impasse, and it does so by emphasizing the need to study phenomena at the levels of their emergence, oriented by the realizations that new stable patterns of activity arise and that those patterns embody emergent rules and laws that are native to the systems.

This requires that researchers pay particular attention to the paces of evolution at hand. For example, biological structure transforms over millennia and eons, and is thus sufficiently stable to lend itself to the assumptions of analytic science. By contrast, other phenomena, such as a culture's symbolic tools, not only evolve more quickly, but are also subject to very different sets of influences. Analytic methods are not just inadequate, but inappropriate for making sense of such dispersed, rapidly changing, and intricately entangled sets of phenomena.

It is thus that I would describe complexity thinking as a sort of *interdiscourse*, where *discourse* is understood as a structurally coherent domain of language use— along with the activities associated with the use of that language—that organizes and constrains what can be said, done, and thought. Every discourse has its own distinctive set of rules, usually operating implicitly, that govern the production of what is to count as meaningful and/or true. Discourses always function in relation or in opposition to other discourses. No discourse stands alone, although some (such as scientism, modernism, or fundamentalist religion) lay claim to certain totalized and exclusive knowledges of the universe.

Post-structuralist theory has contributed to understandings of interdiscursivity—that is, how discourses intersect, overlap, and interlace. But post-structuralism has been less effective at providing insight into how discourses intersect, overlap, and intersect with phenomena, in part because of a tendency within post-structuralist thought to limit discussions to the realm of human interest and interpretation. Phrased in terms of the contents of Table 2, post-structuralism is very useful for interpreting the mutual effects of *disciplines* and *discourses* (the second and third columns). However, it has been less useful or effective in untangling the influences of disciplines and discourses (again, the second and third columns) on *phenomena* (first column). Complexity thinking helps here by pressing beyond the boundaries of intersubjective constructions, as it refuses to collapse *phenomena* with *knowledge of phenomena*. These are inextricably entangled, but not coterminous.

As such, complexity thinking enables a simultaneous appreciation of the insights of such disparate discourses as post-structuralism and analytic science. Notably, as a collective, educational researchers have acknowledged this point. The discourses mentioned in the third column of Table 2 (among many, many others) are prominently represented in the current research literature. What is not so well represented—within single publications, at least—is the necessity of interdiscursivity. Indeed, most often in the contemporary literature, discourses are presented as oppositional rather than complementary. Such a conclusion is inevitable if the transphenomenal character of educational 'objects' is not taken into consideration.

Simultaneity 5—Descriptive and Pragmatic Insights

As noted at the start of this chapter, there has been a longstanding problem with many of the theoretical frames imported by educational researchers from other domains. A major issue is that, very often, the discourses adopted and adapted from psychology, sociology, literary criticism, and elsewhere are not well fitted to the particular, pragmatic concerns of educationists. For the most part, those theories tend to be strictly descriptive, focused much more on the characterization of a specific phenomenon than on how one might go about affecting that phenomenon.

Also mentioned, a contemporary, and highly problematic example is the incorporation of constructivist theories into discussions of teaching and schooling. Explicators of constructivist epistemologies have repeatedly asserted that these frames cannot be construed as theories of education—at least insofar as teaching is understood in terms of the project of prompting learners toward particular sets of desired competencies or predispositions (cf., Glasersfeld, 1995; Davis & Sumara, 2005; Lave & Wenger, 1991). This is not to say that their descriptive insights are inappropriate; obviously it is useful to know about the dynamics of the process(es) involved in, for example, human cognition and social interaction. However, it is just as obvious that an individual learner, a classroom, a disciplinary domain, and a culture are four among many qualitatively different phenomena. To derive guidelines for teaching based on an isolated knowledge of just one is to commit a category error.

As Johnson (2001) notes in his popular account of the emergence of complexity science, the domain might be construed as both descriptive and pragmatic. In particular, over the past decade, the emphasis in complexity research has shifted beyond careful accounts of complex phenomena toward deliberate attempts to prompt the emergence and affect the character of such phenomena. Of course, complexity thinking is not the *only* discourse to offer a pragmatics of transformation. Others that have been taken up by educational researchers in recent decades include psychoanalysis (e.g. Britzman, 1998; Grumet, 1988) and, to a much lesser extent, Eastern mindfulness traditions (e.g. Aoki, 2004). Complexity thinking shares with these frames the conviction that transformations of learning systems cannot be understood in linear or mechanical terms and that any attempt at such transformation is necessarily a deeply ethical matter than must be undertaken with caution, humility, and care.

This assertion is as relevant to the project of educational research as it is to educational practice, which prompts the question (for me, at least) of how educational researchers might frame their own ethical responsibilities.

Simultaneity 6—Representation and Presentation

If one were to take seriously the transphenomenal concerns, the transdisciplinary nature, and the interdiscursive character of education, along with the need for both descriptive and pragmatic advice, one could well find oneself faced with unwieldy reports that undermine the practicality of important insights.

Complexity thinking, then, requires that the teacher or researcher be consciously attentive to strategies to balance attention to and ignorance of detail. Acts of perception and interpretation are always more about bracketing out possibilities than about including detail—and, clearly, such bracketing can be troublesome. The underlying issue here, however, is not really about bracketing; it is about the role of the published work. As Borgmann (1989, p. 110) notes:

> What remains unexamined ... is the power of products, of the material results of production, to shape our conduct profoundly. Any moral theory that thinks of the material setting of society as an essentially neutral stage is profoundly flawed and unhelpful; so, in fact, is most of modern and contemporary ethics.

The written product, then, is not an endpoint, but a particular sort of participation—one that, by virtue of its lingering presence, may well have a more profound influence on life than that actual act of producing.

Complexity thinking prompts me to assert that this understanding must be brought to bear on understandings of academic discussions. Research reports and theoretical accounts must be considered as forms that contribute to the shape of possibility. They are partial rather than comprehensive, active rather than inert, implicated rather than benign. They are parts of an always-evolving reality. How, then, might one structure one's representations in ways that are mindful of such moral layerings? I confess to having few answers here. As this text indicates, I have a personal preference for the standard (re)presentational tools of the academic trade. However, along with others, I have also devoted considerable attention to other strategies. I present some preliminary thoughts on a few of them here, insofar as the forms of these strategies have enabled me to be attentive to my own complicity in the projects of education and educational research.

The post-structuralist strategy of deconstruction (Derrida, 1980) is one that is readily aligned with complexivist emphases. Understood as an interpretive approach to textual representations through which one attempts to flag the multitude of diverse and often conflicting 'voices' that are speaking in a text, deconstruction is already attentive to the inevitable interdiscursive character of any knowledge claim. Derrida and others have steadfastly avoided formal definitions or fixed strategies for deconstruction. As such, and in a manner that is analogous to the complexity scientific recognition that modes of inquiry must be specific to the objects of inquiry, definitive statements on deconstruction as an attitude or method are impossible (and undesirable). It can be said that they engender a certain suspicion of metaphysical assumptions as they endeavour to foreground the internal contradictions of texts. In particular, Derrida saw dichotomies (binary oppositions or discontinuities, in contrast to simultaneities) and hierarchies as hallmarks of Western thought. He sought to expose them in his writing while, at the same time, avoiding the creation of new ones (hence the need for fluidity of the notion of deconstruction—to fix it would be to suggest it complete or sufficient, thus superior to other approaches and attitudes). The refusal to create hierarchies or binaries and the attentiveness to flexible possibilities are obvious sites of compatibility between deconstruction and complexity thinking. (A difference is that complexity compels attentiveness to the biological as well as the social, whereas deconstruction is overwhelmingly focused on human-made texts.)

A further post-structuralist contribution is the notion of rhizomes, developed by Gilles Deleuze and Felix Guattari (1983), who actually borrow extensively from the language and imagery of complexity theory in their work. In brief, they point to the need to be aware of multiple interacting flows that, like the concealed root structures of some plants, give rise to similar structures in diverse domains, even though the interconnection and shared reliance of those structures remain hidden from view. Mindsets, Deleuze and Guattari argue, are fractal-like, concealing intricate patterns of supposition and conjecture beneath a veneer of coherence.

A lesson of deconstruction, rhizomatics, and associated notions is that the expository text (such as this one) is just one of many possible forms—one that tends to fall into traps of reductive explanation and conclusive certainty. Other modes are thus encouraged, provided that they too are subject to the same sort of deconstructive scrutiny. One would not want to critique one form only to be seduced by another.

One means to avoid such a seduction/reduction is articulated by Hans-Georg Gadamer (1990) in his description of the work of art. For him, art has a two-fold function. It both *represents* (in the sense of calling something to mind, not in the sense of precise or fixed depiction) at the same time that it *presents* (that is, it opens up new interpretive possibilities). I would argue that the two-fold function of representation and presentation—this vital simultaneity—can (and should) also be a possibility for texts written in standard academic prose.

Such has, in fact, been my intention and hope with this chapter, throughout which I have operated mainly in an expository mode. In other writing, I and others have attempted to present deconstructive readings, rhizomatics, and level-jumping more poetically, in manners that more actively and explicitly implicate readers or audiences (e.g. Counternormativity Discourse Group, 2006; Davis, Sumara, & Luce-Kapler, 2008). The intention with this sort of presentational strategy is to 'marry complex narrative structure with complex subject matter', as Johnson (2005, p. 68) describes it. More familiar forms that utilize similar multi-episodic or multiple-threaded strategies include such popular television series as *Seinfeld*, *Six Feet Under*, and *The Sopranos*. Within such texts, there is no dominant theme or plot, no clear distinctions among coincident threads. However, a single 'scene' might serve to connect two or more strands at the same time, layering them atop one another. Notably, it is expected that each strand will have its own coherence. The driving idea is essentially complexivist: new interpretive possibilities can arise in the interplay of already-coherent threads of thought.

This manner of presentation does not assume or pretend to offer a complete, unambiguous argument or depiction of some aspect of reality that is somehow intended to stand on its own, independent of author or audience. Rather, the partialities of the presenters are foregrounded at the same time as the listeners/readers are implicated in the text/performance. This is not to say that presenters are abdicating responsibility for coherence or interpretation. Quite the contrary, there should be a point (or, more likely, multiple points). However, the mode of presentation (versus representation) does not allow for simplistic reductions of complex issues.

This structure is merely one of many possibilities—and I re-emphasize that I do not mean to suggest that the standard format of an academic paper is inappropriate for addressing complex phenomena. It is more a case of its being *inadequate* for *all* reporting, especially when a vital aspect of that reporting is level-jumping. Multiple threaded texts are a complement to, not a substitute or replacement for more conventional academic reporting strategies. With current and emergent technologies, it is not difficult to imagine other modes of representation—involving, for example, hypertext or interactive web pages. Many powerful techniques have also been developed in the dramatic and visual arts, some of which might be appropriate for use in academic and educational contexts. Other structures that I have explored with others have been drawn explicitly from fractal geometry (see Davis & Sumara, 2005).

In brief, no-one's work can be perceived in strictly representational terms, regardless of the intentions of the author. Even those research products oriented by a desire to depict or replicate the existing possible inevitably contribute to the expansion of the space of the possible—that is, just like the educational project, they serve in presentational as well as representational capacities simultaneously.

Simultaneity 7—Affect and Effect

Further to the point that education is a net importer of theory and research, one might characterize the domain as having a rather startling trade deficit. Whereas the educational literature is rife with theories and conclusions derived from other domains, the insights of educators or educational researchers are rarely encountered in academic literatures outside the field.

The situation is unlikely to change any time soon, in part because description-oriented and phenomenon-specific disciplines may not have the means to embrace the transphenomenal and pragmatic character of educational inquiry. Nevertheless, complexity thinking offers a challenge to the mindset that seems to underlie educationists' willingness to take on methods and discourses developed elsewhere, without seeking to influence those methods and discourses.

Educators and educational researchers are uniquely positioned to contribute to complexity thinking, in several ways. The most obvious arises in the transphenomenal nature of the educational project, the transdisciplinary character of educational research, and the necessarily interdiscursive nature of educational thought. Educational research thus provides an opportunity to complexify the methods and discourses that it draws on, and I would argue that it has a concomitant responsibility in some manner to 'reply' to the domains to which it listens.

Just as importantly, education sits at the intersection of virtually all domains of inquiry, including the disciplines that serve as source domains for curricula. It is becoming increasingly clear that the knowledge needed to teach these disciplines might be understood as a legitimate branch of inquiry within those disciplines, as evidenced by journals devoted to engineering education, medical education, and so on. This point has perhaps been best developed within mathematics education, where teachers' mathematics knowledge is coming to be recognized as a legitimate branch of mathematical inquiry (see Davis & Simmt, 2006) in which attention is paid to the largely tacit bits of knowledge—the metaphors, analogies, images, applications, and gestures—that bubble to the surface in moments of teaching. The fact that educational insights are being, in effect, exported to domains such as mathematics is instructive. The relationship between education and other domains need not be understood strictly in terms of unidirectional affect. Educators and educational researchers can and should have some effect on other realms.

Complexity thinking provides the elaboration that, not only *should* this be the case, it inevitably *is* the case. This assertion is informed by emergent realizations that initiates exert profound influences on knowledge domains. For example, children, not adults, represent the most potent force in the ongoing evolution of language as they even out inconsistencies in grammar, invent new associations, and impose other modifications to render verbal communication more user-friendly (Deacon, 1997). Similarly, with regard to specific disciplinary domains, such pedagogical acts of selecting topics, structuring classroom experiences, and defining acceptable standards of academic performance contribute profoundly to the shape of a realm of knowledge—especially those realms that are included in grade school curricula. Formal education does much more than draw from established disciplines; it helps to establish them. The dimension highlighted here is that the effects of educational inquiry on other domains could be more conscious and deliberate.

Simultaneity 8—Education and Research

There appears to be a deep compatibility between complexity thinking and herme-neutic inquiry. Hermeneutics is oriented by the entangled questions, 'What is it that we believe?', 'How is it that we came to think this way?', and 'What is being taken for granted about the natures of reality, truth, and existence?'. Complexity thinking addresses each of these questions—and, importantly, does not settle on conclusive answers. The point, then, is not that everyone should agree, but that there should be an attitude of openness toward new possibilities.

Over recent years, an increasing number of educators and educational researchers have demonstrated just such an openness (e.g. Doll *et al.*, 2005; Doll & Gough, 2003; Fleener, 2002). For my own part, the need to attend to theory has meant endeavouring to keep pace with the latest literature in the field. As well, I feel an obligation to tinker with vocabulary. In this regard, I follow Richard Rorty's description of *ironists*:

> The ironist ... takes the unit of persuasion to be a vocabulary rather than a proposition. Her method is redescription rather than inference. Ironists specialize in redescribing ranges of objects or events in partially neologistic jargon, in the hopes that by the time she is finished using old words in new senses, not to mention introducing brand new words, people will no longer ask questions phrased in the old words. (1989, p. 78)

A brief illustration of how one might take up Rorty's exhortation: consider, for a moment, human consciousness, a phenomenon that depends on social collectivity at the same time as it is always personal and individual. As Donald (2002) explains, human cognitive systems (or minds) are hybrid; they depend on both an individual brain and various levels of collectivity. To understand consciousness, one must be willing and able to think in transphenomenal terms and engage in transdisciplinary ways. Yet it is only recently that consciousness studies have developed into a domain in which, for example, neurologists routinely work with psychologists and anthropologists to better understand how electronic technologies are transforming the very nature of human awareness (see Johnson, 2005).

Endeavouring to put an ironical twist on the notion, I would assert that education falls into the same class of phenomena as consciousness and thus demands a similar attitude of its practitioners and its researchers. In fact, it is tempting to suggest a metaphor of 'formal education as cultural consciousness'. Just as one's consciousness serves to bring certain aspects of personal experience to awareness, formal education is a means by which certain aspects of collective experience are foregrounded within the body politic. Developing the analogy a bit further, it is interesting to note that one's consciousness does not control one's experience (cf. Norretranders, 1998), although it does play an important orienting role. Phrased differently, perception, interpretation, and identity are not *determined by* consciousness, but they are *dependent on* consciousness. In a similar sense, formal education does not play a deterministic role in the unfolding of society, but does play an important orienting role that profoundly affects culture.

An obvious problem with this analogy is, of course, the deliberate nature of formal education, which, in effect, can be understood in recursive terms of conscious efforts to organize individual consciousnesses. In comparison, human self-awareness seems much more contingent, even accidental. Yet even here the contrast is probably less pronounced than might be expected. For example, the extent to which curricula reflect emergent worldviews, knowledge, technologies, and social issues illustrates that formal education is highly dependent on evolving circumstances. Just as individual consciousness seems to lag behind the personal experience, in a very strong sense, formal education lags behind the events of the world. Like consciousness, education offers commentary, it orients, it helps to render events sensible, it contributes to the ongoing reorganization of the system's resources, and it assists in the co-ordination of other aspects of the grander unity—all while dealing with only a tiny portion of the vast corpus of knowledge of the grander body.

My purpose in presenting this example of irony, in Rorty's sense of the word, is to develop the suggestion that educational research and educational practice might be considered aspects of the same project—namely, expanding the space of human possibility by exploring the space of the existing possible.

A Closing Note on Complicity: The Need for Critical Reflection

One of the grand errors of classical inquiry has been the conflation of the theoretical, the descriptive, and/or the experimental result with stable and secure knowledge. Complexity thinking does not permit this error—and not only because phenomena that learn cannot be pinned down with certainty. The major issue here is the tendency for the theorist/observer/experimenter to write herself or himself out of the research result. The complexity researcher has an obligation—an ethical imperative, I would argue—to be attentive to how she or he is implicated in the phenomenon studied.

This is especially the case for educational research, which must become more aware of its consequences. Interpretive frames that are powerful at the level of research have been distorted in textbooks and other resources for teachers, giving rise to claims and practices that are simply indefensible. Yet one hears very little from the theorists and researchers who continue to publish at pace, either oblivious to the troublesome consequences of their efforts or unwilling to accept any responsibility.

In foregrounding the overlapping and interlaced characters of social systems—such as research communities and teacher collectives—complexity thinking does not allow for such ignorance and abdication. To the extent possible, complexity researchers are obligated to be attentive to the consequences and implications of their efforts. As such, among the intertwining questions that I ask myself within any research project are the following:

- How am I complicit in (i.e. affecting or hoping to affect) the phenomenon that I study?
- How is this research *educational*—that is, how does it educate?
- How might this research be taken up?
- How might I represent/present these interpretations?

In brief, this issue is a moral one, and I use the word *moral* in the complexified sense of implying an 'ethics of care, responsiveness, and responsibility' (Johnson, 1993, p. 207). As Levin explains, there are two different ways of thinking about moral problems:

(1) a competitive model, which gives primacy to the individual and relies on the supervenience of formal and abstract rules to achieve co-operation and consensus and (2) a cooperative model, which given primacy to relationships and relies on contextual narratives and dialogue—communication ... . (1989, p. 210)

The notion of complicity invokes the latter conception of morality. And that is where I will leave this discussion—not with a sense of conclusion or finality, but with an acknowledgement that in the profoundly moral-ethical domain of education, we must give primacy to relationship and rely on communication.

References

Aoki, T. T. (2004) *Curriculum in a New Key: The collected works of Ted T. Aoki.*, W. F. Pinar & R. L. Irwin, eds (Mahwah, NJ, Lawrence Erlbaum).

Borgmann, A. (1989) *Crossing the Postmodern Divide* (Chicago, University of Chicago Press).

Britzman, D. P. (1998) *Lost Subjects, Contested Objects: Toward a psychoanalytic inquiry of learning* (Albany, NY, State University of New York Press).

Burton, L. (ed.) (1999) *Learning Mathematics: From hierarchies to networks* (London, Falmer).

Counternormativity Discourse Group. (2006) Performing an Archive of Feeling: Experiences of normalizing structures in teaching and teacher education, *Journal of Curriculum and Pedagogy*, 2:2, pp. 173–214.

Davis, B. & Simmt, E. (2003) Understanding learning systems: mathematics teaching and complexity science, *Journal for Research in Mathematics Education*, 34:2, pp. 137–167.

Davis, B. & Simmt, E. (2006) Mathematics-for-Teaching: An ongoing investigation of the mathematics that teachers (need to) know, *Educational Studies in Mathematics*, 61:3, pp. 293–319.

Davis, B. & Sumara, D. (2002) Constructivist Discourses and the Field of Education: Problems and possibilities, *Educational Theory*, 52:4, pp. 409–428.

Davis, B. & Sumara, D. (2005) Challenging Images of Knowing: Complexity science and educational research, *International Journal of Qualitative Studies in Education*, 18:3, pp. 305–321.

Davis, B. & Sumara, D. (2006) *Complexity and Education: Inquiries into learning, teaching, and research* (Mahwah, NJ, Lawrence Erlbaum Associates).

Davis, B., Sumara, D. & Luce-Kapler, R. (2008) *Engaging Minds: Changing teaching in complex times*, 2nd edn. (New York, Routledge).

Deacon, T. (1997) *The Symbolic Species: The co-evolution of language and the human brain* (New York, W.W. Norton).

Deleuze, G. & Guattari, F. (1983) *Anti-Oedipus: Capitalism and schizophrenia* (Minneapolis, University of Minnesota Press).

Derrida, J. (1980) *Writing and Difference*, A. Bass, trans. (Chicago, The University of Chicago Press).

Dewey, J. (1902/1956) *The Child and the Curriculum and The School and Society* (Chicago, The University of Chicago Press).

Doll, Jr., W. E., Fleener, M. J., Trueit, D. & St. Julien, J. (eds) (2005) *Chaos, Complexity, Curriculum, and Culture: A conversation* (New York, Peter Lang).

Doll, Jr., W. E. & Gough, N. (2003) *Curriculum Visions* (New York, Peter Lang).

Donald, M. (2002) *A Mind So Rare: The evolution of human consciousness* (New York, W.W. Norton).

Fleener, M. J. (2002) *Curriculum Dynamics: Recreating heart* (New York, Peter Lang).

Gadamer, H-G. (1989) *Truth and Method*, 2nd rev. edn., J. Weinsheimer & D. G. Marshall, trans. (New York, Crossroad).

Glasersfeld, E. von. (1995) *Radical Constructivism: A way of knowing and learning* (London, The Falmer Press).

Grumet, M. (1988) *Bitter Milk: Women and teaching* (Amherst, MA, University of Massachusetts Press).

Johnson, M. (1993) *Moral Imagination: Implications of cognitive science for ethics* (Chicago, The University of Chicago Press).

Johnson, S. (2001) *Emergence: The connected lives of ants, brains, cities, and software* (New York, Scribner).

Johnson, S. (2005) *Everything Bad is Good for You: How today's popular culture is actually making us smarter* (New York, Riverhead Books).

Lave, J. & Wenger, E. (1991) *Situated Learning: Legitimate peripheral participation* (Cambridge, Cambridge University Press).

Levin, D. M. (1989) *The Listening Self: Personal growth, social change and the closure of metaphysics* (London, Routledge).

Norretranders, T. (1998) *The User Illusion: Cutting consciousness down to size* (New York, Viking).

Rorty, R. (1989) *Contingency, Irony, Solidarity* (New York, Cambridge University Press).

Senge, P., Cambron-McCabe, N., Lucas, T., Smith, B., Dutton, J. & Kleiner, A. (2000) *Schools That Learn: A fifth discipline fieldbook for educators, parents, and everyone who cares about education* (New York, Doubleday).

Skinner, B. F. (1964) New Methods and New Aims in Teaching, *New Scientist*, 122, May 21, pp. 483–484.

Zull, J. E. (2002) *The Art of Changing the Brain: Enriching the practice of teaching by exploring the biology of learning* (Sterling, VA, Stylus).

5

Three Generations of Complexity Theories: Nuances and ambiguities

MICHEL ALHADEFF-JONES

Teachers College, Columbia University
EXPERICE Research Centre, University of Paris 8

[What is] complex cannot be summarised in the word complexity, brought to a law of complexity, reduced to the idea of complexity. Complexity cannot be something which would be defined in a simple way and would replace simplicity. Complexity is a word-problem and not a word-solution. (Morin, 1990, p. 10, free translation)

Introduction: Complexity versus Complexities

In 2002, the US Department of Education asked the Washington Center for Complexity and Public Policy to describe how 'complexity science' was being used in the federal government, in private foundations, in universities, and in independent education and research centres. The Center's ensuing report provided a broad overview of the 'complexity science' landscape around the country (Washington Center for Complexity and Public Policy, 2003), revealing the increasing recognition given to theories informing the idea of complexity. At the same time, it also conveyed some misleading views probably representative of a trend: 'Complexity' considered as a unified concept might appear to be progressively reified. Reduction to a singular form ('complexity theory' or 'complexity science') could well lead to a neglect of the range of different theories that deal with the implications related to the notion of complexity.

Sharing the conviction of other scholars that the background of this notion has important potential with regard to contemporary developments in educational sciences (Ardoino, 1963/1999, 1998, 2000; Ardoino & De Peretti, 1998; Morin, 2000) this chapter suggests the importance of a more nuanced use of the term, thereby avoiding simplification of the concept to some of its dominant expressions only. More radically, the position developed here suggests that within this notion reside deep ambiguities. In this context, tracing its history would seem a particularly relevant way to enrich the debate around its legitimacy and to reposition its meaning in a broader cultural landscape, including Latin traditions of research that often remain unknown in English-speaking countries. Following a chronological logic that discriminates among at least three contemporary generations of complexity theories (Le Moigne, 1996, 2001a), the chapter aims to illustrate both their epistemic and their socio-cultural roots. Switching then from a historical perspective to epistemological and anthropological ones, the chapter illuminates some competing interpretations underlying the definition of complexity. Scientific research is accordingly conceptualised as a learning process that requires not just reducing antagonisms and exploring complementarities, but also reviewing the contributions and the limitations that have shaped its own complexity (Morin, Motta & Ciurana, 2003).

Etymological Roots

The notion of complexity refers to the quality or condition of being complex. Adapted from the Latin expression '*complexus*' (14th century) and adopted from the modern French, the term derives from '*cum*' and '*plectere*', meaning surrounding, encompassing, encircling, embracing, comprehending, comprising. Originally denoting 'embracing or comprehending several elements', its use in English tended to be akin to the sense of 'plaited together, interwoven' (Simpson *et al.*, 1989/2005). Referring to things or ideas 'consisting of or comprehending various parts united or connected together' or 'formed by combination of different elements', 'complex' is often understood as a synonym either for composite and compound, or complicated, involved and intricate (ibid., para. 1). More specifically, it often characterises personality, society, feelings or thoughts that the mind finds difficult to comprehend and are not easily analysed or disentangled. During the past few centuries the adjective 'complex', denoting a plural of both quantity and quality, has conveyed various specific meanings: in mathematics (complex fraction, complex number); in linguistics (complex sentence) and semiotics (complex term); in music (complex note or sound) (Institut National de la Langue Française, 2005). As a noun, 'complex' refers to a 'whole comprehending in its compass a number of parts', especially interconnected ones (Simpson *et al.*, 1989/2005, para. 1a). Initially used in physiology (18th century), the expression migrated to economy, chemistry, biology and geometry. In the early 20th century, it appeared in psychoanalysis, in psychology (Gestalt theory) and in medicine (Institut National de la Langue Française, 2005). The terms 'complex' and 'complexity' are usually used as the opposite of simplicity. Their meanings pertain to the holistic, global or non-linear form of intelligibility needed to comprehend a phenomenon; sometimes they stress a pathological, dense, entangled dimension appearing as rebellious to the normal order of knowledge (Ardoino, 2000). Here is a probable source of the confusion between the words 'complex' and 'complicated', which are frequently but sometimes erroneously interchanged in their usage. It is important to keep in mind this rich semantic and conceptual background associated with the use of the notion of complexity in order to avoid the risks of reduction. Being aware of this diversity of use encourages us to explore the most salient meanings and uses, knowing that they are part of a semantic whole, richer than the sum of its parts.

Contemporary Genesis

In 1934, formulating his conception of a non-Cartesian approach to science, Bachelard was probably the first to legitimate epistemologically the role of complexity as an ideal for contemporary sciences (Le Moigne, 1996). If a Cartesian epistemology reduces complex phenomena to an analysis of their components, understood as simple, absolute and objective, a complexity-oriented epistemology favours understanding phenomena as part of a fabric of relations: 'There is no simple idea, because a simple idea ... is always inserted, to be understood, in a complex system of thoughts and experiences' (Bachelard, 1934/2003, p. 152, free translation). The recognition of complexity appears then at the origins of a new kind of scientific explanation which perceives simplicity as a specific provisional phenomenon. If complication refers to the idea of an intricate situation waiting to be disentangled, complexity supposes then the fundamental non-simplicity of studied phenomena (Ardoino, 2000).

Appropriation of the concept of complexity by the scientific community followed a decade later. In '*Science and Complexity*', Weaver (1948) considered the transformation of sciences since the 17th century and identified the successive emergence of three specific ways of conceiving the complexity of problems tackled by scientists. The first, identified later as the 'paradigm of simplicity' (Morin, 1977/1980), emerged from the 17th to 19th century. Grounded in the models offered by classical physics, it valorises objectivity, causal explanation, quantitative data and certainty. In this paradigm, complex problems are tackled by their reduction into more simple issues, explained or solved independently and successively. Since the second half of the 19th century, the discovery of disordered phenomena at various levels of organisation (the principle of entropy in thermodynamics, discontinuity in quantum mechanics, the explosive nature of stellar phenomena, etc.) contributed to a challenge to this paradigm of rational mechanics. Weaver identified a second paradigm that emerged at this period: one having to deal with problems of 'disorganised complexity'. Associated with the development of models proposed by the machinery of statistics and the theory of probability, this perspective included the consideration of disorder as an integral part of natural phenomena. In spite of their important contribution, Weaver observed that such frameworks did not allow the solving of some of the questions scientists still had to handle. Considering the contemporary problems tackled by biology, medicine, psychology, economy and political sciences as being too complicated to be interpreted through the models of rational mechanics, and not sufficiently disordered to be interpreted through the metrics associated with the second paradigm, Weaver identified them as problems of 'organised complexity', grouping in this expression 'all problems which involve dealing simultaneously with a sizeable number of factors which are interrelated into an organic whole' (Weaver, 1948, para. 3).

These initial distinctions enable the location of the main stakes related to the development of an original but dispersed body of research during the 20th century. From the 1940s until today, three generations of theories have emerged, suggesting a progressive shift from the study of 'organised complexity' to issues related to 'organising complexity' (Le Moigne, 1996), and thus reintroducing the fundamental uncertainties of the researcher as envisaged by Bachelard.

First Generation

Weaver recognised the value of two embryonic scientific trends that emerged from the Second World War—the study of electronic computing devices and the 'mixed-team' approach of 'operations analysis'. A set of new approaches—information and communication theories, automata theories, and cybernetics and operation analysis—can be found at the roots of these trends.

Mathematical Theory of Communication

Information and communication theories emerged with the mathematical theory of communication formulated in 1947 by Shannon (see Shannon & Weaver, 1963). Grounded in the practical issues raised by developments in the Bell telephone company and in his previous work on military encryption, Shannon developed a theory where an exchange of information (defined as 'binary digit' or 'bit') may be observed and measured statistically. Through concepts such as 'noise' and 'redundancy', the theory enabled the evaluation of the reliability of transfers of information by taking into consideration forms of disorder affecting channels of communication. Information theory contributed to explaining the phenomenon of organised complexity as the reduction of entropy (disorder) observed when a system (living or artificial) absorbs external energy and converts it into organisation or structures (order).

Automata Theories and Neural Networks

Based on previous work in formal and symbolic logic, and grounded in the contributions of Turing in the 1930s, automata theories were developed to deal with the body of physical and logical principles underlying the operation of any electromechanical device that converts information from one form to another according to a specific procedure. Automata are governed by operations whose principles can be perceived as a sequence of states which can be considered abstractly, as a set of inputs, outputs and rules of operation (Nelson, 1967). Automata theory contributed to a new perception of organised complexity when it was enriched by the research of McCulloch and Pitts on neural networks (1943) and by the work of Von Neumann on 'self-reproduction' (see below). Based on their neurophysiological research, McCulloch and Pitts offered a mathematical description of some features of the neural system. The concept of a neural network supposed a geometric configuration constituted by a large number of 'formal neurons' operating parallel basic operations. Enabling the description of complex operations engaged by automata, the concept of neural networks offered at the same time a powerful conceptual tool to represent a possible ontology of organised complexity.

Cybernetics

In 1941, as a consequence of research conducted by the US Army on the aiming of anti-aircraft guns, the concept of cybernetics emerged (from the Greek *kubernetes*, the art of governing), and from 1948 it designated a broad subject area concerned with 'control and communication in the animal and the machine' (Wiener, 1948/ 1961). Grounded in the development of information theory and automata theory, cybernetics introduced the concept of 'feedback' to describe how a system can operate by adapting itself to its environment following a pre-defined finality. Linking the idea of feedback to the concept of information, as theorised by Shannon, cybernetics offered a framework to represent the process through which information is assimilated and used by an organism to orient and control its own action. Following a behaviourist tradition, cybernetics grounded the understanding of organised complexity in the study of systems, conceived in a teleological perspective (instead of aiming to identify causes producing observed effects). From 1949, a series of ten successive conferences, known as 'Conference Macy', was initiated by Von Foerster, Wiener, Von Neumann, Savage, McCulloch, Bateson, Mead and Lewin. Despite the lack of a strong epistemological anchorage, these events contributed to the legitimacy of a research trend that provided a powerful pragmatic foundation to the idea of complexity (Le Moigne, 1996, 2001a).

Operations Analysis and Operational Research

The development of mixed-teams approaches, also known as 'operations analysis groups', was initiated during the Second World War by the British to answer problems of tactics and strategy. The procedure was applied to the Navy's anti-submarine campaign and the Air Forces:

> Although mathematicians, physicists, and engineers were essential, the best of the groups also contained physiologists, biochemists, psychologists, and a variety of representatives of other fields of the biochemical and social sciences ... . Under the pressure of war, these mixed teams pooled their resources and focused all their different insights on the common problems ... . It was shown that these groups could tackle certain problems of organised complexity, and get useful answers (Weaver, para. 14)

Progressively institutionalised as 'Operational Research' at the end of the war, this trend contributed to the emergence of a field of study focusing on the development of algorithms to tackle multidimensional decision processes involving uncertainty. Thus, problems of organised complexity with hundreds or thousands of variables were transformed and reduced into linear mathematical expressions which could be handled by computers (Beer, 1959; Churchmann, Ackoff & Arnoff, 1957).

Second Generation

Challenges raised by the Second World War thus accelerated the emergence and institutionalisation of the first body of research informing the concept of complexity. In the early 1960s, the notion was introduced for the first time in a significant American journal of epistemology (Simon, 1962). During the following decades, the development of large corporations, the progress of technology and the context of the Cold War provided the socio-cultural environment favouring the exponential development of new theories revisiting the idea of complexity.

Computer Sciences and Engineering Sciences

During the 1950s, with the extension of telephone networks and the development of large insurance companies, engineering sciences and computer sciences were confronted with the difficulty of conceiving and controlling broad systems perceived as complex ones. Using innovations introduced during the previous decade and the development of new generations of computers, various mathematical models were conceived (Ashby, 1956; Marcus, 1977), and the notion of 'algorithmic complexity' was established (Knuth, 1968). The perspectives opened by this research helped to reinforce an understanding grounded in a quantitative evaluation of complexity that considered, for example, the length of the account that must be given to provide an adequate description of a system (descriptive complexity), the length of the set of instructions that must be given to provide a recipe for producing it (generative complexity), or the amount of time and effort involved in resolving a problem (computational complexity) (Rescher, 1998). Allowing for comparison of the complexity of different systems, and based on mathematical measurement, these approaches contributed to providing instrumental definitions of complexity that bypassed the question of their epistemological legitimacy (Le Moigne, 2001a).

Management Sciences and Artificial Intelligence

In parallel with these developments, and intertwined with the institutionalisation of operational research and the extension of cybernetics to management (Beer, 1959/1970), the study of problems of organised complexity took root in the emerging sciences of management decision-making. Incorporating the contribution of game theory as formulated by Von Neumann and Morgenstern, the work of Simon on 'decision-making processes' in administrative organisations (Simon, 1947) and on 'heuristic problem solving' (Simon & Newell, 1958) contributed to the progressive emergence of an autonomous body of work designated as 'artificial intelligence' (AI). Located at the interface between economic sciences, computer sciences, psychology and logic, and grounded in heuristic methods of research, AI provided approximated representations of real situations more accurately than those calculated through operational research's algorithms. Being able to cope with any situation that can be represented symbolically (i.e. verbally, mathematically or through diagrams), AI extended the use of computers to problems more complex and less structured, including the highest form of reasoning, reserved until then for human judgement (Simon, 1996). The development of AI also contributed to the emergence of an epistemological reflection on the legitimacy of its disciplinary roots. Simon, along with others, initiated what might be interpreted today as a constructivist epistemology of complexity (Le Moigne, 2001a).

Systems Sciences

After prolific use during the 18th century and intense criticism during the 19th, the notion of 'system' emerged again with the development of cybernetics. In 1945, Von Bertalanffy developed the idea that organised wholes of any kind should be describable, and to a certain extent explainable, by means of the same categories, and ultimately by the same formal apparatus. His 'general systems theory' (Von Bertalanffy, 1951) and the initial contribution of Boulding, Gerard & Rapoport triggered a movement during the 1950s that tried to identify invariant structures and mechanisms across different kinds of organised wholes (Schwaninger, 2005). During the next decades, this trend helped to bring about the elaboration and the implementation of a set of methodologies that aimed to represent phenomena of organised complexity by allowing both for the anticipation of their behaviours and the consequences of intentional intervention. Since the 1970s, the influence of systems theories followed two different paths, epistemologically antagonistic. The first, as it appears, for example, in the work of Forrester (1961) on 'system dynamics' and the work of Churchman (1968) on 'system approach', allowed for the emergence of techniques reducing the complexity of a system to the study of its components and their relationships understood as objective phenomena. Influenced by the con-tributions of Piaget, Bateson, Simon, Von Foerster and Morin, a second tradition favoured a definition of complex systems by acknowledging the constructivist nature of their modelling. Such a perspective contributed to an understanding of complexity that recognised the importance of the relationship binding the observer to a phenomenon (Le Moigne, 2001a).

Self-Organisation

The concept of self-organisation—used in the 1930s by Von Bertalanffy to characterise the central feature of organismic development and by Gestalt psychologists to describe the way humans process experience (Fox Keller, 2004)— benefitted from a lot of attention during the early 1950s. Its definition was energised by the contribution of several theories: the work of Von Neumann (1966) on 'self-reproducing automata' (developing the idea of an artificial machine capable of reproducing itself); the research of Ashby (1956) on 'cybernetics variety' (describing the correspondences between the behaviours of a system and the configuration of relations among its components); the invention by Rosenblatt (1958) of the 'Perceptron' (a device whose neuron-like connections should allow it to perceive, recognise and identify its surroundings without human training or control); and finally, the contributions of Von Foerster (1960, 1996) on 'non-trivial systems' (describing autonomous organisations as systems whose inputs are not totally independent of the feedback produced by their outputs). These contribu-tions helped shift the orientation of cybernetics (identified later as 'second-order cybernetics') toward conceiving complex organisations as autonomous systems whose evolution is a function of both their environment and the relationships among their own components. Enriched by the work of Atlan (1972), this renewed conception of self-organisation helped to redefine complex organised phenomena as emergences, produced not only from their constituting order, but also from the disorder (noise or fluctuation) characterising the relations among their own components.

The Study of Non-Linear Dynamics: Dissipative structures, catastrophe, chaos and fractal theories

During the same period, progress in the understanding of self-organised phenomena had major consequences for the study of non-linear dynamics. In 1969, Prigogine's discovery of 'dissipative structures' marked a shift in thermodynamics that sparked a reconsideration of the idea of entropy. His team demonstrated the possibility that an irreversible process (dissipation of energy) far from a steady-state is able to play a constructive role and become a source of order. His description of dissipative structures brought new insights into the way molecular disorder is able to regress (steady zone) and the ways in which circumstantial fluctuations can amplify themselves (bifurcation) to bring the system into a new state characterised by a specific stability (Prigogine & Stengers, 1984). Allowing for a categorisation of the dynamics of non-linear systems depending on their behaviour, the 'catastrophe theory' elaborated by Thom (1975) contributed to an understanding of the relationships between stationary states, changes and ruptures affecting the transformation of regular physical phenomena in discontinuous and singular manifestations. Emerging in the early 1970s, 'chaos theory' provided a framework to describe system behaviour depending so sensitively on its precise initial conditions that it is unpredictable and cannot be distinguished from a random process, even though it is deterministic in a mathematical sense (Gleick, 1987). Finally, the concept of 'fractality', introduced in 1975 by Mandelbrot (1983), referred to the geometrical characteristics of natural phenomena that are statistically self-similar (a fractal is an infinitely complex recursively constructed shape: a magnification of a part of one sample can be matched closely with some other member of the ensemble), allowing geometrical order to be perceived in apparent disorder. Through these developments, the study of non-linear dynamics drastically renewed the vocabulary associated with complexity and the resources available to describe it. Contributing to the development of mathematical and conceptual resources that enabled a revisiting of the relationships between fluctuation and stability, non-linearity and linearity, randomness and non-randomness, the study of non-linear dynamics also provided a framework that helped to describe the complexity of any morphogenesis (Dahan Dalmedico, 2004; Morin, 1977/1980).

Evolutionary Biology

During the 1960s, the progress of technology and developments associated with cybernetics and with self-organisation challenged traditional approaches to biology. On one hand, with the discovery of DNA, new theories were developed to explain the emergence of life as the predictable, even if improbable, consequence of physical and chemical laws characterised by the presence of disorder (Monod, 1972). Evolution was revisited through new statistical models (Dawkins, 1989), illuminating in particular its chaotic nature (Gould & Eldredge, 1977). On the other hand, new theories built new bridges between the development of life and the emergence of cognition, among them the contributions of Bateson (1973) and the work of Maturana and Varela (1992), grounded in Maturana's initial research on *autopoiesis*. (An autopoietic system is organised as a unified whole, the parts of which continue, through multiple interactions and transformations, to realise and produce relations that have themselves produced the network of processes in the first place. Autopoiesis affirms living systems as without essence [see Semetsky, 2008, in this volume].) Providing new representations of 'adaptation', 'evolution', 'self', 'autonomy' and 'emergence', this research positioned the study of the evolution of life at the centre of the ensuing developments informing the understanding of complex phenomena.

Third Generation

During the 1980s, complexity research followed two different paths. The first, more visible in the English-speaking field through the study of 'complex adaptive systems', is perhaps best understood to lie at the border between recent developments in non-linear dynamics, evolutionary biology, and artificial sciences. The second, more prevalent in Latin countries, is characterised by a reflexive dimension that aims to explore new ways of representing multiple complexities and that promotes an epistemology driven by the will of scientists to determine, conceive and construct the rules of their own action, including ethical ones.

Complex Adaptive Systems

In the early 1980s the expression 'complex adaptive systems' (CAS) emerged with the creation of the Santa Fe Institute in New Mexico:

> [E]mphasising multidisciplinary collaboration in pursuit of understanding the common themes that arise in natural, artificial, and social systems [t]his unique scientific enterprise attempts to uncover the mechanisms that underlie the deep simplicity present in our complex world. (Santa Fe Institute, 2005)

Among the theories informing this trend were: the work of Holland (1992) on a 'genetic algorithm' (an attempt to model the phenomena of variation, combination and selection underlying most processes of evolution and adaptation); the research of Kaufmann (1993) on 'Boolean networks' (grounded in the study of properties related to networks of genes or chemical reactions in an evolutionary perspective informed by self-organisation); the research of Bak (Bak & Chen, 1991) on 'self-organized criticality' (aiming to describe the evolution of physical or living phenomena toward a 'critical edge' located between stability and chaos); and the work of Wolfram (2001) on 'cellular automata' (using mathematical models and computer simulations to describe evolution of chaotic phenomena). As illustrated by the work initiated by Langton (1989) on 'artificial life' (software and hardware created to reproduce behaviours similar to those characterising natural living systems), the study of CAS reinforced an ascendant logic of research: aiming to model and simulate behaviours presenting analogies with organic, ecological or socially complex phenomena (Helmreich, 2004; Heylighen, 1997), it reinforced an understanding of complexity requiring researchers to create and organise the rules of its conception, instead of trying to infer them from empirical observation.

Intelligence de la Complexité

In spite of a rich proliferation of theories, the development of epistemological reflections around the concept of complexity is relatively recent. Between 1945 and 1975, the status and epistemological legitimacy of sciences constituted within the paradigm of organised complexity was rarely investigated and the term 'complexity' seldom used (Le Moigne, 1996). Books published in the late 1970s that are now considered classics, contributed to the new wave of epistemological and conceptual research developed at that time (see, for example, University of the United Nations, 1986). In France, the work of Morin is located at the core of these contributions.[1]

In the 1960s Morin's research on the anthropology of knowledge (Morin, 1973, 1977/1980, 1980, 1986, 1991) developed an approach that involved a reorganisation of the various conceptions of complexity from the 1940s. Morin framed significant epistemological critics by going beyond the usual dualisms (positivist and realist versus constructivist; Cartesian versus non-Cartesian, etc.), and used these contributions to question the limitations of contemporary processes of knowledge production. Located at the intersection of philosophy, physics, biology and human sciences, his reflection created an epistemic loop that associated the emergence of 'organised' knowledge (sciences) with the creation of 'organising' knowledge (Le Moigne, 1996). His paradigm of 'self-eco-re-organization' (*auto-éco-ré-organisation*) criticised the epistemological and institutional compartmentalisation of the contemporary sciences and philosophies. Advocating the emergence of a kind of science that endorsed an 'en-cyclo-paedic' process (which builds in cycles rather than in a linear accumulation of knowledge), his approach related fragmented scientific fields of study with each other. Grounded in an open network of concepts and principles of thought, Morin advocated a conception of complexity that dispensed with the antagonist, contra-dictory and complementary tensions which shape its own understanding. Aware of its own biological, physical and anthropological foundation, a complex thought involves the integration of both the complexity of our identity as human beings (Morin, 2001) and the complexity of ethical issues generated by a conception of science understood through its own uncertainty (Morin, 1973, 2004). Reinterpret-ing both the epistemological and the political nature of these theories, the work of Morin contributed to the legitimacy of several trends of research sharing the same ethical commitment with regard to the construction of new models of knowledge production (see for example, the European programme, MCX '*Modélisation de la complexité*', 2005).

Keeping Complexity Complex

In one sense, the genealogy sketched in this chapter may lead one to believe that the development of theories today associated with complexity has followed a linear path, representative of the order which constitutes them. But in another, the heterogeneity of meaning and the multiplicity of definitions, trends and fields of study in which they have taken their roots illuminate the constitutive disorder which shaped their evolution. To identify the contributions associated with this notion requires that we position ourselves with regard to such ambiguity. To do so, it seems relevant to consider from a socio-cultural point of view the epistemological variations underlying complexity theories and some of the ambiguities they convey.

Epistemological Variations

From an epistemological point of view, the ambiguity associated with the development of complexity theories is linked to the fact that historically they have evolved in a space of representations, constituted simultaneously by antagonistic, contradictory and complementary positions. Complexity may be considered an ontological dimension of the object of study, some understandings of which suggest reduction to specific characteristics and representation through a set of all-embracing algebraic expressions. Its states and behaviours can in these views be described and calculated with certainty, following a computing process. In these perspectives, the evolution of this kind of system can be predicted, more or less accurately, through programmable algorithms. The possibilities are considered as foreseeable. The behaviours observed are considered as being explainable, and then predictable, by a theory, a rule, or an invariant structure. If the computational capacity of the observer practically limits such a prediction, the development of more sophisticated computing devices allows its advocates to believe in the great potential of this position (Le Moigne, 1996). Historically, such an approach is at the core of the development of an understanding of 'organised complexity' as predicted by Weaver. Today, it underlies various trends recognised by many as 'reductionist', whose limitations brought them to be associated with the notions of 'complication' or 'hyper-complication' (Ardoino, 2000; Le Moigne, 1996, 2001a; Lissack, 2001; Morin, 1977/1980, 2007).

However, since the 1970s, a 'softer' position has emerged. Considering concepts associated with complexity as powerful metaphors to describe or understand socio-cultural phenomena, this position contributed to a new vocabulary to interpret reality. Recognising similarities and differences between various levels of organisations (physical, biological, social, etc.), this position contributed to the development of analogies between them. Because of the relative paucity of reflection on the validity of these comparisons, their epistemological legitimacy remains largely unchallenged, but some authors have identified them as 'pseudo-scientific' (Le Moigne, 2001a; Phelan, 2001).

In parallel with these perspectives, a third position may be identified. In contrast with 'hyper-complication', it suggests that complexity is associated with situations where the observer is aware of the impossibility of defining the list of potential states of a system, or the list of contributing factors. It invites an approach to complexity that is no longer a matter of explanation or prediction. Conceived as an interpretation, complexity is a characteristic attributed by the observer to a phenomenon. It is, above all, a key element of a representation built by the researcher, and not necessarily an aspect of the ontology of the object of study. It is thus in some senses a constructivist understanding of complexity (Le Moigne, 1996, 2001a, 2001b, 2003).

These positions are prototypical, and as such invite consideration of at least two issues that influence the positioning of complexity as a point of view. The first refers to the level of closure attributed to the definition of complexity. Associated with a set of identified components, complexity is reduced to (hyper-)complication; extended to an open-ended list, its definition loses its specificity. In between, it involves a process of negotiation of its meanings, thus adding a layer of ambiguity. A second issue concerns the type of representation privileged to describe it. The contemporary success of complexity is embedded in both the power of the metaphors and the efficiency of the algorithms associated with it. To be represented and discussed, complexity involves translations between symbolic, formal, and informal languages. These interpretations necessarily add a layer of uncertainty.

Socio-Cultural Ambivalences

Besides or because of their epistemological ambiguity, theories related to complexity are also ambivalent from a socio-cultural point of view. On one hand, complexity theories have substantial emancipatory potential. Concepts like 'control', 'autonomy', 'organisation' or 'self' may enrich our representations of alienation and emancipation as complex processes. They might encourage reconsideration of the meaning of social and philosophical critique (Alhadeff, 2003, 2004; Alhadeff-Jones, 2007b; Geyer, 1980; Morin, 1977/1980, 1980, 1986). The development of complexity theories is also associated with the emergence of new formal logics (Morin, 1991) and new ways of knowing (Fabbri & Munari, 1984/1993). Complexity theories have contributed to the promotion of non-dualistic, non-hierarchical and non-linear representations, reframing ways of understanding contemporary issues. Trends initiated around this body of research also invite reconsideration of a plurality of (old and new) disciplines by challenging their epistemological legitimacy (Le Moigne, 2001b; Morin, 1999). From 'multireferentiality' (Ardoino, 1993) to 'transdisciplinarity' (Nicolescu, 1996, 2005; Paul & Pineau, 2005), complexity has contributed to a critique of traditional modes of organising knowledge. Transversal approaches have emerged, renegotiating ways of conjugating heterogeneous forms of knowledge and of crossing institutional compartmentalisation, without falling into the trap of eclecticism or relativism.

At the same time, complexity theories also carry the potential of perpetuating new forms of intellectual and social alienation (Lafontaine, 2004). Through the importance they give to technological development and the concepts and metaphors they convey, these theories perpetuate a set of values, a vocabulary, even an ideology, which may contribute to perpetuating specific forms of domination

(Lafontaine, 2004; Morin, 1977/1980, 1980, 1986, 1991; Musso, 2003; Boltanski & Chiapello, 1999)[2].

Complexity theories can be accused of the reduction of phenomena to a set of mathematical variables and abstract models, and also of the production of pseudo-scientific analogies grounding new theories and practices in illegitimate frames of interpretation. Furthermore, as a result of their heavy anchorage in physics, biology, engineering, management, etc., some of the concepts framing the contemporary understanding of complexity in connection with, say, the study of education, represent a risk of reducing education's associated concepts and issues to a narrow set of perspectives.[3]

Towards a New Form of Critique?

Complexity theories do not of course necessarily bring about an improvement in research into education, especially from an ethical and socially aware point of view. Because science is also the result of complex processes (Alhadeff-Jones, 2007a, 2007b, in press; Morin, 1986, 1991), the benefits of any of these contributions cannot be taken for granted. To go beyond the fashion of a 'new' set of concepts, one has first to consider how these theories might enable us to rethink educational theories. Critical consideration of education, grounded in contemporary theories related to complexity, as well as in a critical appraisal of their epistemological and ethical legitimacy, has to be considered by following the loops and dynamics they constitute (Alhadeff, 2005; Alhadeff-Jones, 2007b). One of the new challenges for educational theorists is probably to be able to work on the following at the same time: the construction of an original form of critique able to deal with phenomena perceived as complex and the elaboration of a critique able to dialogue with a body of theories which do not fit traditional epistemic frames of reference. Complexity is a 'word-problem' and not a 'word-solution' (Morin, 1990). In the study of education, it should invite us to consider the problems raised by its own irreducibility to existing frames of thought at least as much as the solutions it appears to offer. Complexity should invite us to challenge our ways of interpreting science and philosophy, as well as our ways of interpreting the world. A specific kind of learning may thus be reinforced in these challenges: the ability of educational researchers and practitioners to build systems of representation that allow them to confront more systematically their own transformation, as they conceptualise the transformation they are studying.

Notes

1. Although the research of Morin has been translated into many languages, references to his work are relatively few in English-speaking countries. Among the rare texts related to complexity that are easily available in English are: Morin, E. (2007) Restricted Complexity, General Complexity, in: C. Gershenson, D. Aerts & B. Edmonds (eds) *Worldviews, Science and Us, Philosophy and Complexity* (London, World Scientific) pp. 5–29; Morin, E. & Kern, A. B. (1999) *Homeland Earth* (Creskill, NJ, Humpton Press); Morin, E. (1992) *Method: Towards a study of humankind. Volume 1: The nature of nature* (New York, Peter Lang); Morin, E. (1992)

From the Concept of System to the Paradigm of Complexity, *Journal of Social and Evolutionary Systems*, 15:4, pp. 371–385; Kofman, M. (1996) *Edgar Morin: From big brother to fraternity* (London, Pluto Press).

2. See, for example, the historical work of Musso (2003) grounding a critique of the concept of 'network'; see also the sociological work of Boltanski and Chiapello (1999) illustrating and theorising how, since the late 1970s, the introduction in management of concepts associated with complexity affected and reinforced the discourse legitimising the mutation of capitalism, redefining ways to negotiate power dynamics and social critiques.

3. It seems relevant to consider the fact that several key theories informing the idea of complexity find their roots in military research during the Second World War and the Cold War (Fox Keller, 2004; Lafontaine, 2004), and have contributed to major business-oriented development as well. In the same way, contemporary developments like 'artificial life' appear to be grounded in Western masculine world-views that perpetuate a specific set of representations (Helmreich, 2004).

References

Alhadeff, M. (2003) Rethinking the Concept of 'Critically Reflective Practice' through the Paradigm of Complexity: Some epistemological, theoretical, and practical issues. Paper presented at the 44th Annual Adult Education Research Conference (San Francisco, San Francisco State University).

Alhadeff, M. (2004) Conjuguer l'Hétérogénéité de la Critique en Sciences de l'Education: De l'hypocrit(iqu)e à l'hypercritique, in: R. Arce, Farina, F., Novo, M., Egido, A., Ardoino, J. & Berger, G. (eds), *La Pensée Critique en Education* (Santiago de Compostela, Spain, Universidade de Santiago de Compostela) pp. 34–46.

Alhadeff, M. (2005) Complexité de la Critique et Critique de la Complexité en Formation, in: J. Clenet & D. Poisson (eds) *Complexité de la Formation et Formation à la Complexité* (Paris, L'Harmattan) pp. 227–241.

Alhadeff-Jones, M. (2007a, May) *Scientific Mind, Critical Mind and Complexity: Learning from a Scientist's Life History*. Paper presented at the 2nd International Conference of the Learning Development Institute (Vancouver, Canada, Emilie Carr Institute).

Alhadeff-Jones, M. (2007b) Education, Critique et Complexité: Modèle et expérience de conception d'une approche multiréférentielle de la critique en Sciences de l'éducation. Doctoral dissertation in Educational Sciences (Paris, Université de Paris 8).

Alhadeff-Jones, M. (in press) Promoting Scientific Dialogue as a Lifelong Learning Process, in: F. Darbellay, M. Cockell, J. Billote & F. Waldvogel (eds), *For a Knowledge Dialogue between Natural and Social Sciences* (Paris, Odile Jacob).

Ardoino, J. (1963/1999) *Education et Politique* (Paris, Anthropos).

Ardoino, J. (1993) L'Approche Multiréférentielle (Plurielle) des Situations Educatives et Formatives. *Pratiques de Formation / Analyses*, 25–26, pp. 15–34.

Ardoino, J. (1998) Education et Politique aux Regards de la Pensée Complexe. Paper presented at the AFIRSE international conference (Lisbon, Portugal, Faculty of Psychology and Educational Sciences, University of Lisbon).

Ardoino, J. (2000) *Les Avatars de l'Education* (Paris, Presses Universitaires de France).

Ardoino, J. & De Peretti, A. (1998) *Penser l'Hétérogène* (Paris, Desclée de Brouwer).

Ashby, W. R. (1956) *An Introduction to Cybernetics* (London, Chapman & Hall).

Atlan, H. (1972) *L'Organisation Biologique et la Théorie de l'Information* (Paris, Hermann).

Bachelard, G. (1934/2003) *Le Nouvel Esprit Scientifique* (Paris, Presses Universitaires de France).

Bak, P. & Chen, K. (1991) Self-Organized Criticality, *Scientific American*, 264, pp. 46–53.

Bateson, G. (1973) *Steps to an Ecology of Mind* (London, Paladin).

Beer, S. (1959) What has Cybernetics to do with Operational Research? *Operational Research Quarterly*, 10, pp. 1–21.

Beer, S. (1959/1970) *Cybernetics and Management* (London, English University Press).

Benkirane, R. (ed.) (2002) *La Complexité, Vertiges et Promesses. 18 histoires de sciences* (Paris, Le Pommier).

Boltanski, L. & Chiapello, E. (1999) *Le Nouvel Esprit du Capitalisme* (Paris, Gallimard).

Churchman, C. W. (1968) *The Systems Approach* (New York, Dell).

Churchman, C. W., Ackoff, R. L. & Arnoff, E. L. (1957) *Introduction to Operations Research* (New York, Wiley).

Dahan Dalmedico, A. (2004) Chaos, Disorder, and Mixing: A new fin-de-siècle image of science? in: M. Norton (ed.) *Growing Explanations: Historical perspectives on recent science* (London, Duke University Press) pp. 67–94.

Dawkins, R. (1989) *The Selfish Gene* (2nd edn.) (Oxford, Oxford University Press).

European Program MCX 'Modélisation de la Complexité' (2005) Retrieved September 20, 2005, from http://www.mcxapc.org.

Fabbri, D. & Munari, A. (1984/1993) *Stratégies du Savoir. Vers une psychologie culturelle* (Geneva, Switzerland, Université de Genève).

Forrester, J. (1961) *Industrial Dynamics* (Cambridge, MA, MIT Press).

Fox Keller, E. (2004) Marrying the Premodern to the Postmodern: Computers and organisms after World War II, in: M. N. Wise (ed.) *Growing Explanations. Historical perspectives on recent science* (London, Duke University Press) pp. 181–198.

Geyer, R. F. (1980) *Alienation Theories: A general systems approach* (Oxford, Pergamon Press).

Gleick, J. (1987) *Chaos: Making a new science* (New York, Penguin Books).

Gould, S. J. & Eldredge, N. (1977) Punctuated Equilibria: The tempo and mode of evolution reconsidered, *Paleobiology*, 3, pp. 115–151.

Helmreich, S. (2004) The Word for World is Computer: Simulating second natures in artificial life, in: M. N. Wise (ed.) *Growing Explanations. Historical perspectives on recent science* (London, Duke University Press) pp. 275–300.

Heylighen, F. (1997) *The Evolution of Complexity*. Retrieved August 20, 2004, from http://pespmc1.vub.ac.be/Papers/PublicationsComplexity.html

Holland, J. H. (1992) *Adaptation in Natural and Artificial Systems: An introductory analysis with applications to biology, control and artificial intelligence* (Cambridge, MA, MIT Press).

Institut National de la Langue Française (2005) *Le Trésor de la Langue Française Informatisé* [Electronic resource] (Paris, Centre National de la Recherche Scientifique & Editions Gallimard). Retrieved September 15, 2005, from http://atilf.atilf.fr/tlf.htm

Kauffman, S. A. (1993) *The Origins of Order: Self-organization and selection in evolution* (New York, Oxford University Press).

Knuth, D. E. (1968) *The Art of Computer Programming (vol. 1): Fundamental algorithms* (Reading, MA, Addison-Wesley).

Lafontaine, C. (2004) *L'Empire Cybernétique. Des machines à penser à la pensée machine* (Paris, Seuil).

Langton, C. G. (ed.) (1989) *Artificial Life: The proceedings of an interdisciplinary workshop on the synthesis and simulation of living systems* (Redwood City, CA, Addison-Wesley).

Le Moigne, J.-L. (1979/1984) *La Théorie du Système Général. Théorie de la modélisation* (Paris, Presses Universitaires de France).

Le Moigne, J.-L. (1996) Complexité, in: D. Lecourt (ed.), *Dictionnaire d'Histoire et Philosophie des Sciences* (Paris, Presses Universitaires de France) pp. 205–215.

Le Moigne, J.-L. (2001a) *Le Constructivisme. Les enracinements (vol. 1)* (Paris, L'Harmattan).

Le Moigne, J.-L. (2001b) *Le Constructivisme. Epistémologie de l'interdisciplinarité (vol. 2)* (Paris, L'Harmattan).

Le Moigne, J.-L. (2003) *Le Constructivisme. Modéliser pour comprendre (vol. 3)* (Paris, L'Harmattan).

Lissack, M. R. (ed.) (2001) *Emergence, a journal of complexity issues in organization and management*, 3:1 (Mahwah, NJ, Lawrence Erlbaum Ass).

Mandelbrot, B. (1983) *The Fractal Geometry of Nature* (New York, Freeman).

McCulloch, W. S. & Pitts, W. (1943) A Logical Calculus of the Ideas of Immanent in Nervous Activity, *Bulletin of Mathematical Biophysics*, 6, pp. 115–133.

Marcus, M. (1977) *The Theory of Connecting Networks and their Complexity: A review.* Proceedings of the IEEE, 65:9, pp. 1263–1271.

Maturana, H. R. & Varela F. J. (1992) *The Tree of Knowledge: The biological roots of understanding* (Boston, Shambhala).

Monod, J. (1972) *Chance and Necessity* (London, Collins).

Morin, E. (1973) *Le Paradigme Perdu: La nature humaine* (Paris, Seuil).

Morin, E. (1977/1980) *La Méthode (vol. 1) La nature de la nature* (Paris, Seuil).

Morin, E. (1980) *La Méthode (vol. 2) La vie de la vie* (Paris, Seuil).

Morin, E. (1986) *La Méthode (vol. 3) La connaissance de la connaissance* (Paris, Seuil).

Morin, E. (1990) *Introduction à la Pensée Complexe* (Paris, ESF).

Morin, E. (1991) *La Méthode (vol. 4) Les idées. Leur habitat, leur vie, leurs mœurs, leur organisation* (Paris, Seuil).

Morin, E. (ed.) (1999) *Relier les Connaissances, le Défi du XXIe siècle* (Paris, Seuil).

Morin, E. (2000) *Les Sept Savoirs Nécessaires à l'Education du Futur* (Paris, Seuil).

Morin, E. (2001) *La Méthode (vol. 5) L'humanité de l'humanité, l'identité humaine* (Paris, Seuil).

Morin, E. (2004) *La Méthode (vol. 6) Ethique* (Paris, Seuil).

Morin, E. (2007) Restricted Complexity, General Complexity, in: C. Gershenson, D. Aerts & B. Edmonds (eds) *Worldviews, Science and Us, Philosophy and Complexity* (London, World Scientific) pp. 5–29.

Morin, E. & Le Moigne, J.-L. (1999) *L'Intelligence de la complexité* (Paris, L'Harmattan).

Morin, E., Motta, R. & Ciurana, E.-R. (2003) *Eduquer pour l'Ere Planétaire. La pensée complexe comme méthode d'apprentissage dans l'erreur et l'incertitude humaines* (Paris, Balland).

Musso, P. (2003) *Critique des Réseaux* (Paris, Presses Universitaires de France).

Nelson, R. J. (1967) *Introduction to Automata* (New York, Wiley).

Nicolescu, B. (1996) *La Transdisciplinarité. Manifeste* (Monaco, Editions du Rocher).

Nicolescu, B. (2005, September) *Transdisciplinarity—Past, Present and Future.* Paper presented at the Second World Congress of Transdisciplinarity: 'What education for sustainable development? Attitude—research—action' (Vitória, Vila Velha, Brazil).

Paul, P. & Pineau, G. (eds) (2005) *Transdisciplinarité et Formation* (Paris, L'Harmattan).

Phelan, S. E. (2001) What is Complexity Science, really? *Emergence*, 3:1, pp. 120–136.

Prigogine, I. & Stengers, I. (1984) *Order out of Chaos* (New York, Bantam Books).

Rescher, N. (1998) *Complexity. A philosophical overview* (New Brunswick, NJ, Transaction Publishers).

Rosenblatt, F. (1958) The Perceptron: A probabilistic model for information storage and organization in the brain, *Psychological Review*, 65, pp. 386–408.

Santa Fe Institute (2005) Homepage. Retrieved September 15, 2005, from http://www.santafe.edu.

Schwaninger, M. (2005) *System Dynamics and the Evolution of Systems Movement. An historical perspective* (Diskussionsbeiträge des Institus für Betriebswirtschaft, #52) (St-Gallen, Switzerland, Hochschule für Wirtschafts-, Rechts- und Sozialwissenschaften).

Semetsky, I. (2008) On the Creative Logic of Education, or: Re-reading Dewey through the Lens of Complexity Science, *Educational Philosophy and Theory*, 40:1 (this issue).

Shannon, C. E. & Weaver, W. (1963) *The Mathematical Theory of Communication* (5th edn.) (Chicago, University of Illinois Press).

Simon, H. A. (1947) *Administrative Behavior* (New York, MacMillan).

Simon, H. A. & Newell, A. (1958) Heuristic Problem Solving: The next advance in operations research, *Operations Research*, 6, pp. 1–10.

Simon, H. A. (1962) Architecture of Complexity, *Proceedings of the American Philosophical* Society, 106, pp. 467–482.

Simon, H. (1996) *The Sciences of the Artificial* (3rd edn.) (Cambridge, MA, MIT Press).

Simpson, J. & al. (ed.) (1989/2005) *Oxford English Dictionary Online* (2nd edn.) [Electronic resource] (Oxford, Oxford University Press).

Thom, R. (1975) *Structural Stability and Morphogenesis* (Reading, MA, Benjamin).

University of the United Nations (Dir.) (1986) *Sciences et Pratiques de la Complexité* (Paris, La Documentation Française).

Von Bertalanffy, L. (1951) *General System Theory: A new approach to unity of science* (Baltimore, John Hopkins Press).

Von Foerster, H. (1960) On Self-Organizing Systems and their Environments, in: M. C. Yovits & S. Cameron (eds) *Self-Organizing Systems* (London, Pergamon Press) pp. 31–50.

Von Foerster, H. (1996) *Cybernetics of Cybernetics* (2nd edn.) (Minneapolis, MN, Future Systems).

Von Neumann, J. (1966) *Theory of Self-Reproducing Automata* (Urbana, University of Illinois Press).

Washington Center for Complexity and Public Policy (2003, October) The Use of Complexity Science. A survey of federal departments and agencies, private foundations, universities and independent education and research centers. Retrieved August 20, 2004, from http://www.complexsys.org

Weaver, W. (1948) Science and Complexity [Electronic version], *American Scientist*, 36, p. 536. Retrieved August 20, 2004, from http://www.ceptualinstitute.com.

Wiener, N. (1948/1961) *Cybernetics, or Control and Communication in the Animal and the Machine* (New York, Wiley & Sons).

Wise, M. N. (ed.) (2004) *Growing Explanations. Historical perspectives on recent science* (Durham, NC, Duke University Press).

Wolfram, S. (2001) *A New Kind of Science* (Champaign, IL, Wolfram Media).

6

Re-reading Dewey through the Lens of Complexity Science, or: On the creative logic of education

INNA SEMETSKY
University of Newcastle, Australia

John Dewey's philosophy remains a source of inspiration for educational theorists. This chapter adopts an unusual stance: reading Dewey's works through the lens of complex systems theory. It came as no surprise, when I opened Stephen H. Kellert's book, *In the Wake of Chaos*, and found that its first chapter starts with the following quotation from Dewey's *Experience and Nature*, from three quarters of a century ago: 'The world must actually be such as to generate ignorance and inquiry: doubt and hypothesis, trial and temporal conclusions ... . The ultimate evidence of genuine hazard, contingency, irregularity and indeterminateness in nature is thus found in the occurrence of thinking' (in Kellert, 1993, p. 1). Still, against nature as contingent and unpredictable, we, as Dewey says, safeguard ourselves in our quest for certainty in the complex, uncertain and 'aleatory world' (Dewey, 1929/1958, p. 41). We tend to deny the existence of chance by positing universal and necessary laws and by asserting 'the ubiquity of cause and effect' (ibid., p. 44) so as to secure through science our power for prediction and control. Yet, mathematical models based on strictly linear cause-and-effect connections do not always work, and the paradoxes of the complex world are such that it is 'change [that] gives meaning to permanency and recurrence [that] makes novelty possible' (ibid., p. 47).

Non-linearity enters our thinking. Ludwig von Bertalanffy, who founded the general systems theory, addressed the insufficiency of the analytical procedures of classical science based on linear causality connecting two basic variables, and attracted our attention to 'new categories of interaction, transaction, teleology' (1972, p. xix) that problematise mathematical models of systems dynamics. In the framework of systems thinking, knowledge is not reduced to given facts but becomes a function of 'an interaction between knower and known' (ibid.), very much in accord with Dewey's prophetic conceptualisations and pragmatic theory of inquiry (Dewey, 1938). Let us clarify vocabulary: in the most general terms, complexity theory is a conceptual framework used for the purpose of analysing the behaviour of systems that consist of a large number of interacting components. Human culture is a prime example of a complex system; but so may be the natural world too, should Newtonian laws prove insufficient to describe its dynamics. Importantly, the 'interactions do not have to be *physical*; they can also be thought of as a transference of *information*' (Cilliers, 1998, p. 3). A dynamical system is a model for the time-dependent behaviour of any real-life system. If the equations describing such a system contain non-linear, algebraic terms that represent interactions, then an exact, closed-form solution to such an equation is impossible, and the long-term behaviour of such a system would be described in terms of qualitative accounts rather than a single numerical prediction about its precise future state.

The dynamics of complex systems are first and foremost *relational*: it is a relation or an interaction that serves as a unit of analysis. Moreover, the interactions constituting the system's dynamics act in a non-linear manner. Chaos theory, for example, focuses on unstable and aperiodic, or complex, behaviour, one example of which may be human history, consisting as it does of *events* that involve competing agents and conflicting outcomes. Recognising the difference between linear and non-linear laws is paramount for conceptualising the relationship between cause and effect in a system. Non-linearity (that is, the absence of a direct causal connection as a feature of Newtonian science based on the laws of classical mechanics) between a complex system's many components is its major qualitative feature. A single cause may in fact lead to a multiplicity of effects; conversely, a single effect may be produced by a multiplicity of causes. A system may be rendered deterministic, albeit unpredictable, which means that the boundaries of such a system are open. An open-ended system is thus posited to exist in constant dynamic interaction with its environment, thus forming a continuum, or an organised complex whole, which cannot be reduced to the sum total of its isolated parts. Interestingly, the inter-relations of the parts are highly coordinated to yield some observable patterns at the level of behaviour of the whole system. For example, complicated dynamic behaviour can exhibit a shape known, in mathematical language, as an attractor. The uncertain motion of an attractor displays specific instability described, from the viewpoint of possible (un)predictability, as a system's sensitive dependence on initial conditions.

The mathematics of interdependent constitutive complexes can be equally applied to physical, biological, psychological and social systems (see Laszlo, 1972). Both Dewey and Charles S. Peirce acknowledged continuity in nature. Dewey described it as being 'the intimate, delicate and subtle interdependence of all organic structures and processes with one another' (Dewey, 1929/1958, p. 295). According to Dewey's naturalistic logic (1938), there is no breach of continuity between the operations of inquiry and biological and physical operations—that is, cognitive operations grow out of organic activities, without, however, being identical to that from which they emerge. As inquiry into inquiry, Dewey's naturalistic logic is recursive—that is, its function does not depend on anything extraneous to inquiry. Instead, it establishes continuity between the less complex and the more complex activities and forms comprising the multiplicity of heterogeneous levels. From the perspective of postmodern science (Cilliers, 1998; Byrne, 1998), complex systems, their being social or natural and including living systems, language and education, are indeed *complex* by virtue of the impossibility of either a single unified theory prescribing their behaviour, or even a single meta-narrative as being sufficient at the descriptive level.

A complex system has its dynamics that preclude permanency or the constancy of any theory. The interactions within the system change with time; and time itself is one of the intervening variables, a directional, irreversible 'arrow'. The analysis of complex systems proceeds historically: at every present moment a system has its past temporal history and is also future-oriented. Complexity theory regards the reductive analysis of the individual components of any system, such as the supposedly speaking, thinking and knowing 'selves' having in their centres the Cartesian *cogito*, to be an insufficient condition to come to terms with the system's dynamics as a whole, which has to take into consideration many contingencies and intervening variables inscribed in the dynamics of the process. Overall correlations, because of multiple interactions, are modulated and may spread or be distributed from immediately neighbouring regions to distant territories. Many non-local connections are formed by loops creating interactive feedback that contributes to the self-organising dynamics of the system as a whole. Such dynamics are characterised by new properties emerging at levels that are not immediately connected with the preceding ones but are nevertheless continuous with the latter by virtue of the (non-local) effect produced at a new level. The whole is by necessity greater than the sum of its parts, because the system's non-linearity precludes its dynamics being described by a simple addition of its individual components.

As a whole, the system remains open-ended; that is, it functions by means of constant interactions and transformations of matter/energy—or information, in the case of communication—with its environment, thereby belying the notion of a strictly defined border between itself and its environment. Philosophically, meanings— that make communication significant—cannot be defined as determined by either: the interactive dynamics are effectuated by feedback loops, which create multiple recurrences and self-referential closures as the very features that enable the system's dynamics. Human decision-making, from a systems theory perspective, is continuous with the entire situation that would have ensured system control based on adaptive reorganisation. Analogously, Dewey considered the reorganisation of experience to have its origin in what he called the problematic situation. It is the perplexity of a particular situation that demands a constructive process based on reflective thinking grounded in the 'superpropositional' (Dewey, 1934/1980, p. 85); that is, irreducibility to linear syllogistic inferential logic. Instead, it becomes the 'creative logic of artistic construction' (Dewey, 1998, p. 199). Interactions are established between, as Dewey said, what is done and what is undergone, and it is by means of apprehending these connections and interrelations that 'an organism increases in complexity' (Dewey, 1934/1980, p. 23); in other words, it learns.

The interaction between a system and its present environment induces a selective mechanism so that the environment does not directly determine the system's internal structure, but influences instead the system's developmental dynamics to the effect of producing new relations and making new connections. Significantly, Cilliers (1998) comments that such dynamics, in neural network terminology, would be understood as unsupervised learning (1998, p. 100) and contrasted with the direct information-processing model of knowledge structure. Such unsupervised learning, which would be above and beyond educational models based on direct instruction, is therefore part of what I call the creative logic of education. The total experiential situation, and not just a teacher's instruction, enables one's learning from experience (Semetsky, 2004) and studying 'by experience' (Lehmann-Rommel, 2000, p. 194).

This implies learning as an increase in complexity, but what would this mean? There are two kinds of systems understood as ordered wholes in relation to their environment. First-order systems effectuating adaptation, or stabilisation, by means of negative, or error-reducing feedback. 'Error' describes initial instability, fluctuation, or disequilibrium. For Dewey, it is some *tension* between an organism and its environment that makes the very situation problematic and uncertain. However, of greater interest to us, in view of Dewey's conceptualisations, are the second-order systems based on error-amplifying, positive feedback enabling the evolution of a system towards ever higher levels of complexity—that is, the progressive reorganisation of the total structure of a system, or what Dewey, employing a biological metaphor, would have called *growth*. Systems thus become transformed: they evolve towards increasingly adapted yet further unstable states. This transformation, understood as a transfer to a new level of complexity, can be expressed in terms of 'the focal culmination of the continuity of an ordered temporal experience in a sudden discrete instant of climax' (Dewey, 1934/1980, p. 24). Dewey was adamant that the more an organism learns, the more it still has to learn. The system keeps itself going by means of continuously reorganising itself so as to achieve a series of unsteady temporary equilibria from initial disequilibrium: 'otherwise death and catastrophe' (Dewey, 1929/1958, p. 281) would result. The metaphor of death is poignant: in systems-theoretical discourse, death would represent a state of complete equilibrium of the system, or its total closure in the absence of any tension that would otherwise have triggered interaction as the exchange (or, in technical terms, dissipation: see, e.g. Prigogine, 1980; Allen, 1981) of matter, energy, or information.

It is a self-organising communicative process that leads to growth and an increase in complexity; for Dewey, it ensures the added capacity for growth: as embedded in experience, 'learning naturally results' (1916/1924, p. 154). Dewey's *tension*, thereby, is the necessary presence of instability or uncertainty that serves as a precursor for the system's self- or re-organisation. Tension enables an import of negative entropy, as a measure of information, from a system's environment under the necessary 'condition of tensional distribution of energies' (Dewey, 1929/1958, p. 253). The system thereby self-organises or re-structures itself: indeed, what takes place is the system's *growth* in terms of its expanding its own boundaries: the re-organisation of experience. For Dewey, growth is possible only through participation in the dynamical process enacted in the rhythmic fluctuations between disequilibria and the restoration of equilibrium at a new level. Tension is embedded in the constant rhythm represented, first, by the loss of integration with the environment and, second, by the recovery of a new union (see Dewey, 1934/1980, p. 15). These rhythmic fluctuations enable human evolution and growth as a function of the continuous reconstruction of experience based on the 'integration of organic–environmental connections' (Dewey, 1929/1958, p. 279). The dynamics of organisation were envisaged by Dewey as organic and vital, and therefore irreducible to the paradigm of classical mechanics and the causal model of scientific explanation.

The emergence of order out of unstable, chaotic fluctuations is, however, not a miracle presiding over and above science. In the language of non-linear mathematics, in which complexity *science* 'speaks', the system *converges* on an attractor despite the fact that chaos theory defies deductive logic because of the system's dependence on initial conditions and its inherent uncertainty leading to *divergent* dynamics. Laszlo (1972) pointed out that there is nothing supernatural about such a self-organising process toward states of higher negative entropy, because 'the decrease of entropy within an open system is always offset by the increase of entropy in its surroundings' (Laszlo, 1972, p. 44), maintaining an exchange of entropy in every open system–environment complex. Dewey has given a specific name to such a mutual exchange whenever a 'response to another's act involves contemporaneous response to a thing as entering into other's behaviour, and this upon both sides' (1929/1980, p. 178): a transaction. Contrary to spectator theory of knowledge, a transaction is an 'unfractured observation' (Dewey, 1991, p. 97), which may seem a contradiction in terms if not for realising that it represents a spatio-temporal event encompassing 'the observer, the observing, and the observed' (ibid.).

In biological living systems, processes of a similar kind are referred to as autopoietic (Varela, 1979). An autopoietic system, by definition, is organised as a unified whole, the parts of which continue, through multiple interactions and transformations, to realise and produce relations that have themselves produced the network of processes in the first place. Autopoiesis affirms living systems as without essence—albeit not predicated solely on the interference of some action from outside the system—and the world as open-ended. The dynamics of autopoietic processes are analogous to Dewey's asserting that the reorganisation of experience is not a function of some external influence. He suggested that 'order is not imposed from without' (Dewey, 1934/1980, p. 14)—which would be an extraneous intervention, making a system allopoietic rather than autopoietic—'but is made out of the relations of harmonious interactions that energies bear to one another. Because it is active (not anything static ...) order itself develops ... . Order cannot but be admirable in a world constantly threatened with disorder' (1934/1980, p. 15). For Dewey, human emotions, desires, wishes, purposes—as ends-in-view—are 'informed ... when ... spent indirectly in search of material and in giving it order' (1934/1980, p. 70): hence we participate in the self-organising process of producing order out of chaos.

The fact that, as Dewey says, order itself develops means that the system's dynamics are such that its evolution tends towards greater complexity. Order can *develop* only when a system is open—that is, it exists by means of a continuous network of relations that demonstrate themselves as interactions with the environment. The operational closure in question is itself a transactional event, and its nature 'is the opposite of arrest, or *stasis*' (Dewey, 1934/1980, p. 41). The world constantly threatened with disorder constitutes an objective uncertainty, which cannot be reduced to the personal uncertainty of a Cartesian subject. In fact a problematic situation would be as yet subject-less or 'selfless' (Varela, 1999). Literally, autopoiesis means self-making and, figuratively, the making of the self. What is customarily called the self is an outcome of the whole series of experiential events: 'among and within these occurrences, not outside of them nor underlying them are those events which are denominated selves' (Dewey, 1929/1958, p. 232). An individual experience, for Dewey, is never exclusively personal: 'it [is] nature's, localised in a body as that body happened to exist by nature' (1929/1958, p. 231). It is a transaction that, itself being an event in the dynamical time-series, culminates in such an intercourse, the latter constituting the so-called autopoietic structural coupling that produces a series of 'interlocked ... *communicative interactions*' (Varela, 1979, p. 48). For Dewey, the human mind virtually comes in contact with the world—and therefore ensures the aforementioned structural coupling—because human attitudes, dispositions and habits are always relational in character and should never be taken as 'separate existences. They are always *of, from, toward*, situations and things' (1929/ 1958, p. 238). The transformation of the whole situation is then equivalent to an increase in complexity because of the reorganisation of experience. And *transformation* always presupposes *information* or, as we said earlier, the flow of negentropy, which is possible due to the openness of a system.

The Deweyan reorganisation of experience is 'always mutual: both organism and environment undergo transformations' (Maturana & Varela, 1992, p. 102) as a necessary condition of autopoietic systems' information exchange and creation of meanings. Significantly, in such a 'continuum ... there is no attempt to tell exactly where one begins and the other ends' (Dewey, 1934/1980, p. 227): both are involved in 'the intercourse of the live creature with his surroundings' (Dewey, 1934/1980, p. 22). Transaction ensures the operational closure of the system at large, making each end-in-view a temporary means to a new end, thereby correcting and ordering the course of events. The relations embedded in the continual and recursive feedbacks and constituting a network of mutual interactions establish the exchange of information as a sort of conversation (see Varela, 1979), or a metaphoric communication between the many levels in a complex system. The communicative process, in which transactions are embedded, is itself responsible for the continuously changing relations, and the system as a whole is inherently capable of maintaining itself by virtue of continuous coping and adaptation. The complex system therefore has flexibility and plasticity enabling its own self-organisation. Similar dynamics have been noted by Dewey who, seemingly in accord with the systems-theoretical viewpoint, emphasised that it is 'processes ... [that] are self-maintaining' (1938, p. 26), and not the individual components of a system.

This dialogic communication is not of course limited to verbal exchange: its meaning is much broader. Dewey asserted that nature itself speaks a language that must be interpreted. For Dewey, when communication takes place, all events in nature are subject to reconsideration, revision and re-adaptation: 'they are re-adapted to meet the requirements of conversation, whether it be public discourse or that preliminary discourse termed thinking' (1929/1958, p. 166), as internal communication. The logic of relations ensures re-adaptation, and new meanings are created because 'events turn into objects, things with meaning' (Dewey, 1929/1958, p. 166) as the outcome of complex relational dynamics. Dewey's naturalistic logic, irreducible to the laws of mechanical certainty, is again in agreement with the theory of autopoiesis. Through interactions, the unity of a system, or, in Dewey's words, its total pervasive quality, is differentiated, while at the same time these differentiations are connected, further sustaining such a pervasive and internally integrating quality. An operational closure represents a moment when a meaning emerges, and it is the relations between the structural components of the system at large that confer the range of possible meanings. Complex systems always operate under the far from equilibrium conditions that create a tension between the levels enabling interaction as a mutual transformation of energy or information.

The dynamics of the process are *cooperative*, as we have seen in the following passage from Dewey cited in part earlier: the 'response to another's act involves contemporaneous response to a thing as entering into the other's behaviour, and this upon both sides ... . It constitutes the intelligibility of acts and things. Possession of the capacity to engage in such activity is intelligence' (Dewey, 1929/1980, pp. 179–180). Dewey addressed intelligence in terms of habits that he described as the *organisations* of human nature. For Dewey, habit is a mode of organisation: it both commands an action—for example, a certain decision-making under the circumstances— and it also has 'a hold upon us because we are the habit' (1922/1988, p. 21). The transformation of habits is then tantamount to the reorganisation of experience on the basis of intelligent inquiry. An *inquiry* must precede the very fact of *acquiring* new habits, or modifying the old ones, because such a modification effects some predisposition, as Dewey asserted, to the easier and more effective action in a like direction in the future. The organism's interaction with the environment is capable of generating what Dewey called an intelligence in operation. Dewey positioned habits as capable of constituting one's self by way of forming desires and ruling thoughts. 'They *are* will', says Dewey (1922/1988, p. 21), but in the affective sense of being an 'immensely more intimate and fundamental part of ourselves than are vague, general, conscious choices' (1922/1988, p. 21). Sinking toward the very bottom of consciousness, habits 'perpetuate themselves, by acting unremittingly upon the native stock of activities. They stimulate, inhibit, intensify, weaken, select, concentrate and organise the latter into its own likeness' (Dewey, 1922/1988, p. 88), seemingly acting in the mode of some strange, yet natural, attractors.

Habits are 'active means, means that project themselves, energetic and dominating ways of acting' (Dewey, 1922/1988, p. 22). They act as though being real forces defined by Dewey as dynamic and projective, yet by virtue of their functioning below the level of consciousness, they may manifest in human behaviour as 'routine, unintelligent habit[s]' (Dewey, 1922/1988, p. 55). The reorganisation of habits then becomes a mode of inquiry so as to make a habit enter consciousness as perceived and, subsequently, intelligently controlled. Such a mode of organisation, effected by 'cooperating with external materials and energies' (Dewey, 1922/1988, p. 22), is capable of reaching our internal perceptions and thoughts. The transformation of the unconscious, and unintelligent, habit into the conscious and intelligent is made possible by means of transactions. Because a habit, for Dewey, is a way or manner of action, a change at the level of human choices, decisions, and actions would reciprocally bring forth changes and transformations in modes of thinking, feeling and perceiving. An inferential process, by definition, 'reaches down into nature, ... it has breadth ... to an indefinitely elastic extent. It stretches' (Dewey, 1929/1958, p. 1), therefore contributing to overcoming the limitations of perceptible reality by fine-tuning the perception *per se*. Perception thereby merges into inference because '[t]hat stretch constitutes inference' (Dewey, 1929/1958, p. 1). Among conflicting and uncertain experiences, this enriched thinking represents a potential tendency to form a new habit: as such, it 'cuts across some old habit' (Dewey, 1929/1958, p. 281). The act of cutting across betrays the further linear progression in the direction of an old habit and instead contributes, much in accord with non-linear dynamics describing complex behaviours, to the 'emergence of unexpected and unpredictable combinations' (Dewey, 1929/1958, p. 281) as genuine novelty.

Novelty, for Dewey, may be created precisely at such a critical point where the human mind, as we said earlier, 'comes in contact with the world … . When the new is created, the far and strange become the most natural inevitable things in the world' (Dewey, 1934/1980, p. 267). It is the background of organised meanings that is capable of converting the problematic situation from being obscure into clear and determined. Autopoiesis may be understood as describing a process, which cannot be explained either in merely causal or even teleological terms: it functions on the basis of *self-cause* (cf. Juarrero, 1995; Semetsky, 2003). An autopoietic process is one of continual renewal and self-organisation as it pertains to living and social systems so as to maintain the integrity of systems' structures—the latter arising as a result of transactional dynamics. Sure enough, transaction points to the occurrence of potential transformations and 'modifications on both sides' (Lehmann-Rommel, 2000, p. 197) and considers all human activities including 'behavings [and] knowings … as activities not of [man] alone … but as processes of the full situation of organism-environment' (Dewey, quoted in Biesta, 1995, p. 279). The human mind existing in contact with the world is not just an attractive metaphor, but acquires an almost physical reality in the capacity of being a possible catalyst that would have contributed to overcoming the dualistic split between the knower and the known by means of expanding the boundaries of a system. Its function is irreducible to the role of the agent or Cartesian *Cogito*.

As Dewey emphasised, the mode of communication in a creative process is not an agency but 'a release and amplification of energies that enter into it, conferring upon [human beings] the added quality of meaning. The quality of meaning thus introduced is extended and transferred, actually and potentially, from sounds, gestures and marks, to all other things in nature. Natural events become messages to be enjoyed and administered, precisely as are song, fiction, oratory, the giving of advice and instruction' (Dewey, 1929/1958, p. 174). The giving of advice and instruction is traditionally the prerogative of a teacher. As the catalyst, though, a teacher would have to find herself embedded together with students and subject-matter (cf. Garrison, 1999a) and her function would be equivalent to one of 'efficiency in action, … capacity to change the course of action, to experience novelties … . [I]t signifies the power of desire and choice to be factors in events' (Dewey, 1922/1988, p. 209; see also Garrison, 1999b, pp. 304–305). Novelty, as a change in a system's behaviour, is described in non-linear mathematics as a phase transition, which, sure enough, may be produced by a state 'of uneasy or unstable equilibrium' (Dewey, 1929/1958, p. 253). The method of intelligent inquiry as 'dynamic understanding'

(Kellert, 1993) differs in principle from predictability and knowledge of facts. It is 'the striving to make stability of meanings prevail over the instability of events' (Dewey, 1929/1958, p. 50) that remains a driving force behind the reorganisation of experience. Perception itself is capable of differentiating between, as Dewey says, what may be and is not, so that both human actions and their consequences become joined in perception. Dewey defined the art of perception as an ability to acknowledge many unattained possibilities so as to be able to 'refer the present to consequences' (Dewey, 1929/1958, p. 182). Such a thought-experiment is capable of containing in its present phase also 'affairs remote in space and in time' (Dewey, 1929/1958, p. 279). Functioning in a mode of an imaginary excursion into some possible future, an inquiry assumes the function of deliberation.

Deliberation has been defined by Dewey as 'a dramatic rehearsal (in imagination) of various competing possible lines of action ... . Deliberation is an experiment in finding out what the various lines of possible action are really like' (Dewey, 1922/ 1988, p. 132). An expanded perception enables one—in an unprecedented, as Dewey says, response to conditions—to creatively reorganise the change in a given direction. The new categories of interaction, transaction and purpose, as we said earlier, citing Von Bertalanffy, enter the picture vis-à-vis old mechanical determinism. For Dewey, there exists a peculiar 'feeling of the direction and end of various lines of behaviour' (Dewey, 1922/1988, p. 26); he distinguished between the realm of thinking traditionally represented in terms of symbols and an expanded thinking in terms of relations of qualities. Despite non-linear dynamics precluding certainty and predictability, continuity ensures a sense of potential anticipation. The dynamical process comprises 'the past [that] is carried into the present so as to expand and deepen the content of the latter' (Dewey, 1934/1980, p. 24) but it also involves a sense of anticipation of future consequences. The creative 'will is thus not something opposed to consequences or severed from them. It is a cause of consequences' (Dewey, 1922/1988, p. 33), which is capable of creating novelty.

The newly created process-structure is in fact a decision made, an *end-in-view* that, by virtue of its being also the *means*, may open up new possibilities. Each decision-making represents a change described by a novel distribution of parts acting within the overall dynamics of the complex system. In agreement with the systems-theoretical perspective, Dewey considers a part as always 'already a part-of-a-whole ... conditioned by the contingent, although itself a condition of the full determination of the latter' (Dewey, 1929/1958, p. 65). For Dewey, we give way *in our mind*, to some impulse; we try, *in our mind*, some plan. Following its development through various steps, we find ourselves *in imagination* in the presence of the consequences that would follow. Imagination functions by providing the opportunities to see what is possible in the actual, and 'deliberation has the power of genesis' (Garrison, 1997, p. 121). It results in a modification, as Dewey says, of the whole objective order and involves dissolution of old objects together with creative and unpredictable 'suddenness of emergence' (Dewey, 1934/1980, p. 75) of new *objects*, among which the self, as emerging *subject*, is just one: hence the aforementioned anti-Cartesian subject-less-ness of a problematic situation, the transformation of which inherently leads to the autopoietic making of the self.

The core of autopoietic systems that function on the aforementioned basis of self-cause is that they in some sense, as stated by Maturana and Varela (1992), produce their own identity. Dewey envisaged that 'personality, selfhood, subjectivity [become] eventual functions that emerge with complexly organised interactions (Dewey, 1929/1958, p. 108). The self-organising dynamics of the process of inquiry ensure 'a continual beginning afresh' (Dewey, 1916/1924, p. 417), that is, the emergence of new experiences and novel meanings. Respectively—and in the autopoietic manner—'the created can continue the creation' (Garrison, 1997, p. 79): creativity is what characterises the process of self-organisation. An open-ended process 'is determined but unpredictable,' as Doll (1993, p. 72) says, addressing the issue of transformative and creative pedagogy and relating the concept of self-organisation to a postmodern perspective on curriculum development. The organisation of the process is enabled by continuous, recursive and self-referential interactions that defy an absolute dichotomy between such binary opposites of modern discourse as objective reality and subjective experience, facts and fantasy, profane and sacred, private and public, thereby overcoming 'a process–product, objective–subjective split' (Doll, 1993, p. 13). The blurring in a complex system of divisions between rigid customary opposites is another qualitative feature complementing its potential increase in complexity—that is, a system's functioning on a succeeding level that would have incorporated a previous one.

The relations in question establish a coordination that may be defined as 'the dialogue between the present construct and the problems of the environment that determines the emerging, next stage' (Doll, 1993, p. 72). The role of the teacher will have been shifting from strictly 'causal [to] transformative' (Soltis, in Doll, 1993, p. xi). By its very nature, a self-organised system *opens* itself to 'challenges, perturbations, disruptions [that are] the *sine qua non* of the transformative process' (Doll, 1993, p. 14). New meanings are capable of creative (self)-expression only as eventual outcomes of the total process by virtue of the active self-cause—in the guise of what Dewey called *interest*, perhaps—and not as externally given in a forceful and often destructive manner. Rather than conforming to some special educative aim imposed from without the process, education is posited by Dewey as a coordinated movement in which subjective desire is completely integrated with an object. But we have to be careful here. Self-reference of a dynamical system would be impossible unless the capacity of a system to maintain itself is complemented by the respective capacity of such a system also to modify itself. In other words, a system is capable of sustaining itself by virtue of, as recently noted by Horn and Wilburn (2005) with respect to new approaches in the philosophy of learning, its 'both conservative and expansionary aspects' (2005, p. 752).

It is the self-reference of a system that, in a way, makes it self-transcending. Self-transcendence, defined by systems-theorist Erich Jantsch as 'the creative overcoming of the *status quo*' (1981, p. 91), is equivalent to the Deweyan process of growth when 'the old self is put off and the new self is ... forming' (Dewey, 1929/1958, p. 245). Pragmatic inquiry is concerned with organising information into knowledge, and the dynamics of self-organisation necessarily combines in itself two complementary processes, novelty and confirmation, as illustrated in Figure 1, with reference to the Shannon-Weaver model of communication.

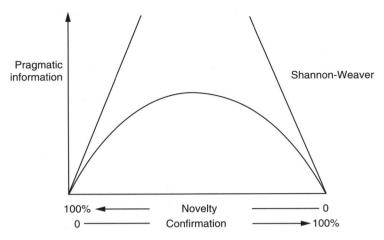

Figure 1: Reproduced from Figure 3 in Jantsch, 1981, p. 96.

An open-ended system would transform novelty into confirmation just as much as it creates novelty. Philosophy of education would do well to take notice of this delicate principle. The symbolic 'death', discussed earlier, quoting Dewey, means the arrest of movement, a state of equilibrium when total confirmation is achieved. Analogously, total novelty would imply ending up in chaos. As noted by Jantsch, there won't be any 'pragmatic information content in either extreme' (1981, p. 98). The role of the teacher becomes highly significant in this regard, especially in that our emphasis so far has been on unsupervised learning. To maintain a balance of novelty and confirmation so that pragmatic information reaches its maximum means complying with the creative logic of education. Yet, under continuously shifting classroom conditions, would this logic work? What is the scope of flexibility and plasticity (as features of self-organising dynamics) embedded in the actual pedagogical space? These are empirical questions and are, as such, beyond the scope of this chapter. They need, however, to be further developed and addressed in future research programs in the light of the theory advanced here.

References

Allen, P. (1981) The Evolutionary Paradigm of Dissipative Structures, in: E. Jantsch (ed.), *The Evolutionary Vision: Toward a unifying paradigm of physical, biological, and sociocultural evolution (American Association for the Advancement of Science Selected Symposia Series)* (Boulder, CO: Westview Press), pp. 25–72.

Bertalanffy, von L. (1972) Foreword, in: E. Laszlo, *Introduction to Systems Philosophy: Toward a New Paradigm of Contemporary Thought.* New York. London, Paris: Gordon and Breach Science Publishers, pp. xvii–xxi.

Biesta, G. (1995) Pragmatism as a Pedagogy of Communicative Action. *Studies in Philosophy and Education*, 13, pp. 273–290.

Byrne, D (1998) *Complexity Theory and the Social Sciences, An Introduction* (London and New York, Routledge).

Cilliers, P. (1998) *Complexity and Postmodernism: Understanding complex systems* (London and New York, Routledge).

Dewey, J. (1916/1924) *Democracy and Education* (New York, Macmillan Company).

Dewey, J. (1922/1988) *Human Nature and Conduct* (Carbondale: Southern Illinois University Press).

Dewey, J. (1929/1958) *Experience and Nature* (New York, Dover Publications).

Dewey, J. (1934/1980) *Art as Experience* (New York, Perigee Books).

Dewey, J. (1938) *Logic: The theory of inquiry* (New York, Henry Holt and Company).

Dewey, J. (1991) *Knowing and the Known* (with Arthur F. Bentley), in: J. A. Boydston (ed.), *The Later Works, 1925–1952, Volume 16: 1949–1952* (Carbondale and Edwardsville: Southern Illinois Press).

Dewey, J. (1998) Qualitative Thought, in: D. Browning & W. T. Myers (eds) *Philosophers of Process* (New York, Fordham University Press), pp. 192–210.

Doll, W. A. (1993) *A Postmodern Perspective on Curriculum* (New York and London, Teachers College Press).

Garrison, J. (1995) Introduction: Education and the new scholarship on John Dewey, in: J. Garrison (ed.) *The New Scholarship on Dewey* (Dordrecht, Kluwer Academic Publishers), pp. 1–6.

Garrison, J. (1997) *Dewey and Eros: Wisdom and desire in the art of teaching* (New York and London, Teachers College Press).

Garrison, J. (1999a) John Dewey's Theory of Practical Reasoning, *Educational Philosophy and Theory*, 31:3, pp. 291–312.

Garrison, J. (1999b) John Dewey, Jacque Derrida, and the Metaphysics of Presence. *Transactions of Charles S. Peirce Society*, XXXV (2), pp. 346–372.

Horn, J. & D. Wilburn (2005) The Embodiment of Learning, in: Paul Hager (ed.), *Educational Philosophy and Theory, special issue New Approaches in the Philosophy of Learning*, 37:5, pp. 745–760.

Jantsch, J. (1981) Unifying Principles of Evolution, in: E. Jantsch (ed.), *The Evolutionary Vision: Toward a Unifying Paradigm of Physical, Biological, and Sociocultural Evolution (American Association for the Advancement of Science Selected Symposia Series)* (Boulder, CO: Westview Press), pp. 83–116.

Juarrero, A. (1998) *Dynamics in Action: Intentional behavior as a complex system* (Cambridge, MA, The MIT Press).

Kellert, S. H. (1993) *In the Wake of Chaos: Unpredictable order in dynamical systems* (Chicago and London: The University of Chicago Press).

Laszlo, E. (1972) *Introduction to Systems Philosophy: Toward a new paradigm of contemporary thought* (New York. London, Paris: Gordon and Breach Science Publishers).

Lehmann-Rommel, R. (2000) The Renewal of Dewey—Trends in the Nineties. *Studies in Philosophy and Education*, 19: 1–2, pp. 187–218.

Maturana, H. R. & F. J. Varela (1992) *The Tree of Knowledge: The biological roots of human understanding*, trans. R. Paolucci (Boston, Shambhala).

Prigogine, I. (1980) *From Being to Becoming* (San Francisco, Freeman).

Semetsky, I. (2003) The Magician's autopoietic action, or Eros contained and uncontained, *Trickster's Way*, 2:3 http://www.trinity.edu/org/tricksters/TrixWay

Semetsky, I. (2004) Learning from Experience: Dewey, Deleuze, and 'becoming-child', in: H. Alexander (ed.) *Spirituality and Ethics in Education: Philosophical, theological and radical perspectives* (Eastbourne, UK, Sussex Academic Press), pp. 54–64.

Varela, F. J. (1979) *Principles of Biological Autonomy* (New York: North Holland).

Varela, F. J. (1999) *Ethical Know-How: Action, wisdom, and cognition* (Stanford, CA, Stanford University Press).

7

Foucault as Complexity Theorist: Overcoming the problems of classical philosophical analysis

Mark Olssen
University of Surrey

In my book, *Michel Foucault: Materialism and Education* (original Bergin & Garvey, 1999, ch. 11; paperback edition, Paradigm Press, 2006, ch. 12), I consider Foucault as a complexity theorist and relate him to contemporary conceptions of complexity as they are being utilised in the physical and social sciences. In order to set the background to a discussion of Foucault as complexity theorist it is necessary to consider briefly both his appropriation of Nietzsche and his rejection of Marx in relation to the themes of chance and pluralism within his work.

Foucault's rejection of structuralism and Marxism, and his turn to genealogy and Nietzsche as the basis of his pluralistic conception became clearer at the close of the 1960s. With his growing interest in genealogy, Foucault became more concerned with power and history, and with the historical constitution of knowledge. Although history was a process, it was a process that recognised no integrative principle or essence. If the genealogist studies history 'he finds that there is "something altogether different" behind things: not a timeless and essential secret, but the secret that they have no essence or that their essence was fabricated in a piecemeal fashion from alien forms' (Foucault, 1977a, p. 142).

Foucault's conception of history explicitly reflects his Nietzschean heritage and his belief that certain aspects of Marxism and structuralism distorted the liberatory potential of the discourse.

> The interest in Nietzsche and Bataille was not a way of distancing ourselves
> from Marxism or communism—it was the only path towards what we expected
> from communism. (Foucault, 2001, p. 249)

It was in terms of the philosophy of difference and Nietzsche's conception of multiplicities through a rejection of Platonic hierachies that Foucault enunciates a theory of discursive formations, rejects Marxist and Hegelian conceptions of history and establishes an approach which broadly parallels contemporary complexity theories. The utilisation of Nietzsche signalled a rupture from Marxism in relation to a series of inter-related conceptual, theoretical and methodological precepts, including power, knowledge and truth, the subject, and the nature of historical change and determination.

Nietzsche focussed on power in an altogether different way to Marx. In 'Prison Talk', Foucault (1980a, p. 47) states:

> It was Nietzsche who specified the power relation as the general focus, shall we say, of philosophical discourse—whereas for Marx it was the productive relation. Nietzsche is the philosopher of power, a philosopher who managed to think of power without having to confine himself within a political theory in order to do so.

Power, for Nietzsche, was conceived as a relation of forces within an analytics of power/knowledge/truth, which became important for Foucault to understand in the later 1960s after the publication *of The Archaeology of Knowledge* and his growing friendship with the French Nietzschean, Gilles Deleuze. Foucault accredits Nietzsche as the source of his interest in the question of truth and its relation to power. As he states in 'Truth and Power' (Foucault, 1980, p. 133), 'The political question ... is not, error, illusion, alienated consciousness or ideology, it is truth itself. Hence, the importance of Nietzsche'. Nietzsche's importance to Foucault can be seen as 'correcting Marx', especially in relation to the linkage between power–knowledge–truth, and the functioning of knowledge as an instrument of power. As Alan Schrift (1995, p. 40) notes, Nietzsche's influence drew attention away from 'substances, subjects and things, and focussed attention instead on the *relations between* these substantives'. In a related way, Foucault 'draws our attention away from the substantive notion of power and directs our attention instead to the multifarious ways that power operates through the social order' (ibid.). For Nietzsche, such relations were relations of forces. Foucault thus focussed on new relations as the relations of forces that existed and interacted within social systems as social practices. These were forces of repression and production that characterised the disciplinary society: forces that enable and block, subjugate and realise, and normalise and resist. In this model, power is not a thing, but a process, a relation of forces.

Beyond these concerns with power–truth–knowledge, and language and discourse, Foucault acknowledges the influence of Nietzsche in reference to the decentring of the subject, and the constitutive ethics of self-creation.

In the *Genealogy of Morals* Nietzsche (1967) traces the processes of descent (*Entstehung*) and emergence (*Herkunft*), but distinguishes these from a concern with origins (*Ursprung*) or essences. Nietzsche's thesis is that the subject is historically constituted and does not exist as something given metaphysically in advance. This is what Nietzsche (1967, 1, 13) means when he says 'there is no "being" behind doing, effecting, becoming; "the doer" is merely the fiction added to the deed—the deed is everything'. For Foucault, accepting this view, the subject is an ideological product, an effect of power, whose identity is defined in relation to the functionality of discourse.

Nietzsche constitutes important background to understanding Foucault as a complexity theorist in relation to his critique of mechanical philosophy and his writings on causation, determinism and free will. In his book *The Will to Power*, which had a central influence on both Heidegger and Foucault, Nietzsche (1968, p. 339) attacks the mechanical physicalistic world view:

> Physicists believe in a 'true world' in their own fashion: a firm systematization of atoms in necessary motion, the same for all beings—so for them the 'apparent world' is reduced to the side of universal and universally necessary being which is accessible to every being in its own way. But they are in error. The atom they posit is inferred according to the logic of perspectivism of consciousness—and is therefore itself a subjective fiction.

One way of interpreting the significance of such a statement from Foucault's perspective is to indicate the measure of his constructivism, or non-realism over concepts and categories of science. While Foucault subscribed to the view that sciences like physics clearly maintain parallels to the extractive powers of the universe, judged purely by the fruits of its efforts, such a science does not imply the actual existence of atoms or the workings of a mechanical system or a particular individualist representation of the world.

For Nietzsche, the Will to Power operates as a general metaphysic of which 'life is merely one special case' (Nietzsche, 1968, p. 369). In Nietzsche's view, all being is *becoming*. As a method of critique it aims to expose illusion and falsehood. And on this basis Nietzsche criticises the concepts of necessity and law, determinism and freedom. As he states (1968, p. 337):

> Let us dismiss the two popular concepts 'necessity' and 'law': the former introduces a false constraint into the world, the latter a false freedom. Things do not behave regularly, according to a rule; there are no things (—they are factors invested by us); they behave just as little under the constraint of necessity. There is no obedience here: for that something is as it is, as strong or as weak, is not the consequence of an obedience or a rule or a compulsion—

Or, in even starker terms (1968, p. 297):

> From the fact that something ensues regularly and ensues calculably, it does not follow that it ensues necessarily. That a quantum of force determines and conducts itself in every particular case in one way and manner does not make it into an 'unfree will'. 'Mechanical necessity' is not a fact.

In his rejection of mechanical philosophy and organicism Nietzsche asserts a radical ontology whereby the conception of the totality or whole is reconfigured as an always open, relatively borderless system of infinite interconnections, possibilities and developments. Nietzsche's 'fundamental metaphysical position', as Heidegger (1984: II, ch. 12) reminds us, posits a philosophical ontology that, while it comprises a semiotic system of *finite* particulars, is nevertheless a system which is open-ended and contains *infinite* possibilities for reinvestment. The conception of an infinite relational order liberates conceptions of the whole from the traditional finitude associated with Hegel. This can be seen as an opening towards a non-linear system of dynamics and change. In relation to a politics of space, the conception of the community becomes reconfigured as an open borderless arena where changes are instrumented both internally and externally as elements within and without themselves undergo change.

This applies to any system, including language, and can be represented in relation to the economy of the metaphor. In the words of David B. Allison (1977, p. xvi),

> metaphorical signification amounts to a chain of substitutions ... . While the number of possible substitutions ... is finite, i.e., is bounded by resources of a given language—the process of substituting one for another is open-ended. The constitution of the metaphor is thus a process that is at least temporarily open to infinity. The metaphor, then, enjoys a 'finite' but 'open' economy.

This finite but open economy of signification also works, says Nietzsche, in relation to the will to power. While the field of forces is finite, it can be continually expended and recombined. Allison (p. xvii) cites Nietzsche from s639 of *The Will to Power*:

> Regarded mechanistically, the energy of the totality of becoming remains constant; regarded economically; it rises to a high point and sinks down again in an eternal circle. This 'Will to Power' expresses itself in the interpretation, in the manner in which force is used up.

In his own representation, Heidegger (1991, Vol. II, Ch. 12) summarises the 'Presentation and grounding' of Nietzsche's doctrine with regards to 'Being as a whole as Life and Force', and 'the World as Chaos'. Heidegger lists several core theses which are central to Nietzsche's world view:

1. Force is the pervasive character of the world. Force, for Nietzsche, is the will to power (ibid., Vol. II, p. 86).
2. Force is limited, because it is finite. 'In itself' force is 'determinate' and 'inherently limited' (ibid., Vol. II, p. 87). 'Because force, which is essentially finite, is the essence of the world, the totality of the world itself remains finite' (ibid., Vol. II, p. 88). Hence there is a 'firm confinement within boundaries' (ibid., Vol. II, p. 88).
3. 'The lack of diminuation and accretion in universal force signifies not a "standstill" ... but a perpetual "Becoming"'. There is no equilibrium of force. Heidegger continues, 'We must grasp "Becoming" here quite generally in the sense of transformation or— still more cautiously—change.' (ibid., Vol. II, p. 88).
4. 'Precisely because the world is perpetual Becoming, and because as a totality of force it is nonetheless inherently finite, it produces "infinite" effects'. Nietzsche uses the phrase 'infinitely waxing' to describe force in relation to its potentials (ibid., Vol. II, p. 87).
5. 'In contrast to the imaginary character of space, *time* is *actual*' (ibid., Vol. II, p. 90). Furthermore, 'It is also—in contrast to the bounded character of space— unbounded, infinite'. He quotes Nietzsche from *The Gay Science* (S. 341), where he speaks of 'the eternal hourglass of existence'. For Heidegger (1991, Vol. II, p. 90), 'Such actual, infinite time, Nietzsche grasps as *eternity*'.
6. Heidegger (1991, Vol. II, p. 91) cites Nietzsche from *The Gay Science* (S. 109): 'The collective character of the world is ... to all eternity—chaos'—and this is 'the fundamental representation of being as a whole' (Heidegger, 1991, Vol. II, p. 91).

In this representation, as Nietzsche notes (S. 109), chaos applies not in the sense of a 'lack of necessity, but a lack of order' (Heidegger, 1991, Vol. II, p. 90). Hence, the world lacks order or lawfulness, as well as predictability.

7. The idea that beings proceed according to 'laws' is a 'humanization', or 'moralistic-juridical mode of thought', says Heidegger (1991, Vol. II, p. 92). It is 'anthropomorphic'. He continues: 'Nor are there in beings any "goals" or "purposes" or "intentions"; and if there are no purposes, then "purposelessness" and "accident" as well are excluded' (ibid., Vol. II, p. 92). Just as mechanics is wanting, so too is the idea of the universe as an 'organism'. Such a notion is for Nietzsche just a further 'humanization', says Heidegger (1991, Vol. II, p. 93).

Heidegger draws his summary of Nietzsche's position largely from *The Gay Science* and *The Will to Power*. But most of Nietzsche's texts from the 1880s until his death could be drawn upon for support. With Nietzsche, then, we have an ontological position which stresses 'force, finitude, perpetual Becoming, the innumerability of appearances, the bounded character of space, and the infinity of time' (1991, Vol. II, pp. 90–91). And these relate back to the collective character of the world. While, as Heidegger (1991, Vol. II, pp. 91–92) notes, 'although Nietzsche distinguishes the concept of the world from the notion of fortuitous and arbitrary jumble, a sort of universal cosmic porridge, he nevertheless fails to liberate himself from the transmitted sense of chaos as something that lacks order and lawfulness'. Such are the labyrinths of Nietzsche's thought.

That Foucault's agreement with the broad philosophical ontology of Nietzsche's approach has influenced his own epistemological constructivism, social constructionism, as well as the theory of social forces and power, is now well known. In general terms, Nietzsche's constructivism and his belief in chance were to become hallmarks of Foucault's own approach. The view of history as pluralist and not accounted for within a context of causal, 'iron-law' determinism was thus important in Foucault's debt to Nietzsche, and also contributes background to understanding the affinities with complexity theory. Whereas Marxists like Althusser adopted a totalistic programme of seeking to explain the whole by understanding the interrelations between its component parts, for Foucault the totality always eluded analysis or understanding in terms of structure, but rather was characterised by *incompleteness, indeterminacy, complexity* and *chance*. This was the core of his pluralism. As Foucault says, 'though it is true that these discontinuous discursive series each have, within certain limits, their regularity, it is undoubtedly no longer possible to establish links of mechanical causality, or of ideal necessity between the elements which constitute them. We must accept the introduction of *aléa* (chance) as a category in the production of events' (1981, p. 69).[1]

In seeking to characterise the nature of his 'pluralism' and how it effects the analytics of discourse as operating through complex laws, Foucault (1978, p. 11) explains how he 'substitutes the analysis of different types of transformation for the abstract, general, and monotonous form of "change" in which one so willingly thinks in terms of succession'. In this, he seeks to define with the greatest care the transformations which have constituted the change, replacing the general theme of *becoming* ('general form, abstract element, primary cause, and universal effect') by the analysis of the transformations in their specificity, an examination of 'the diversity of *systems* and the play of discontinuities into the history of *discourse*' (1978, p. 15). This involves, says Foucault (1978, pp. 11–12), within a given discursive formation, (1) detecting the changes which effect the operations, objects, theoretical choices, etc.; (2) detecting the changes which effect the discursive formations themselves (e.g. changes in the boundaries that define the field); and (3) detecting the changes which effect simultaneously several discursive formations (e.g. reversal of the hierarchy of importance, as happened, for instance, in the Classical period when the analysis of language lost the 'directing role' that it had in the first years of the nineteenth century to biology, which in turn led to the development of new concepts such as 'organism', 'function', 'organisation', etc., which in turn effected other sciences). All of these types of changes, says Foucault, characterise changes to both individual discourses and effect modifications in the episteme itself: its 'redistributions', i.e. 'the different transformations which it is possible to describe concerning ... states of a discourse'. In opposition to totalising models Foucault sees his own analysis as more limited: to searching for the empirical historical grounds for discursive consistency or coherence; to recognising in discourse its empirical worldly features— 'the work of the author. And why not?—His juvenilia or mature work, the patterns of a linguistic or rhetorical model (an idea, a theme)'; and acknowledging that the transformatory operations are all carried out 'prior to discourse and outside of it' (1978, p. 17).

In his later reflections on method, in response to interviews on the subject of *Discipline and Punish*, Foucault (1987) asserts the 'pluralist' nature of his project through his use of concepts like 'eventalisation'; that 'specific events' (*événements signuliers*) cannot be integrated or decoded simply as an application of a uniform and universal regularity. In this non-unified sense, the analysis of discourse effects a non-unified method. As Foucault (1972, p. 8) explains it:

> It has led to the individualisation of different series, which are juxtaposed to one another, follow one another, overlap and intersect, without one being able to reduce them to a linear schema. Thus, in place of the continuous chronology of reason, which was invariably traced back to some inaccessible origin, there have appeared scales that are sometimes very brief, distinct from one another, irreducible to a single law, scales that bear a type of history peculiar to each one, and which cannot be reduced to the general model of a consciousness that acquires, progresses, and remembers.

The notion of 'eventalisation' itself contains a number of elements. First, it treats all objects of knowledge as historical *events*. Second, it refers to a 'pluralisation of causes' (Foucault, 1987, pp. 104–105):

> Causal multiplication consists in analysing an event according to the multiple processes that constitute it ... . '[E]ventalization' thus works by constructing around the singular event analysed as process a 'polygon' or rather a 'polyhedron' of intelligibility, the number of whose faces is not

given in advance and can never properly be taken as finite. One has to proceed by progressive, necessarily incomplete saturation. And one has to bear in mind that the further one decomposes the processes under analysis, the more one is enabled, and indeed obliged to construct their external relations of intelligibility.

In addition, says Foucault (1987, p. 104) eventalization refers to the rediscovery of the 'connections, encounters, blockages, plays of forces, strategies, etc. that at a given moment establish what consequently comes to count as being self evident, universal and necessary'. In this sense, it constitutes a 'breach of self evidence', i.e.:

> It means making visible a *singularity* at places where there is a temptation to invoke historical constants, an immediate anthropological trait, or an obviousness that imposes itself uniformly on all. To show that things 'weren't as necessary as all that; that it wasn't a matter of course that mad people came to be regarded as mentally ill; it wasn't self-evident that the only things to be done to a criminal were to lock him up, it wasn't self-evident that the causes of illness were to be sought through the individual examination of bodies; and so on'.

In this sense, eventalisation opposes the evidences upon which knowledge sequences and practices rest. Its theoretical quest is endlessly open. It operates in Foucault's (1987, p. 105) view, 'as a procedure for lightening the weight of causality'.

Alongside the concept of *eventalisation* are those of *exteriority/interiority*, which Foucault (1972, pp. 120–122, 125, 140) discusses in *The Archaeology of Knowledge*, as well as in his inaugural lecture at the College de France (see Foucault, 1981), and also in his essay on Blanchot (Foucault, 1990). What Foucault means by 'exteriority' is that the being of discourse resides in the 'pure dispersion' of the socio-historical processes of reproduction and change; in the 'particular events, regularities, relationships, modifications and systematic transformations', which constitute an 'autonomous (although dependent)' domain, and 'which can be described at its own level' (1972, pp. 121–2). As expressed in his essay on Blanchot (1990, p. 15), it is 'the breakthrough to a language from which the subject is excluded ... : the being of language only appears for itself with the disappearance of the subject'. This places the emphasis on 'speech' rather than on the Cartesian *Cogito*. As he states (1990, p. 13):

> 'I speak' runs counter to 'I think'. 'I think' led to the indubitable certainty of the 'I' and its existence; 'I speak', on the other hand, distances, disperses, effaces that existence and lets only its empty emplacement appear. Thought about thought, an entire tradition wider than philosophy, has taught us that thought leads us to the deepest interiority. Speech about speech leads us, by way of literature as well as perhaps by other paths, to the outside in which the speaking subject disappears. No doubt that is why Western thought took so long to think the being of language: as if it had a premonition of the danger that the naked experience of language poses for the self-evidence of the 'I think'.

Manfred Frank emphasises the ontological and methodological functions of exteriority. What Foucault means by exteriority, he says (1992, p. 108) is that each individual element in discourse is irreducible 'to the unified discursive principle, or to an internal core of meaning to be found in the discourse'. As he continues:

> What the rule of exteriority of discourse means then, is: 'not moving from the discourse towards its internal, hidden core, towards the heart of the thought or the meaning, which is manifest in it'. So the procedure of the analytic of discourse is external because it wishes to leave the series (série) of single events, mutually irreducible (in terms of a deductive or teleological principle), just as they are 'external' to any totalizing general concept.

In a methodological sense, in that events and instances are individualised, 'individualised' means here, as Frank (1992, p. 110) states it, 'not predictable from the point of view of their structure, and contingent with respect to the way they happen to be'. What is important in terms of the analytics of discourse is not seeking such a reduction: hence the analytics of discourse is *external* to the process of analysis. What is important to Foucault (1990, pp. 15–16) is that:

> thought stands outside subjectivity, setting its limits as though from without, articulating its end, making its dispersion shine forth, taking only its invincible absence; and that at the same time stands at the threshold of all positivity, not in order to grasp its foundation or justification but in order to regain the space of its unfolding, the void serving as its site, the distance in which it is constituted and into which its immediate certainties slip the moment they are glimpsed—a thought that, in relation to the interiority of our philosophical reflection and the positivity of our knowledge, constitutes what in a word we might call 'the thought from the outside'.

As well as referring to consciousness, interiority thus refers also to any foundation or centre to the social formation which the events or parts echo or reflect. Hence, again, this can also be seen as consistent with, and expressing, his opposition to the notion of a determined causality embodied in the Hegelian conception of an 'expressive totality' and, by derivation, also embodied in the notion of a primary causal necessity (*un causalisme primaire*) which he sees as central to Marxism. In this sense, the analytics of discourse must resist interiorisation, 'forsaking the wordy interiority of consciousness', as well the appeal to a centre or foundation, and become, as in Bataille, the 'discourse of the limit' (1990, p. 18).

What Foucault, following Nietzsche, Blanchot and Bataille, also elaborates as a theme, is the 'uniqueness' and 'unpredictability' of the singular historical instance, and it is this that I will claim below enables us to forge links between Foucault and complexity theory. What he seeks to do is introduce conceptions of *indeterminacy, irregularity, openness, complexity, and uniqueness* as integral to his conception of the historical process. This means that any event contains an element of uniqueness. In *The Archaeology of Knowledge* (Foucault, 1972, p. 101) examples abound: it takes the form of establishing the spatio-temporal co-ordinates that ensure the novel aspect of the 'statement' (énoncé): 'The enunciation is an unrepeatable event; it has situated and dated uniqueness that is irreducible. Yet this uniqueness allows of a number of constants—grammatical, semantic, logical—by which we can, by neutralising the moment of enunciation and the co-ordinates that individuate it, recognise the general form'. Or again (ibid., 1972, pp. 146–7): 'every statement belongs to a certain regularity—that consequently none can be regarded as pure creation, as the marvellous disorder of genius. But we have also seen that no statement can be regarded as inactive, and be valid as the scarcely real shadow or transfer of the initial statement. The whole enunciative field is both regular and alerted: it never sleeps'. This fact that the future never simply reproduces the past, but adds always elements of novelty, means that the self is never simply the reproduced habitus of its socialisation, but due to its necessarily distinct location in time and space and culture, as well as its progressively growing capacity for agency, is characterised by elements of difference and uniqueness. Yet this difference and uniqueness is not an artefact of language but a real phenomenon. In addition, it means that ethical values can never simply be expressed merely as *repeatable* rules of conduct—which increases, rather than decreases, our sense of ethical responsibility in action.

Such a conception also expresses an 'internalist' view of history, which is central to how Foucault understands change and how issues like freedom and determinism are resolved. Such a view of history means that there is no guiding principle underlying structures or their emergence. Difference then is historical, and resists both the univocity of being, as well as transcendence in all its forms, whether God, *Cogito*, Forms, Economy. There is nothing outside of history. Although such a conception does not adopt a uniform ahistorical model of temporalisation, or prioritise one element (economy) over others, neither does it deny that invariant necessities may exist which can express themselves through the different discursive lenses of particular historical periods. In this sense, as Joseph Margolis (1993, p. 204) notes, Foucault does not deny a world of 'things': he

> does not dismiss de re necessities of this or that episteme; they are rightly recognised there as the necessities they are. But they are also not enshrined as universal, changeless structures of any kind (regarding world or reason). [Rather] we are always invited to 'test' for the 'limits' that we may go beyond. That's to say: the invariances of any proposed transcendental limits of reason may be tested by exploring whether we can alter such a model of coherence convincingly, in a way that rests on historical change.

Similarly, such a conception can be claimed to resist the charge of epistemological relativism. As Foucault (1984a, p. 335) puts it in the *Preface* to the *History of Sexuality, Volume II*, he says that he is not denying the possibility of universal structures:

> Singular forms of experience may perfectly well harbor universal structures: they may well not be independent from the concrete determination of social existence ... : (t)his thought has a historicity which is proper to it. That it should have this historicity does not mean that it is deprived of all universal form but instead the putting into play of these universal forms is itself historical.

Like Heidegger, in *Being and Time*, Foucault manifests a pragmatic anti-foundationalism. Such an approach bares a similarity to parallel developments in Western Anglo-American philosophy in writers like Dewey, Quine, Davidson, Putnam, Kuhn, and Goodman, and in the continental tradition to writers like Habermas, Bourdieu and Apel. While all developed versions of historicism, all denied any total pernicious form of relativism and all claimed a measure of objectivity. For Foucault, the maxim that 'everything is historical' means that while we remain forever imprisoned by contingency, non-correspondence, relativity and ideological prejudice, there are some 'footholds', even if they do not lead easily to a uniform consensus. Foucault's anti-essentialism places him alongside a possible (pragmatic) reading of Popper, who also rejected essentialist ontologies, in that there is nothing that prevents testing and attempted falsifications in order to 'take a bearing', or 'check the situation out'. While this will give a certain form of confidence on some issues, on others, the conditions of what constitutes falsifiability will not be so easy to foresee.[2] Foucault's realism holds to the view that correspondence or synchronisation of discourse and reality is not required. Rather than correspondence, we must speak of isomorphism. There is no assurance, pace Kant, either, of transcendentally valid and universally reliable cognitive schemata, for such a conception relies on a conception of a subject posited prior to history. What justified Kant's cognitive schemata depends on various historically contingent conditions within what Heidegger would call the 'horizon' within which they appear. This doesn't mean there are no historical justifications (survival), and nor does it mean there are no footholds of any sort. But with Heidegger, Foucault's thesis of the historicity of existence would deny that there is any eternal 'point of view'.

Although Foucault acknowledges a debt to Nietzsche, it would be an error to represent his approach as simply Nietzschean, and this would misrepresent his relation to Marx and to radical politics. As well as Nietzsche, Foucault has debts to Heidegger: Herbert Dreyfus (1992, pp. 80–81) claims that 'it was through Heidegger that Foucault came to appreciate Nietzsche'. As Foucault (1985, p. 9) says: 'it is possible that if I had not read Heidegger, I would not have read Nietzsche. I had tried to read Nietzsche in the fifties but Nietzsche alone did not appeal to me—whereas Nietzsche and Heidegger, that was a philosophical shock'. Ultimately, Foucault 'nevertheless recognised that Nietzsche outweighed [Heidegger]'. But both exacted an influence. One of the central themes which Foucault shared with Heidegger and Nietzsche, as well as with Althusser, was their challenge to the Cartesian and Kantian conceptions of the subject. He was also influenced by Heidegger in terms of the understanding of Being as indicating the presuppositions, things, tools, language, institutions, shared understandings, and other people which determine what is deemed possible or impossible, or what counts as important or unimportant, or meaningful or unmeaningful. Like Heidegger, Foucault came to reject the view of a constant, ahistorical, universal truth, which came to influence his rejection of essentialism and other forms of foundationalism, thereby influencing the precise nature of his materialism. Yet another writer that Foucault has course to refer to is Spinoza, whom he refers to and summarises in several of his papers over the course of his writing career.[3] While Spinoza cannot be represented as a direct influence, and one must be cautious about attribution of themes or concepts, Foucault's detailed understanding of Spinoza is suggestive in that Spinoza's concepts of power, politics, of collective and individual praxis, and of republican constitutionalism, and general theme of complexity can, if suitably modified according to the dictates of difference, be rendered broadly compatible with Foucault's approach.[4]

Complexity and Openness

In that Foucault talks of 'chance' and 'unpredictability', such a conception of historical openness is not technically incompatible with deterministic Newtonian physics, in the sense that events and outcomes are still the result of antecedent conditions. Foucault, however, follows Nietzsche who introduced indeterminacy into the Newtonian theory. Rather than postulate a closed universe with a small number of invariable, universal laws which could explain everything, and predict the future, the universe is theorised as an infinitely open, complex whole, characterised by unpredictability, uncertainty and change. Causation in Foucault's view is conceived of *systemically*, in terms of a model of holism-particularism, or complex causation, which makes events, which are the outcomes of interactions in open systems, effectively unpredictable, in that the full range of possible combinations or effects cannot be specified in advance. Complex systems, moreover, are contingent and dynamic—the structure of the system is continuously transformed through the interaction of the elements—and are not explainable by reference to any external principle, origin, or foundation. In this process, says Cilliers (1998, pp. 107–108), 'no complex system, whether biological or social, can be understood without considering its history ... . To be more precise, the history of a system ... co-determines the structure of a system'. In this theory, while change is understood as the outcome of contingent complex activity, human agency is understood as an emergent property of the historical and social system.[5]

In insisting on the open nature of the historical system, Foucault's approach to understanding history parallels Derrida's critique and revision of Saussure in stressing the open and incomplete character of the totality of social relations. In Foucault, however, the analysis proceeds beyond the textual to an analysis of the historical relations between the discursive and pre-discursive, whereas for Derrida and Saussure the analysis is synchronic and confined to language. Throughout his career, in fact, it can be said that Foucault maintains a distinction between the discursive and the pre-discursive. In his early period, prior to the *Archaeology of Knowledge*, published in 1968, Foucault sees discourses formed on the basis of *epistemes* that provide a unified view of intellectual life during a particular period or age. After his turn to genealogy, he developed such an approach more directly in relation to how the practices discursive and pre-discursive were related. As a consequence, in retaining the poststructural emphasis on the open and incomplete nature of the totality, but applied to history and social relations, rather than language, Foucault's more materialist approach has radical implications for our understanding of concepts like determinism, predictability, and the future.

In this context, it is worth noting the parallel between Foucault's systemic conception of change, linked closely to a system of open possibilies or variations, and what is now known as complexity theory. Although having roots in ancient Chinese and Greek thought, versions of complexity theory are a relatively new field of scientific enquiry, and are perhaps one of the most notable new developments since the advent of quantum theory in the early 1900s. Such theories are not only compatible with materialism, but are systemic, or holist, in that they account for diversity and unity in the context of a systemic field of complex interactional changes. Chaos theory is one version of complexity. Partly with origins in computing technology, and partly in the development of new non-Euclidean structures of fractal geometrical mathematics, chaos theory became concerned with explaining 'the qualitative study of unstable aperiodic behaviour in deterministic non-linear dynamical systems' (Sardar & Abrams, 1999, p. 9).[6] It is complexity theory more broadly, however, that has drawn off poststructural methods, and establishes them as a form of critical realism.[7]

In the recent history of science, the work of Ilya Prigogine (1980, 1984, 1989, 1994, 1997, 2003) has advanced the field of post-Quantum complexity analysis at the macroscopic and microscopic levels, based in non-equilibrium physics, linked to the significant work of the Solvay Institutes for Physics and Chemistry. Prigogine received a Nobel Prize in 1977. Like Nietzsche and others before him, he translated the effects of a theory of becoming, based on an Heraclitean idea of ceaseless change, and providing a post-Quantum understanding of the universe in terms of dimensions of chance, unpredictability, uncertainty, chaos, non-equilibrium systems, and change. Prigogine's central contribution was to non-equilibrium statistical mechanics, thermodynamics and the probabilistic analysis of complex systems (Prigogine, 2003, pp. 45, 82). His main ideas (expressed non-mathematically) were that 'nature leads to unexpected complexity' (ibid., 2003, p. 8); that 'self-organization appears in nature far from equilibrium' (ibid., p. vii); that 'the universe is evolving' (ibid., p. 9); that the messages of Parmenides (that nothing changes) must be replaced by those of Heraclitus (that everything always changes) (ibid., pp. 9, 56); that 'time is our existential dimension' (ibid., p. 9); that 'time is an invention' (ibid., p. 10); that 'the direction of time is the most fundamental property of the universe' (ibid., p. 64); that nothing is predetermined (ibid., p. 9); that non-equilibrium, time-irreversibility, and non-integration, are features of all systems, including evolution, which is to say that our universe is full of non-linear, irreversible processes (ibid., p. 59); that life creates evolution (ibid., pp. 61, 65), and that everything is historical (ibid., p. 64).[8]

In his book *Complexity and Postmodernism*, Paul Cilliers (1998: p. viii) defines complexity in the following way:

> In a complex system ... the interaction of constituents of the system, and the interaction between the system and its environment, are of such a nature that the system as a whole cannot be fully understood simply by analysing its components. Moreover, these relationships are not fixed, but shift and change, often as a result of self-organisation. This can result in novel features, usually referred to in terms of emergent properties. The brain, natural language and social systems are complex.

Poststructuralism, says Cilliers, has introduced a new conception of complexity based on 'distributed' or 'relational' representation, following Saussure.[9] Such a system is complex in relation to the fact that it has a large number of elements which interact dynamically in a non-linear and asymmetrical manner. Interactions take place in open systems through 'self-organisation' by adapting dynamically to changes in both the environment and the system. Self-organisation is an *emergent* property of the system as a whole. An emergent property is a property that is constituted due to the combination of elements in the system as a whole. As such it is a property possessed by the system but not by its components.[10] Cilliers (1998, p. 90) defines 'self-organisation' as 'the capacity of complex systems which enables them to develop or change internal structure spontaneously and adaptively in order to cope with or manipulate the environment'. Such systems are not in equilibrium because they are constantly changing as a consequence of interaction between system and environment, and, as well as being influenced by external factors, are influenced by the history of the system (1998, p. 66). Cilliers identifies social systems, the economy, the human brain, and language as complex systems.[11]

Hence one could characterise Foucault's conception of societies as 'non-equilibrium systems', where no general laws can predict the detailed behaviour of such systems. As much that develops does so as a consequence of emergence, life is created as a consequence of the collective interactions of parts. This entails not only the limitless possibility of combinations that can occur in open environments, but also that as the collectivity possesses properties and energies not possessed by the parts, but through which change can take place, new forms and patterns can develop. Relatively small changes in initial conditions can trigger major changes throughout the system, in part or whole. Such a perspective gives a new insight to the 'contradictions of capitalism'.[12] Although for Foucault the economy cannot be represented as a transhistorical foundation permitting an understanding of change in history, it can be analysed internally, i.e. a genealogy of capitalism in terms of the history of economic structures, and the effects they engender throughout the social structure. Although I realise that this brief account cannot possibly do justice to the topics of complexity theory, emergence, chance or critical realism, it is broadly in this direction that Foucault's historical materialism leads.

The Nature of Identity

Such a notion of Foucault as complexity theorist also enables us to understand his views about identity, as well as many other philosophical conundrums. Let me start with identity. Given that structural linguistics seeks to define identity relationally, Saussure (1974, p. 120) argued that it cannot posit a theory of identity as a substantive entity, or as a concrete 'positive' unique particularity. This was retained by Derrida in his revision of Saussure's view, seeing identities as constituted by the series of *traces* of the differences in the system.[13] But if one conceives of identity in purely relational terms, as Mark Currie (2004, p. 13) notes, 'it could be said that the concept of difference is no respecter of difference'. As he continues, in explaining Saussure's view:

A theory of subjectivity, or personhood, for example, might locate identity not in the body of the individual but in the relations between that person and others. In other words a person might not be defined by inherent characteristics, but like Saussure's train or chess piece, be understood as an identity only because of the relationships that person has with other people, in a system of family, friendship and social relations. This would be referred to as a relational view of personal identity. The same might be said of collective identities. It might be argued for example, that a national identity is not one that is made up of inherent qualities (of 'positive terms' in Saussure's language) but of relational ones concerned with how a nation distinguishes itself from other nations.

For Nietzsche, Deleuze and Foucault, difference operates historically and has a dynamic quality that the theories of Saussure and Derrida lack. On this basis there is no reason why the traces that infuse identity could not be seen as leaving a residue or mark, developing into a positive conception of self constituted through complex interactions in the push and pull of the historical process. The stress on historical praxis creates a more enduring sense of identity in this sense. While this still leaves identity as relational in terms of its constitution, an identity which can be represented as positive and substantial (in the sense of its being irrepressible or non-reducible) is the outcome of self-creation or constitutive praxis in history.[14]

Such a view has the advantage over Saussure's and Derrida's view in that it can account for a substantial conception of the self and can explain, in the context of historical and social contructionist views of the self, how identities can emerge that are both *distinct* and *unique*,[15] which are non-reversible, and irreducible to the social whole.[16] For Nietzsche and Deleuze, following Duns Scotus, Spinoza and Hume, identities are constituted in experience, which is defined in terms of complex effects and relations, as practices (or, for Deleuze, *haecceities*) whose complex modes of operation are individuating (but not personalising or privatising). For Deleuze (1985, 1987, ch. 1), such patterns show parallels to nomadology or rhizomatic (rather than arborescent) development. For Foucault (1990), it is 'outside thought'; for Nietzsche, 'gay science'. In twentieth century Marxist thought, Althusser's conception of structural causality, as outlined at the start of this chapter, partly fits such a model.[17] Similar models of organisation and development are also evident in Spinoza's 'ethics', as what Spinozian interpreters like Damasio (2003, p. 37) call 'nesting' theories of development, where the 'parts of simple reactions [are] incorporated as components of more elaborate ones, a nesting of the simple within the complex'.[18] Yet other approaches utilizing complex models, although in somewhat variable ways, are cybernetics, or the early theories of Gregory Bateson (see Bateson, 1972).

Holism-particularism, Uniqueness and Creativity

We can see how Foucault's general method enables uniqueness to emerge from antecedent conditions. I have described his method elsewhere as one of 'holism-particularism' (Olssen, 1999, ch. 11). Foucault (1994b, pp. 824–5) himself talks about his own method in *Dits et Écrits* as a 'logical analysis of reality', and distinguishes it from 'the determinist ascription of causality' in Marx, as well as from 'logic of the Hegelian type'. Arnold Davidson (1997, p. 11) in a review of *Dits et Écrits* to which my own analysis is indebted, characterises Foucault's methodological strategy in terms of a 'non-reductive' and 'holistic' analysis of social life. As he puts it (Davidson, 1997, p. 11):

> This kind of analysis is characterized, first, by anti-atomism, by the idea that we should not analyze single or individual elements in isolation but that one must look at the systematic relations amongst elements; second. it is characterized by the idea that the relations between elements are coherent and transformable, that is, that the elements form a structure.

Thus, in his dissertation on the knowledge of heredity as a system of thought, submitted as part of his application for his position at the Collège de France, Foucault seeks to describe the changes, transformations, and conditions of possibility that made genetics possible, that constituted it as a science based on a series of discourses concerning breeding, just as in *The Order of Things* (1970) he had done for natural history and biology. What factors led to the emergence of these fields as sciences? What elements changed to make such developments possible? What made them possible as systems of thought? Thus Foucault seeks to describe the relations among elements as structures which change as the component elements change, in an always open system where unexpected outcomes and novel features are contingent inevitabilities of the process of history.

Such an approach makes it possible to explain how individuals are on the one hand the outcome of social and historical processes and yet how, on the other, novelty, uniqueness and creativity are possible. By interpreting Foucault in such a light, we can begin to make sense of his comments and general sense of incredulity in response to questions that were put to him on the general dimension of 'social construction/individuation'. As he says in *The Archaeology of Knowledge* (1972, p. 200):

> If I suspended all reference to the speaking subject, it was not to discover laws of construction or forms that could be applied in the same way by all speaking subjects, nor was it to give voice to the great universal discourse that is common to all men at a particular period. On the contrary, my aim was to show what the differences consisted of, how it was possible for men, within the same discursive practice, to speak of different objects, to have contrary opinions ... . [I]n short I want not to exclude the problem of the subject but to define positions and functions that the subject could occupy in the diversity of discourse.

It is not unrelated to his general conception of complexity that Foucault also seems to suggest the genuine possibility of free agency and creativity. With reference to thought, for instance, he describes it as an original and creative response in relation to social determinants. As he (1984b, pp. 388–389) puts it:

For a domain of action, a behaviour, to enter the field of thought, it is necessary to have made it lose its familiarity, or to have provoked a certain number of difficulties around it. These elements result from social, economic, or political processes. But here their only role is that of castigation. They can exist and perform their action for a very long time, before there is effective problematization by thought. And when thought intervenes, it doesn't assume a unique form that is the direct result or the necessary expression of these difficulties; it is an original or specific response—often taking many forms, sometimes even contradictory in its different aspects—to these difficulties, which are defined for it by a situation or a context and which hold true as a possible question.

Thought, then, arises as a unique event from a context of rules. Hence it is always the case, says Foucault (1984b, p. 389), that:

to a single set of difficulties, several responses can be made ... . But what has to be understood is what makes them simultaneously possible: it is the point in which their simultaneity is rooted; it is the soil that can flourish them all in their diversity and sometimes in spite of their contradictions.

A similar line of reasoning, dissecting the general from the particular, and the social from the individual, is evident in his debate with Chomsky (Foucault & Chomsky, 1997, pp. 119–120) where he refers to 'free creation within a system of rules':

One can only, in terms of language or of knowledge, produce something new by putting into play a certain number of rules ... . Thus we can roughly say that linguists before Mr Chomsky mainly insisted on the rules of construction of statements and less on the innovation represented by every new statement ... . And in the history of science or in the history of thought, we place more emphasis on individual creation, and we had kept aside and left in the shadows these communal general rules, which obscurely manifest themselves through every scientific discovery, every scientific invention, and even every philosophical innovation.

In this sense, Foucault explains the originality and uniqueness of the subject in the same way, and using the same arguments as he explains the originality of statements (*énoncés*). In the interview with Chomsky, Foucault agrees that 'rules and freedom are not opposed to each other'. In fact, the point he is at pains to stress in the interview with Chomsky is that within any system of rules, in the long run 'what is striking is the proliferation of possibilities by divergences' (p. 122). As he says (p. 123):

[C]reativity is possible in putting into play a system of rules; it is not a mixture of order and freedom ... . [W]here I don't completely agree with Mr Chomsky is when he places the principle of these regularities, in a way, in the interior of the mind or of human nature ... . If it is a matter of whether these rules are effectively put to work by the human mind, all right; all right, too, if it is a question of whether the historian and the linguist can think it in their turn; it is all right also to say that these rules should allow us to realise what is said or thought by these individuals. But to say that these regularities are connected, as conditions of existence, to the human mind or its nature, is difficult for me to accept; it seems to me that one must, before reaching that point ... replace it in the field of other human practices, such as economics, technology, politics, sociology, which can serve them as conditions of formation, of models, of place, or apparition, etc. I would like to know whether one cannot discover the system of regularity, of constraint, which makes science possible, somewhere else, even outside the human mind, in social forms, in the relations of production, in the class struggle, etc.

While Chomsky is interested in the 'intrinsic capabilities of mind', Foucault is interested in explaining how infinite possibilities of application arise from a limited number of rules which constitute the social conditions of existence.

In insisting on the open nature of the historical system, Foucault's approach to understanding history parallels Derrida's critique and revision of Saussure's in stressing the open and incomplete character of the totality of social relations. In Foucault, however, the analysis proceeds beyond the textual to an analysis of the historical relations between the discursive and pre-discursive, whereas for Derrida and Saussure the analysis is synchronic and confined to language. For Foucault, what is analysed is social practices—both discursive and non-discursive. Although this establishes a sociological holism and social objectivism which is anterior to the individual human subject, it is not a 'spirit' or 'mind' in the Hegelian (*Geist*) or Durkheimian (collective representations or consciousness) sense, but, influenced by the linguistic turn, a series of practices—habits, actions, mores, customs, languages—which function like a language, and from which individuals derive and alter meanings. In this sense, Foucault's sociological objectivism is akin to Wittgenstein's (*forms of life*), or Lévi-Strauss's (*symbolic systems*), in that objective social reality, while having ontological status, is not posited as a superior mind or intelligence which presides over other (mere ordinary) individual actors in history.

Notes

1. In his review of Deleuze's books, ('Theatrum Philosophicum') Foucault (1998, p. 366) reinforces the importance of chance: 'The present as the recurrence of difference, as repetition giving voice to difference, affirms at once the totality of chance. The univocity of being in Duns Scotus led to the immobility of an abstraction, in Spinoza it led to the necessity and eternity of substance; but here it leads to the single throw of chance in the fissure of the present. If being always declares itself in the same way, it is not because being is one but because the totality of chance is affirmed in the single dice throw of the present'.
2. As, for example, when they tried to test Copernicus's theories in astronomy by dropping stones from church spires to test to see whether the earth was rotating on its axis.

3. See, for instance, Foucault's essay 'Truth and Juridical Forms', originally published in May 1973, where he summarises Spinoza in relation to Nietzsche (Foucault, 2001, pp. 11–12); again, Foucault refers to Spinoza in the debate with Chomsky (Foucault, 1997, p. 136); in 'Theatrum Philosopicum' (Foucault, 1998, pp. 359–60 and pp. 366–67); and in 'Afterword to The Temptation of St Anthony' (1998, p. 105), just to name a few. It is also noteworthy that Deleuze was influenced by Spinoza, as Deleuze had a strong influence on Foucault. See Paul Veyne (1997, pp. 63–64), 'Foucault Revolutionizes History'. Also see index entries to Deleuze and Guattari (1987), Deleuze (1990, 1994) and others. Like Deleuze, Foucault (1998, p. 364) 'adapts' Spinozist concepts to express his views. For example: 'The univocity of being, its singleness of expression, is paradoxically the principal condition that permits difference to escape the domination of identity, frees it from the law of the Same as a simple opposition within conceptual elements'.

4. Michael Hardt has already noted the importance of Spinoza's conception of power on Foucault. See 'Translator's Foreword: The Anatomy of Power' in Antonio Negri's *The Savage Anomaly: The power of Spinoza's metaphysics and politics* (1991). On the theme of complexity, see Damasio (2003).

5. Foucault, like Nietzsche, wrote philosophically, and hence his use of terms like 'chance' and 'unpredictability' possibly lack technical translatability to the language of natural science. An account of the classical definition of concepts such as 'stability', 'chance', etc is given by Cilliers (1998). One way to define 'chance' might be to see it as not incompatible with a Newtonian universe. In complex systems, as Cilliers (1998: 109) says, 'novel, unpredicted behaviour need not be a result of chance. It can be 'caused' by the complex interaction of a large number of factors … . Complexity is not to be confused with randomness and chance, but cannot be confused with first-order logical terms either'. In this sense, we can speak of events which are theoretically unpredictable, which are not explainable in terms of 'chance'.

6. For other accounts of chaos theory, see Swinney (1983), Holden (1985), Gleick (1987), Sappington (1990) and Ayers (1997).

7. Chaos theory and complexity theories are distinct, although chaos theory can be seen as one type of complexity theory, which emphasises the importance of sensitivity to initial conditions. This is not so important with complex systems in general, which stresses the interaction of a large number of components (see Cilliers, 1998: ix).

8. Prigogine mostly applies these ideas to physical systems, but does sometimes demonstrate their applicability to the social and human world. Discussing his theories of time and irreversibility, he notes how all events are irreversible events. The consequence of irreversibility is that 'it leads to probabilistic descriptions, which cannot be reduced to individual trajectories or wave functions corresponding to Newtonian or Quantum mechanics' (Prigogine, 2003, p. 75).

9. Meaning is conferred not by one to one correspondence with the world but by relationships between structural components of the system. See Cilliers (1998, p. 81). His analysis of poststructural complexity is based on Saussure's well-known analysis in the *Course in General Linguistics* (1974). Having said this, it is interesting that Cilliers translates poststructural philosophy into western analytic schemas rather than elaborate his thesis in relation to difference theory as elaborated by Foucault or Deleuze. I have done the same here simply to convey something of the tenor of the poststructural innovation.

10. For other forms of emergentist materialism in western thought, see Bunge (1977), Haken (1977, 1990), Rapp *et al.* (1986) or Skarda and Freeman (1990). Although such theories are broadly analogous to Foucault's materialism, the emphasis in poststructuralism on the open and incomplete character of the totality presents new insights into issues like determination and chance. Again, see Cilliers (1998).

11. For another view of complexity theory, see Kauffman (1991, 1993, 1995). Kauffman suggests that while events can be seen as having antecedent conditions which explain them, in open environments the possible combinations are unpredictable. Other characteristics of complex systems are that they do not operate near equilibrium; the relationships between

components are non-linear and dynamic; elements do not have fixed positions; the relationships between elements are not stable; and there are always more possibilities than can be actualised.

12. The form of complexity may itself change, as is happening with globalisation. The notion, for example, that carbon emissions can trigger climate change, which can have potentially unpredictable effects of unimaginable severity, is one illustration of how determination works in relation to complex causality.

13. For Derrida (1981, p. 26) the sign has no positive identity but comprises only the collection of traces of all the other signs that run through it.

14. If we think of someone like Winston Churchill, there is something trite in representing him as the outcome of the play of differences (Churchill is not Balfour, not Astor, not Baldwin, etc.), for agency in history established a substantial, yet non-essential sense. Yet this identity is still always precarious, incomplete, fragmented, inconsistent, and transitional. It represents at any particular time, a 'settlement'.

15. Liberals, especially Rawls (1971), bemoaned in *A Theory of Justice* that it was necessary to retreat to deontology (return to a rights discourse) because social approaches (including utilitarianism) could not account for the *distinctness* of identity.

16. Such theories of complex emergentist materialism can also account for the origins of mind as irrepressible (non-reducible) yet wholly material, or physical.

17. Such complex non-linear models are historically contingent in terms of their internal, substantive arrangements. In Althusser, the variability of the effectivity of the levels of practices of the social formation conforms to such a complex formula, albeit in structuralist and decidedly non-nominalistic terms. The ultimate necessity of the economic, however, does not conform, as it introduces a causal factor which is historically invariant across successive modes of production. In this sense, to use Deleuze and Guattari's (1987) language, Althusser's model of structural causality conforms to both *rhizonomic* and *arborescent* forms.

18. Damasio (2003) uses examples of social emotions, including sympathy, embarrassment, shame, etc., to exemplify the nesting principle. As he states (pp. 45–46): 'a whole retinue of regulatory reactions along with elements present in primary emotions can be identified as subcomponents of social emotions in varied combinations. The nested incorporation of components from lower tiers is apparent. Think how the social emotion 'contempt' borrows from the facial expressions of 'disgust', a primary emotion that evolved in association with the autonomous and beneficial rejection of potentially toxic foods'. The appropriate image for these reactions 'is not that of a simple linear hierarchy' (p. 38).

References

Allison, D. B. (1977) (ed.) *The New Nietzsche* (New York: A Delta Book).

Ayers, S. (1997) The Application of Chaos Theory to Psychology, *Theory and Psychology*, 7:3, pp. 373–398.

Bateson, G. (1972) *Steps Towards an Ecology of Mind* (New York, Ballantine Books).

Bunge, M. (1977) Emergence and the Mind: Commentary, *Neuroscience*, 2, pp. 501–509.

Cilliers, P. (1998) *Complexity and Postmodernism* (London and New York, Routledge).

Currie, M. (2004) *Difference* (London and New York, Routledge).

Damasio, A. (2003) *Looking for Spinoza* (London, Verso).

Davidson, A. (1997) *Foucault and His Interlocutors* (Chicago & London, University of Chicago Press).

Deleuze, G. (1985) Nomad Thought, in D. B. Allison (ed.) *The New Nietzsche* (Cambridge Mass., MIT Press).

Deleuze, G. & Guartari, F. (1987) *A Thousand Plateaus: Capitalism and Schizophrenia*. Trans. and Foreword by Brian Massumi (London and New York, Continuum).

Deleuze, G. (1990) *The Logic of Sense*, ed. C. V. Bourdas, trans. M. Lester with C. Stiavale (New York, Columbia University Press).

Deleuze, G. (1994) *Difference and Repetition*, trans. P. Patton (London, Continuum).

Derrida, J. (1981) *Positions* (Chicago, University of Chicago Press).

Dreyfus, H. (1992) On the Ordering of Things: Being and power in Heidegger and Foucault, in: T. J. Armstrong (ed.), *Michel Foucault: Philosopher* (New York and London, Harvester/ Wheatsheaf) pp. 80–98.

Foucault, M. (1970) *The Order of Things* (New York, Random House).

Foucault, M. (1972) *The Archaeology of Knowledge*, trans. A. Sheridan (London, Tavistock).

Foucault, M. (1977a) Nietzsche, Genealogy, History, in: D. Bouchard (ed.) *Language, Counter-Memory, Practice: Selected Essays and Interviews* (Ithaca, N.Y., Cornell University Press) pp. 139–164.

Foucault, M. (1977b) *Discipline and Punish*, trans. A. Sheridan (New York, Pantheon).

Foucault, M. (1978) Politics and the Study of Discourse, trans. C. Gordon, *Ideology and Consciousness*, 3(Spring), pp. 7–26.

Foucault, M. (1980) Truth and Power, in: C. Gordon (ed.) *Power/Knowledge: Selected Interviews and Other Writings 1972–1977* (Brighton, Harvester Press) pp. 109–133.

Foucault, M. (1980a) Prison Talk, trans. C. Gordon, in: C. Gordon (ed.) *Power/Knowledge: Selected Interviews and Other Writings, 1972–1977* (Brighton, Harvester Press) pp. 37–54.

Foucault, M. (1981) The Order of Discourse, trans. I. McLeod, in: R. Young (ed.) *Untying the Text* (London, Routledge & Kegan Paul).

Foucault, M. (1984a) Preface to the History of Sexuality, Volume II, in: P. Rabinow (ed.) *The Foucault Reader* (New York: Pantheon).

Foucault, M. (1984b) Polemics, Politics, Problematizations, trans. L. Davis, in: P. Rabinow (ed.) *The Foucault Reader* (New York, Pantheon) pp. 381–389.

Foucault, M. (1985) Final Interview, trans. T. Levin and I. Lorenz, *Raritan*, 5(Summer), 1–13 (interview conducted by G. Barbedette, published in *Les Louvelles*, June 28, 1984.

Foucault, M. (1987) Questions of Method, in: K. Baynes, J. Bonman & T. McCarthy (eds) *After Philosophy, End or Transformation* (Cambridge, Mass., MIT Press).

Foucault, M. (1990) Maurice Blanchot: The Thought from Outside, in: *Michel Foucault and Maurice Blanchot, Foucault/Blanchot*, trans. J. Mehlman & B. Massumi (New York, Zone Books).

Foucault, M. (1994a) La Philosophie Analytique de la Politique, in: D. Defert & F. Ewald (eds) with J. Lagrange, *Dits et écrits, 1954–1988*, Vol. 3: 232 (Paris, Éditions Gallimard) pp. 534–551.

Foucault, M. (1994b) Linguistique et Sciences Sociales, in: D. Defert & F. Ewald (eds) with J. Lagrange, *Dits et écrits: 1954–1988* Vol. 1: 70 (Paris, Éditions Gallimard) pp. 821–842.

Foucault, M. (1998) Theatrum Philosophicum, in: J. D. Faubion (ed.) *Michel Foucault: Aesthetics, Method, and Epistemology* (the essential works, volume 2) (Allen Lane, The Penguin Press), pp. 343–368.

Foucault, M. (1998a) Afterword to the Temptation of Saint Anthony, in: J. D. Faubion (ed.) *Michel Foucault: Aesthetics, Method, and Epistemology* (the essential works, volume 2) (Allen Lane, The Penguin Press), pp. 103–123.

Foucault, M. (2001) Interview with Michel Foucault, in: J. D. Faubion (ed.) *Michel Foucault: Power* (the essential works, volume 3) (Allen Lane, The Penguin Press), pp. 239–297.

Foucault, M. & Chomsky, N. (1997) Human Nature: Justice vs. power, in: A. I. Davidson (ed.) *Foucault and His Interlocutors* (Chicago and London, University of Chicago Press).

Frank, M. (1992) On Foucault's Concept of Discourse, in: T. J. Armstrong (ed.) *Michel Foucault: Philosopher* (New York, Harvester/Wheatsheaf).

Gleick, J. (1987) *Chaos: Making a New Science* (London, Abacus).

Haken, H. (1977) Synergetics—An Introduction (Heidelberg, Springer-Verlag).

Haken, H. (1990) Synergetics as a Tool for the Conceptualization and Mathematization of Cognition and Behaviour—How Far Can We Go? In: H. Haken & M. Stadler (eds), *Synergetics of Cognition* (Berlin, Springer) pp. 2–31.

Heidegger, M. (1991) *Nietzsche*, (two volumes), trans. D. Farrel Krell (San Francisco, Harper Collins).

Holden, A. (1985). Chaos is No Longer a Dirty Word. *New Scientist*, 106:1453. pp. 12–15.

Kauffman, S. A. (1991) Antichaos and Adaptation, *Scientific American*, August, pp. 64–70.

Kauffman, S. A. (1993) *The Origins of Order: Self-organisation and selection in evolution* (New York, Oxford University Press).

Kauffman, S. A. (1995) *At Home in the Universe: The search for laws of complexity* (London, Viking Press).

Margolis, J. (1993) *The Flux of History and the Flux of Science* (Berkeley, University of California Press).

Negri, A. (1991) *The Savage Anomaly: The power of Spinoza's metaphysics and politics*. Trans. Michael Hardt (Minneapolis, University of Minnesota Press).

Nietzsche, F. (1967) *On the Genealogy of Morals. Ecce Homo*, trans. W. Kaufmann (New York, Random House).

Nietzsche, F. (1968) *The Will to Power*, trans. W. Kaufman and R. J. Hollingdale, ed. W. Kaufmann (New York, Vintage Books).

Olssen, M. (1999) *Michel Foucault: Materialism and education* (Westport, Bergin and Garvey).

Olssen, M. (2006) *Michel Foucault: Materialism and education* (Boulder/London, Paradigm Press).

Prigogine, I. (1980) *From Being to Becoming* (San Francisco, W.H. Freeman and Co.).

Prigogine, I. (1994) *Time, Chaos and the Laws of Chaos* (Moscow: Ed. Progress).

Prigogine, I. (2003) *Is Future Given?* (New Jersey, World Scientific).

Prigogine, I. & Nicolis, G. (1989) *Exploring Complexity* (New York, W.H. Freeman).

Prigogne, I. & Stengers, I. (1984) *Order Out of Chaos* (New York, Bantam).

Prigogne, I. & Stengers, I. (1997) *The End of Certainty: Time's flow and the laws of nature* (New York, The Free Press).

Rapp, P. E., Zimmerman, I. D., Albano, A. M., de Gusman, G. C., Grenbauri, M. N. & Bashmore, T. R. (1986) Experimental Studies of Chaotic Neural Behaviour: Cellular activity and electronencephalographic signals, in: H. G. Othmer (ed.), *Nonlinear Oscillations in Biology and Chemistry* (Berlin, Springer).

Rawls, J. (1971) *A Theory of Justice* (Oxford, Oxford University Press).

Sappington, A. A. (1990) Recent Psychological Approaches to the Free Will versus Determinism Issue. *Psychological Bulletin*, 108, pp. 19–29.

Sardar, Z. & Abrams, I. (1999) *Introduciing Chaos* (Cambridge, Icon Books Ltd).

Saussure, F. de (1974) *Course in General Linguistics* (London, Fontana).

Schrift, A. D. (1995) *Nietzsche's French Legacy: A Genealogy of Poststructuralism* (New York, London, Routledge).

Skarda, C. A. & Freeman, W. J. (1990) Chaos and the New Science of the Brain, *Concepts in Neuroscience*, 1, pp. 275–285.

Swinney, H. L. (1983) Observations of Order and Chaos in Non-linear Systems, *Physica*, 7, pp. 3–15.

Veyne, P. (1997) Foucault Revolutionizes History, in: A. Davidson (ed.) *Foucault and His Interlocutors* (Chicago & London, University of Chicago Press).

8
Complex Systems and Educational Change: Towards a new research agenda

Jay L. Lemke* & Nora H. Sabelli**
*University of Michigan
**SRI International

1. Studying the Complexity of Educational Change

How might we usefully apply concepts and procedures derived from the study of other complex dynamical systems to analyzing systemic change in education?

This seemed a natural question to the diverse group of about 40 leading natural science and education researchers who met first in 1999 at MIT's Endicott House under the sponsorship of the National Science Foundation and the New England Complex Systems Institute (NECSI, 1999) to consider the future role of complex systems science in the K-16 curriculum. It was clear that whatever recommendations for curriculum development might eventually emerge, the curriculum change process itself would pose challenges to making this important new area of the sciences accessible to large numbers of students. The Endicott House conference participants were hopeful that complex systems theory could offer insights into the processes of curriculum change and, more generally, of systemic reform in education. A working group was formed to examine this question, and it produced an initial report (Lemke et al., 1999).

A key recommendation from the Endicott House conference was to bring these issues to wider attention in the education community, and at a smaller second meeting sponsored by NECSI, plans were developed for a symposium at the American Educational Research Association annual meeting in 2002 (Jacobson et al., 2001). At the same time a number of the participants also convened in 2001 at the Balcones Springs conference sponsored by NSF and the University of Texas to discuss issues of urban systemic reform with leaders of four major NSF-sponsored projects and about 16 other experts in the science and mathematics education community (Confrey et al., 2001). This chapter describes a number of the important concepts and research issues regarding the application of complex systems approaches to education that have developed out of this continuing discussion.

New conceptual approaches to the study of complex systems have been developed in the last two decades by mathematicians, physicists, chemists, biologists, and computer scientists (cf. Bar-Yam, 1997). They are being applied and extended by economists, psychologists, organizational scientists and researchers in many disciplines whose insights are being scaffolded not only by new quantitative techniques, but by new qualitative conceptions of phenomena common to many different complex systems. Concepts such as multi-scale hierarchical organization, emergent patterning, agent-based modeling, dynamical attractors and repellors, information flows and constraints, system-environment interaction, developmental trajectories, selectional ratchets, fitness landscapes, interaction across timescales, and varieties of self-organization are becoming key tools for qualitative reasoning about complex socio-natural systems as well as for quantitative modeling and simulation.

Can the new tools of complex system analysis help us understand the potential impact on the educational system of new technologies and help us predict the paths that different efforts at systemic reform follow? Can they help us design new educational systems to meet the needs of all citizens in the new century? Can they help us identify critical relationships within the educational system that resist systemic change or afford opportunities for new alternatives? Can we realistically hope for an educational system that will teach large numbers of students to use the new tools for thinking that complexity theory has developed? Can we find ways to make the value of these tools sufficiently evident and attractive to large numbers of students and teachers so that they will seek them out?

If the answers to any of these questions are to be 'yes', we will require collaboration within a diverse new community of researchers seeking a common framework for sharing ideas from different disciplines and approaches to both complex system analysis and to education. There is an urgency to the formation of such a community. If the response of the educational system to the new demands of the public for reform and to the new opportunities technology affords is not guided by the best ideas of the research community, and by research- and data-driven decision-making, it will be guided by other forces, in which we may have less confidence.

The concepts and tools we consider in this chapter have been put to use in practice and tested in managing complex and ill-defined ecological systems, e.g. in what has been called the 'active adaptive management' technique, which could serve as a case study of handling the complexity inherent in a multifaceted system merging scientific knowledge and public-interest goals (see Farr, 2000, for definitions and references and Gunderson & Holling, 2002, for a related approach). Active adaptive management is a 'process of testing alternative hypotheses through management action, learning from experience, and making appropriate change to policy and management practice'.

2. Developing a Conceptual Framework

It is not our aim here to present a complete conceptual framework for the analysis of education as a complex system. Our purpose is to begin to define possible agendas for further research toward such a framework. Towards this end, we will try to illustrate the plausibility of defining such a framework, and raise the question of the relation between such frameworks and the crucial aggregation of data across 'systemic experiments' (Sabelli, in preparation; Confrey *et al.*, 2002). Even within what we might eventually agree on as a common framework and terminology for describing such a complex system, there will continue to be room for many existing alternative models and, over an extended period of research, for the emergence of new data-driven models and syntheses appropriate to various specific tasks. We will describe the core issues for a framework under the following headings: *Defining the System, Structural Analysis, Relationships among Subsystems and Levels, Drivers for Change,* and *Modeling Methods.* Much of this sketch towards a possible framework will be presented in the form of questions because we believe that the primary contribution that complex systems theory can make to such an enterprise right now is to guide what questions we ask and how we frame them in relation to one another and to prospective data sources. Questions matter: they are the seeds from which new theories grow, and like all seeds they carry forward the prior theories from which they come.

Defining the System

The US K-16 educational system is conventionally defined as the system of public and private schools and colleges that offer students formal education from kindergarten to college graduation. For research purposes, however, the system must ultimately be defined by our analysis of its constituent elements and environmental dynamics, such as which institutions and social practices and which sources and users of information and material and human resources are tightly enough coupled and interdependent in their behavior that they must be included within the system? Likewise, what is the range of timescales characteristic of the critical processes that enable the system to maintain itself? What are its significant levels of organization, not simply or primarily in terms of lines of authority (control hierarchies), but in terms of characteristic structures and characteristic emergent processes and patterns at each level? What kinds of material resource and information flows connect adjacent and non-adjacent levels? How is information transformed, filtered, re-organized, and added to from level to level? How is information-overload avoided by emergent systems through pattern-recognition that extracts from large data-flows only what matters for the dynamics of the next higher level?

If we consider the longest timescales experienced by students within the system, we will need to extend its definition to consider pre-school education, post-graduate study, and continuing adult education. If we examine all the source institutions that contribute to students' understanding of particular topics within the formal curriculum, we must include informal educational institutions such as science museums and information sources and learning sites afforded by mass media, print publishing, and interactive communication technologies. If we look at resource constraints and decision-making bodies, we will add school boards and trustees and state education authorities. If we include ourselves within the system, we will consider our roles as teachers and researchers, and the relationship between research institutions and sponsors and the communities that make use of research results.

Structural Analysis

Formal organizational hierarchies propose one starting point for identifying levels within the core educational system: individual learners and teachers, small groups, classrooms, departments, schools, districts (LEAs), states (SEAs), federal agencies, the total system. What would a dynamical analysis propose—one that takes into account the differing timescales at which different levels of the system function? If we analyze the system in terms of dynamical processes and emergent phenomena on different timescales, what would the units of analysis be? How do brief actions by teachers and students add up to coherent activities over periods of minutes and hours, days and months? How do curriculum change processes that occur over periods of years exchange information with classroom activities that occur over periods of minutes? How do learning events in a laboratory or at a computer workstation and those in classrooms and hallways and cafeterias add up to a coherent longer-term process of educational development, or perhaps the development of facility with a particular concept? How do networks of social interaction with peers in the classroom, in the wider neighborhood community, and in virtual online communities contribute to long-term processes of identity development and formation of lasting attitudes and values, which affect decisions and actions on very short timescales? How do the changing priorities, populations and problems of a local community influence the larger educational system's agendas and programs?

Having focused on some of the characteristic educational processes that involve the student, we could raise similar questions about those in which teachers participate but which may not always involve students, and similar questions about supervisors and administrators, teacher educators, curriculum developers, educational materials publishers, and ourselves as researchers.

Relationships among Subsystems and Levels

Whatever level of organization or subsystem is the focus of our concerns at a particular point, we can always ask a series of key questions motivated by the perspectives of complex system theory:

- What next higher level of organization determines constraints on the dynamics at the focal level?
  - How do all subsystems subject to those constraints interact to constitute the dynamics of the higher level?
  - What degrees of freedom remain at the focal level after the constraints are allowed for?
- What units of analysis at the next level below interact to constitute units (or processes or patterns) at the focal level?
  - What characteristics of those lower level units determine the range of dynamical possibilities at the focal level?
- What are the typical attractors of the focal level dynamics?

- ○ Under what conditions is each attractor dominant for the (sub-) system?
- ○ How do new attractors emerge over the history of the system's development and the evolution of this kind of system?
- Which features of system behavior are determinate and which are not?
  - ○ Which regions of the space of possibilities are accessible and which are not?
  - ○ What manifolds describe the conditions on the range of values of all other parameters that must be met to achieve some value of the parameter of interest?
- At a given level of organization, how are the different units and processes coupled with one another?
  - ○ What kinds of matter, information, and energy do they exchange?
  - ○ How tightly coupled are they and what is the topology of the coupling network?
  - ○ What are the significant branchings, closed loops, and connectivity decompositions?
- What is system and what is 'environment'?
  - ○ How do system and environment form a supersystem from the viewpoint of some still larger-scale unit or process?

As an example, we will see that any focal pedagogical 'innovation' introduced into a tightly constrained school system is in fact a series of embedded innovations at levels *above and below* the focal intervention, and strategies for all levels have to be considered coherently.

Drivers for Change

How is the educational system as a whole driven by external events and pressures such as advances in scientific understanding, the increasing complexity of problems addressed by communities and societies, changing technologies, and public demands for reform? How is educational change constrained by resource limitations, standardized curricula and testing, or deeply held cultural beliefs? How is educational change enabled or made possible by bringing new kinds of people into contact with one another or utilizing new technologies (e.g. cross-age tutoring, or tele-mentoring)? How would educational processes be affected by creating new feedback loops, such as research data that systematically describes outcomes back to teachers, students, and parents? How might new educational institutions (e.g. charter schools, online courses) create niches for themselves in the educational ecology? How might new spontaneous networks, such as online communication groups of teachers within a school or across the country, affect the rate of educational change at each scale of organization?

Modeling Methods

How would we model and analyze issues like these using the concepts and techniques of ecosystem theory and adaptive management, developmental biology, reaction-diffusion chemistry, non-equilibrium statistical mechanics, nonlinear dynamical systems analysis, cellular automata models, artificial life systems, neural networks, parallel distributed computation, agent-based modeling theory, informatics and infodynamics? Given access to data and expertise about the educational system, how would you yourself approach one of these issues? Given collaboration with others who could offer different insights about complex system behavior, how would you and other educators and researchers begin to formulate any one of these problems for actual study?

How well, for example, could we design today a 'SimSchool' or 'SimDistrict' school- or school district-simulation program? Not just to model an existing system, but to enable us to create alternative systems and study their evolution over time, their needs and problems, their probable outcomes? We could then ask, for instance, what kinds of schools would students design if given access to an appropriate version of this software? How would they evaluate various designs proposed by others? Who would we enlist in the team to create such a software package? What research literatures would we want to consult? What is not yet known that would be needed to complete the project?

Do we even know what kinds of data would be needed to realistically attempt such a project? Insofar as we are only interested in easily quantifiable parameters of the system, such as school budgets, teacher qualifications, and student test-scores, we still need to know how much value added there might be from a complex dynamic system model compared to more static statistical analyses. Good use has been made of static and isolated case analyses, particularly when the dynamics of the relation with the environment or with environmental variables are taken into account, usually by statistical methods, and more recently, by the dynamical inclusion of environmental variables (e.g. Jost, 2003). Agent-based dynamical and simulation models hold the promise of enabling us to explore potential effects of changes in quantitative parameters and assumptions about how variables interact to produce observable statistical relationships. Complex systems models are designed to model change and dynamics, especially qualitative change: the emergence of new social networks, changes in daily routines or actor preferences. In a human social system, these kinds of changes are mediated by the meanings and values assigned by actors, individually and collectively, to the more objectively definable affordances of their environments. To build effective dynamical models of educational institutions we will need to know not just what people do, but why they do it, how they might imagine things being different, and what they would really want to do.

Even if such system models are not predictive in any detailed way, they can still be useful in identifying possible alternatives, potential problems, and overall qualitative features of the change process that may not be intuitively evident to a linear logic of cause and effect. In complex systems every causal chain is mediated, and many chains branch and loop back on themselves in complicated webs of mutual interdependence, self-regulation, and amplification of effects. This conceptualization is consistent with Michael Fullan's 'systems at the edge of chaos' view of education (Fullan, 1999).

No mention of the data needed for analysis and the development of theoretical models should leave out considerations of the importance of sharing information across projects (i.e. across localized case studies). This sharing and aggregation is a major problem for a topic so dependent on localized conditions as education reform is.

We report next on one such effort to begin this process across a set of long-term projects on systemic reform in science and mathematics education in the USA.

3. Lessons for Modeling from Real Cases

The important report from the Balcones Springs conference (Confrey *et al.*, 2001) summarizes the lessons learned from four major educational reform projects (see Table 1). Such lessons represent hard-won long-term information about the specificity and diversity of implementations of various closely related curriculum- and system-wide reform models. The projects were related in being implemented in urban schools and districts with highly diverse students, being guided by the same meta-model of systemic change 'drivers' (NSF, 2001), but using different models of how to achieve sustainable improvement of teaching and learning. Any research effort to develop a complex system model of educational change would do well to take into account this data about what matters to the success of existing systemic reform initiatives.

Perhaps the most important of these lessons is that adaptation of models for system reform to local conditions matters more than efforts to replicate successes elsewhere, without extensive knowledge of how the systemic variables differ between environments. This 'localization effect' points to the importance of determining whether any single complex system model can be both general and specific enough that it can include design templates to identify key local parameters that need to be set. Alternatively,

Table 1: Four Major Educational Reform Projects

Project	Research Organization	Urban Sites	Participants	Years in Operation
LeTUS (Learning Technology in Urban Schools) http://www.letus.org	NWU U Michigan	Chicago IL Detroit MI	62 schools	9
SYRCE (Systemic Research Collaborative for Education) http://syrce.org	U Texas	Austin TX	6 schools	4
(SFT) School For Thought http://peabody.vanderbilt.edu/projects/funded/sft/general/sfthome.html	Vanderbilt	Nashville TN	125*	6
Union City Online http://www2.edc.org/CCT/cctweb/project/descrip.asp?2	EDC	Union City NJ School District	11 schools	6

*The number is approximate because the configuration of Nashville schools and teachers was in a continuous state of flux throughout the project. Accordingly, many teachers changed schools throughout the project. This makes it difficult to provide an exact number of schools because many of the teachers take the reform with them but the project has no access to data on what they do after leaving, how the reform survives, or the impact on student learning.

more heuristic guidance needs to be developed to aid in the design of quite different models for each educational system (i.e. differing structurally and not just parametrically from one another). Here are some of the more detailed lessons learned from these research projects that seem especially relevant to the design of realistic system models.

Timescales and Stepwise Structure

It was found that in most cases it takes a long time, of the order of 5–10 years, to establish effective collaborations between researchers and school systems, and that during this period there may be a need to re-negotiate and re-commit to goals and strategies developed together whenever there are major changes in leadership or personnel on either side of the partnership. The development of effective partnerships takes 5–10 years, and the fruits of reform efforts tend to become visible only after at least 3–5 years. Any evaluation and tests of scalability require at least a second or third cycle of enlargement or replication, implying a minimum of 10 years' scope for models of effective change.

For reform efforts to be maximally adaptive to changing environmental conditions, an iterative process is needed in which plans are continually modified in response to issues that come to light only once implementation has begun, or to the mere change of individuals in either the research or implementation personnel. Successful multi-year reform processes include periods of consolidation of gains; these periods provide a respite to plan for needed changes and for people to become comfortable with one set of changes before contemplating others. In this sense, reform should be viewed as a 'stepwise' process, in which advances alternate with such periods of reflection and consolidation. This stepwise strategy promotes buy-in from skeptics, allows for non-disruptive change and establishes a culture of continuous improvement. Under these conditions, modeling the likely effects of different 'schedules for innovation' may lead to a more integrated and sustainable organization that is resilient with respect to changing future conditions.

Sustainability and Scaling

Reforms often begin locally and then face the problem of 'scaling out', i.e. including more units at the same level of organization (e.g. from a few teachers, or one grade level, to all teachers in a school or all grades), and also of 'scaling up', i.e. from small-scale systems (e.g. a small suburban district) to much larger-scale systems (e.g. a large urban system or an entire state). As reform scales, there is no guarantee that it will maintain validity with respect to its fundamental principles or goals. For this to happen, some self-regulatory feedback must exist within the system to assess whether such validity has been maintained and to provide an incentive for maintaining it.

Agents of Scaling

There were found to be a number of agents of scaling. For example, student cohorts can motivate scaling up as they move through a system, carrying the reform 'upward' with them. This type of spread appears to require a critical mass of students and an initial phase that includes a plan for such 'vertical' growth. Another model of spread is to systematically plan for horizontal growth, or scaling out. In doing so, pressures on the reform implementation can create situations that indicate problems with the model, or its limits of applicability (e.g. whole school models in contexts where there are not sufficient resources to support that model). Scaling is a useful strategy for testing the robustness of the process, making it more sustainable, and finding its weakest spots. This points to the *interdependence of scaling and sustainability* as a key issue for any model.

Role of Sustainability

Sustainability, it was found, has two key aspects. The first is the need for a match between stakeholders' expectations regarding the nature and pace of results and the ability to provide persuasive demonstrations of timely effects. Early successes, as judged by stakeholders, appear to be crucial for sustaining the reform process. The second aspect depends on relationships among the timescales of change processes in different elements of the system and between the system and larger social-political-economic systems in which it is embedded and on which its functioning depends.

Sustainability is threatened by normal processes of change in larger-scale systems within which the educational system operates (e.g. changes in political administrations, new superintendents with new policies, changes in state regulations or funding formulas, etc.). Widespread commitment by many stakeholders and a critical mass of committed practitioners can ensure that maintaining gains in achievement will move the community to keep updating policies and practices needed to sustain reforms while responding to other inevitable social changes.

Many of these lessons point to the importance of multi-scale modeling techniques for educational change, and particularly to multiple timescale models (Lemke, 2000a, 2000b). When we consider that many key structural features of educational practice (e.g. student-teacher ratios, use of textbooks, age-grading, local-taxation funding, curriculum areas, teacher training institutions) have been stable on timescales of a century or longer, we can infer that there are powerful system-regulatory relationships maintaining this stability. Reform mandates and implementations, on the other hand, are formulated and expect results on timescales of the order of a decade or less. Complex system models need to help us understand why so many features of the educational system do not change, as well as under what conditions they will change. Many current reform policies assume that no major structural changes are necessary to achieve reform goals. Realistic models, based on detailed case studies of reform efforts, as well as on general system modeling principles, may help us understand if such assumptions are realistic or not. We need to know whether or not current modest reforms have any realistic chance of producing major gains at the large-scale in realistic timeframes. If it should appear that more radical re-engineering of the educational system is needed, we will need to understand the functional roles and interdependencies of current structural features all the more.

4. A Philosophical Note

The perspective of this chapter has been largely instrumental and externalist, continuing the research and philosophical tradition of trying to view systems we are actually a part of as if we were outside them, in order to gain some ability to intervene in them. The logic of complex systems, however, pulls us away from this expected perspective. In the case studies at the Balcones Springs conference it was clear that the researchers were very much a part of the systems they were reporting on, and that how they participated, what their roles were, and how they were perceived by others all mattered very much both to what happened and to how they reported on it. In many cases their most interesting reports included very personal observations, more experiential and phenomenological than objectified and structural. The development of their models, both for change processes and for good practice, often depended critically on the experiential insights that came from direct participation, over extended periods of time, gaining, in a now classic phrase, 'a feeling for the organism' (Keller, 1983). The further lesson, across the cases studied, that change is local, and each case as much a unique individual system as an instance of more general processes, was taken very seriously. Complex systems are, in some special sense, 'individuals', whether or not they are also members of some species.

Our philosophical traditions in natural and social science have not prepared us very well to study the internalist, phenomenological, and individual aspects of complex systems. Our traditions doubt the very possibility of a science of the individual, a science of the particular, and yet other traditions, e.g. in the humanities, have long dealt with their objects of study as both unique and typical. Even reflexive sociology balks short of internalism, of putting ourselves squarely inside our models, of stipulating just how systems look different depending on where we sit inside them, or alongside them (Haraway, 1997).

If complex socio-natural systems are individual, surprising, recalcitrant; if we have to get to know them over time, and in person; if we know them only insofar as we participate in them, and then in specifically partial or participation-dependent ways, then our traditional epistemologies may fail us and good science for these systems looks somewhat different from what science has imagined itself doing (though perhaps not, as Latour [1987] argues, from what it has actually been doing). Relative to our human viewpoint and ways of participating in them, socio-natural systems of interest may indeed be a little perverse, may actually display an independent sense of humor. The last word about the real has not been said, and the study of complex systems may still be able to teach us new lessons in intellectual humility. Not every frame of mind on the part of an investigator may prove equally fruitful in learning those lessons.

Conclusions

The conceptual basis of complex systems ideas reflects a change in perspective about our world. This perspective emphasizes both the limits of predictability as well as the possibility of understanding indirect consequences of actions taken, both positive and negative, through the modeling of interdependence. The study of complex systems involves experimental, computational, and theoretical approaches for observation, analysis, modeling, and dynamical simulation.

Complex systems concepts are used in science to provide organization for the otherwise bewildering properties of diverse and often unpredictable systems in a common framework and language. These systems are often unpredictable because small changes in one variable may result in major changes in overall outcomes (critical thresholds), while other, larger, local changes might not disrupt the system significantly (robustness).

The application of these concepts in conjunction with computational models and visually compelling data-driven simulations yields unprecedented means for understanding complex phenomena and revealing new, sometimes counter-intuitive patterns and relationships. Such understandings lead to new and essential questions and to viewing educational systems with new eyes. Understanding complex systems also seems to be critical to our ability to apply knowledge and techniques across very different individual contexts.

The education system is one of the most complex and challenging systems for research. Much as we know about cognitive aspects of learning, pedagogical strategies, and reform implementation, we currently lack the modeling capability needed to help practitioners and policymakers explore the potential impact of proposed interventions, since efforts in this area are still at a very preliminary stage of development. Indeed, in this perspective there are no independent interventions: proposed changes at the classroom level have implications at school and district levels (e.g. for teacher development, parental expectations, school resources, accountability, and so on) and need to be supported by related interventions across multiple levels. A technical ability to explore such dynamic linkages could be a significant tool for educators and policy makers.

Most important perhaps is a change in the paradigms of our thinking about research on education. Away from input-output 'black-box' causal models to modeling the specific, local linkages that actually interconnect actors, practices, and events across multiple levels of organization. Away from single interventions and simplistic solutions to recognition of the need for coordinated changes throughout the system and to its 'external' relations to its constraining and enabling contexts and resources. And even perhaps away from the Enlightenment dream of universal laws, perfect predictability and rational control to a new recognition that all genuinely complex systems are individual, surprising, and not a little perverse. Just like us.

References

Bar-Yam, Y. (1997) *Dynamics of Complex Systems* (Reading, MA, Perseus).

Confrey, J., Lemke, J. L., Marshall, J. & Sabelli, N. (2001) *Conference on Models of Implementation Research in Science and Mathematics Instruction in Urban Schools* (Austin, TX, University of Texas).

Confrey, J., Sabelli, N., and Sheingold, K. (2002) A Framework for Quality in Educational Technology Programs, *Educational Technology*, Vol. 42, 7–20.

Farr, D. (2000) Defining Active Adaptive Management. [Online] http://www.ameteam.ca/About%20Flame/AAMdefinition.PDF

Fullan, M. (1999) *Change Forces: The Sequel* (New York, Routledge/Falmer).

Gunderson, L. & Holling, C. S. (2002) *Panarchy: Understanding transformations in human and natural systems* (Washington, DC, Island Press).

Haraway, D. (1997) *Modest_Witness@Second_Millennium.FemaleMan(c) _Meets_OncoMouse(TM)* (New York/London, Routledge).

Jacobson, M., Kaput, J., Wilensky, U. & Lemke, J. L. (2001) Complex Systems in Education: integrative conceptual tools and techniques for understanding the education system itself. [Online] http://edtech.connect.msu.edu/Searchaera2002/viewproposaltext.asp?propID=6203

Jost, J. (2003) External and Internal Complexity of Complex Adaptive Systems, SFI Working Paper Abstract. Available at: www.santafe.edu/sfi/publications/wpabstract/200312070

Keller, E. F. (1983) *A Feeling for the Organism: The Life and Work of Barbara McClintock* (San Francisco, Freeman).

Latour, B. (1987) *Science in Action* (Cambridge, MA, Harvard University Press).

Lemke, J. L., *et al.* (1999) Toward Systemic Educational Change: Questions from a complex systems perspective. Working Group 3, Systemic Educational Change. Report of an NSF-funded Workshop, Endicott House, MA. [Online] http://necsi.org/events/cxedk16/cxedk16_3.html

Lemke, J. L. (2000a) Across the Scales of Time: Artifacts, activities, and meanings in ecosocial systems, *Mind, Culture, and Activity*, 7:4, pp. 273–290.

Lemke, J. L. (2000b) Opening Up Closure: Semiotics across scales, in: J. Chandler & G. van de Vijver (eds), *Closure: Emergent Organizations and their Dynamics* (New York, New York Academy of Sciences) pp. 100–111.

National Science Foundation [NSF], Educational System Reform (2001) Six Critical Drivers. [Online]. http://www.ehr.nsf.gov/esr/drivers/

New England Complex Systems Institute [NECSI] (1999) Planning documents for a national initiative on complex systems in K-16 education. [Online] http://necsi.org/events/cxedk16/cxedk16.html

Sabelli, N. (in preparation) Crafting a Shared Framework for Systemic Change Research in Education.

9

Human Research and Complexity Theory

JAMES HORN
Monmouth University

Introduction

In a paper presented in 1940, Gregory Bateson described the divergent and convergent dance, or 'the whole fluctuating business', that accompanies the historical advance of science:

> [Y]ou see both elements of the alternating process—first the loose thinking and the building up of a structure on unsound foundations and then the correction to stricter thinking and the substitution of a new underpinning beneath the already constructed mass. And that, I believe, is a pretty fair picture of how science advances ... . Sometimes, as in physics, we find centuries between the first building of the edifice and the later correction of the foundations—but the process is basically the same (1972, p. 86).

Bateson's long view seems particularly appropriate to keep in mind now during our early enthusiasms for the new sciences of complexity that are finding entry points to thinking and research questions across many disciplines that range from anthropology (Lansing, 2003) to zoology (Parrish & Edelstein-Keshnet, 1999).

In 1994, in the early heyday of thinking 'loosely' about complexity, a colleague and I attended a conference sponsored by the Society for Chaos Theory in Psychology and Life Sciences. We were there to present a paper (Horn & Wilburn, 1994) that aimed to provide links from the philosophical and empirical literature on chaos and complexity to the field of education. Immodestly, perhaps, we wanted to help clear a path to an understanding of schools as complex organizations that could be re-conceptualized by using the emerging principles of self-organizing and adaptive systems (Maturana & Varela, 1987; Waldrop, 1992). Even though our own experiences told us that schools most often are externally controlled and not controlled from within, we believed that an understanding and acceptance of the new sciences could change all that. Our own experiences told us, too, that transformative learning communities could emerge, grow, and sustain themselves as a result of the interactions of constituents within boundary conditions, or parameters, which enable those interactions to develop and flourish. We knew, too, that those interactions could, in recursive fashion, strengthen those boundary conditions, thus sustaining the interactions that give further direction to these dynamic learning communities. We thought we were, in fact, ready to lead the evolution of schooling.

That non-blushing optimism was based, in part, on the emancipatory notions we had extrapolated from a body of work (Maturana, 1980; Ulrich & Probst, 1984; Kelso, 1990) that characterized social phenomena as too complex to be sustained healthily by pre-established goals and external controls far removed from the local-ized contexts of schools. The bubbling up of order and freedom derived from local interactions seemed to present the potential realization of a Deweyan agenda begun a hundred years prior. We were a bit surprised, then, to encounter very few papers at the conference that seemed to share our excitement for the democratizing potential that self-organizing, adaptive systems seemed to herald. Instead, the buzz at the conference centred on the search for algorithms that could provide testable models for anticipating the unpredictable or for simulating the indescribable. In short, the search was on to capture chaos and simplify complexity. These efforts were, however, brought back to earth by Rapp's (1994) somewhat dispirited report at the conference on the application of the Grassberger-Procaccia algorithm in an unsuccessful search for a predictable chaos in the human central nervous system as measured by EEG data. Quite abruptly, there emerged the realization that the search would have to continue for a mathematics that could render the chaotic manageable and the complex simple. It would not be found in any algorithm available at that time.

My partner and I did present our paper, which was completely lacking in computational gyrations and breathy suppositions on how logistical equations might advance the study of education. And even though we may have helped to metaphorize the concepts of the complexity sciences to the study of education, our presentation fell short of providing empirically derived examples that could link the new sciences with our own field of study. We were not, however, alone in this regard. Nor were we alone in our impatient sense to move on beyond the metaphorical stage of 'thinking loosely'. The goal of 'stricter thinking' would come to preoccupy most of us there who believed that we were onto something either new or profoundly forgotten, and there was a worrisome sense that the longer we had to wait for complexity theory to advance beyond the metaphorical stage, the greater the likelihood would be for these ideas to become (for the time being, at least) another 'fad *de jour*' destined for the dustbin of scientific oddities. This was a fate that seemed undeserving for a set of propositions that, not even fully developed, had already begun to deepen perspectives on understanding, if not predicting, phenomena in the physical, biological, social, and linguistic worlds.

Impatience to get beyond the 'loose thinking' stage, however, presents its own dangers. Scientific or philosophic gestalts do not occur overnight, and even though complexity carried on a tradition that began with Vico, it was not Vico, but Descartes, who inspired the scientific enlightenment based on the principles of reductionism that guided its development until today. In designing philosophical or empirical studies inside the new complexity box, there could easily develop the temptation to limit research questions to that which could be answered with what we presently know (or don't know) of complexity, thus sustaining our current level of metaphorical understanding and moving us no closer to rendering 'general laws of pattern formation' (Waldrop, 1992) regarding interactive, open systems—systems that are not self-contained but that take in and dissipate energy through interactions. A second danger resides in attempts to resolve ambiguities, or to simplify complexities, through the use of methodologies and methods that may be rigorous, yet reductive—or comprehensively abstract, though experientially removed from the phenomena to be understood (as in C. Wright Mills's (1959) criticism of the 'abstracted empiricism' of his day). Nor is Cilliers (1998) alone in warning that 'the obsession to find *one* essential truth blinds us to the relational nature of complexity, and especially to the continuous shifting of those relationships' (p. 112, emphasis added). Thus the defining of complexity itself carries with it the dangers just noted. Even so, that seems to be an important place to begin if we are going to move beyond Bateson's loose thinking stage and toward a clearer delineation of an expanded boundary of science that may, in fact, represent a reclamation of a wider world that has historically been out of bounds for scientific sense-making.

What Complexity Is

Complexity focuses on emergent behaviours that result from interactions within and among self-organizing and adaptive systems (Barlow & Waldrop, 1994; Richardson, 2005). The goal of the complexity sciences is to comprehend and explain general laws of pattern formation (Waldrop, 1992) that signify transitions within autonomous, open systems. Because complexity is concerned with pattern *formation*, the focus of research is on transformations or phase transitions that provide the markers for growth, change, or learning. For educational researchers, the study of learning communities as self-organizing systems offers an opportunity to understand the conditions that are in place when phase transitions occur. This, of course, does not allow us to predict the exact timing or consequences of particular transformations, but it does give us good clues about the appropriate parameters for the likelihood for subsequent phase transitions. Kelso (1990) points out 'the reason why phase transitions are crucial is because qualitative change allows a clear distinction of one behavioral pattern from another, thereby enabling one to identify the order parameters or collective variables for different patterns' (p. 249).

The sciences of complexity are concerned with understanding emergent behaviours and behavioural pattern formations that result from interactions of system agents. A system in which complexity operates is an entity whose operations are determined by agent interactions as 'structure-determined' systems (see Maturana & Varela, 1998, pp. 95–99) within boundaries that make the system identifiable from its background. These boundaries or parameters remain stable for as long as the system maintains itself as viable within the larger medium, or domain, that it helps to sustain through interactions with other systems that, too, are self-produced, yet adaptive within the larger medium. Thus, the study of complexity is bounded by the capacity of self-sustaining systems to interact and adapt autonomously within the self-defining boundaries that sustain the agent intra-actions and inter-actions (I-actions) (Horn & Wilburn, 2005).

A complex system's capacity to be self-organizing does not, however, guarantee that it operates as such. Historically, the management of social organizations of all types has been maintained by control measures that work to block the capacity of systems to operate autonomously. We may look to any number of social systems to see the not so invisible hands of control parameters that are institutionalized for the primary purpose of assuring externally imposed order that would otherwise be maintained by internally occurring I-actions of system agents. In many cases, these 'enforced mechanisms' (Maturana & Varela, 1998, p. 199) create unhealthy systems that regularly exhibit the pathologies of impaired systems.

In their discussion of how biological systems and social systems differ, Maturana and Varela (1998) point out that the organism or biological system is sustained by the contributions of its agents whose unrestrained expressions are held in check for the good of the organism. The aggressive policing by the human immune system provides an example of how our own personal organism works to maintain equilibrium, and thus our physical wellbeing. In essence, the restraints on sub-systems within organisms assure the organism's overall wellbeing. There are important distinctions in what constitutes healthy functions within biological and social systems, respectively. As Maturana and Varela (1998) have pointed out, the components of *organisms* exist for the continued maintenance and adaptation of the organism, and each component's autonomy is regulated and sometimes sacrificed toward that end. Human social systems, however, whether they are kindergarten classrooms or adult study groups or corporations, remain viable and capable of growth and change through the continued capacity of interacting members to experience autonomous growth and change: 'The organism restricts the individual creativity of its component unities, as these unities exist for that organism. The human social system amplifies the individual creativity of its components, as that system exists for these components' (Maturana & Varela, 1998, p. 199).

In healthy human social systems that operate to provide for the expression and exploration of its individual agents, agents' I-actions, in turn, sustain the boundary conditions that assure the continued self-production of individual paths. These varied and complex paths occur within the supportive limitations that constitute the organizational boundary of a system that simultaneously is sustained by the I-actions that the organization confers. Where the autonomy of agents is sacrificed for organizational needs, however, we see social systems understood and organized more as organic systems, rather than as the languaging social systems that are grown from the communicative I-actions in order to sustain each individual agent. To disregard these distinctions between organic and social systems confuses, and thus confounds, the self-organizing capacities of either type of system, whether biological or social:

> Organisms and human social systems, therefore, are opposite cases in a series of metasystems formed by the aggregation of cellular systems of any order. Among them we have ... those human communities which, because they embody enforced mechanisms of stabilization in all the behavioral dimensions of its members, constitute impaired human social systems: they have lost their vigor and have depersonalized their agents; they have become more like an organism, as in the case of Sparta (Maturana & Varela, 1998, p. 199).

The historical misappropriation of scientific principles across domains of analysis has also occurred in the way that social systems are viewed in terms of energy and information production. Complexity sciences are only now offering a needed corrective in the way that thermodynamic laws have come to be understood in relation to living systems. Laws of thermodynamics tell us that energy can neither be created nor destroyed, and, furthermore, that the physical universe is moving inexorably toward an entropic state in which all energy will become equally dispersed. As Gell-Mann (1994) recounts the old physics joke, the First Law reminds us that we can never win, and the Second reinforces the fact that we cannot even hope to break even (pp. 217–218). The 19th century discoveries by Clausius, Maxwell, and Boltzmann regarding energy dynamics in physical systems, then, were incorporated in how the new social sciences, and the social engineering they inspired, would develop. As Steven Jay Gould and others have noted, the social sciences came to suffer a case of 'physics envy' that continues to hang on even today. The upshot of this attempted appropriation of mechanical laws came to be demonstrated in the way that social systems were viewed by 20th century social science as dependent upon continuing energy injections and/or control measures to head off the possibility of either, 1) a running down of the system to where the amount of usable energy is minimized (maximum entropy), or, 2) runaway social engines that would lead to explosions into social anarchy (maximum entropy), thus achieving the same entropic end, just achieved differently. In either case, the social system is viewed as dependent upon external sources of energy and a functioning governor (an interesting metaphor to describe a mechanical device) to head off the same inevitable entropic destiny that Clausius laid out in the late 19th century. The developments, I think, of the scientific management movement in education in the early 20th century were clearly aimed at imposing order upon a system that would otherwise, it was thought, lose energy and eventually disintegrate without such imposition.

Historically, these efforts have most often ignored or rejected the possibility that social systems have the capacity to self-organize, adapt, and undergo transitions that lead to sustained, or even higher, levels of effectiveness and efficiency. Essentially, social institutions have been treated as closed (self-contained) systems, rather than the permeable, dissipative open systems that they would be if allowed. The label of 'self-contained classroom' is no misnomer, for that is the implicit conception in the historical management of them as closed systems in need of endless energy injections and control measures. Thus, we have become the inheritors of institutionalized social systems governed by the application of scientific principles that are more applicable to, let's say, steam engines than to the interactive social systems that depend upon the continuing I-actions of their constituent members, or agents, for the production of informational energies for maintenance and growth. The counterproductive results of such treatments most often bring more draconian systems of motivation and control, a phenomenon pithily noted by Axelrod and Cohen (1999): 'it is ironic that in our efforts to stabilize systems against ... failures, we often transform them into more tightly coupled systems that redistribute stress' (p. 108). It would seem that even negative energy cannot be destroyed.

Such stabilization efforts occur through the use of corrective (negative) feedback mechanisms that seek to maintain systems or to increase performance toward a pre-defined goal. Interactive and open social systems, however, depend upon a mix of negative and positive (amplifying) feedback that occur as a result of I-actions of the agents that comprise the system in the light of environmental contexts. These two types of feedback constitute, in fact, the centrifugal and centripetal forces that intermittently move systems toward expansion and contraction, depending, again, on larger environmental circumstances. It is, in fact, this relative balance of feedback mechanisms that shapes the spiralling boundary of systems marked by stability and growth. And just as drought or flood does not determine the size of particular tree rings, there would be none to study if the tree's metabolism did not remain consistent with environing conditions. In short, complex, adaptive systems are self-organizing, or structure-determined systems, but they remain so only to the extent that they are capable of environmental adjustments that are consistent with environmental parameters.

Complexity theory introduces an orientation that allows consideration of social systems in terms of both the information and communication exchanges that make social systems distinct from their biological foundations, as what Maturana and Varela (1998) call 'third order unities' (p. 191). In significant ways, complexity signals the meeting up once again of two roads that diverged in the late 1940s, when cybernetics split into two research programmes, one destined to create information theory (concerned with the communicative aspect of signal transfer) and the other communication theory (concerned with the communicative aspect of meaning derived from those signals). As Conway and Siegelman (2004) point out in their biography of Norbert Wiener, the inventor of cybernetics, information theory focused on the effective transmission of signals and would become the more dominant strand of research, leading, of course, to the development of computer science and artificial intelligence. The other road, communication theory, would travel the margins of scientific respectability, trying to make sense of the meanings and significance of the cultural messages that link humans together in social systems constituted by language. Followers of this strand of research included Margaret Mead, Bateson, Warren McCulloch, and Walter Pitts, all of whom influenced the young Humberto Maturana, whose research on the neurophysiology of frogs would come to have a lasting impact on the way humans see the world. From this early work Maturana and Varela would develop the theory of autopoiesis, or self-production, which would represent a breakthrough in the understanding of emergence as the mechanism enabling complex systems to exhibit self-organization and autonomy. While complexity, then, does not attempt to re-write the laws of thermodynamics, the focus is shifted from the battle against entropy to the production of negentropy as the continuing internally-generative process that characterizes self-organizing, adaptive systems as long as they remain living systems. What the study of complex systems strongly suggests is that, given the proper environmental conditions, human systems quite naturally produce repertoires of I-actions that are self-sustaining despite, in fact, elaborate interventions to accomplish the same end by artificial means.

Understanding how to allow and sustain self-organizing social systems will require an expansion of the current scientific repertoire used in schools to include 'a science of qualities that is not an alternative to, but complements and extends, the science of quantities' (Goodwin, 1994, p. 198). Such an expansion will allow science to acknowledge configurations of phenomena that have heretofore remained either beyond the purview of acceptable science or else have become abstracted in ways that allowed for empirical investigation only within the confines of existing methodologies based on traditional measurements. In so doing, however, the system that began as the focus of understanding inevitably becomes transformed from its naturalistic manifestation into an imposed design that can be rendered by the science used to study it. In order to understand schools and classrooms as the complex environments that they are capable of becoming, we must first allow them to be so. This will require new methodologies that acknowledge the necessity of the emergent and enduring relational spaces that characterize and enable learning within systems whose I-actions produce those systems; and it will require methodologies that do not reduce the phenomena studied to fit within the prevailing research repertoires or management goals.

Toward a Qualitative Approach to a Science of Qualities

Educational research, both qualitative and quantitative, continues to undergo methodological shifts that are influenced from a number of directions, some of which are in reaction to the perceived hegemony of a positivist scientific tradition that has been the major influence on the organization and study of schooling. The tenacity of the scientific management movement in education has, in fact, contributed to a rejection of science by some educational theorists, so much so that we sometimes find ourselves as markedly negative toward science at the beginning of the 21st century as we were pro-scientific at the beginning of the 20th. The resulting disdain for much of empirical science has led to a postmodern elevation of language that creates a hazardous bifurcation between language and behaviour, thereby risking the loss of the material connection that links the linguistic domain to that which it is intended to describe. Without an appreciation of and an interest in the co-originating process of knowing *and* doing that unifies the cognitive and the behavioural, or the informational and the communicative, the research goals of understanding and interpretation are deprived of the full range of empirical research possibilities that include both the concrete event and the sense making of those events that characterizes the embodied nature of human acts, scientific or otherwise.

Complexity holds out the potential to re-establish the lost link to science that resulted from a denunciation of positivist assumptions. With the lens of complexity, we are able to see whole systems as irreducible examples of knowledge in action, thus establishing a clear link between behaving and thinking, or between 'data of sense and data of consciousness' (Lonergan, 1958). It is, after all is said and done, the evidence of behaviour coordination, or shared meaning, that allows us to observe that information expression has, indeed, resulted in communication. What we may aspire to, then, in terms of science is a hermeneutic social science whose intent is not social engineering but, rather, description and explanation of the emergence, sustenance, and transitioning of healthy social systems defined in terms of information and communication. As such, the intent of research shifts from control within a set of reified parameters toward the exploration of our own limits within the consensual domains that we, as autonomous social actors, create and sustain in ways that assure our continued autonomy. So, while the positivist insistence on an 'objective' view from nowhere may assuredly be denounced as a simplistic assumption by those who do not acknowledge their own complicity in the act of thinking and communicating, complexity acknowledges the need for a systematic and principled empirical approach to investigating behaviour and thought, while recognizing that every investigation includes an investigator. The recognition of 'objectivity in parenthesis' (Maturana, 1988) has profound implications for the ways that humans may come to view the world within which they operate and make knowledge claims.

From Simplicity to Complexity

From wide-ranging studies of dynamical systems, a new dialogue has begun to examine what constitutes evolution, learning, organizations, and life itself. It is an interdisciplinary dialogue that focuses on the self-organization of complex adaptive systems, from the cellular to the social level. While being mapped within various scientific disciplines, these developments (Wolfram, 2002) offer scientific alternatives to the predominantly reductionist assumptions that have informed science to date. Table 1 presents a summary of Morin's thirteen points (as cited in Redner, 1994, p. 375) in distinguishing the 'paradigm of complexity' from 'the paradigm of simplicity'.

The further development of complexity theory will offer a paradigmatic lens through which a deeper and more encompassing view of the study of social learning systems by educational researchers becomes possible. Complexity focuses necessarily on 'coarse-grained' (Gell-Mann, 1994, pp. 29–30) descriptions and explanations of systems whose self-organizing I-actions define them as too complex to be rendered by the standard repertoire of educational research tools, unless the complexity of the phenomena is abstracted and reduced to a workable level of statistical generalization. Complexity does not replace statistical manipulations to control for variables within phenomena that would otherwise make their examination impossible, and nor does it intend to hinder the prediction of outcomes within certain abstracted elements of a system; rather, complexity offers a theoretical framework for acknowledging and helping to sustain the self-organizing capacity of fully embodied systems that are only realized through the I-actions of agents within the boundary that those activities help to generate and sustain. Out of necessity, a certain amount of uncertainty must be sustained. As Axelrod and Cohen (1999) have put it, 'harnessing complexity involves acting sensibly without fully knowing how the world works' (p. 45).

Researching the 'Edge of Chaos'

In the absence of external controls, conditions may be established that greatly enhance the likelihood for the emergence of communicative behaviours that are

Paradigm of Simplicity	Paradigm of Complexity
Adheres to the principle of universality and treats all individual and local phenomena as residual and contingent	Without denying universality, also adopts the complementary principle that the individual and the local are intelligible in themselves
Rejects temporal irreversibility and, in general, the historical	Seeks to bring irreversibility into physics, biology and systems theory so as to give events in these fields a temporal direction
Seeks to reduce wholes to their simple constituents	Integrates elements into their ensembles or complexes
Seeks principles of order within complexes	Looks for self-organization among elements of complexity
Employs linear causality	Searches for principles of causal interrelations
Assumes total determinism and thus excludes chance	Allows for chance in its 'dialogic' of the process order-disorder-interaction-organization
Isolates the object from its environment or context	Places the object back into interaction with its environment or context
Separates subject from object, observer from observed	Puts the observer back into the experimental situation and relocates human subjects into their normal environments
Ultimately eliminates the subject from objective scientific knowledge	Provides for a scientific theory of the subject
Eliminates being and existence through formalization	Pursues a view of self-organization and self-production which enables being and existence to be acknowledged scientifically
Does not recognize autonomy	Considers autonomy in terms of self-organization and self-production
Treats contradiction as error and logic as absolute	Sees logic as limited, and regards contradictions and paradoxes ... as indices of a deeper reality
Thinks mono-logically	Thinks dialogically and so relates contrary concepts in a complementary manner

Table 1: Scientific orientations of simplicity and complexity

self-organizing and adaptive. The understanding of the dynamics involved in such autonomous systems has been enhanced greatly by the use of powerful computers that can simulate variations in control parameters. A growing number of computer programmes, which simulate a wide range of self-organizing behaviours, from birds flocking to the dynamics of ant colonies, can now be downloaded from the Internet. Developed by the Epistemology and Learning Group at MIT's Media Lab, StarLogo (2005) is a good example that can be used as a teaching tool to understand the complexities of those systems that operate in the absence of central control mechanisms.

The optimal parameter values for growth and reproduction within autonomous systems were first discovered by Chris Langton (Waldrop, 1992, pp. 225–34). In experimenting with conditions for interactions of agents within the virtual world of cellular automata, Langton found, through a glitch in his computer programme that occurred as he adjusted interaction rules, what he came to term the 'lambda parameter'. When interactions were absent, the cellular automata exhibited zero growth. When interactions were sparse, some self-organization was apparent, but soon the dots on the computer grid coalesced into static blobs. Interaction levels were not sufficient to sustain the community. When the interactions between agents were extremely numerous, the computer grid became chaotic, with cycles of accelerated growth followed by mass extinctions. But when the parameters for interactions were established at a certain mid-point, the automata exhibited 'coherent structures that propagated, grew, split apart, and recombined in wonderfully complex ways' (p. 226). This was the lambda parameter, the condition for interactions that produced continued growth, transformation and, in the terms of computer science, maximum computation.

What became most interesting to Langton was the repeated tendency for these systems to experience growth, transformation, or phase transitions, and then to reorganize themselves at the same point—at the edge of chaos. As Goodwin (1994) discusses these findings, he points out that Langton's cellular automata do not move to the edge of chaos spontaneously. Goodwin suggests that the organizational relations must be established for a 'maximum dynamic interaction' (p. 184) in order for individual transitions to cascade back and forth through the system, thus producing community as well as individual effects. By doing so, the individual partakes of a community continually enriched by her own individual interactive capacities.

The contours of complexity research aimed at identifying optimum I-action parameters will be clearly distinct from the 'abstracted empiricism' (Mills, 1959) of the social engineering sciences. We know the pitfalls associated with applying assumptions and methodologies from one domain to another: the development of the social sciences through the application of physical science methodologies provides an example not easily forgotten. In attempting to make the human sciences objective, the human became turned into an object. Smith and Thelen (1993) point out this perceived problem in their discussion of the current state of dynamic systems theory:

> [Dynamic systems theory] is being used by researchers and theorists for many different levels of analysis, for behavior ranging from the physiologic to the social, and for describing change over time scales from seconds to years. We see this diversity, however, not as a failing of the approach, but indeed as its real strength ... . [W]e are now alert to the pitfalls of explaining too much by single, overarching organization. It seems to us that the future of [dynamic systems theory] will lie with very general principles of process and change, applicable in many domains, over many levels and time scales, but also allowing the multiple local details to emerge from the necessary empirical work (p. xii).

The translation or extrapolation of these findings into research theory and practice is a compelling possibility, particularly if optimal and adjustable parameters can be established as research aims within self-organizing learning communities where longitudinal, observational, and experimental methods can be applied. Although a daunting prospect, there is a growing body of theory and research that provides some directions to pursue. Thelen (1989) has indicated that there is nothing new in this approach, but that 'what may be new, however, is the systematic linking of these practices to synergetic principles'. She outlines these linkages as follows:

1. The focus is on process not just outcome measures.
2. No agent or subsystem has ontological priority.
3. Task and context, not instructions, assemble behavior.
4. Control parameters are not stationary. (The state space itself evolves through time.) (p. 105).

Other clues as to what constitutes the adjustable boundary conditions for sustained growth within organizations come from organizational theory (Goldstein, 1994, 2005; Stacey, 1996). Stacey, for instance, points out that 'complex adaptive systems are driven by three control parameters: the rate of information flow through the system, the richness of connectivity between agents in the system, and the level of diversity within and between the schemas of the agents' (1996, p. 99). From these beginnings, then, the vastness of the unexplored territory seems limitless. For the time being, perhaps, we should post what Bateson (1972) would call a proper sign for all who would move forward with the humane science agenda, 'such that these terms will forever stand, not as fences hiding the unknown from future investigators, but rather as signposts which read: "UNEXPLORED BEYOND THIS POINT"' (pp. 86–87).

Ethics and Complexity Research

In conceiving a research process that is both self-organizing and reflexive, it is necessary to recognize the ontological parity that characterizes the 'observer community' (Varela, 1979, 1999) comprised of researchers and research participants. Cilliers (2005) has noted that the sheer scope of the variables within complex systems makes modelling them a tricky, if not impossible, task. Such models would have to be as complex as the original, since the distributed, nonlinear features of complex systems do not allow for the compression of data. This creates the need to observe complex human systems as comprised of fully embodied interactive agents, which then highlights the importance of viewing the researching of such systems from an ethical perspective. It will be the interactive and reflexive research practice based upon this recognition that instantiates the ethical ideal, which would yield a research practice in which humans are not subjected to research but, rather, are acknowledged as participants engaged in the ongoing elaboration of the communicative behaviours that include researchers as well.

Because of the limitations imposed by parenthetical objectivity, social interactions reside within a system such that an explanation on an operational level (*Erklärung*) is not possible (Varela, 1979). The level, then, of explaining and understanding (*Verstehung*) that is available to researchers through description and interpretation is symbolic rather than operational. Researchers of human social systems are left with the possibility of interpreting descriptions of descriptions or describing interpretations of interpretations. This mode of explanation is used not only in understanding the vagaries that characterize communicative behaviours; symbolic explanations are used also in understanding biological phenomena (Varela, 1979) that regularly display high degrees of complexity and change. Thus, the interpretations we derive from lived experiences are communicated through symbols chosen to characterize a process that would otherwise remain unknown to us. This is accomplished through an examination of interactions among participants whose lived experiences remain beyond the scrutiny of an observer whose ontological bearing is grounded in his biological fact. Here, this observer readily concedes the difficulty posed in deriving direct causal explanations or predictive proof for complex phenomena within which he is embedded—and the folly of attempting to derive a true understanding if he were otherwise.

How then do such possibilities and pronouncements fit with the reality of schools and the needs of teachers and students? I would argue first that every teacher can and should understand the underlying big picture of the new sciences, for with that understanding necessarily comes the realization that she has been placed in charge of a sensitive learning ecology whose directions can be altered by small changes in the boundary conditions and interaction patterns of the classroom. In the most tangible sense, complexity places the teacher and the students at the locus of control in terms of classroom learning, while at the same time acknowledging the larger institutional systems with which classrooms and individual schools are linked. While political factors may attempt to turn science into a means of control by insisting on experimental protocols that would eliminate much of what has previously passed as human research, the sustainability of such schemes should be clear to anyone who has not been blinded by the reflection of his own search beam. Complexity offers the insight that the study of human systems is best done where it is happening, with students and teachers whose I-actions form the learning patterns that can be shifted without major infusions of motivational energy or continuing intrusions of control measures, either of which stands in the way of growing humans who aspire to freedom and autonomy in the absence of external motivators or control measures.

References

Axelrod, R. & Cohen, M. (2000) *Harnessing Complexity: Organizational implications of a scientific frontier* (New York, Free Press).

Barlow, C. & Waldrop, M. (1994) Worldview Extensions of Complexity Theory, in C. Barlow, (ed.), *Evolution Extended: Biological debates on the meaning of life* (Cambridge, MA, MIT Press).

Bateson, G. (1972) *Steps to an Ecology of Mind* (New York, Ballantine Books).

Gell-Mann, M. (1994) *The Quark and the Jaguar: Adventures in the simple and the complex* (New York, W. H. Freeman).

Cilliers, P. (1998) *Complexity and Postmodernism: Understanding complex systems* (New York, Routledge).

Cilliers, P. (2005) Knowing Complex Systems, in: K. Richardson (ed.), *Managing the Complex Volume One: Philosophy, theory and application* (Greenwich, CT, Information Age Publishers).

Conway, F. & Siegelman, J. (2004) *Dark Hero Of The Information Age: In search of Norbert Wiener, the father of cybernetics* (New York, Basic Books).

Goldstein, J. A. (1994) *The Unshackled Organization: Facing the challenge of unpredictability through spontaneous reorganization* (University Park, IL, Productiviy Press, Inc.).

Goldstein, J. A. (2005) Emergence, Creative Process, and Self-transcending Constructions, in: K. Richardson (ed.), *Managing the Complex Volume One: Philosophy, theory and application* (Greenwich, CT, Information Age Publishers).

Goodwin, B. (1994) *How the Leopard Changed its Spots: The evolution of complexity* (New York, Charles Scribner's Sons).

Horn, J. & Wilburn, D. (1994) Toward an Emergent Educational Design: A complex systems approach. Paper presented at the Society for Chaos Theory in Psychology and the Life Sciences Fourth Annual Conference, The Johns Hopkins University, Baltimore, Maryland, June 24–27, 1994.

Horn, J. & Wilburn, D. (2005) The Embodiment of Learning, *Educational Philosophy and Theory*, 37:5, pp. 745–760.

Kelso, J. (1990) Phase Transitions: Foundations of behavior, in: H. Haken & M. Stadler (eds), *Synergetics of Cognition* (Berlin, Springer-Verlag).

Lansing, J. (2003) Complex Adaptive Systems, *Annual Review of Anthropology*, 32, pp. 183–204.

Lonergan, B. (1958) *Insight: A study of human understanding* (New York, Philosophical Library).

Maturana, H. (1980) Man and Society, in: F. Benseler & W. Koch (eds), *Autopoiesis, Communication and Society: The theory of autopoietic systems in the social sciences* (Frankfurt, Campus Verlag).

Maturana, H. (1988) *Ontology of Observing: The biological foundations of self consciousness and the physical domain of existence*, Retrieved November 12, 2005 from http://www.inteco.cl/biology/ontology/

Maturana, H. & Varela, F. (1980) *Autopoiesis and Cognition: The realization of the living* (Dordrecht, Riedel).

Maturana, H. & Varela, F. (1987) *The Tree of Knowledge: The biological roots of human understanding* (Boston, Shambhala Publications).

Maturana, H. & Varela, F. (1998) *The Tree of Knowledge: The biological roots of human understanding* (Revised Edition) (Boston, Shambhala Publications).

Mills, C. W. (1959) *The Sociological Imagination* (New York, Oxford University Press).

Parrish, J. & Edelstein-Keshnet, L. (1999) Complexity, Pattern, and Evolutionary Trade-offs in Animal Aggregation, *Science*, 284, pp. 99–101.

Rapp, P. (1994). Is there Evidence for Chaos in the Human Central Nervous System? Paper presented at the Society for Chaos Theory in Psychology and the Life Sciences Fourth Annual Conference, The Johns Hopkins University, Baltimore, Maryland, June 24–27, 1994.

Redner, H. (1994) *A New Science of Representation: Towards an integrated theory of representation in science, politics and art* (Boulder, CO, Westview Press).

Richardson, K., (ed.) (2005) *Managing the Complex Volume One: Philosophy, theory and application* (Greenwich, CT, Information Age Publishers).

Smith, L. & Thelen, E. (1993) *A Dynamic Systems Approach to Development: Applications* (Cambridge, MA, MIT Press).

Stacey, R. (1996) *Complexity and Creativity in Organizations* (San Francisco, Berrett Koehler).

Thelen, E. (1989) Self-organization in Developmental Processes: Can systems approaches work?, in: M. Gunnar & E. Thelen (eds), *Systems and Development: The Minnesota symposia on child psychology, Vol. 22* (Hillsdale, NJ, Lawrence ErlbaumAssociates).

Ulrich, H. & Probst, G. (eds) (1984) *Self-organization and Management of Social Systems: Insights, promises, doubts, and questions* (New York, Springer-Verlag).

Varela, F. (1979) *Principles of Biological Autonomy* (New York, McGraw-Hill).

Varela, F. (1999) *Ethical Know-how: Action, wisdom, and cognition* (Stanford, StanfordUniversity Press).

Waldrop, M. (1992) *Complexity: The emerging science at the edge of order and chaos* (New York, Simon and Schuster).

Wolfram, S. (2002) A New Kind of Science (Champaign, IL, Wolfram Media, Inc.).

10

Complexity and Truth in Educational Research

MIKE RADFORD

Canterbury Christ Church University

Introduction

The problem of objectivity and the truth of propositions in relation to educational situations and events may be contextualised within the current trend (not least in the United Kingdom) towards the demand for 'objective' inspection of schools, notions of 'evidence-based practice and policy', and attempts to control the social development of schools through development plans. Sutherland, quoted in Wilcox & Gray (1996), suggested that:

> Inspectors (of schools) are there to formulate and present a picture of the school as it really is; to judge how well a school is meeting the various demands placed upon it and the needs of its pupils.

Statements in such inspection reports depend for their truth upon how they correspond to that which they seek to represent. This is sought through the systematic gathering of evidence, collectively agreed by the inspection team and consistent within the framework of the inspection process. Observations are neutral and the judgements made by the inspection team, being rooted in these observations, are objectively justifiable. The epistemological assumptions of this social technological view are of course positivist in character. There is an assumption that a school can be objectively observed within a range of observational categories, and that virtually every aspect of educational provision can be reduced to basic units of observational evidence, much of which can be articulated in terms of numerical values. This approach to observing and researching schools is centred on the assumptions that objective research is the avenue to improvement and that through research-generated knowledge we can exercise greater levels of control in and over educational environments.

Although philosophy has witnessed a general retreat from the correspondence theory of truth that is reflected in this social technological approach, the concept of correspondence between propositions and their objects, of a mind-independent reality that is represented in our language, remains a necessary assumption of rational empirical enquiry. The only way in which we can understand our propositions as bearing truth is, at least theoretically, in relationship to that which they represent and which is accessible to us through our experience. There is an assumption that reality is potentially stable and open to division and classification in the ways to which our descriptions and explanations aspire. The perspective that is offered by complexity theory might lead to scepticism in relation to this view. Complexity theory, while accepting the necessity of some kind of theoretical correspondence in relation to truth, draws attention to the assumption of a degree of homogeneity in both the reality that is being described and explained and the propositions that are generated in relation to it. Complexity theory recognizes the virtually infinite number of divisions and classifications to which phenomena, and particularly social phenomena, are potentially subject. Further, it recognizes the dynamic and non-linear nature of interactions among the objects of these classifications and divisions, of a continuously shifting and indeterminate field of study. In the light of this, conceptual analyses that emphasize the importance of recognizing correspondence as the source of truth, and the positivist social technology that may be associated with this, are both undermined.

The first part of the chapter offers an analysis of the argument that truth and correspondence are necessary assumptions of rational inquiry. Without some kind of concept of truth, some kind of regulating idea, rational argumentation, it is suggested, falls into incoherence (Bridges, 1999, p. 597; Pring, 2000a, pp. 252–3). There is a necessary assumption within any form of knowledge discourse that statements require supporting analysis and that there is the possibility of some of them being true, or at least more likely to be true than others. What would be the purpose of rational analysis if not that it somehow brings us towards a 'truer' perspective on the state of affairs under consideration? Truth in this context becomes a kind of regulative principle. We do not need the expectation of a 'monolithic concept' of truth (Bridges, 1999, p. 597), a notion of absolute and potentially attainable certainty, to hold onto the assumption that an understanding of truth has a part to play in our arguments. We do need, however, a theory of truth as regulated by something beyond or exterior to human perception and its propositions, and the theoretical possibility of our statements corresponding with this state of affairs. This, it is argued, is the only possible 'theory of truth', others being reducible either to this position or to arguments centred on subjective interests in which the concept of truth is little more than a rhetorical device.

Complexity theory provides an explanatory framework within which to re-examine the way in which our representations come together in our explanations but may be seen to put pressure on the notion of truth by correspondence. Representation in the sense of 'stands for', assumes a degree of stability and homogeneity in both experience and the representational symbol. Complexity theory challenges this view. Representation, it is argued, is part of a flexible organization of symbols, distributed across experiences, relating to experience and to other representational symbols in non-linear and dynamic ways. Information contained within a representational system consists both in the way in which the system explains that which is represented, and in the nature of the organization itself. Relationships between symbols are weighted and the pattern of weightings might in part be understood in terms of the purposes that the representation serves.

Just as our representational system, the symbols that come together within it and the language within which they are articulated, is complex, so also is experienced social reality. Reality is complex, susceptible to 'infinite classification and divisibility' (Pring, 2000b, p. 51), and 'inherently contingent, ungrounded, diverse, unstable and indeterminate' (Eagleton, 1996, p. vii). As such we may be led to ask how it can act as an anchor in our pursuit of objective truth. If it is limitless in its nature, reality becomes a kind of blank sheet upon which any kind of description and explanation might be possible. Research, rather than focusing on creating stable or coherent sets of descriptions and explanations, becomes more a matter of helping us to survive. If correspondence is undermined in this way, we may be left asking what is left of our concept of truth.

The Primacy of Correspondence

David Bridges (1999) describes five theories of truth: correspondence, coherence, 'what works', consensus, and warranted belief.

The coherence theory of truth suggests that statements about the world are true because they cohere with other statements, that my knowledge of the world hangs together in a coherent bundle of propositions representing beliefs and understandings. My inclination to believe in the truth of particular statements rests on the fact that they fit in with others. This is an important principle of human understanding for teachers: Jerome Bruner writes about the ways in which pupils 'scaffold' their thought and how new concepts, if they are to make sense, must be incorporated into that scaffolding (David, 1999, p. 4). In an interconnecting bundle of mutually dependent propositions, however, there must be at least one proposition that is true by virtue of criteria other than coherence, and that acts as guarantor for all the rest (Bridges, 1999, p. 604). The proponent of the coherentist position might argue that we do not need to go beyond the fact that propositions cohere and that truth does not belong to each proposition but to the bundle as a whole. This begs the question why statements should cohere in the first place. The fact that there is coherence does not tell us why. If coherence is to be identified in our understanding we can justifiably ask whence this coherence arises.

There are two possibilities. The first is that the coherence of sets of beliefs represents some kind of coherence that is intrinsic to the reality to which they are related by correspondence. The orderliness in the relationships among my statements corresponds to an orderliness in the world. A second possibility is that this coherence is a product of our psychology, an orderliness that we impose on diverse experiences by virtue of our 'self-organizing minds'. Why the mind 'self organizes' in this way might be explained by reference to its own complex needs and interests, and how it has evolved to meet them. Coherence can be explained in terms of 'what works' for me, given the complex combination of my own needs and the environment in which I find myself. This coherence does not represent the pattern of interaction between my needs and the environment, but is explained by them.

A similar argument may be advanced in relation to consensus as a theory of truth. I am more likely to hold a statement to be true if everybody around me believes it to be so, but this begs the question why consensus arose in the first place. It may be that consensus about the truth of statements is explained by the fact that these statements represent and correspond to reality by virtue of commonality in experience. I do not believe that *x* state of affairs is true because everybody else does, but the fact of such agreement is an indicator to me that *x* state of affairs does in fact correspond to what is externally the case. Alternatively, it may be that there is consensus in belief about the truth of *x* because such a belief has evolved to suit socially shared needs and interests. Thus, as with coherence, consensus can offer an explanation, but not a theory of truth. Rather, it rests either on an idea of correspondence that is identified through consensus, or on a pragmatic notion of 'what works' given the social circumstances of our understandings (Pring, 2000b, p. 74).

The fifth theory of truth is what Bridges refers to as warranted belief: that a statement can be shown to be true if it 'satisfies the relevant tests for the truth of propositions of its kind' (1999, p. 607). It is this theory of truth that comes under attack from Lyotard when he refers to rational inquiry as 'self-legitimating' (1996, p. 482). Lyotard's critique attacks the circularity in the following: a statement is held to be true by virtue of the process of legitimation, but the process of legitimation is the process of identifying true statements. Lyotard argues that the legitimation of statements rests on a more fundamental interest in how such statements work in relation to the power of the social group that controls the legitimation process—in other words, on their 'performativity' or pragmatic value in supporting the power relationships represented by knowledge.

Against Lyotard, one might argue that the processes of legitimation, the methodological disciplines, rather than being based in ideological or political interests, actually reveal correspondence between statements and their objects. In Popper's 'evolutionary epistemology' of science, hypotheses are generated to explain human experience of the world. Subsequent formally organized experience is used to challenge those hypotheses, to test them for their survival value, and those found wanting are discarded. In this way our hypotheses 'die in our stead' (Popper, 1979, p. 244). The pursuit of statements that are absolutely true by virtue of their correspondence to reality lies at the heart of this epistemological position. Whether our statements ever actually obtain this absolute truth is another matter. Popper's notion of truth is of something either unattainable or of something that if it were attained would not necessarily be recognized as such (1963, p. 226). Truth is therefore regarded as a regulative principle, with verification a 'dynamic and continuing process' (Bridges, 1999, p. 608).

Thus from five theories we come down to two possibilities. Truth is assigned to statements either on the basis of their correspondence (at least potentially) to some kind of independent reality, or on the basis of their place in the network of subjective human needs—social, ideological, political, practical and individual. Of these two, only those aspiring to the first can argue unequivocally that theirs is a 'theory of truth' (Pring, 2000b, p. 74). Those taking the latter position might argue that it is perfectly legitimate to speak of the truth of a statement, but that this is relative to the particular circumstances of its utterance, that there may be many different truths depending on such circumstances, or that there is no such thing as truth at all, merely a variety of human constructions that exist within a sea of possibilities. Different contexts of need will yield different statements and different forms of knowledge about the world, and what one individual or group hold to be the case will only be so within its arena of interest.

Lyotard's criterion of the 'performativity' of statements ensures that should we choose to ascribe truth to a proposition, this can only be on a local, provisional and temporary basis. This position is similar to that taken up by Guba and Lincoln in their *Fourth Generation Evaluation* (1989), who argue that there is no universal reality, at least not in social research, that stands as a criterion for truth, which statements approximate in terms of correspondence, or by which we can understand truth as a regulative principle. Instead, we construct our sets of descriptions and explanations on the basis of 'human meanings' (ibid., 1989, p. 266), by which they presumably mean what human beings take to be the case within a given context of human interests and actions.

Bridges wants to avoid the 'monolithic' concept of truth that is targeted in the critiques of both Lyotard and Guba and Lincoln, but it may be argued that ultimately a notion of truth must come back to some kind of relationship between statements and the state of affairs to which they refer. Pring argues that even if the criterion for the truth of statements lies in agreement about their 'reasonableness', or is based on 'best judgements', as suggested by the constructivist position of Guba and Lincoln, the implication of this is that 'reality' must be something that is not entirely:

> ... created or constructed or negotiated, but constraining and limiting, something that is independent of us and which shapes the standards of what we can *justifiably* say or think or the conclusions which can be *correctly* drawn from the evidence given (Pring, 2000a, p. 254).

He goes on to argue that the fact that we make the distinctions we do in relation to our perception of the world depends upon there being features of the world that exist independently of us, which in turn makes such distinctions possible. The fact that there is an infinite number of ways in which we could divide and classify the world, Pring continues, does not entail that just any kind of distinction is possible. This is, however, problematic. If the world is indeed amenable to infinite division and classification, then it may be difficult to avoid the conclusion that any kind of distinction is possible. The constraints and limitations that Pring argues are necessary for rational enquiry would imply that reality presents us with boundaries, but in an infinitely divisible and classifiable universe there can be no such boundaries. Complexity theory suggests that in any inquiry, although the possibilities are not limitless, they are nevertheless of such multiplicity, and in some instances involve such precision, that they might just as well be infinite.

Correspondence and the Retreat from Reality

It is debatable as to how far science has ever seen itself as seeking to draw an exact picture of reality. Science, it may be argued, is a pragmatic kind of activity dealing with what can be explained within certain parameters and in the context of certain kinds of inquiry. Given the complexity of the natural world, philosophers of science may be the first to admit to the relative crudity of scientific measurements and their theoretical explanations. One characteristic in relation to the complexity of the natural world is its subtlety with regard to the precision of its quantities, such that there is an inherent inexactitude in our abilities to measure it. As Peirce, quoted in Popper (1979, pp. 212–213), noted,

> ... the most refined comparisons or masses and lengths, ... far surpassing in precision all other measurements, ... fall behind the accuracy of bank accounts; ... the determinations of physical constants are about on a par with an upholsterer's measurements of carpets and curtains.

This observation may relate to Peirce's experimental work on measurement, completed for the US Coastal and Geodetic Survey in the 1880s (Mounce, 1997, p. 3). The problem of accuracy in relation to measurement is compounded by the fact that measurement requires relatively static phenomena. Complexity, on the other hand, assumes that values in relation to variables are in a state of continuous change in relation to other variables and in time. Clearly measurement is a central feature of both social and natural scientific inquiry, but its value is more likely to depend on its temporary usefulness within an inquiry rather than to reside in claims to a permanent relationship between its quantities and that to which it refers (Stroup, in Eve *et al.*, 1997, p. 135).

Another characteristic of the 'real' world is its resistance to exhaustive explanation of any particular natural event while remaining susceptible to almost endless explanation and re-explanation. Hempel, in Brown *et al.* (1981, p. 164), argues that complete explanations of events are never possible:

> ... it might seem ... important and interesting to consider the notion of a complete explanation of some concrete event ... : we might want to regard a particular event explained only if an explanatory account ... (is provided in respect of) ... all its aspects. This notion however is self defeating, for any particular event may be regarded as having infinitely many different aspects of characteristics which cannot all be accounted for by a finite set, however large, of explanatory statements.

For this reason, insofar as certain features of the event being explained, or general theoretical principles of the explanation are assumed and thus omitted from explicit attention, explanations in rational and scientific inquiry are invariably elliptically formulated, and inevitably partial in nature. What governs this partiality? How do we decide the extent and limits of our explanations? Since these are invariably selective, where does this selection end and what makes one selective explanation better than another? One might argue that explanations are constrained by that to which they refer, but in a multiply divisible and classifiable reality why should we not simply select other reference points to justify our particular explanation?

Popper turns the problem around by arguing that the explanations themselves have limitless consequences in terms of that which they explain. His response (1979, p. 299) is to resort to a kind of epistemological pragmatism:

... understanding a theory is something like an infinite task, so that we may well say that a theory is never fully understood ... . [A] full understanding of a theory would mean understanding all of its logical consequences. But these are infinite ... ; there are infinitely many situations of infinite variety to which the theory might be applicable ... , upon which its logical consequences might bear ... . Nobody, neither its creator nor anybody who has tried to grasp it, can have a full understanding of all the possibilities inherent in a theory. The decisive point is that of how well our theories solve our problems, how effectively they lead to error elimination.

But what are the problems that our theories are established to serve and how do we decide what counts as error? Popper's conclusion is to move away from a theory of truth that is dependent upon a correspondence between our representations and reality, to that of truth, mentioned above, as a kind of 'regulative principle' (1979, p. 266). He might, however, be understood to be offering a theory of 'performativity': how well do our theories perform in the context of our problems and in exposing our errors? If so, how far does this retreat from the idea of truth as correspondence extend?

Complexity and Correspondence

The problem that complexity theory brings to the idea of representation and correspondence may be seen at two levels: that of the nature of reality in itself, and that of the nature of our understandings, the representations that we form of that reality. The idea of reality as complex comes from our experience of particular phenomena such as weather systems, fluid dynamics and neurological systems. These phenomena are unstable and resistant to reductive and determinist analysis. Rather, they call for a more holistic approach that emphasizes the interactions between variables within the system as equally if not more significant than the variables themselves.

The Nature of Complexity Theory

Complexity theory has been presented as an empirical theory, discovered in the context of investigation into certain natural phenomena (Byrne, 1998, p. 37). From its emerging identification in natural phenomena some social theorists have argued that, as a matter of empirical fact, it applies equally to the social world (Eve *et al.*, 1997, pp. 7–9). There is a sense, however, that we might see it less as something discovered in the real world and more as a way of conceptualising it. The inspiration for this theory may have arisen in the context of studies, for example, of weather systems, but finding the necessity of looking at these systems in new ways, it may be that we can choose to use the explanatory categories in other contexts. Just as Hempel's scientist simplifies the world by adopting a reductionist methodology, the complexity theorist may simply be choosing to view the world as complex.

Popper (1979) suggested that everything in the universe might be viewed on a continuum between, on the one hand, determinate, reducible and therefore relatively predictable and closed systems, such as clocks, and, on the other, indeterminate, unpredictable, and open systems, such as clouds. Everything, however, at every point on the continuum, even clouds, might be understood in terms of 'clockishness', the amenability to deconstruction down to the molecular level, where they can be explained in terms of a myriad either determinate or indeterminate interactions between elements. On the other hand everything might also contain a degree of 'cloudishness'. Even the most 'clockish' phenomena at the molecular level contain a degree of indeterminacy, an unpredictability that, in clocks themselves, for example, arises from metal fatigue, corrosion, or the environmental conditions within which they are working.

The difference between 'clockish' and 'cloudish' perspectives is that of their usefulness in terms of explanations for the ways in which the universe seems to work—although the question is begged, usefulness for what? As suggested earlier in connection with Popper's evolutionary epistemology, human survival seems to be one criterion—'our hypotheses die in our stead' (ibid., p. 244). The epistemological approaches that arise in the context of Hempel's analysis of explanations suggest that empirical enquiry, if it is to make sense, must be reductive, involving focus on the more 'clocklike' aspects of reality and choosing to some extent which facts to include and which relationships to notice. Since everything in the world is potentially complex, in order to understand we reduce that complexity by a process of selection. But such reduction comes, of course, with some cost. If we accept that the characteristics attended to by complexity theory are those that we experience in the world, then we may come to the conclusion that the reductive analytical approach may be limited and misleading, as well as impracticable. Clouds do not lend themselves to this kind of analysis. The question for educational researchers is whether schools, for example, are more like clocks or clouds.

What are the characteristics to which complexity theory draws our attention? First, within complex systems it is argued that there are too many variables to account fully for any event. Even if we could take account of all internal operational variables or elements within a system, complex systems have 'fuzzy' or open boundaries, and there may well be other influential factors at those boundaries that could not have been foreseen. The decomposition of an event must invariably be selective, and the principles of that selection cannot be determined by the event itself but rather by the agenda that the inquirer brings to it. Second, the information that is contained in the system is as much invested in the relationships among variables as in the variables themselves. The relationships among variables are non-linear: in other words, the impact of any one set of variables upon any other is disproportionate and variable, depending on local and temporary conditions. Relationships among variables are weighted in such a way as interactions among them may excite or inhibit the impact of the interactions. Third, interactions are rarely reducible to an observable set of variables. Many variables might impact on a particular event and particular events may have a rippling effect through the system that in turn involves many changes in neighbouring variables. In this way interactions are dynamic. Finally for the purposes of this chapter, interactions among variables give rise to emergent properties that could not have been identified from analysis prior to the interaction.

In the study of naturally occurring complex phenomena there are regularities, recursive symmetries and attractors that, through a process of modelling, can be detected at the level of the system as a whole. The discovery of these qualities may be useful in trying to simulate the behaviour of naturally occurring complex systems so as to gain some knowledge of how we might predict their development and, within technological systems, control them. In the application of complexity theory to our understanding of social systems we may be less optimistic. We have yet to establish the presence of recursive symmetries or attractors within social systems that could help us to predict their future development. Rather, in the first instance, a recognition of social systems as complex will incline us to step back from current reductionist methodologies and associated aspirations to control. Research, rather than vaunted as prescriptive, may be seen to take on a more passive role, one of description and critical explanation. These issues have been discussed elsewhere (Wrigley, 2004; Radford, 2006). Our interest is philosophical, and the question addressed here is how complexity theory affects our understanding of representation, correspondence and truth in educational research.

Complexity, Representation and Correspondence

If we view the social world as complex, we may find that we need to reconsider our view of truth in terms of how our propositions represent their objects. It was the verifiability of representative statements as corresponding to experienced reality that, for the logical positivists, marked out their meaningfulness (Ayer, 1946, p. 5). This somewhat restrictive definition of meaning is commensurate with a reductionist view of atomistic propositions representing individual and relatively isolated units of experience. At the centre of this conceptualisation is the 'fact'. A fact is an irreducible feature of the real world, independent of our ability to state it. The task of the inquirer is to uncover facts about the world and from these individual irreducible states of affairs, to construct a coherent picture of reality. All arguments can be reduced to basic statements of fact that are either correct or incorrect. This tendency to try to discover facts about, for example, the school, represented in terms of units of observational evidence, which in turn support judgments, persists in the advice to school inspectors (Ofsted, 1995, p. 66). The objective of this atomistic approach is to simplify what is a complex event and to create coherence in our understanding that may not be apparent in the observations of the event as a whole. It is illustrated in the view that by altering particular aspects of a field of educational activity, 'tinkering', as David Hargreaves has put it (1999, p. 246), all other things might adjust accordingly, and 'better' results will prevail.

As a theory of meaning, the view of propositions as reducible to elemental statements of fact has been frequently challenged. For Quine there is no clear relationship between specific statements and the facts that they are supposed to represent. He argues that propositions achieve meaning only in relation to other propositions. The facts of reality, insofar as they impinge on us via experience, might be considered as a boundary condition to rational inquiry: there is 'much latitude of choice as to what statements to re-evaluate (in terms of meaning) in the light of single contrary experiences' (Quine, 1980, p. 65) or facts. The questions for us are those of how much latitude there is in choice and what the conditions of such choices might be. Quine writes about the under-determination of these boundary conditions, i.e. the fact that there will always be more than one theory consistent with any body of empirical data. How do we evaluate these different theories? What might be our criteria for determining the truth of one or the other?

Putnam takes up this analysis in relation to meaning and truth. He introduces qualities that we have associated with complexity theory, identifying a number of features that are important to our understanding of meaning (Putnam, 1988, pp. 8–15). The first is that meaning is holistic. The positivist view of meaning, he argues, seeks to reduce complex descriptive words to an 'epistemologically primitive level', a level of basic and irreducible meaning at which particular symbols can be seen as representing specific facts. At this level meaning is stabilised, homogenous and generally inflexible. In Putnam's view the relationship between symbols and the things to which they refer is elastic and a product of the ensemble. The idea that we seek to justify explanations by reducing them to their basic propositions and setting these individually against experience is mistaken. Rather, they can only be seen as part of a larger body of statements to which they bear a consequential relationship. 'Sentences', argues Putnam, 'meet the test of experience as a "corporate body" and not one by one: hence the term "holism"' (ibid., pp. 8–9). Our expectations in terms of the meanings of particular statements depends upon a whole set of interconnecting beliefs, and as such, 'if language describes experience it does so as a network, not sentence by sentence' (ibid., p. 9). There are no 'epistemologically primitive' symbols, irreducible units of meaning. Meanings are interconnected and definition is continuous, open and expanding.

A second feature of meaning is that it is, in part, a 'normative notion'. Testing a theory, Putnam argues, involves intangibles such as 'estimating simplicity', weighed against the desire for successful prediction, and the preservation of a certain amount of past doctrine. Rational inquiry is a process of 'having the nose for the "right" trade off between such values' (ibid., p. 11). In our definitions we give the benefit of the doubt in relation to the meanings of words and statements. Meanings have an 'open texture', a flexibility in meaning that demands a degree of charity in interpretation. The degree of charity that can be tolerated in any discourse before participants lose each other's meaning and communication breaks down must depend in part on how far participants share the normative judgements that are implicit in the theoretical explanations being offered.

A third feature of meaning is that it is an evolving system. As we interact with the environment the ways in which we conceptualise it change, partly as a result of new experiences and partly as a result of the constructions that emerge from our ability to reflect on and describe the world differently. In this way, meaning might be understood to be a product of the history of the symbol system of which it is a part (Cilliers, 1998, p. 66). Having said that, a study of the history of particular meanings gives no indication as to how they might change in the future. The interrelationships between symbols and the objects to which they refer is non-linear and dynamic—that is, particular symbols may relate more or less closely to many objects, and many symbols may be more or less closely related to particular objects.

Thus, to the extent that language is the means by which we represent the world to ourselves and to others, what Putnam says about meaning and representation bears closely on the qualities that we have identified in complexity theory. Just as we can generate a multiplicity of meaningful sentences, so may be the case with representations. We can represent the world in as many different ways as our imaginations will permit. There are no particular articulations representing a singular homogeneous reality. Meaning and representation are distributed across language. In the process of describing objects or events, hypothetical or otherwise, in different ways, we are representing them differently. These representations form part of an interconnecting network and these interconnections lend weight to particular representations and their relationship with others. They may be seen as 'openly textured'—in other words, they change depending upon the context in which they are reproduced. Not only can many representations be present in a network that is focused on singular situations, events, and objects, but also singular representations can be distributed across many situations, events or objects.

Cilliers suggests that this theory may be described as one of 'distributed representation' and that it substantially undermines the conventionally understood notion of representation (ibid., p. 72). The main characteristics of this theory are, first, taking its cue from Putnam's analysis of meaning, that the relationships among the representations that come together within a concept are non-linear and dynamic. Interaction between representations is creative to the extent that it produces changing or newly emerging conceptualisations that are unpredictable within the given conditions. A second characteristic of distributed representation is that representations contain a degree of openness. Symbols may stand for a range of objects and may be fuzzy at their boundaries. Experience is distributed across a representational network, generating a rich set of explanatory opportunities. A large amount of information is available to support different explanations; the informational network is complex, consisting of many non-linear and dynamic interconnections. New experiences are accommodated even if they barely resemble existing ones, and no existing units are encoded in fixed or fully constrained representations.

Contrary to the specific or non-distributed representation in which abstraction reduces and constrains opportunities for recognition and explanation (a paradigm which may be necessary for some forms of representation, e.g. mathematical), the distributed network allows for imaginative and creative analysis of data. There is an evolution of concepts as the weightings within the network of which they are a part change. In this way, distributed representation may be seen as robust. No specific responsibilities in the 'processing' of experience are tied to specific representations, and as one way of representing an object may weaken or fail, so other parts of the system might take over its functions.

The network that marks this distribution of representations is not arbitrarily organized. There is information contained within the system represented by the weightings, the emphases that are put on particular conceptual units in the processing of information. The task of the researcher in this context is to critically describe and explain the weightings that exist between the interacting components of the system. Clearly in this analysis we have not discarded the notion of correspondence. We could not do so since the idea of an object is logically contained by the notion of representation, but the truth or accuracy of our representations cannot be explained in any way by reference to that correspondence. Representations are working features of a complex system and are determined by their relationships with each other. This is not an anti-representationalist analysis, but one that makes representation and its claims as a basis for the ascription of truth redundant. This is particularly visible in the context of social and educational research. Representation does not work in the way that is expected of it, since there is insufficient stability both within the linguistic system and in the reality itself to create a fixed point of truth.

Conclusions

Many questions follow from this analysis. The first is what has happened to our theory of truth and objectivity. Doubt has been raised with respect to what, I have argued, is the only possible theory of truth—that is, as a result of correspondence between representations and that represented. If, however, we are seen as discarding our theory of objective truth, does this mean that we are inevitably driven to view our understandings as products of our values, of research as the handmaiden to ideology? What is the relationship between research and education? If research constructs a complex and shifting body of understandings set against a complex and shifting social reality then we may see ourselves as rudderless in rough seas.

Although our concept of truth is challenged by complexity, this does not mean that our explanations are unconstrained. We can still distinguish between what we collectively take to be the facts of our social world and what we understand as our values, between explanation and prescriptions, and we can exercise a degree of intellectual discipline that enables us to recognize when the latter are contaminating the former (Hammersley, 2003). We do not have to identify the kinds of research that Tooley and Darby (1998) focused upon for this. Current UK government policies in the form of target setting, league tables, an authoritarian inspection regime, and educational standards identified almost entirely in terms of measurable attainment, have given rise to a whole new field of practical inquiry that provides multiple examples of how research can be contaminated by ideological agenda.

So how does research relate to policy and practice in the context of complexity theory? Complexity theory inclines us to extreme caution in relation to our explanations, and similarly to the degree of control that we have over the complex social technology of schooling. Research cannot deliver the kinds of clear and simplistic lines between evidence and practice or policy that is being demanded. The complexity of the social reality that is being researched and the explanatory frameworks within which new explanations are generated mean that these are invariably fragile and open to layers of interpretation and reinterpretation. The social technology of schooling is like a work of art, rich in interpretive possibilities, and the role of research is to offer tentative identification and critical analysis of these interpretations.

The success of interventions in the interests of one objective or another is unpredictable. There are too many variables to predict clear lines of effect between intervention and result, and it may be just as likely that the technology of schooling is impaired by relatively crude and clumsy interventions.

Metaphors for education are better found in the arts and sport than medicine or engineering. Observation and formal study play important parts in preparation or rehearsal for the activity, but the activity itself cannot be driven by those observations and studies. Furthermore, there are sufficient instances of successful performance where the 'theory' has been thrown aside to keep researchers in a state of continuous evaluation and re-evaluation of their explanations.

References

Ayer, A. J. (1946) *Language, Truth and Logic*, 2nd edn. (London, Victor Gollancz Ltd.).

Bridges, D. (1999) Educational Research: Pursuit of truth or flight into fantasy, *British Educational Research Journal*, 25:5, pp. 597–616.

Brown, S., Fauvel, J. & Finnegan, R. (eds) (1981) *Conceptions of Inquiry* (London, Methuen).

Byrne, D. (1998) *Complexity Theory and the Social Sciences: An introduction* (London, Routledge).

Cilliers, P. (1998) *Complexity and Postmodernism* (London, Routledge).

David, T. (ed.) (1999) *Young Children's Learning* (London, Paul Chapman).

Eve, R. A., Horsfall, S. & Lee, M. A. (eds) (1997) *Chaos, Complexity and Sociology* (London, Sage).

Eagleton, T. (1996) *The Illusions of Post Modernism* (Oxford, Blackwell).

Guba, E. G. & Lincoln, V. S. (1989) *Fourth Generation Evaluation* (London, Sage).

Hammersley, M. (2003) Can and Should Educational Research be Educative?, *Oxford Review of Education*, 29:1, pp. 3–25.

Hargreaves, D. (1999) Revitalising Educational Research: Lessons from the past and proposals for the future, *Cambridge Journal of Education*, 29.2, pp. 239–249.

Lyotard, J. (1996) *The Postmodern Condition: A Report on Knowledge*, G. Bennington & B. Massumi, trans., in: L. Cahoone (ed.), *From Modernism to Postmodernism* (Oxford, Blackwell).

Mounce, H. O. (1997) *The Two Pragmatisms, from Peirce to Rorty* (London, Routledge).

Ofsted (1995) *Guidance on the Inspection of Nursery and Primary Schools* (London, HMSO).

Popper, K. R. (1963) *Conjectures and Refutations* (London, Routledge).

Popper, K. R. (1979) *Objective Knowledge: An evolutionary approach* (Oxford, Oxford University Press).

Pring, R. (2000a) The 'False Dualisms' of Educational Researc, *Journal of Philosophy of Education*, 34:2, pp. 247–260.

Pring, R. (2000b) *Philosophy of Educational Research* (London, Continuum).

Putnam, H. (1988) *Representation and Reality* (Cambridge, MA, MIT Press).

Quine, W. V. (1980) Two Dogmas of Empiricism, in: H. Morick (ed.), *Challenges to Empiricism* (London, Methuen).

Radford, M. A. (2006) Researching Classrooms, Complexity and Chaos, *British Educational Research Journal*, 32:2, pp. 177–190.

Tooley, J. & Darby, D. (1998) *Educational Research: A critique* (London, Ofsted).

Wilcox, B. & Gray, J. (1996) *Inspecting Schools* (Buckingham, Open University Press).

Wrigley, T. (2004) 'School Effectiveness'—the problem of reductionism, *British Educational Research Journal*, 30:2, pp. 227–244.

11

'Knowledge Must Be Contextual': Some possible implications of complexity and dynamic systems theories for educational research

TAMSIN HAGGIS

University of Stirling

It is now widely accepted that qualitative and quantitative research traditions, rather than being seen as opposed to or in competition with each other (Hammersley & Atkinson, 1995; Furlong, 2004) should be used, where appropriate, in some kind of combination (Bryman & Cramer, 1999; Moore *et al.*, 2003). How this combining is to be understood ontologically, and therefore epistemologically, however, is not always clear. After looking briefly at the wide variety of different practices and epistemologies that are conflated in the use of qualitative/quantitative as a binary concept, the chapter will explore this area of 'critical connections' in relation to the analysis of data. Complexity/dynamic systems theory will be explored as offering the basis of a different kind of ontology, which might open up possibilities for creating different types of knowledge (see Byrne, 1997).

How is the Combining of Qualitative/Quantitative Methods to be Understood?

The assumption that qualitative and quantitative traditions can be 'fused' (Bryman & Cramer, 1999), or at least combined meaningfully (for example, in mixed method approaches), raises a number of questions about how such fusion/combining is to be understood, in terms of the meaning and interpretation of different kinds of research results (whether these are based on realist, interpretive or other philosophical orientations). Although some researchers seem to suggest that the relationship between these different approaches to research is relatively unproblematic (e.g. Silverman, 2001[1]); others claim that the different approaches start from contradictory ontological, epistemological (Yanow, 2003) and philosophical (Clark, 2005) bases, resulting in a tendency for theorising to 'remain bifurcated' (Flyvbjerg, 2001, p. 138), and for social scientists to 'tend to generate macrolevel or microlevel explanations' whilst 'ignoring the critical connections' (ibid.).

As a binary category, quantitative/qualitative is intrinsically problematic, referring to a wide range of different methods that can be allied to many different intentions and philosophical orientations. 'Qualitative' can refer, amongst other things, to 'small *n*' studies in psychology (where a case study is in effect a smaller unit of focus for a largely numerical approach), as well as to various types of 'ethnographic study' in sociology or anthropology (where the case study attempts to elucidate a complexity of meanings and interpretations). In terms of method, interview data can be treated quantitatively (Strauss & Corbin, 1998), in the sense that occurrences of words or concepts may be counted, and statistical data collection may include qualitative elements (such as open-ended questions in a questionnaire). Qualitative data which attempts to elucidate meanings can also be analysed in a variety of ways: using semiotic analysis in relation to 'thick descriptions' (Geertz, 1973); analytic induction in relation to increasing numbers of single cases (Smelser & Bates, 2001; Hammersley, 1989); or 'constant comparative analysis' (Strauss & Corbin, 1998), to name but a few different approaches. In addition, qualitative analysis may be underpinned by realist, interpretive or postmodern assumptions and/or intentions, which all produce different kinds of results in relation to bodies of data (Yanow, 2003).

'Critical Connections'?

The different, and possibly contradictory, philosophies/ontologies which can underpin different approaches to research have been discussed by many (e.g. Hammersley, 1989). Rock's distinction between 'phenomenalism' ('the need to faithfully reproduce the social world as it is known by its inhabitants', 1973, p. 17) and 'essentialism' ('the search for the underlying properties of social order', ibid.) suggests one way of understanding what might also be framed as a distinction between a desire for explanation and a desire for understanding (Hollis, 2003). Whilst some researchers appear simply to accept the existence of different research intentions *as* different, (Law & Urry, 2003), others attempt to bridge or reconcile such differences, as, for example, in grounded theory's attempt to create a 'genuine interplay' between qualitative and quantitative approaches (Strauss & Corbin, 1998).

Is the choice in these 'recurrent discussions about the relationship between qualitative and quantitative work' (Hammersley, 2005) only between attempting to reconcile different philosophical orientations and/or purposes, and accepting that they may be irreconcilable? Perhaps, alternatively, there is something to unearth here, in relation to more fundamental and largely invisible cultural orientations. It has been argued, for example, that approaches which declare themselves to be distinct theoretically are often surprisingly similar methodologically, in the sense that many declaredly interpretive types of qualitative research are informed by principles that underpin realist, statistical approaches. Thomas (2002), drawing on Stronach, suggests that 'the search for theory in qualitative research is characterised by an unqualitative approach to qualitative enquiry' (2002, p. 430), and claims that naturalist ethnography takes a 'neo-positivist stance' that represents a 'modernist pursuit of a post-modern goal' (ibid., p. 422). In the same vein, Law and Urry (2003, p. 13) suggest that:

... method, in practice, whatever its theoretical stance, and whatever its particular research tools, tends to a kind of empiricist realism: the assumption that in any given context and given the purposes of the study, there is a single reality.

Prevailing Epistemologies: Similarity Categories, Key Factors, and Deep Structure

The first way in which this empiricist realism is demonstrated is in the assumption that in order to make sense of data it is necessary to create abstractions that *transcend* the complex particularity of the data in specific ways. Although abstraction could, theoretically, be created in relation to the longitudinal history of each sub-unit within the case, the data is instead usually analysed cross-sectionally, on the assumption that comparison between different sub-cases will lead to the identification of key elements or themes that will have some meaning *beyond* each individual sub-history: '(Analytic) concepts may be "observer identified" ... . [T]he analyst ... (draws together) under the aegis of a single type what for members is a diverse and unrelated range of phenomena' (Hammersley & Atkinson, 1995, p. 211).

In the analysis of narratives, for example, the smaller unit within a case is often the individual, with the comparative analysis taking place in relation to what can be seen to be shared across different narratives when these are viewed in relation to each other. In approaches such as grounded theory (Strauss & Corbin, 1998) or phenomenography[2] (Marton *et al.*, 1997), the smaller unit is not necessarily the individual, but the overall intention is the same: to look across different elements of data and find a pattern of similarity which appears to transcend (and therefore, at some kind of deeper level, to unite) these smaller units. The creation of such categories of 'things held in common' (e.g. correlations, 'key factors', typologies, hierarchies), occurring in both quantitative and qualitative types of analysis, is fundamental to research in the social sciences (Llewelyn, 2003).

In creating a similarity pattern the researcher is, in effect, trying to 'see through' difference and variety to 'what lies beneath', in order to try to establish a sense of generative principles (Gomm & Hammersley, 2001). This is arguably a search for a subtle form of 'deep structure'. Whether or not such structure is seen instrumentally[3] or in more realist terms, the implication in both cases is that its identification will lead to the possibility of other manifestations of variety becoming, at least in theory, more predictable. This approach certainly does identify meaningful patterns: patterns which do often relate to other, similar, situations; and which can be successful in terms of facilitating certain kinds of generalisation and prediction (developments in science and technology show how productive an approach this can be.) What is of interest here, however, is the observable reality that possibilities of generalisation and prediction based upon this approach are often limited when attempts are made to use it in relation to human and social phenomena (Gomm & Hammersley, 2001; Byrne, 2005a). One way in which attention has been drawn to these limitations is the recent criticism of educational research (Tooley & Darby, 1998; Hargreaves, 1996). Whether or not such limitations are the 'problems' or 'failings' that this critique suggests is a matter of debate, but the existence of the debate itself points to some problematic areas in relation to epistemology.

Limitations in applying this approach to social phenomena are also suggested by the theoretical shift in fields such as anthropology and sociology towards an interest in difference, particularity, and local, contextual concerns. This shift accommodates a sensitivity to areas which conventional approaches are forced to downplay, such as time, process and connectivity. It has been suggested that approaches based on the prevailing ontology are not able to deal well with 'the fleeting', 'the distributed', 'the multiple' and 'the complex' (Law & Urry, 2003, p. 10). Such concerns have impacted on the development of educational theory to some extent, but these effects do not usually extend to an examination or questioning of the ontological and epistemological assumptions that underpin the practices of educational research, particularly in relation to methods of analysis. Though there have been critiques of these assumptions from postmodern and feminist perspectives, these tend to be based on approaches from areas such as literary theory and the visual arts. Complexity theory, on the other hand, offers a way of thinking about these issues from a perspective closer to the theoretical orientation of social scientists, and appears to open up a different way of thinking about individuals, classes, groups, cultures and societies.

Problems Conceptualising and Researching Difference, Specificity and Context

The theoretical shift in the social sciences towards an interest in understanding 'things in context' implies the need to investigate difference and particularity. This is arguably of particular relevance to educational research, as it attempts to create knowledge that can be used in relation to practices in specific contexts. But practices, and people, in specific contexts are particularly difficult to investigate from the dominant epistemological, and ontological, position.

Many forms of case study research do, of course, make 'people in context' the focus of their investigations. Different types of qualitative study focus on small groups of individuals, attempting to capture the richness of individual experience and to understand how meaning functions and is made. But these studies arguably face a problem when it comes to writing up their results. The dominant ontology requires that it has to be possible to relate some aspect of the particular study to other, similar situations, but researchers at the same time know that they are not easily able to generalise from small samples. The final sections of research reports are often thus forced to present a kind of conceptual 'fudge', which may involve discussion of such things as 'lessons to be drawn', the possibility of 'illuminating' problems (Newton, 2003), or the drawing of conclusions that 'might apply' to other situations (Stein *et al.*, 2004). Although qualitative case study researchers are usually careful to make it clear that they cannot generalise, this caveat itself indicates how such research is still firmly located within particular ontological and epistemological assumptions which privilege the capacity for a particular kind of generalisation. Clearly, some kind of connection between the results of a case study and other potential situations *is* possible, but these connections are subtle, interpretative, and to some degree speculative. They are not always convincing to those who fund educational research, and do not really overcome the problem of how such subtle forms of connection may be understood to relate to the kinds of patterns described by other, more quantitative (e.g. survey-based) forms of investigation.

A different approach to these problems is suggested by forms of analysis such as 'thick description' (Geertz, 1973) and 'analytic induction' (Smelser & Bates, 2001; Roberts, 2002), both of which take the individual case as their starting point, rather than trying to stand back from a range of different cases and decide what they have in common. These approaches, however, although different from each other, both still reflect aspects of the approach discussed above, in that the aim is to gradually identify a principle which will be able to explain, and hopefully to predict, aspects of future, different occurrences of similar cases. Though these approaches are 'bottom up' (starting with concrete, individual cases), rather than 'top down' (looking across a range of individuals or elements within the case), the idea that a given phenomenon can be characterised in this way is based on the assumption that the only way to understand a phenomenon is to try to define central/underpinning tendencies or mechanisms (which ultimately pertain to the 'class' of which the case is assumed to be an instance).

Cross-sectional and comparative analyses clearly do identify important types of pattern and linkage. These forms of analysis can describe what is amenable to description in terms of variables or categories, and what is amenable to some form of counting or measurement. There are other aspects of the data, though, which cannot be described in relation to either of these areas. First, what is *different* between the various transcripts becomes invisible, in the sense that what is similar becomes a category or theme. Second, in order to create a theme, the focus of attention is named, bounded, and *removed* from the complex web of its contexts. Third, the focus on articulating *key aspects* of phenomena means that many aspects of the data are disregarded. Fourth, it is difficult to conceptualise *time* and *process* using this approach. Fifth, this overall approach is underpinned by a desire to infer *causal processes*, despite the fact that these can seldom be measured directly.

In relation to the first two, difference and local context, Guba and Lincoln (1998) discuss how what they call 'context-stripping' removes other variables in the context of the research which could 'greatly alter findings' if they were 'allowed to exert their effects' (p. 197), a point also made by Strathern (1992) in relation to the analysis of anthropological data. In more qualitative types of data analysis, 'context-stripping' not only removes the details of individual lives and histories, but also aspects of the data that could disturb the analyst's creation of apparent regularities (Walsh, 1994, p. 24, in Ashworth & Lucas, 2000, p. 298). The aggregated, unifying category or theme is created at the expense of the acknowledgement of other, less easily-disciplined situational factors which, it could be argued, are nonetheless crucial, either in making what is being examined *functional*, in realist/explanatory terms, or *meaningful*, in more interpretative terms. This is arguably partly the cause of some of the problems that can be experienced when attempts are made to 'apply' a general principle created in this way to a particular case, in the sense that the specifics of the situation can appear to refute, confound, or at least complicate such application.

Part of the problem here seems to be the way that context is conceptualised in relation to the boundaries of the case, and the relationship of this conceptualisation to the contexts of the individual sub-units within the case. If the intention is to 'interpret meanings in context', then comparative analysis of different interview narratives from a particular context appears to make this possible. The meanings that are represented by the interview transcripts, however, in one sense do not so much relate to the group or class which has been defined as the case, but rather to the local contexts inhabited by the different individuals who have been interviewed. In terms of generative forces, it is arguably these individual contexts (which include but also go beyond the membership of the defined group or class) that have created the meanings expressed in the narratives.

A similarity pattern created through comparative analysis of different interview texts (e.g. a 'theme', or group of themes) arguably says more about the group which has been defined as the case than it does about the individuals within the group. Paradoxically, however (given that individual contexts are not considered in the analysis), the theme is far more likely to be presented as information about the individuals ('these adults are all motivated by career prospects' rather than 'this university setting, in the context of current political and cultural agendas, encourages these adults to talk about learning in terms of career prospects'). This kind of theme is often presented as if it points towards some kind of 'deep structure' that might help to explain the diversity of individuals. An example of this is Goodwin's (2002) study of adult learners at university, which identifies three categories of individual: 'pleasers', 'searchers' and 'sceptics'. These transcendent categories appear to unify certain aspects of the different narratives that have been analysed, although all of these were generated from within very *different* contextual settings.

Whether or not this is problematic depends on the purpose of the research. If the researcher is trying to understand how individuals within the context defined as the case understand that particular context (e.g. the university class), then comparative analysis of smaller units, from one perspective at least, makes this possible.[4] Similarly, if the researcher wanted to investigate how larger discourse patterns transcend the individual contexts within which language is generated, this could also be done using comparative analysis. But if the researcher were trying to understand individual experience, to 'give voice' to individual perspectives, then the comparative analysis of interview texts would seem to contradict this intention. Describing a particular group as a case allows for patterns that transcend individual uniqueness to be identified, but it does not allow examination of the ways in which individuals are, in some aspects, *also unique*. Each individual within a case could, from a different perspective, be seen as a case in themselves, but current epistemologies do not really provide a way of conceptualising either the unique individual (other than as an example of a larger class) or of investigating uniquely individual differences in a meaningful way.

The third issue, that of having to disregard certain aspects of the data because of the assumption that it is necessary to articulate 'key aspects' of phenomena, arguably reflects what Thomas (2002, p. 430), citing Derrida, refers to as a 'desire for center in the constitution of structure'. By definition, what is 'key' has to be separated out from a complexity of other factors that are deemed to be less important.

But what if all of the factors in a particular situation were *equally* important, or if something that was determined to be unimportant was actually creating an effect on the phenomena being studied (a realist question, but one which works equally well if asked from a more interpretative stance)? This possibility could not be accommodated within dominant conceptual frameworks. The reason that much of social life 'escapes our capacity to make models of it' (Law & Urry, 2003, p. 7) could be because it is currently difficult to imagine and discuss a world in which multiple factors might be interacting 'equally', rather than in relation to definable 'driving forces' (not that imagining such multi-factor interactions would necessarily make it easier to *model* the world, but it might make it easier to talk about aspects of social life).

In relation to the fourth issue, difficulties conceptualising time and process, the removal of 'spatial and temporal grounding' (Nespor, 1994, p. 152) is an important casualty of the necessary eradication of 'contextual imperatives' (Unwin *et al.*, 2005). Although interview studies may sometimes gather data at two or three different points in time, the range of conceptual resources available for the discussion of fluidity and change in relation to process and interaction is currently limited (Seibt, 2003), and this limitation is enhanced by cross-sectional methods of analysis (Stehr & Grundmann, 2001).

Complexity Theory: Redefining Order (and Chaos)?

Complexity theory (Cilliers, 1998; Byrne, 1998), sometimes also referred to as dynamic systems theory (Fogel *et al.*, 1997; Valsiner, 1998), or as theories of emergence (Goldstein, 2000; Johnson, 2001), appears to provide a different way of conceptualising the issues so far discussed. 'Complexity theory' does not refer to a specific body of literature. Emerging from a surprising range of different disciplines, its ideas appear in fields as diverse as archaeology, biology, economics, psychology and law. Richardson and Cilliers (2001), in an overview of the many uses of complexity theory, define what they call three themes, or communities, in the literature: 'hard, reductionist complexity science' (which aims to understand the principles of complex systems), 'soft complexity science' (which uses complexity as a metaphorical tool to understand organisations) and 'complexity thinking' (which considers the epistemological implications of assuming 'the ubiquity of complexity' (2001). More recently, Byrne (2005a) has distinguished between 'simplistic' complexity (similar to the first of Richardson and Cilliers's categories) and 'complex' complexity (which seems related to Richardson and Cilliers's third category, discussed in the context of research methodology). The use of complexity theory here is related to this last category, with a focus particularly on ontology. As a set of ideas about process and formation which can be used in relation to both realist/explanatory and interpretive approaches, complexity appears to offer not just another theory, but a completely different starting point for theory, and also for the conceptualisation of method.

Of course not everything that is complicated manifests features of 'complexity'. Cilliers (1998) distinguishes between 'complicated' (having many parts, but each part can be explained—e.g. a mechanical engine) and 'complex' (having many parts, but not all of which can be named, and not all processes involved can be tracked or described). With regard to the complex, Johnson, following Weaver (1948 in Johnson, 2001), suggests that there are three types of scientific inquiry. The first deals with problems involving very limited numbers of variables, and concerns issues such as the movement of the planets around the sun (the approach underpinning Newtonian mechanics). The second approach deals with problems that are characterised by 'millions or billions of variables that can only be approached by the use of statistical mechanics and probability theory' (2001, p. 46), which he calls 'disorganised complexity'. He suggests, however, that there is a field between these two approaches which deals with a still substantial number of variables, but with one crucial difference:

> ... much more important than the mere number of variables is the fact that these variables are all interrelated ... . [T]hese problems, as contrasted with the disorganised situations with which statisticians can cope, *show the essential feature of organisation*. We will therefore refer to this group of problems as those of *organised complexity*. (Weaver, 1948, in Johnson, 2001, p. 47; italics in original)

Much large-scale social science research could be conceptualised as attempting to deal with 'disorganised complexity'. However, although the complexity of the social world, taken as a whole, could be conceptualised as being characterised by 'millions or billions of variables', such complexity could also be conceptualised as consisting of a large number of smaller, overlapping types of 'organised' (but open) systems. Cultures, discourses, practices, social groupings, institutions, and individuals could all be seen as 'open systems', which manifest different types of organisation.

In terms of the methods that have commonly been used to investigate such systems, cross-sectional and comparative types of analysis (whether in large-scale surveys or qualitative case studies) function by deliberately discounting the relationships which exist within the smaller units bounded by the population or case (e.g. people, classes, schools), in order to focus on the patterns which can be seen when these smaller units are viewed in relation to each other. The interconnectedness of the elements within these types of units is seen to be too specific to be useful for the purpose of extracting a general principle. By contrast, dynamic systems theories focus upon the interactions and relationships that occur *within* open systems, however the idea of 'system' may be applied.

A dynamic system consists of a large number of components, which are interacting dynamically at a local level (Cilliers, 1998). These multiple interactions are non-linear, involving complex feedback loops which continually adjust and modify both the 'parts' of the system, and the system itself. As the system is open, the interactions can also affect the boundaries of the system itself, and indeed have effects beyond it. Moreover, because the interactions are always local, such effects are distributed, rather than emanating from any central cause (Osberg, 2002; Johnson, 2001). If there is a sufficient number of these interactions, and if they take place over a sufficiently long period of time, specific forms of order, or organisation, will periodically *emerge* from within the system (Johnson, 2001). An example of this discussed by Holland is the way that neighbourhoods within cities organise themselves around social class, and the way that cities themselves continually change and adapt in ways that have not been planned:

> Cities have no central planning commissions that solve the problem of purchasing and distributing supplies ... . How do these cities avoid devastating swings between shortage and glut, year after year, decade after decade? The mystery deepens when we observe the kaleidoscopic nature of large cities. Buyers, sellers, administrators, streets, bridges and buildings are always changing, so that a city's coherence is somehow imposed on a perpetual flux of people and structures. Like the standing wave in front of a rock in a fast-moving stream, a city is a pattern in time.
> (Holland, 1998, in Johnson, 2001, p. 27)

Discussion of the unpredictability of emergence in this kind of description of dynamic processes is often misunderstood to imply randomness, chaos or non-determinism. Non-linear systems, however, are in fact understood, at least in some ways, to be deterministic, although the idea of determinism is perhaps differently nuanced in this context. There is causality, but not of the 'a causes b' kind. For some writers properties 'emerge deterministically from non-linear rules of interaction', and are thus 'merely *unexpected*' in relation to 'the principles governing the lower-level domain' (Osberg, 2005, p. 169). For others, however, emergence suggests a more radical kind of novelty that cannot be traced back to antecedent conditions, however well these conditions may be understood (Goldstein, 2005).

However emergence is understood, it is largely impossible, due to the sheer number of interacting variables, for most of the processes involved to be tracked or observed (Goldstein, 2000). The results of the interactions also cannot be predicted, beyond certain general parameters, because it is not possible to know in advance what will interact with what, or indeed, what has interacted with what up to that point, and what has resulted from previous unknown interactions. This untrackable history of interactions (both within and beyond the system) is crucial in determining the form of future emergences, making time and history of central importance. In addition, these processes are completely decentralised, in that the order which is produced is seen to emerge solely from the multiple interactions. There is no key variable, no centrally-guiding programme or brain, and no one principle factor which makes everything happen. This does not, however, imply that anything at all can emerge, as emergence is ultimately constrained by certain features of the system itself (the idea of 'sensitive dependence on original conditions', for example, describes the effects of differing initial circumstances), and by the system's interaction with (and partial constitution by) factors and systems beyond its own boundaries (Fogel *et al.*, 1997).

A Complexity-Based Ontology

Even the simplified overview of complexity outlined above begins to gives an idea of how an ontology based on these ideas might produce some very different ways of approaching the conceptualisation and analysis of data in social research (see

Byrne, 1997). First, the interactions are *multiple*, and *multiply connected*, and it is the multiplicity of the interactions through *time* that produces effects. Causality in this situation cannot be reduced to single or limited numbers of factors, as the factors are all crucially implicated in relation to each other. Byrne (2005b) has suggested that the impossibility of tracking these multiple interaction histories suggests a shift from a focus on *cause* to a focus on *effects*.

Second, because of this connected, multi-factor causality, elements that are isolated and conceptually 'removed' from the system of connected interactions in effect cease to have meaning in terms of understanding that system (though they might have meaning in relation to other such isolated elements abstracted from other systems). The *system itself* has to be studied, and studied in terms of its *interactions* (rather than defining 'key elements' in relation to smaller units within the system and comparing these to elements from other systems). However, studying systemic interactions involves understanding that some of the interactions pertaining to the system being investigated are at the same time also interactions of other, larger/different systems which the system that is the focus of attention is embedded in and connected to.

As this kind of open system evolves through time, it is in constant 'interaction with' environmental factors, i.e. factors that exist beyond its boundaries. But the language used here immediately suggests a 'thing' with a 'context'. From a dynamic systems point of view, the system, itself consisting of interactions, is at any point in time *partly constituted* by interactions that are part of the dynamic structures of other, different systems (both larger and smaller). These other systems will have their own interaction characteristics which, in the case of larger systems, means that smaller systems within them will be sharing in the same larger system interactions. However, the interactions of larger systems are themselves constantly combining and reforming uniquely within each open system, as they combine with interactions that are *particular* to that system. Because all of the systems involved are composed of interactions among constituent elements, they cannot not be reduced to objects or categories, so some other way has to be found of conceptualising 'event rather than structure' (Dallmayr, 1992, p. 20, in Thomas, 2002, p. 430).

Third, causality based on untrackable histories of multiple interactions means that *irregularity* and *unpredictability* have to be accepted as being a 'structural' aspect of the interactions that are to be investigated; these features cannot be 'evened out' or ignored. This unpredictability is not random 'noise' or chaos, but is part of the structuring dynamics of this type of system. The causal paths involved in multiple interactions through time may be too varied, too fast, and too simultaneous to ever be tracked or observed, but this does not mean that such causal paths are absent. It does mean, however, that researchers have to accept limits to what can be described or explained (and perhaps redirect their attention to effects, as indicated above).

Fourth, though focussing on process, denying the existence of underpinning deep structures, and highlighting (rather than simply accommodating) unpredictability, this approach differs from post-structuralist, or postmodern critiques in offering an account of structure and also of coherence. Structure, however, here relates to processes of dynamic, de-centralised *emergence*, which are continually being created as a result of local interactions, and which take place in relation to constraints that exist both within and beyond the system. The idea of constraint usually implies something 'external' that operates 'on' 'something' which can be bounded, and which is at the centre of an external 'environment'. In a dynamic system, however, the constraints are as much internal to the system as they are external. Each dynamic system has a starting point in time (it emerges as a result of other sets of interactions); a specific set of 'initial conditions', and a specific and particular history of interactions through time. In this sense, every dynamic system is unique, in that even similar types of system will have emerged out of slightly different combinations of original interactions; will have 'initial conditions' that consisted of *specific* combinations of the many different interactions which were theoretically possible at that time and in that place; and will have specific *histories* which involve further particular interactions with particular combinations of factors.

Coherence, from this perspective, is not an underlying logic or set of principles which might be seen to 'underpin' different individual systems. Coherence is *the existence of the system itself*, and the processes that continue, through time, to maintain the system *as* a system. If an individual human being is thought of as a dynamic system, genetic, environmental, biological, sensory, emotional and conscious processes all continually work together to keep the person healthy, sane and socially integrated (to whatever degree ...). Similarly, a social group, or an educational institution, has a coherence in the sense of a shape and an identity, although from a complexity perspective this shape and identity are in a process of continual formation, rather than resulting from essential, generative structures.

This view of coherence indicates why it can be difficult to understand individuals when they are studied in relation to each other, or why it is difficult to apply generalised results to particular individuals. In a cross-sectional analysis, what an individual says or does at a particular point in time could be seen as an emergence, generated by an unseen history of interactions through time. As people all have different starting points, and different histories, when these emergences are compared to each other, they can appear to be messy, idiosyncratic and generally mystifying. But this is the case only when a system is observed from a vantage point which is *outside* of that system: if one were to try to understand the interactions, both past and present, that constitute the individual as if from *within* their situation, what emerges is likely to be consistent with this history of interactions (even if these cannot be tracked or measured) and with the overall impulse towards maintaining the vitality and coherence of the system.

Conceptualising Difference, Specificity and Context

> Complexity theory challenges the nomothetic programme of universally applicable knowledge at its very heart—it asserts that knowledge must be contextual. (Byrne, 2005a)

A complexity ontology provides a way of thinking about institutions, cultures, groups and individuals as systems of interactions which are, in some important ways, always unique. This uniquely presenting system of interactions, however, is partially

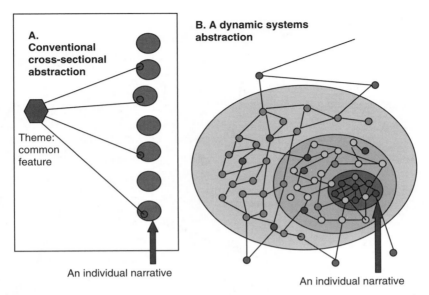

Figure 1: Conventional, cross-sectional abstraction and Dynamic systems abstraction

A. Conventional, cross-sectional abstraction

The individual cases (oval shapes on the right hand side) are compared cross-sectionally, and a theme is identified in relation to features that the different cases have in common. Aspects of the data that are not found to be similar cannot be reported.

B. Dynamic systems abstraction

The individual case (the smallest oval here is equivalent to the row of ovals in diagram A) is analysed in terms of different systemic interactions. The oval shapes represent different systems embedded within each other. The interactions are represented as smaller circles of different shades—each smaller circle represents a type of interaction, rather than a static category or variable.

An individual narrative (the darkest oval) consists of the interactions that make up 'the person': sense of identity, self and purpose (agency), personality, consciousness (including bodily awareness and emotions), memory (history), body, genetic makeup, etc. The paler grey area within which this is embedded represents one of the contexts (systems) within which the person operates. The interactions of this larger system maintain its own (dynamic) boundaries, but some of these interactions are also constitutive of the smaller 'person' system. Similarly, the interactions of the still larger (palest) system partly constitute the other two systems. Figure 2 applies this to an example of an individual person's narrative.

constituted by the interactions of other, larger systems; systems of governance, for example, of culture, language, policy, or of funding. Other individuals, groups or institutions will be partly constituted by the same larger system interactions in the same way. Whilst a more conventional approach might try to track the workings of these larger system interactions in relation to the idea of 'underpinning structures' which cut across individual examples (such as 'gender', for example), a complexity framing might suggest investigating the ways in which aspects of these larger system interactions function within particular, smaller cases (how is this woman 'gendered' compared to this one?). The first approach privileges the similarities observable by comparison (leading to the ability to formulate a category such as 'gender' in the first place), while the complexity approach is as likely to find difference as it is to find similarity (see Figures 1 and 2). When it does find patterns of similarity, these will relate to quite different aspects of the focus of study.

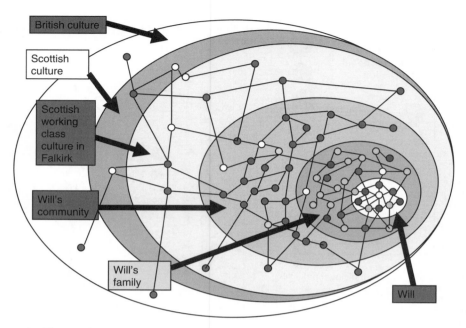

Figure 2: Dynamic system abstraction (detail)

The white circle in the centre represents the person known as 'Will'. The darkest dots within this are the interactions that create his consciousness (sense of self, agency, emotional experience etc.), his body, his genetic makeup and predispositions. Will is, however, partly constituted by the interactions that take place with his family (the system most immediately 'surrounding' him in this diagram); he is partly constituted by the actions, reactions and practices that go on in this area of his life (how they eat, their weekly routines, how they cope with his son's dyslexia, etc.). At the same time, his family is partly constituted by its interactions with Will's 'personality'; the way he interacts with his children, his behaviour in relation to his work, the language he uses when talking to his partner, etc.

Both Will and his family are, in turn, partly constituted by the interactions that make up the still larger system that is their local community: norms in relation to visits to the pub; conversations and meetings at the local supermarket; accompanying values and discourses in relation to things such as what is regarded as suitable attire for young girls, or the age that sons should start drinking. He and his family also contribute to the interactions that make up the community, in terms of their involvement in these and other practices. Aspects of Will's personality partly constitute this larger community, mediated both directly, through actions such as his leadership of a local band, or his participation in pub conversations, and indirectly, through the effects of his actions and practices in relation to his partner and children. Similarly, the interactions which involve Will, his family and his local community are partly constituted by, and partly constitute, the interactions of larger systems of interaction such as 'Scottish working class culture', or 'British society in 2007'.

This perspective is a tool for analysis, rather than any kind of description of 'what is'—it could be used in relation to narratives alone, or to a combination of narrative, observation notes, documentary evidence, etc.

With respect to the problems discussed above, a complexity approach is helpful in relation to the conceptualisation of context, and the confusion that results from the conflation of the context of the case with the contexts of the wider lives and histories of those being interviewed within the case. Thinking of people and social/ institutional/cultural contexts as complex, dynamic systems allows for the separation of these two distinct types of context, even though (and perhaps crucially because) they may be embedded in each other[5]. If the intention is to find out something about, say, the area that has been bounded as the case (an access course, a class, a school), then interviews with individuals are potentially quite limited. The researcher, attempting to 'draw together ... a diverse and unrelated range of phenomena' (Hammersley & Atkinson, 1995, p. 211) is positioned, conceptually, 'outside' the smaller sub-units within the case (in the sense that he/she creates a category or theme that relates to narratives generated by these sub-units, rather than looking at multiple elements of the case), trying to understand something that is likely to be multi-factorial in relation to a comparison of only one type of element in the dynamic system (i.e. the individuals).

Gomm and Hammersley's (2001) discussion of the possible relevance of complexity theory to educational research provides an example of this kind of problem. In the study they discuss, the researchers wanted to find out why exam results were so similar over a period of time within a particular context. They point out that if the research had only interviewed examiners, producing an account of 'assessing according to the views of assessors', they could not have come to their final conclusion, which was that 'the selective function was smeared across the system as a whole':

> ... features of ... examining at the time (were) to be found embedded in the selection of students, in their tuition, in the design and use of assessment instruments, in the formal talk of examination boards, in the informal talk in staff rooms, in the career trajectories of staff, and in the rich folklore there was about how to elicit—and interpret—evidence about students. (Gomm & Hammersley, 2001, p. 12)

In order to understand how this complexity of factors worked together, over time, to produce a certain result, the researchers had to make the shift discussed above. Rather than looking from 'outside' at a collection of narratives produced by a group of separate individuals ('the view from above'), they looked as if from 'inside' what was conceptualised as a dynamically interacting system of multiple elements (the examination system within which the assessors were embedded). Although in this particular example this may seem like an obvious way of approaching the problem of understanding assessment results, it is quite a good example of the potential problem of assuming that interview narratives can 'say something' about the multiple interactions of the dynamic system within which they are embedded (although such interviews might 'say something' about how such interactions affect the individuals). This conceptualisation of the researcher looking as if from 'within' larger dynamic systems of connected factors is quite common in sociological research, but less so in many forms of small-scale educational research. Whilst ethnographic approaches do operate from this position, justifying these approaches, as discussed above, is problematic within conventional epistemologies. Complexity offers a way of explaining ethnography on the basis of a different ontology.

The second problem is how to deal with the wider contexts (both historical and present) of the individuals who are bounded by the case. Here, the assumption is often that talking to individuals will tell the researcher something about the 'type' (in the sense of larger class) of individuals who are believed to be represented within the case (see Figure 1). Once again, the researcher is usually conceptualised as being 'outside' the smaller sub-units within the case, and attempts to 'see' a transcendent analytical category that will hopefully indicate some kind of connection which could link to underpinning causal processes. If, however, the researcher were to shift to a position that tried to see the relevant dynamic system as if from 'inside', this would imply a need to conceptualise each person as a dynamically interacting system of multiple elements with a history through time (Figure 2).

As dynamic systems, each with unique starting points and histories, and yet each also partially constituted by the interactions of larger cultural and linguistic systems, individuals could, from this perspective, now be considered as systems which could justifiably be the focus of a research study. If the aim of this approach is *not* to identify 'deep' structural principles, and therefore not to try to generalise in relation to such principles, then other types of connection, and of generalisation, may become possible. For example, comparisons could be made in relation to data on individuals which had be analysed longitudinally in relation to the history and evolution of factors within that person's life, rather than at one or two points in time in relation to factors from other people's lives.

The shift from analysing sub-units within bounded cases as if from outside such sub-units, to thinking about both the case and its sub-components as open systems which might be understood in relation to patterns of multiple interactions that take place *within* them (rather than the structures *beyond* them), makes it possible to examine specificity in relation to individuals from a very different ontological position. Within the dynamic system which is the case, each person might be seen as a point within a number of different interlocking dynamic systems, only one of which will be the 'case' in research terms. This 'point', however, also has its own history through time.

Thinking of individuals as dynamic systems, however, requires a reconceptualisation of 'the individual' that moves beyond the terms of cultural assumptions relating to ideas of an essential self or core personality. The details of this are beyond the scope of this chapter.[6] In brief, self becomes replaced by a 'sense of self', with this 'sense of self' being seen as a continually emerging property of the interactions of the system (there is no central, generative core), which functions to maintain the individual's sense of their own coherence. In the context of dynamic systems, a reconceptualised, non-essential individual begins to make space for a different understanding of both *individual* and *context*. An analysis that examines histories, traces and emergences in relation to the multiple contexts within which a 'sense of self' emerges, still, of course, employs various forms of 'reduction' and abstraction (a mistaken interpretation of complexity theory is that it somehow can 'account for' or model the totality of things [Cilliers, 1998]). This analysis reduces and abstracts, however, in relation to the history and multiplicity of each different individual, rather than by creating a transcendent category that deliberately ignores these histories and multiplicities.

Conclusion

This chapter has attempted to use complexity thinking to draw attention to conceptual limitations of the epistemologies that underpin a large amount of qualitative research. The purpose of this is not to try to build an argument that attacks or tries to undermine these epistemologies. The discussion represents an attempt to highlight some aspects of what has, inevitably, been cast into the shadows by the strong beam of established ontologies and epistemologies, and to experiment with the potential of complexity theory for suggesting different ways of thinking.

Current conceptual framings were found to be problematic in relation to the conceptualisation of difference, context, processes through time, multi-factor causality, and the specificity of situations. The concept of open, dynamic systems, embedded within and partly constituting each other, whilst at the same time maintaining their own coherence, allows for different ways of thinking about *context*, and provides a rationale for the investigation of *individuals*, *difference* and *specificity*. By focusing on interactions, rather than static categories, complexity theory also makes it possible to consider different aspects of *process*. It does this not only in the general sense of providing a language with which to talk about dynamic interactions, but also specifically in relation to the importance of histories of *interactions through time* (without time, there is no emergence). In addition, complexity theory articulates a notion of causality that is *multi-factorial*. It is impossible to talk about isolating 'key' factors, because all of the 'factors' work together, with no one factor being more important than any other (whether or not it is helpful to even talk about 'factors' as things which 'work together' is another question). The causality implied by complexity theory is also *de-centred*, in the sense that there is no 'pacemaker cell' (Johnson, 2001), no gene-type entity in a dynamic system that could be said to 'cause' a particular effect, or set of effects. Causation is too multi-dimensional, too fast, and in some senses (though not others) too unpredictable to be a viable focus of attention. Complexity therefore suggests a shift from the habitual preoccupation with *causes* to a focus on *effects* (Byrne, 2005b).

The combination of multi-factor causality, occurring through time, in the absence of a central, generative force, results in the quite radical notion of *emergence*, and a reframing of the notion of *structure*. From a complexity perspective, things 'emerge' at certain points in the history of a set of multiple interactions through time, simply as a result of the interactions, rather than as the result of 'deep', generative causal structures. This is partly what makes emergence, to some extent at least, unpredictable; what emerges will depend upon what interacts, which is at least partly determined by chance encounters and changes in environments. Emergence, however, though unpredictable, is nonetheless also constrained: by features that are both internal (in terms of initial conditions and interaction histories) and external (in the sense that the system is partly made up of the interactions of larger systems, and also in the more conventional sense of physical, 'environmental' factors) to the system which is the focus of study. Though complexity theory may be seen by some as providing a way of talking about random, intuitive, even 'spiritual' phenomena, this is not what has been argued here. The causalities involved in the interactions may be untrackable, but what emerges from them is not 'mysterious', in this sense: it is consistent with the nature and histories of the interactions involved (for discussion of a research project based on these ideas, see Haggis, 2006).

Notes

1. Although Silverman warns elsewhere against a simplistic view of multiple methods, here he states that 'the proper relationship' between quantitative and qualitative work 'is a division of labour in which qualitative researchers seek to answer "how" and "what" questions and then pass on their findings, so that causes and outputs of the phenomena identified ("why" questions) can be studied by their quantitative colleagues' (2001, p. 259).
2. This refers to the influential body of work in higher education that describes 'deep' and 'surface' approaches to learning.
3. '[T]he issue of realism and instrumentalism ... is typically understood as the question of whether various terms in statements making up scientific theories refer to real objects or merely serve the role of facilitating inferences among claims about observations' (Giere, 2000, p. 515).
4. Students in a class, for example, could all comment on what they thought was happening: how the interaction was working, what the teacher was teaching, which aspects of the subject were difficult, etc.
5. For a further development of these ideas that takes account of a third type of context, that of the dynamic systems of culture and society within which the case is embedded, see Haggis, 2006.
6. The idea of a dynamic and non-essential 'self' is unusual only in the context of the Western tradition (and recent 'Western' thinkers such as Derrida have, of course, worked on similar questions). Underpinned by the very different, dynamic ontology represented by the idea of 'impermanence' (which reflects many aspects of what has been discussed here in relation to complexity theory), Theravada Buddhism presents the following account of self: 'One thing disappears, conditioning the appearance of the next in a series of cause and effect ... (but) there is no unchanging substance in them. There is nothing behind them that can be called a permanent self, individuality, or anything that can in reality be called "I"' (Rahula, 1990, p. 26).

References

Ashworth, P. & Lucas, U. (2000) Achieving Empathy and Engagement: A practical approach to the design, conduct and reporting of phenomenographic research, *Studies in Higher Education*, 25:3, pp. 295–308.

Byrne, D. (1997) Complexity Theory and Social Research, *Social Research Update*, 18, pp. 1–6.

Byrne, D. (1998) *Complexity Theory and the Social Sciences* (London, Routledge).

Byrne, D. (2005a) Complexity, Configurations and Cases, *Theory, Culture and Society*, 22:5, pp. 95–111.

Byrne, D. (2005b) Focusing on the Case in Quantitative and Qualitative Research, *ESRC Research Methods Programme, Workshop 4, The Case Study* January 12–13, 2005 (oral communication).

Bryman, A. & Cramer, D. (1999) *Quantitative Data Analysis with SPSS Release 8 for Windows* (London, Routledge).

Cilliers, P. (1998) *Complexity and Postmodernism* (London, Routledge).

Clark, C. (2005) The Structure of Educational Research, *British Educational Research Journal*, 31:3, pp. 289–308.

Flyvbjerg, B. (2001) *Making Social Science Matter* (Cambridge, Cambridge University Press).

Furlong, J. (2004) BERA at 30. Have we come of age?, *British Educational Research Journal*, 30, pp. 343–358.

Fogel, A., Lyra, M. & Valsiner, J. (1997) *Dynamics and Indeterminism in Developmental and Social Processes* (Hillsdale, NJ, Lawrence Erlbaum).

Geertz, C. (1973) On Thick Description, in: *The Interpretation of Culture* (New York, Basic Books).

Giere, R. (2000) Theories, in: W. H. Newton-Smith (ed.), *A Companion to the Philosophy of Science* (Oxford, Blackwell).

Goldstein, J. (2000) Emergence: A construct amid a thicket of conceptual snares, *Emergence*, 2:1, pp. 5–22.

Goldstein, J. (2005) Impetus Without Teleology: The self-transcending construction of emergence. Paper given at the *Complexity, Science and Society Conference*, Liverpool, September 2005.

Gomm, R. & Hammersley, M. (2001) *Thick Ethnographic Description and Thin Models of Complexity*. Paper presented at British Educational Research Association Annual Conference, Leeds University, 13–15 September.

Goodwin, L. (2002) *Resilient Spirits* (London, Routledge Falmer).

Guba, E. & Lincoln, Y. (1998) Competing Paradigms in Qualitative Research, in: N. Denzin & Y. Lincoln (eds), *The Landscape of Qualitative Research* (London, Sage).

Haggis, T. (2006) Context, Agency and Time: Looking at learning from the perspective of complexity and dynamic systems theory. Paper presented at ESRC Teaching and Learning Research Programme Thematic Seminar Series: *Contexts, Communities, Networks; Mobilising learner's resources and relationships in different domains*, University of Stirling, June 2006.

Hammersley, M. (1989) *The Dilemma of Qualitative Method* (London, Routledge).

Hammersley, M. (2005) Review of Key Themes in Qualitative Research: Continuities and Change, *British Educational Research Journal*, 31:3, pp. 405–408.

Hammersley, M. & Atkinson, P. (1995) *Ethnography: Principles in practice*, 2nd edn. (New York, Routledge).

Hargreaves, D. (1996) Teaching as a Research-Based Profession (London, Teacher Training Agency).

Hollis, M. (2003) Explaining and Understanding, in: N. Bunnin & E. Tsui-James (eds), *The Blackwell Companion to Philosophy* (Oxford, Blackwell).

Johnson, S. (2001) *Emergence* (London, Penguin).

Law, J. & Urry, J. (2003) Enacting the Social (Lancaster, Department of Sociology and the Centre for Science Studies, Lancaster University) available at http://www.lancs.ac.uk/fss/sociology/research/resalph.htm#lr

Llewelyn, S. (2003) What Counts as 'Theory' in Qualitative Management and Accounting Research?, *Accounting, Auditing and Accountability Journal*, 16, pp. 662–708.

Marton, F., Hounsell, D. & Entwistle, N. (eds) (1997) *The Experience of Learning* (Edinburgh, Scottish Academic Press).

Moore, L., Graham, A. & Diamond, I. (2003) On the Feasibility of Conducting Randomised Trials in Education: Case study of a sex education intervention, *British Educational Research Journal*, 29:5, pp. 673–689.

Nespor, J. (1994) *Knowledge in Motion: Space, time and curriculum in undergraduate physics and management* (London, Falmer).

Newton, J. (2003) Implementing a Teaching And Learning Strategy, *Studies in Higher Education*, 28:4.

Osberg, D. (2002) Complexity, Science And Education: Some insights and possibilities. Paper presented at the 32nd SCUTREA Annual Conference, University of Stirling, 2–4th July.

Osberg, D. (2005) *Curriculum, Complexity and Representation*. Unpublished PhD Thesis, The Open University, Milton Keynes.

Rahula, W. (1990) *What the Buddha Taught* (London, The Gordon Fraser Gallery).

Roberts, B. (2002) *Biographical Research* (Buckingham, Open University Press).

Rock, P. (1973) Phenomenalism and Essentialism in the Sociology of Deviance, *Sociology*, 7:1, pp. 17–29.

Richardson, K. & Cilliers, P. (2001) What is Complexity Science? A view from different directions, *Emergence*, 3:1, pp. 5–22.

Seibt, J. (2003) (ed.) *Process Theories* (London, Kluwer).

Silverman, D. (2001) *Interpreting Qualitative Data*, 2nd edn. (London, Sage).

Smelser, N. J. & Bates, P. B. (eds) (2001) *International Encyclopedia of the Social & Behavioral Sciences* (Oxford, Pergamon Press).

Stein, S., Isaacs, G. & Andrews, T. (2004) Incorporating Authentic Learning Experiences within a University Course, *Studies in Higher Education*, 29:2, pp. 237–258.

Stehr, N. & Grundmann, R. (2001) The Authority of Complexity, *British Journal of Sociology*, 52:2, pp. 313–329.

Strauss, A. & Corbin, J. (1998) *Basics of Qualitative Research* (Thousand Oaks, CA, Sage).

Strathern, M. (1992) *Partial Connections* (London, Rowman & Littlefield).

Thomas, G. (2002) Theory's Spell—On Qualitative Inquiry and Educational Research, *British Educational Research Journal*, 28:3, pp. 419–435.

Tooley, J. & Darby, D. (1998) *Educational Research: A critique* (London, Office for Standards in Education).

Unwin, L., Felstead, A., Fuller, A., Lee, T., Butler, P. & Ashton, D. (2005) *Worlds within Worlds: The relationship between context and pedagogy in the workplace*. Paper presented at ESRC Teaching and Learning Research Programme Thematic Seminar Series: Contexts, communities, networks: mobilizing learner's resources and relationships in different domains.

Valsiner, J. (1998) *The Guided Mind* (Cambridge, MA, Harvard University Press).

Yanow, D. (2003) Interpretive Empirical Political Science: What makes this not a subfield of qualitative methods, *Qualitative Methods Section (APSA) Newsletter 2nd Issue*.

12
Complexity and Educational Research: A critical reflection

LESLEY KUHN
University of Western Sydney

Introduction

This chapter critically reflects on issues associated with bringing a complexity (here used as an abbreviation of 'complexity science' or 'complexity theory') approach to educational research. Complexity offers a way of envisaging and working with complex phenomena. As such it is apparent that complexity has implications for how we conceive of social interactions and institutions, such as educational endeavour. However, in taking seriously complexity's commitment to 'radical relationality' (Dillon, 2000, p. 4), assuming that 'nothing is without being in relation, and that everything is in the way that it is—in terms and in virtue of relationality' (ibid.), it is no simple matter to bring together discourses that have different relational histories. So in considering complexity in connection with educational phenomena, this chapter will make visible some aspects of the relationality between complexity and education.

Utilising complexity in the sphere of human interactions, our social and institutional world, has long been of interest to me. Together with two colleagues in the School of Social Ecology at the University of Western Sydney I have been engaged over the past ten years in bringing to life a complexity approach to social inquiry. Two of our group of three have backgrounds in transdisciplinary approaches to social inquiry (psychology, sociology, philosophy) with the third member having a background in cybernetics. The so-called 'new sciences' offered ways of thinking and talking about social reality that matched the complexity of our experiences. At first we immersed ourselves in learning about Chaos Theory and Fuzzy Logic. Over time however, as we continued to research with great enthusiasm and intensity, we came to understand that what we were doing was evolving a complexity approach to social inquiry. Complexity as I use the term refers to a style of thinking or a paradigmatic approach. Others have labelled this as the 'complexity sciences' or 'Complexity Theory'. I do not think however, that complexity has yet been systematically articulated in such a way that it could be termed a single 'theory'. Thus in my usage, complexity constitutes an umbrella description under which researchers have grouped a set of new scientific theories sharing the idea that while certain phenomena appear to be chaotic or random, they are actually part of a larger coherent process (see also Wolfram, 2002; Kauffman, 1995).

In developing our complexity approach, as befitting our view of academics, we have persistently brought critical reflection to all of our work. Given the natural sciences and mathematical aetiology of complexity science, it has been important to persevere in asking about the appropriateness of bringing a complexity approach to social inquiry.

In recent years our small group has found that it is not alone in its fascination with complexity. It is increasingly evident that ideas from complexity science have been utilised and developed by a great many people working in what may broadly be described as social rather than scientific domains. Complexity has been brought to a diversity of fields including psychology (Bütz *et al.*, 1997; Eenwyk, 1997), economics (Hawken, 1994), architecture (Sakai, 2001), sociology (Eve *et al.*, 1997) and education (Morin, 2001). This list is of course indicative rather than comprehensive, reflecting only a few of the works I have come across.

The purpose of this chapter is to critically reflect on some issues implicated in utilising complexity in educational endeavour. In particular the chapter focuses on issues relating to complexity-informed research (inquiry). The chapter addresses two main foci:

1. The appropriateness *per se* of complexity science in educational research; and,
2. Issues relating to the *ways* in which complexity is engaged in the educational domain.

Comments about the Nature of Research

By way of setting a foundation for critical discussion of the appropriateness of complexity science in educational research, I begin by considering the nature of research itself.

Judgements concerning proper or appropriate educational endeavour, methods of investigation and philosophising about education necessarily implicate perspectives, values, assumptions and beliefs. While seeking to be clearly focussed, rigorous, ethically defensible and valid, research is never a neutral enterprise. Underpinning any research activity are the basic assumptions of the researcher about the nature of 'reality' and the way we comprehend it. Ideas about knowledge, about what we can know (an ontological concern) and how we can know it (an epistemological question), long central to philosophical reflection, guide research. So too do beliefs, values (axiological concerns) and aspirations. Often research, particularly when it is thought that knowledge about the world can be made objective, is taken as generating certain or foundational knowledge. Rather than viewing research as seeking foundational knowledge, I find it more useful to regard research as activity undertaken by socially interacting individuals employing various frames of reference that orient meaningful activity. Research in this formulation is constituted by and embedded within discourses, thereby creating identifiable cultures of inquiry.

To explain this idea, let us conceive of the rich history of approaches to research as emerging out of like minded people (holding similar values, assumptions and beliefs) tending to gather together over time (as research teams, or through reading similar literature and attending related conferences, and so on), telling each other stories of what they know and do (developing narratives) thereby evolving particular cultures of inquiry, where certain habits of thought (epistemic, ontological and axiological assumptions), styles of investigation, analysis and synthesis develop. In this sense I see research as undertaken within particular cultures of inquiry.

It can be observed that cultures of inquiry are created over time, through so formed discursive communities. These discursive communities can be viewed as being both somewhat stable and somewhat flexible and fluid, tending to evolve in relation to people having interest in particular styles of research (such as quantitative, qualitative, ethnographic or action research, for example), a substantive area, be this field driven (such as education, early childhood development or education in the middle years) or issue driven (such as retention of Aboriginal students, educational equity, experiences of girls in coeducational schools, and so on), or ideological allegiance (Marxist, humanist, Feminist, Buddhist and so on).

A complexity explanation is that cultures of inquiry (or more generally, communities of understanding) represent an intersection of *phase space* with *phrase space*. Phase space refers to a space comprising all of the possible states of a complex entity. One way of giving shape to this space is to think in terms of time and place dimensions. In human activity, time and place influence a great many possibilities, including possible habits of thought. In this way we could say that phase space provides a structural dimension to the emergence of cultures of inquiry. Along with phase space, we can also think in terms of phrase space (Kuhn, Woog & Hodgson, 2003). Within phrase space, we exercise agency in our languaging of our world to ourselves and others and as we determine to whom and how we communicate. So we could say that cultures of inquiry represent transient expressions of the interface between phase space and phrase space, and that this intersection may alternatively be described as being at 'the edge of chaos' (a positively exciting place to be that is rich with potentiality) or 'the chaotic edge', a rather more scary interpretation!

Qualitative Research: A Quiet Methodological Revolution

When we seek to undertake research, we necessarily join and contribute to a certain culture of inquiry (so exercising agency). We join discursive communities through becoming familiar with and then aligning ourselves with relevant research philosophy, approach, design, methodologies, methods and techniques. Thus researchers may describe their research as quantitative, qualitative, constructivist, feminist, critical, postmodern and so on. With a burgeoning of qualitative research over the past three decades, it can be seen that a 'quiet methodological revolution' (Denzin & Lincoln, 2005, p. ix) has taken place, where to do research no longer means adherence exclusively to such scientific mores as objectivity and reductionism.

As Kuhn (1962) has shown (within science) revolutions or transformations of paradigm are not easily accomplished. This is to be expected as the very nature of a paradigm is that it 'is both underground and sovereign in all theories, doctrines and ideologies', instituting the 'primordial relations that form axioms, determine concepts, command discourse and/or theories' (Morin, 2001, p. 23). The directive influence of a paradigm is such that it engenders a situation whereby, as Brazilian educator Paulo Freire argues, 'It is not the "I think" that constitutes the "we think" but rather the "we think" that makes it possible for me to think' (Freire, 1985, pp. 99–100).

For many, qualitative research is held within a different paradigm to quantitative research. Although I do not believe that a distinction of such huge proportion is always the case, as when, for example, a qualitative piece of inquiry is sought to be, and presented by the researcher as being, 'objective', comparative quantitative/qualitative literature abounds, attesting to this perception of paradigmatic differentiation.

Qualitative research has been, and continues to be met with resistance from people subscribing to other, perhaps what may be described as 'neoconservative' (Denzin & Lincoln, 2005, p. ix) discursive communities. Early qualitative research literature attests to interest in qualitative research as constituting a paradigmatic revolution (albeit beyond what may be in a strict sense referred to as science), with much writing devoted to justification for the new; for qualitative rather than quantitative research.

I have experienced over the past 20 years a change in how qualitative researchers situate their research approach. Around 15 to 20 years ago (what I may call in shorthand form 'then') researchers would typically:

a) Construct arguments regarding the inadequacy of traditional scientific research methods for social inquiry;
b) Build an argument explaining and positioning an improvement-oriented impetus to social inquiry where the research would be intentionally designed to bring about improvement to the situation or issue under investigation; and,
c) Position their research approach within a particular methodology (or method), taking care to demonstrate how their work conforms to 'the requirements' of the method/methodology.

This in my view constitutes a form of championing of methodological purity.
    In contrast, in more recent years, ('now') it seems researchers:

d) Identify the discourse with which they wish to place their research approach;
e) Demonstrate coherence between their ontological, epistemological and axiological (values) assumptions; and,
f) Take for granted the 'primacy of practice' (Ulrich, 1994), where the situation under investigation is taken as guiding the choice of research methodology/methods/techniques, rather than a desire to attain and maintain methodological purity.

This is not to say that my 'then' and 'now' are related to time frames in an exclusive way. Rather, I am interested in depicting an indicative evolution of discourse within qualitative research. The situation, I acknowledge, is far more complex, involving contradictions, contestations and recursions.

For me, however, it remains important that researchers do attend to d), e) and f). Doing so involves depth of thinking, whereby a number of significant questions may be asked: Why do I prefer these research conversations above others? What ethos or disposition do I champion? What form of life do I exemplify or contribute to?

Research as Necessarily Ethical Activity

These questions relating to preferred values and aspirations bring me to my first and overriding concern. It is though, less a critical reflection directly in connection with utilising complexity in educational research *per se,* than a critique relating to principles of 'utilisation' of any particular research approach. My concern is that at times researchers adopt certain methodological stances and employ particular methods, but without much awareness of why, apart from reasons of the most mechanical or 'calculative' kind (to use Heidegger's [1966] term). Ideas and theories, in my view, should not be simply instrumentalised, tyrannically imposing verdicts (Morin, 2001, p. 25); rather, we should engage with them to 'assist and orient the cognitive strategies adopted' (Morin, 2001, p. 25). To not so engage is to give over that which makes us uniquely human, the capacity for 'meta mental ascent' (Lehrer, 1997): our capacity to be deeply critically evaluative.

Research is necessarily and inescapably an ethical activity. This is to take ethics as not relating to socially agreed-upon mores, but rather to view ethics as essentially implicated in all of human being. I concur with Maturana and Varela, in understanding that 'Every human act has an ethical meaning because it is an act of constitution of the human world' (Maturana & Varela, 1988, p. 247). Researchers act as ethical beings in their making of choices about methodology, methods and techniques. Further, these choices will be guided by epistemic, ontological, and axiological assumptions. Paradigmatic embeddedness and/or preference will be apparent. As ethical beings, having the capacity for 'meta mental ascent' (able to make judgements about our judgements) it behoves us to act on (as well as be acted upon by) the noosphere (sphere of accumulated human thought) of our existence. We do this when we are circumspect, critically considering the implications of our paradigmatic, methodological, methods and techniques choices.

Complexity

To continue the process of setting a foundation for critical reflection on utilising complexity in educational research, I offer here a brief conceptual introduction to complexity (more detailed discussions can be found in other chapters in this volume).

I take complexity as constituting a paradigmatic orientation, functioning as an intellectual successor of other previously favoured frameworks for explaining how novelty, order and evolution are present in the world. Extrapolating out from precise scientific and mathematical enterprises, the complexity sciences, or complexity theory, presents particular habits of thought about the nature of the organisation of the world, with complexity narratives and vocabularies generating alternative habits of explanation to those deriving from linear, objective, positivist accounts of the natural and social world. Complexity as paradigm offers evocative metaphors for making sense that are not bound to linearity or certainty (Kuhn, 2005). The habit of thought exemplified by complexity is, as described by Morin (1992), a recognition of 'complex causality', or more specifically, 'an eco-auto-causality where autocausality means recursive causality in which the organising process elaborates the products, actions, and effects necessary for its creation or regeneration' (Morin, 1992, pp. 130–131). In other words, complexity recognises a tightly bound, mutually inducing, pairing of cause and effect.

From a complexity perspective both the nature of the world and human sense-making are dynamic and emergent. Ontologically, complexity depicts the world as self-organising, non-linear, sensitive to initial conditions and influenced by many sets of rules. Epistemologically, human-sense making is also construed in exactly the same way, as self-organising, non-linear, sensitive to initial conditions and influenced by many sets of rules.

A complexity perspective thus emphasises human evolution (be this of an individual over a life time or of humanity in general over eons of time) as radically unpredictable. Human beings are depicted as essentially self-referential and reflexive, and human enterprise as inescapably responsive and participative.

Complexity and Educational Research

Education, or educational enterprise can be viewed (similarly to research), as activity undertaken by socially interacting individuals employing various frames of reference that orient meaningful activity. Educational endeavour, including educational research, in this view is constituted by and embedded within discourses creating identifiable cultures.

Complexity and education may be brought together because in the language of complexity, such human cultural settings, productions and institutions as educational endeavour are complex and dynamic. Individual human beings (learners, educators, and administrators), various associations of individuals (classes, schools, universities, educational associations) and human endeavour (such as educational research) are multi-dimensional, non-linear, interconnected, far from equilibrium and unpredictable. Rather than seek to undertake inquiry that simplifies through reducing this complexity to that which can be measured objectively, a complexity approach begins by acknowledging that human settings and activities are necessarily complex. This is not a new idea. E. B. Tylor's 1871 definition of culture, used as a base definition in cultural studies, is that 'Culture or Civilisation, taken in its widest ethnographic sense is that complex whole which includes knowledge, belief, art, morals, law, custom and any other capabilities and habits acquired by man [sic] as a member of society (quoted in Cohen, 1995, p. 84).

A complexity approach acknowledges that all levels of focus, whether this is the individual, class, school, national or international associations, reveal humans and human endeavour as complex, and that focussing on one level will not reduce the multi-dimensionality, non-linearity, interconnectedness, or unpredictability encountered. A complexity view is that 'in human beings, as in other living creatures, the whole is present within the parts; every cell of a multicellular organism contains the totality of its genetic patrimony, and society inasmuch as a whole is present within every individual in his language, knowledge, obligations and standards' (Morin, 2001, p. 31).

Two Frequently Made Objections to Utilising Complexity in Social Research

Educational research constitutes a form of social inquiry. As such, two frequently made objections to utilising complexity in socially oriented inquiry apply. The first is that as complexity, even when utilised in social domains, draws on images and metaphors from mathematics and science, it is deemed not applicable to work in human oriented domains such as education. On this argument, recourse to complexity as an organising framework (paradigm) would not be desirable in educational research. The second objection is that many discourses outside of science and mathematics, in domains such as philosophy, arts, humanities, social sciences, relating to constructivist, postmodernist, post-structuralist or critical perspectives provide adequate, equivalent or superior means of addressing similar ideas to insights claimed by complexity. This view positions complexity as redundant. Both of these objections indicate issues that do need to be addressed.

The first objection belies a rather linearly organised worldview, whereby discourse emergence is seen as compartmentalised, occurring within separate domains. Rather than conceive of separate evolutions in thinking in the natural and social sciences, I propose a complexity, nonlinearly oriented explanation. It seems to me that with growing acceptance of certain specific theories and worldviews in one domain of inquiry, there can be observed a co-arising of similar ways of thinking across other cultures and domains of knowing. For example, postmodernism, second order cybernetics and complexity all share a sense of implausibility of the 'grand narrative' (Lyotard, 1984) and recognition of the impossibility of independent objective observation.

The idea of theoretic orientations co-arising across many domains of interest may be illuminated using complexity styles of understanding. Histories of intellectual ideas can be thought of as self-organising, and as exhibiting swarming behaviour. In complexity, swarming refers to the way in which multiple agents may in seemingly spontaneous ways come together. So, perhaps as Johnson (2001) suggests, we have secret, undeveloped histories of ideas, where ideas although thought of do not take rigorous hold until there is enough of a swarming of similar thinking. From this view, ideas from the sciences and social domains when they appear to be similar to one another can be thought of as instances when 'isolated hunches and private obsessions coalesce into a new way of looking at the world, shared by thousands of individuals' (2001, p. 64).

While it is evident that in a narrow sense, the language of complexity is emergent directly from recent scientific inquiry, the underlying assumption that there exists a clear separation of mathematics and science from humanities, social science or sociology does not do justice to the complex interrelated nature of human society. It could be argued, for example, that social researchers, in grappling with the complexity and indeterminacy of human beings, influenced natural scientists to think differently and re-narrate their scientific fields of inquiry. Similarly, it may be argued that the high regard for science over the past couple of hundred years led to early social science interest in its methods, while the cultural revolution of the 1960s, wherein science came to be identified with repressive and dehumanising tendencies, meant many social scientists rejected quantification and opted for more hermeneutic approaches.

Of course, if we were to take too literally this objection that complexity is inappropriate in social domains because of its antecedence in mathematics and science, much educational research activity would be disallowed, including all of the vast quantities of quantitative, 'objective' research, as this too is based on images and metaphors from mathematics and science.

It is useful however, to bear this objection in mind, to hedge tendencies towards objectifying theoretical orientations. It is appropriate to recognise that the (complexity) image or metaphor we utilise does have antecedence different from our proposed usage. We can ask, for example: In what context was this image created? What are the aspects of complexity that I find useful, and why? How do these ideas relate to other discourses and beliefs with which I am engaged?

The second objection, in arguing that the similarity of insights between complexity and other social or humanities oriented research is such that complexity is redundant, indicates a rather static, objectifying view of knowledge and discursive communities.

This objection can be thought of as an expression of boundary keeping activity (Kuhn, 2005). It positions some researchers (those who do not subscribe to the hegemonic language) as 'users of' rather than co-creators of discourse. Given the adversarial habit of mind engendered within academia, languaging differently can be perceived as a threat to status. From a complexity perspective, ways of knowing, styles of expression and location of focus can be understood as evolving through ongoing discursive processes, whereby boundary judgements and contestations continually occur, and of themselves contribute to what is considered legitimate within epistemic communities of practice. While a complexity perspective sees this second objection as to be expected, it does not construe alternative languaging as redundant. Rather, of greater interest, is focussing on what can be learned from a complexity perspective that is useful to the problem or issue being investigated.

Language is not neutral, but emerges out of different 'language games' (Wittgenstein, 1953). The images and metaphors we construct are tied to our worldview and this to our languaging practices. Similarly, it is through our use of language that we construct paradigmatic orientations through which we organise our strategic and adaptive responses to the world of our experience. In this analysis, to use different language is to construct different meaning. This argument rebuts the objection that complexity is redundant.

Nevertheless, there is wisdom to be gleaned in seriously responding to the objection. We can ask of ourselves: Am I cognisant of *why* I am choosing a complexity approach? Am I cognisant of *how* I am creating and developing a complexity approach? Are there approaches that would be better suited to the issue under investigation? What is paid attention to, and what is made invisible through a complexity or other approach?

Complexity in Educational Research: Caveats

This final section of the chapter presents a series of five caveats for when considering utilising complexity in educational research.

1. Complexity does not Substitute for Thoughtfulness

Complexity offers principles; it does not substitute for thoughtfulness. Complexity presents preferred ways of thinking about the organisation of the world, while simultaneously pointing to the impossibility of accuracy in knowledge and prediction. I believe this is one of its greatest advantages. Engaged with in this way, complexity fosters reflection and thoughtfulness. Taking complexity as conceptual and theoretical, we engage as imaginative, creative beings in converting complexity ideas into particularities. It is this spaciousness that appeals to me. Complexity in this way does not offer research recipes, 'tried and true', but rather a space for thinking otherwise, for musing on a series of 'as ifs'. Out of a researcher's engagement with complexity, in combination with their history of being and researching preferences, researchers can evolve appropriate complexity inspired or informed research approaches and strategies.

Ulrich (1994) in his critical discussion of what is involved in justifying the validity of research findings, argues that it is not enough to base validity on 'proper choice' combined with 'proper application' of research methods. Ulrich argues that choice of methods should relate to the researcher:

- Understanding his/her own personal quest for improvement;
- Observing the 'primacy of practice' by paying attention to the nature of the domain of inquiry; and
- Recognising the significance of the 'pragmatic axiom' whereby consideration is given to the implications of the research for the domain of investigation.

Ulrich's remarks indicate some of the many inescapably critical judgements made by researchers, by virtue of their engagement in research activities. Complexity does not and cannot prescribe responses for researchers to any of the three points raised by Ulrich.

Complexity is catalytic, enabling rather than determining research processes. In requiring researchers to make links and generate their own thought-out research approaches, engaging with complexity in research can be viewed as fostering cognitive development. I believe it is dangerous when neophyte (and experienced) researchers give over their capacity for critical thinking to others, as is seen when rules of engagement are followed at the expense of critique and thoughtfulness. Complexity, in offering only organisational principles, encourages researchers to:

- engage in critical and reflective discourse about the nature of education and conceptual frameworks, such as complexity science, as well as about impacts and legacies of utilising complexity in educational endeavour; and
- cultivate their latent epistemic resources, through grappling with a range of important and difficult material.

2. Develop Complexity Habits of Thought

To adequately do complexity informed educational research requires researchers to not only familiarise themselves with the language and metaphors of complexity, but to develop within themselves complexity habits of thought. This is necessary, as most people will have been immersed in the predominant western paradigm where linear styles of thinking determine concepts, discourses and theories. The primordial relations of complexity are different from those of Newtonian science (Kiel & Elliott, 1996; Cilliers, 1998), forming different axioms, discourses and theories. As in any new learning, old habits can be difficult to replace because they are so taken for granted, invisible and automatic.

3. Be Aware of 'Is' and 'Ought' Confusion

Often I find that complexity metaphors and descriptions are taken as prescriptive rather than descriptive. Where complexity construes the nature of organic unities, such as individuals, classes, schools or educational systems as self-organising, dynamic and emergent, these characteristics are sometimes interpreted as characteristics towards which we might aspire. Whereas complexity offers explanation of 'how things in fact do stand' (that is, as self-organising, dynamic and emergent), complexity's 'is' is moved into an 'ought', an injunction to change 'how things are' (that is, to make them self-organising, dynamic and emergent). Semetsky, in her paper 'Not by Breadth Alone: Imagining a self-organised classroom', (2005) demonstrates this tendency in writing 'Let me now imagine a classroom which functions in a self-organised manner ...' (2005, p. 30), thus suggesting that self-organisation is not the normal state of affairs. From a complexity perspective, no matter how the classroom functions, it is demonstrating its manner of self-organisation, whether or not the classroom is one in which 'transversal communications flow freely' (Semetsky, 2005, p. 30).

Interestingly, further in the paper Semetsky utilises complexity's 'is' to reinterpret ideas about students' learning. Here there is no 'is and ought' confusion. She states, 'Moreover, by virtue of the complex, interactive and self-organising character of the students' learning process, I suggest the inherent incapacity for students to experience failure at any point within the process. Even when *folded* in conflicting experiences, or precisely *when* enfolded in such an experience, students may learn from this experience rather than perceiving a sense of failure' (2005, p. 31). Staying with Semetsky's classroom, to not confuse 'is and ought' would be to ask something like, 'If we conceive of a classroom as self-organising, how might we participate to promote better coherence between the self-organisation of the students and the aims of the educative institution?'.

4. Complexity and Education are Differently Disposed

It may be argued that there is a fundamental mismatch between complexity and educational enterprise as in essence complexity is descriptive whereas education is normative, or goal-oriented. As stated above, complexity offers organisational principles for describing how the world and humans function. Education, however, is oriented towards achieving certain goals. These goals, many argue, have been continually rehearsed since the time of Plato's *Republic* wherein it was argued that people should be educated in such a way that the outcome would be a just society (Honderich, 1995). Since Plato's time, recurring themes in educational thinking relate to the ideas that: education and individual lives are for the sake of both the individual and the state; education aims to build character as well as intelligence; and that education should transform individuals so as to generate a better society (Honderich, 1995). Egan (1997) similarly suggests that 'educational theorizing' involves 'three significant ideas'. Egan describes these as being 'that we must shape the young to the current norms and conventions of adult society, that we must teach them the knowledge that will ensure their thinking conforms with what is real and true about the world, and thus we must encourage the development of each student's individual potential' (Egan, 1997, p. 3). Again educational enterprise is depicted as a series of things 'we must' do; it is goal driven. In summary, my point is that the difference between complexity and education is that complexity merely describes whereas education aims to make a difference.

Notwithstanding recognition of this statement of difference, research too may be seen as catalytic of change, precisely *through* offering different descriptions. This view has been argued by qualitative researchers (for example, Robottom, 1987; Kuhn-White, 1994). In my own research I came to understand that to enlarge the complexity by which participants (including those identified as the formal researchers) understand their own situation is to facilitate change. Thus description and goal orientation need not be interpreted as incompatibly separate. However, researchers do need to be cognisant of this difference in ethos. Engaging complexity in educational research involves researchers in a complex process of marrying complexity habits of thought with a range of aims. It means recognising that complexity *per se* does not have an ethical intent. It is the researcher who is committed to human betterment.

5. Complexity Does Not Mark the End of Original Thinking

It can often be the case that we come to view the values, assumptions and beliefs of our chosen culture of inquiry as constituting the only correct approach—a dangerous view in light of the human capacity for thinking with originality. Complexity represents one of a range of contemporary modes of understanding and explanation. Taking a broad purview of history, we see time and again the hegemonic ideas of one generation displaced by another. We do well to recognise complexity as socially embedded. Like other paradigmatic orientations before it, complexity represents 'a serious attempt to get in all the phenomena known at a given period' while also reflecting 'the prevalent psychology of an (our) age almost as much as it reflects the state of that (our) age's knowledge' (Lewis, 1964, p. 222). Through critical engagement with complexity we participate in growing or evolving research approaches. We contribute to future 'states of knowledge' (to use Lewis's language) with respect to educational research.

References

Bütz, M., Chamberlain, L. & McCown, W. (1997) *Strange Attractors: Chaos, complexity and the art of family therapy* (New York, John Wiley and Sons).

Cilliers, P. (1998) *Complexity and Postmodernism* (London, Routledge).

Cohen, R. (1995) How Useful is the Complexity Paradigm Without Quantifiable Data? in: A. Albert (ed.), *Chaos and Society* (Amsterdam, IOS Press).

Denzin, N. & Lincoln, Y. (2005) *Handbook of Qualitative Research* (London, Sage).

Dillon, M. (2000) Poststructuralism, Complexity and Poetics, *Theory, Culture and Society*, 17:5, pp. 1–26.

Eenwyk, van J. (1997) *Archetypes and Strange Attractors* (Toronto, Inner City Books).

Egan, K. (1997) *The Educated Mind: How cognitive tools shape our understanding* (Chicago, University of Chicago Press).

Eve, R., Horsfall, S. & Lee, M. (eds) (1997) *Chaos, Complexity and Sociology* (London, Sage).

Freire, P. (1985) *The Politics of Education* (Cambridge, MA, Bergin and Garvey).

Hawken, P. (1994) *The Ecology of Commerce* (London, Phoenix).

Heidegger, M. (1966) *Discourse on Thinking*, J. Anderson & E. Freund, trans. (New York, Harper and Row).

Honderich, T. (ed.) (1995) *The Oxford Companion to Philosophy* (Oxford, Oxford University Press).

Johnson, S. (2001) *Emergence* (Melbourne, Penguin).

Kauffman, S. (1995) *At Home in the Universe: The search for the laws of self-organisation and complexity* (Oxford, Oxford University Press).

Kiel, L. D. & Elliott, E. (eds) (1996) *Chaos Theory in the Social Sciences* (Ann Arbor, MI, University of Michigan Press).

Kuhn, L. (2005) A Critical Reflection on the Legitimacy of Utilising a Complexity Approach in Social Inquiry. Paper presented at the *Complexity, Science and Society Conference*, 11–14 September, Liverpool, UK.

Kuhn, L., Woog, R. & Hodgson, M. (2003) Applying Complexity Principles to Enhance Organisational Knowledge Management, in: D. Nejdet and C. Chiang-nan (eds), *Challenging the Frontiers in Global Business and Technology: Implementation of changes in values, strategy and policy*, (Ne York, Global Business and Technology Association).

Kuhn-White, L. (1994) Action Research Still Has to Buy the Groceries: Some dilemmas in doing action research in an academic setting, in: B. Neville, P. Willis and M. Edwards (eds), *Qualitative Research in Adult Education* (Mawson Lakes, University of South Australia, Centre for Research in Education and Work).

Kuhn, T. S. (1962) *The Structure of Scientific Revolutions* (Chicago, University of Chicago Press).

Lehrer, K. (1997) *Self Trust* (Oxford, Oxford University Press).

Lewis, C. S. (1964) *The Discarded Image* (Cambridge, Cambridge University Press).

Lyotard, J. (1984) *The Postmodern Condition: A report on knowledge* (Manchester, Manchester University Press).

Maturana, H. & Varela, F. (1988) *The Tree of Knowledge* (Boston, Shambhala Press).

Morin, E. (1992) The Concept of System and the Paradigm of Complexity, in: M. Maruyama (ed.), *Context and Complexity: Cultivating contextual understanding* (New York, Springer-Verlag).

Morin, E. (2001) *Seven Complex Lessons in Education for the Future* (Paris, UNESCO Publishing).

Robottom, I. (ed.) (1987) *Environmental Education: Practice and possibility* (Geelong, Deakin University Press).

Sakai, K. (2001) *Nonlinear Dynamics and Chaos in Agricultural Systems* (Amsterdam, Elsevier).

Semetsky, I. (2005) Not by Breadth Alone: Imagining a self-organised classroom, *Complicity: An International Journal of Complexity and Education*, 2:1, pp. 19–36.

Ulrich, W. (1994) *Critical Heuristics of Social Planning: A new approach to practical philosophy* (Chichester, Wiley & Sons).

Wittgenstein, L. (1953) *Philosophical Investigations* (Oxford, Blackwell).

Wolfram, S. (2002) *A New Kind of Science* (Champaign, IL, Wolfram Media).

13
Complexity and the Culture of Curriculum

WILLIAM E. DOLL
Louisiana State University, Baton Rouge

Curriculum, as we know it, has always had a culture: Protestant. That is, since John Calvin in the mid-1500s appropriated the word, obviously Latin in origin, to mean a course, or path, of life (curriculum vitae), instead of a racetrack around which chariots sped (OED online, 2005), the word and concept of curriculum have been embedded in a Protestant, bourgeois, commercial/capitalist culture.[1] The word curriculum, in our educational sense of 'a regular course of study or training, as at a school or university', leading to a degree or certification (OED online, 2005), was first used by a Peter Ramus (Petrus Ramus)—schoolmaster, headmaster, Regius Professor of Logic—in the late 16th century.[2] Ramus' ordering of courses, indeed, all knowledge, is shown in the following Ramist map (or chart).

The word curriculum appears in the center left, classifying and organizing the Seven Liberal Arts as part of the work of philosophy.[3] Prior to such a graphic representation, studies of the *trivium* (grammar, dialectic, rhetoric) and *quadrivium* (arithmetic, geometry, physics and ethics or music) were more loosely organized and there were considerable variations amongst schoolmasters. Utilizing the printing press, Ramus was able to provide—for wide distribution—an organizational chart of his approach to the organization of curriculum, thus 'methodizing' (and indeed universalizing) that which had previously been quite personal. Following in his footsteps, in the early 17th century, the universities of Glasgow (Scotland) and Leiden (the Netherlands)—both strongly Protestant—adopted the concept of curriculum, as a series of disciplinarily oriented courses leading to a degree, here a Bachelor's degree.[4]

Ramus' work in curriculum reform was most controversial: revered by the Protestants, especially the Puritans in England and America for its 'simple order' or 'plain style' (Doll *et al.*, 2005, pp. 26–27; Triche & McKnight, 2004, *passim*), it was dismissed as 'juvenile' and 'textbookish', fit only for 'youngsters in their early teens'—by many university scholars (Ong, 1958/1983, pp. 299–303). The notion of 'textbookizing' knowledge was a major part of Ramus' educational reform effort and part of the legacy he and his followers (of which there were thousands in the late 16th and early 17th centuries) have left us.[5] David Hamilton (2003) makes this point quite explicitly when he states that Ramus' instructional methods have 'served as paradigms in the subsequent history of modern schooling' (2003,

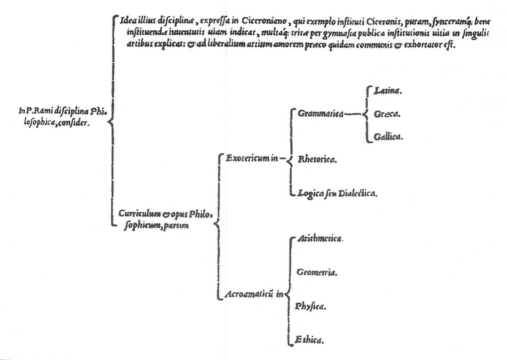

TABVLA ARTIVM, QVAS IN
hoc Volumine coniunximus.

Idea illius difciplinæ, expreffa in Ciceroniano, qui exemplo inftituti Ciceronis, puram, fynceramq, bene inftituendæ iuuentutis uiam indicat, multaq: tritæ per gymnafia publica inftitutionis uitia in fingulis artibus explicat: & ad liberalium artium amorem præco quidam communis & exhortator eft.

In P.Rami difciplina Philofophica, confider.

Curriculum & opus Philofophicum, partim

Exotericum in —

Grammatica —

Latina.

Græca.

Gallica.

Rhetorica.

Logica feu Dialectica.

Acroamaticū in

Arithmetica.

Geometria.

Phyfica.

Ethica.

Figure 1: A Ramist map. Source: P. Ramus, *Professio regia*, Basle, 1576

Abstract). While Ramus was not the first to bring a schooling concept to education, he was among the first in this movement and was undoubtedly the most influential.[6]

Ramus' methods (in both curriculum design and instructional delivery) have a lineage. I and others have argued elsewhere (Doll *et al.*, 2005, Ch. 2; Triche & McKnight, 2004, pp. 53–54) that this lineage runs from himself, through Johann Comenius and René Descartes, into Puritan thought on both sides of the Atlantic, then into New England schooling, to American 19th century schoolbooks and that century's efficiency movement (epitomized by Frederick Taylor), and comes to culmination in what today is known as the Tyler Rationale.[7] This long string of overlapping strands is the background against which we need to place the culture of complexity—a culture which embraces the complex and eschews the 'simplistic [and pietistic] view' of life held by the early founders of America's educational systems.

A reexamination of the Ramus map will show a version of the current corporate line-and-flow chart. Turn the map 90° with the 'philosophy of Peter Ramus' at the north or top, and a corporate chart of organizational responsibilities flows. Power or control flows from the top (the most general) down to the bottom (the particular).

This frame also occurs, although not in chart form, in the Tyler Rationale where broad, general goals permeate all.[8] These goals and their language flow through the whole design. It is this design that dominates most lesson plans teachers are encouraged (often mandated) to develop and use. Virtually all 'methods' courses use this design.[9]

It is interesting to note that in this design the flow is top-down (deductive logic). It could also be bottom-up (inductive logic) but would still need to follow the linear hierarchy set up. Moving abductively, as both Charles Peirce and Gregory Bateson[10] assert human thinking does—across, sideways, diagonally, or skipping over from node to node or idea to idea—is not possible in this frame. In short, Ramus' chart constricts human thinking—certainly it constricts creative thinking – and is an ironic twist on Protestantism's individual interpretation of the Christian Bible. As Andrew Grafton and Lisa Jardine (1986) point out though:

> The individualism verging on hero-worship [of the great teachers] of early humanism gave way in the early seventeenth century to an ideology of routine, order, and above all, 'method'. (p. 123)

This sense of method being an ideology has been explored by myself and colleagues elsewhere (Doll & Gough, 2002; Doll *et al.*, 2005; Triche & McKnight, 2004). There is no better word I know than ideology to explain the fascination, captivation even, Protestant thought had with an ordered and routine 'method'. Peter Dear (1995), in an insightful observation on Protestant method as contrasted with Catholic spirit, says:

> Protestants would not accept the authority of Catholic tradition. Catholics held their tradition to be justified by the continual, behind-the-scenes guidance of the Holy Spirit. Just so, humanisticly informed philosophers had their own functional equivalent of the Holy Spirit. It was something of a consuming interest by the end of the sixteenth century: Method. (p. 121)[11]

I believe the strength of this 'consuming interest', combined with the love of Ramus—he whom Increase Mather called 'that Great Scholar and Blessed Martyr'[12]— which permeated the early American educational scene, helps explain why Frederick Taylor, two centuries later, with his time and motion studies considered it a 'moral duty' to have Schmidt load pig-iron at a rate of 48 tons per day, not at the usual 12 1/2 tons he had previously done.[13]

This Ramist/Protestant sense of method—separating knowledge from oral conversation, and bifurcating such knowledge into a hierarchal sequence of linear steps—has dominated scientific and intellectual thought from the 17th through 20th centuries, and remains a foundation for mainstream pedagogy today.[14]

Chaotic Order

> The law of chaos is the law of ideas, of improvisations and seasons of belief. (Wallace Stevens, 'Extracts')

N. Katherine Hayles in her book on *Chaos and Order* (1991) remarks that in the latter decades of the 20th century an increasing interest in 'the relations between order and disorder (p. 1) developed in both the sciences and the humanities, particularly since the advent of the 'new sciences' (Gleick, 1987; Doll *et al.*, 2005). Traditionally, in a modernist frame, this order/disorder *relation* has been seen as one of opposites; hence from this view, chaos having 'laws' is oxymoronic. By definition chaos is lawless. With the advent of the *new sciences of chaos and complexity*, though, scholars are realizing that both of these sciences are dealing with a complex sense of order, where order and disorder are structurally intertwined. Hayles says that each of these systems (chaos and complexity) deals with 'orderly disorder' (1991, p. 1). Such a phrase is no longer oxymoronic but is, rather, *descriptive*: descriptive of nature and its 'laws'. Hayles further comments, as do I (Doll, 1993), that the chaos/order dichotomous split is but another example of modernism's tendency to categorize. I trace this tendency to Ramus' charting and Aristotle's categorization. Hayles talks only of Aristotle's either/or (excluded middle) logic. Such logic with its sense of domination—right better than wrong—is being challenged today. The name of Michel Serres (1983; Serres & Latour, 1995) comes to mind when one thinks of this challenge. Jayne Fleener's *Curriculum Dynamics* (2002) as well as our *Chaos, Complexity, Curriculum and Culture* (2005) offer insights into both a new logic, one of emergence and its importance for pedagogy (Osberg, 2005).

Important as Isaac Newton's scientific writings have been in the shaping of western science, it is his metaphysical assumptions that have given modernism's cultural milieu its distinctive flavor (Burtt, 1932/1955). Four of these assumptions are (1) that 'Nature is pleased with simplicity'; (2) 'To the same natural effect we must ... assign the same cause'; (3) 'God in the Beginning formed Matter into solid, massy, hard, impenetrable particles'; and (4) that 'Nature is conformable to herself and simple' (cited in Doll, 1993, pp. 20, 33, 36–37). The third listed assumption, that Nature is made of solid atoms, reigned in science from the early 1700s to the early 1900s, at which time quanta concepts produced for us a very different picture (mostly inner space) of the atom. The notion of 'facts' existing as atomistic hardnesses, not as *relations* (as both A. N. Whitehead and Gregory Bateson argue) remains with us still, and dominates our sense of educational 'basics'.[15]

The second assumption, that of cause/effect, shows how in one particular instance chaos theory operates from a different set of presuppositions than do traditional pedagogical theories. Jacob Bronowski points out that since the 18th century a one-to-one relation of cause to effect—small cause, small effect; large cause, large effect—'has been elevated to the rank of the central concept of science', arising as 'its guiding principle ... hence becoming our *natural* way of looking at all problems' (1978, p. 398, emphasis added). Such a mechanistic view (machine metaphor) underlies Pierre Simon de Laplace's linear predictability (understand the initial factors completely and the future history of the cosmos is predictable);[16] behaviorism's deterministic stimulus-response (same effect arises from and indicates same cause); and teachers' faith in direct instruction (limited at best) and its (mis)placed honoring of repetition. Chaos theory, with its emphasis on nonlinearity (most 2nd order and all higher order mathematical equations) helps us realize that 'small causes can lead [not just to small, but also] to large effects' (Hayles, 1991, p. 11). The metaphor here, not mechanistic but dynamic,[17] is that of 'a butterfly flapping its wings in Brazil causing a typhoon in Tokyo'. Such a comment, dealing with the deterministic but unpredictable, is attributed to Edward Lorenz, whose seminal paper—'Deterministic Nonperiodic Flow' (1963)—brought forth the birth of a new science (Gleick, 1987; Bak, 1996; Capra, 1996; Lorenz, 1995) and thereby 'marked a perceptual change which was to alter the face of dynamical systems' (Holton & May, 1993, pp. 98–99).[18] It is this notion of a 'perceptual change'—particularly that dynamically structured—which both Katherine Hayles (1991) and Lee Smolin (2001) emphasize as being so important in seeing the possibilities inherent in chaos and complexity theories.

The first and fourth assumptions, that 'Nature is pleased with simplicity', and that 'Nature is conformable to herself and simple', present not only the sharpest contrast with chaos and complexity theories but also the greatest opportunity for these two theories to develop their senses of being. The simplicity of which Newton speaks has strong Puritan overtones whose worship of 'simple piety' led them to pay great honor to Peter Ramus. In contrast, Prigogine & Stengers (1984) point out that the 'night sky' of today does not show us the simple order of 'stars fixed in their firmament' but shows us rather 'strange objects: pulsars, galaxies exploding and being torn apart; stars that, we are told, collapse into "black holes" irreversibly devouring all they manage to ensnare' (p. 214). In short, the cosmos is turbulent and it is *turbulence* that so fascinated chemist Prigogine. He posits that turbulence, particularly thermodynamic turbulence, with its unstable dynamic and dissipative heat structures actually gives birth to new structures. In Donna Trueit's (2005) sense, *the new* emerges from (indeed needs) the *imbalance* of a dissipative structure. Rather than being conformable to itself in a simple sense, our universe is complexly conformable, continually recreating and transforming itself through the dynamic activity of dissipative structures. 'Orderly disorder' seems to be a fine phrase for this phenomenon, and *imbalance* the state in which this phenomenon occurs.

The phrase 'dissipative structure' is on first look an oxymoron, for with enough dissipation the structure becomes no longer—it wastes away. A heat engine, such as a locomotive, dissipates or wastes energy as it functions. Too much waste or dissipation (escaping of heat/energy) and the machine stops functioning.[19] Lord Kelvin (William Thompson) applied this idea of dissipation to the universe in general, giving us the notion of the universe's 'heat death'—through dissipation of the sun's energy. The second law of thermodynamics states that this wasting away is universal, all objects in the universe tending toward maximum dissipation or entropy. Entropy was one of the big E's of the 19th century (Doll, 1993, ch. 4). But what about living organisms, indeed, living systems? The other big E of the 19th century was Evolution, the progressive development or 'spontaneous increase in organization in living organisms'. Contrasting these two phenomena, Katherine Hayles (1990) comments that Lord Kelvin 'agonized in print over whether living organisms were an exception' to the law of *'universal dissipation'*. He finally concluded it was futile to worry about the matter ... [since] the real phenomena of life infinitely transcend human science' (p. 93).

Ilya Prigogine problematizes the issue of entropy (the dying of the universe) and negentropy (the universe's creative thrust) via his notion of structures far-from-equilibrium—structures which with their inherent unstable dynamics and turbulences (earthquakes, hurricanes, tornadoes, and tsunamis) are *highly unbalanced, but still structured*. Here Prigogine posits imbalance as a source of creativity. In a closed, mechanistic, equilibrium oriented system (as a heat engine) imbalance and disorder are to be avoided, lessened, negated. In an open, living, far-from-equilibrium system (life itself), an orderly disorder is the very source of creativity.[20]

Complexity's Features

Obviously chaos and complexity are intertwined—both accept disorder as a natural part of order, both utilize nonlinear, recursive equations in the mathematical work they rely on, and both see Nature from a non-Newtonian perspective (complex not simple). There are, though, important differences. Chaos theory, often called deterministic chaos theory, uses nonlinear mathematics to study the turbulences of nature (those on the very edge of order/disorder) for the purpose of controlling (at least in the short term) those turbulences. While the determinism it espouses is an unpredictable determinism (due to the myriad of ever changing factors entering any situation or event), the goal is one of control and the *methods* (mathematical in nature) are quite rational.[21]

Chaos theory arose from the turn of the 20th century's three-body problem, one that emerged with the introduction of 'the third' into a dyadic relationship.[22] This is a problem French mathematician Jules Henri Poincaré said was impossible to solve with the conceptual (linear) framework of mathematics of the time: *prediction devient impossible*.[23] Complexity theory, allied with chaos theory through the utilization both make of nonlinear processes (especially iteration and fractal dimensions), came later in the century with the realization that nature itself is fractaled and self-organizing (Bak, 1996). It is these two concepts—fractalness and self-organization—that characterize the 'nature' of complexity.

A Systems View

I will focus here on self-organization and its relation to systems theory, since both chaos and complexity come under the large umbrella of complex adaptive systems (Stanley, 2005, in Doll *et al.*, ch. 5). A modern systems approach is generally credited to Ludwig von Bertalanffy (1901–1972), who formalized his thoughts into a *General System Theory* first in articles in the 1940s and 1950s and later (in a book edition) in 1968. While a practicing biologist all his life—the inventor of the Bertalanffy Method of cellular screening for cancer as a determiner of the need for a biopsy—Bertalanffy was mostly drawn to theoretical biology, which he saw as the interface of biology with philosophy. As his wife, Maria, told him when, as a young student in Vienna, he was deciding what course his career should take: 'A biologist can use what he knows to be a philosopher, but it cannot work the other way around' (in Davidson, 1983, p. 53).[24]

As a theoretical biologist, Bertalanffy was drawn to the notion of organization, particularly developmental organization. Developmental organization, as in evolution, has a hierarchical frame to it.[25] This is to say that the wholeness of the cell, made up of molecule parts, is itself part of a more comprehensive form of organization, the human body, which in turn is part of a social enclave, itself part of a biosphere, etc. Thus, the part-whole relationship is a nested one—each whole, as a collection of interacting elements or parts, being itself part of a more inclusive whole. What fascinated Bertalanffy so much in this doubled relationship of wholes depending upon parts and parts depending upon wholes, is that of elements standing, not alone, but in interrelation. In Chapter 3 of his *General System Theory* (1968) he shows four dots unconnected:

●　●　●　●

and then connects the dots via a linear sequence,

and also as a square.

●—●
|　　|
●—●

He comments that once we see the dots connected, then we know 'not only the elements but also the relations between them' (p. 54). He then goes on to define a system 'as a set of elements standing in *interrelations*' (p. 55, emphasis added). The systems encapsulating these interrelations need to be, for Bertalanffy, *open* systems. While in nature both open and closed systems have external relations, are 'fed' in one way or another by outside forces, closed systems function toward a pre-set goal, such as in the workings of a thermostat. Open systems, in differentiation, function to keep just the right amount of *imbalance*, so that the systems might maintain a creative dynamism. The human body, democratic social systems, and the cosmos itself are all illustrations of open systems. Whereas closed systems 'exchange energy but no matter', open systems 'exchange both energy and matter' (Prigogine, 1961, p. 3) and thus can transform matter into energy, as in an atomic explosion.[26] In simple terms, ones important for education, closed systems *transfer and transmit*, open systems *transform*. Analogously, direct instruction, with its simplicity, would exemplify a closed system approach while interpretative inquiry, with its complexity, would exemplify an open systems approach.

Bertalanffy, with his biological background, definitely advocated the study, in many forms, of open systems. As Davidson (1983, p. 83) notes, Bertalanffy considered his emphasis on and development of open systems to be 'one of his most important accomplishments'. Its importance is certainly evident in Bertalanffy's *General System Theory* (1968) where chapter 6 is devoted to 'The Model of Open System'. In essays put forth under the title *A Systems View of Man* (1981), Bertalanffy makes many cogent remarks about open systems, and especially his belief about their inherent creative power.

Against this background it is quite amazing, but true, that as time went on in Bertalanffy's career he became associated, particularly after the Macy conferences of the post-WW II years,[27] with a closed, mechanistic, engineering view of systems. This view he called 'the darker aspects of this (systems) development' (in Davidson, 1983, p. 208). It remained for Ilya Prigogine and his colleagues to bring forward the positive aspects of open systems, a concept Bertalanffy fathered. The educational implications of an open systems frame are just now beginning to emerge (see Davis & Sumara, 2006; Doll, 1993; Doll & Gough, 2002, with Doll *et al.*, 2005; and Fleener, 2002), and allied with this approach is the work being done by David Jardine, Pat Clifford, and Sharon Friesen, 2003 & 2006).

Quite akin to Jean Piaget's sense of 'equilibration' (a word Bertalanffy uses [1981, p. 36]), Bertalanffy talks of the living organism, the epitome of an open system, as one that "does more than maintain its equilibrium"'. 'As long as it lives, it [the open system] maintains a disequilibrium', a state Bertalanffy defines as 'steady'. Such steadiness though is not the steadiness of a closed, stable system; rather, the steadiness of an open system is a dynamic or unstable steadiness, one where through its own (inter)activity, the system maintains an 'imbalance', neither too great nor too small, but of just 'the right amount' (Doll, 1993, p. 176) for the system to be continually active. In this activity, developmental and progressive, the organism has the power and creative urge to move (transform itself) to 'higher forms of order and organization' (Bertalanffy, 1981, p. 36). In his analysis of this equilibration ('orderly disorder') process, Bertalanffy goes on to make some trenchant and most useful comments about the nature of open systems. An open system, existing in what C. H. Waddington (1957) would call a homeorhetic (as opposed to homeostatic) state, exhibits a dynamic, creative steadiness. This state possesses the power of transformation. Educationally this is not a state of teaching or learning where *mimesis* holds forth, but is one where play, *poiesis*, and possibility reign (Trueit, 2005, in preparation). Bertalanffy goes on to state that while the final conditions of a closed state are 'determined by the initial conditions' [the setting of a thermostat], the further (never final) conditions of transformation in an open system emerge from the long-term interactions within and by the system itself.[28] Educationally such an interactive frame not only calls into question, but actually negates, such time honored practices as setting an I.Q. for each person, averaging grades, and dividing a school into various sequential units. None of these pays attention to transformative development over time. This latter point leads to Bertalanffy's final one regarding open systems—a point central to all of Ilya Prigogine's work. In open systems, especially in the living world, human and ecological, there can be found 'a transition [I'd say transformation] toward states of higher order', states which 'seemingly contradict ... the second principle of thermodynamics' (1981, p. 113). 'Open systems [he goes on to say] may exhibit anti-entropic processes and develop toward states of higher order, differentiation, and organization'.

Complex Organization

> Where monadic physics ends and trajectories become unstable, the world of the irreversible begins, the open world in which, through fluctuations and bifurcations, things are born, grown, and die. (Prigogine & Stengers, 1983, 'Postface' in Michel Serres, *Hermes*)

The systems view is the emerging contemporary view of organized complexity, one step beyond the Newtonian view of organized simplicity, and two steps beyond the classical world views of divinely ordered or imaginatively envisaged complexity. (Laszlo, 1972, *The Systems View of the World*)

One of the most unusual, and most characteristic, features of complex organization is the ability of the complex to develop states of higher (that is more comprehensive) order, differentiation and organization; indeed to create newness from itself via its interactions. In Stuart Kauffman's phrase, the interaction of elements in this complex organization produces 'order for free'. Kauffman, a MacArthur Fellow at the Santa Fe Institute (for the study of complex systems),[29] following in the footsteps of both Ludwig von Bertalanffy and Ilya Prigogine (and certainly alongside those of A. N. Whitehead and Gregory Bateson), focuses on *The Origins of Order* (1993). In this book, the first of three, Kauffman speculates that life began not in Jacques Monod's elegant phrase, as 'chance caught on a wing' (p. xv), nor as the creationists believe as a direct gift from God. Between these two positions, which Kauffman sees as extremes, there lies space for self-organization, indeed self-creation, to arise from 'modestly complex' structures. As he says:

> I want to suggest that we can think of the origin of life as an expected *emergent collective property* of a modestly complex mixture of catalytic polymers, such as proteins or catalytic RNA, which catalyze one another's formation. I believe that the origin of life was not an enormously improbable event, but law-like and governed by new principles of self-organization in complex webs of catalysts. (p. xvi, emphasis in original)

Using Kauffman's ideas as a generative framework (not as a model) for our own educational thoughts I believe it is possible for 'meaning' and 'understanding'—at a deeper, less superficial level than textbooks provide—to come forward in a 'modestly complex mixture', or webs of catalysts. That is, if we modify just a bit A. N. Whitehead's (1929/1967) dictum of 'throwing ideas into every combination conceivable' (p. 2) we might be able to design curricula or instructional strategies where ideas interacting with other ideas will catalyze themselves to develop (create) not only other ideas but ones more adaptable to the issues or problems at hand. As simple and practical (and indeed practiced) as this suggestion is, we have never developed a theory to underpin this suggestion and to carry it forward beyond the cliché of 'brainstorming'. In his next book, *At Home in the Universe* (1995), Kauffman brings forth suggestions around the idea of self-organization, which I believe do help us develop a practical pedagogy based on meaning and understanding arising spontaneously from modestly complex interactions.

The notion of 'modestly complex interactions' is an important one for Kauffman—for while his interactions (computer simulated and biological) are complex, in a *robust and rich* way, they do arise from sets of simples, which, as simples, affect, guide, and ultimately provide a measure of constraint or control over the emergence of the complex interactions.[30] Such modestly complex interactions are generative for those of us using complexity theory to develop educational frames. Before going into some detail regarding Kauffman's argument—that certain (robust) complex systems have a natural 'penchant for exhibiting convergent ... flow' (in Brockman, 1995, p. 337)[31]—I'd like to make a comment about the idea of the sacred, which appears in the opening chapters of his 1995 book and especially in his acknowledgement of the role Johnson played in helping Kauffman 'clarify and structure' his thoughts. As they hiked, together, the rugged landscape behind Santa Fe, chapter after chapter of Kauffman's book emerged.[32] Kauffman even offered Johnson a co-authoring of the book. Johnson graciously declined, writing his own book (1996) on faith and science as Kauffman wrote his on self-organization and complexity. The two books are intertwined though—Johnson talks about Kauffman, while Kauffman echoes Johnson's theme of connecting the sacred with the scientific. To quote Kauffman at the beginning of his book:

> Even though science has advanced over the decades and centuries, 'a spiritual hunger remains', a hunger that cannot be satisfied by science alone but yearns for us 'to find anew our place in the universe ... [a place where] we recover our sense of worth, of the sacred'. (1995, pp. 4–5)

Not many, indeed none I know, have made a connection between the science of complexity and the sacredness of being, yet this is a persistent theme as Kauffman looks at our species and its place or home in the universe. This is a theme, I believe, worth exploring. It is a theme Kauffman returns to in the final paragraphs of his book.

As I have said, Kauffman's scientific and spiritual theme is that in 'living systems' there is an underlying 'deep theory of biological order' (p. 18). When the systems are complex—open and far-from-equilibrium—they may, indeed it is almost certain they will, creatively develop new systems. Order will now emerge 'for free'. Kauffman's theory is deep in two ways—one way is that it applies to multiple situations, those near equilibrium, far-from-equilibrium (which are near the edge of chaos), and even to those in the chaotic realm just on the edge of chaos. For most cellular life 'equilibrium corresponds to death' (p. 21); thus there is neither robustness nor richness to life in an equilibrium situation. I would say the same occurs in teaching where teaching is no more than telling—a situation A. N. Whitehead (1929/1967) calls 'dead', 'inert', 'useless', 'barren' and full of 'mental dryrot' (chs. 1, 2, 3, *passim*).

Behavior in the chaotic realm (where the interactions are more than modestly complex) is overly sensitive to slight changes. Thus, 'any small change in a chaotic system can, and typically does have large and amplifying effects', making such a situation too fragile for any sort of sustained emergence to last (Kauffman, 1995, p. 19).[33] Rather, the robustness of life Kauffman sees outside his Santa Fe window— a 'bubbling activity', rich and generative, an 'ordered complexity'—comes, he believes, from intermediate situations, far-from-equilibrium where 'a kind of collective crystallization of spontaneous structure' emerges (pp. 18–19). This sort of *im*balanced, dynamic situation, one of non-equilibrium (which Kauffman, like Prigogine, believes is the 'natural' one for the universe) is where life and creativity are prominent. This intermediate situation between order and chaos is where self-organization occurs.

The other way in which Kauffman's theory of biological order is 'deep', is that opposed to reductionism and its insistence on the precision of details (a precision Whitehead called 'misplaced concreteness): 'the core phenomena of the deepest importance do not depend on all the details' (1995, p. 18). In the vernacular, focusing on such details leads one to 'miss the forest for the trees', a criticism which can certainly be leveled at the United States' 2000 educational movement of 'No Child Left Behind'.

Taking an approach of 'Unrepentant Holism' (p. 69), Kauffman sets out to explain 'an order whose origin and character ... (are) independent of the details' (p. 18): in other words, this order is ubiquitous throughout the universe, where 'development arises almost without regard to how networks of interacting genes [or elements] are strung together' (p. 18). In common parlance, there are many pathways to development, biological and intellectual; there is no 'one and only way'. Certainly, for an order which 'springs forth', which arises spontaneously from interactions, there is no pre-set way. Whatever 'method' our universe is using for its ordering, it must have flexibility.[34] Kauffman's basic assumption—a metaphysical, sacred,[35] and controversial one—is that inside the universe there is a deep, 'living' order (p. 304)—one of systems self-organizing themselves, via networks, inside these systems, catalyzing themselves (pp. 47–66).

Kauffman approaches his *investigations* (which, incidentally, is the title of his third book [2000]) of self-organizing systems by looking first at the systems structure of Boolean networks. He chooses a Boolean network for its 0 and 1 algebra, which corresponds nicely with switchings (on/off) in both a computer circuit and a genetic, neuronal one. He has spent over three decades *playing with* these structures. Kauffman and his associates apply this structure with its on/off workings first to a network of light bulbs, then speculatively to evolution, and finally, even more speculatively, to social systems.[36]

As a theoretical biologist, Kauffman assumes that 'in a chemical soup', when the number of different kinds of molecules passes a certain threshold—an autocatalytic metabolism suddenly appears (p. 47).[37] To test this hypothesis Kauffman and his colleagues built various circuit boards of connecting light bulbs. The bulbs were connected randomly, one to another: that is, bulb A was connected to bulb B and/or bulb C and/or bulb D, etc. The number of bulbs was labeled N and the connections of each bulb, anywhere from one to twenty, labeled K. Since the connections were random many bulbs, when electrified, became schizophrenic, receiving an order to turn on from one connection and off from another. As electric current was fed into the circuit board, the light bulbs lit—sometimes this lighting produced a stable or 'frozen' state; sometimes the lighting went on and on and on blinking, blinking, blinking with no pattern emerging. To create what he wanted—order arising from random connections ('order for free') Kauffman found he needed a large circuit board with many bulbs (he finally settled on a board of 100,000 bulbs). The connections, though, needed to be sparse—only 1 or 2 connections per bulb. With a higher number of connections, order did not emerge. When many bulbs, though, were connected 'sparsely', the randomness of the blinking bulbs would eventually develop (cycle) into patterns of interesting and varied orders. Kauffman calls this 'order for free' (ch. 4). To quote Kauffman:

> Sparsely connected networks exhibit internal order; densely connected ones veer into chaos; and networks with a single connection per element freeze into mindlessly dull behavior. (p. 85)

Using the above as a heuristic, I interpret the single connection in terms of direct instruction from teacher to student as producing 'mindlessly dull behavior'.[38] From too much richness in curriculum, a chaotic frame emerges. What one needs, from Kauffman's point of view and mine, are networks (or curricular structures) that 'achieve both stability and flexibility' (pp. 86 and *passim*). This notion of a structure or system that aims for stability *and* flexibility is one that has guided my curriculum designs and instructional strategies for the past decade. Obviously this 'and-ness' is in contrast to the Aristotelian logic which has dominated our intellectual thought for so many centuries—namely that logic, epistemology, education should exhibit an either/or (right/wrong) frame. To quote Aristotle's famous phrase: 'An object cannot both be and not be at the same time'. The new science of complexity (Doll, *et al.*, 2005) challenges this dichotomous split.

Educational Implications

In looking at the educational implications I see emerging from the new science of complexity (as well as from the new science of chaos theory), I'd like to go back to Ervin Laszlo's comments about a systems view and 'organized complexity'. In these comments, he mentions (back in the 1980s) that a systems view is the one emerging around organized complexity, a step ahead of the Newtonian/modernist view of organized simplicity, and two steps ahead of the pre-modernist 'classical world views of divinely ordered [and] imaginatively envisaged complexity' (the quote with which I introduced the previous section, Complex Organization). In focusing on organized complexity—Katherine Hayles' 'disorderly order'—Laszlo helps us see contemporary complexity theory's relation to biological, open systems, whence complexity theory emerged. A focus here, I'd say the key focus, is that of relations. The heart of a systems view is one of relations. While relations exist in both pre-modern and modern frames, in neither of these do they take on the dominant role. In a pre-modern world, it is ritual that is dominant; and in a modern world it is observation—reality is what an 'eye-witness' sees. But as I quote in endnote 18, in our contemporary, post-modern world, 'observation disappears in favor of [patterned or webbed] relations': 'relations and their patterns replace observation and its data collection'. Relations then become, to paraphrase Whitehead, the 'really real'. More than just this, relations, in terms of similarities and differences, become the focal point for a developing epistemology. Such an emerging epistemology is aided, indeed guided, by comments made by Bateson, Kauffman, and Whitehead. Once one moves from data collection to relationships, one also moves from isolated facts (with all their 'inertness') to interconnected or webbed patterns (with their ongoing 'aliveness'). Such a switch of focus is illustrated by the way in Fritjof Capra's *The Web of Life* (1996) lies at the heart of complexity science's worldview (Davis & Sumara, 2006).

At the university or college level this has meant for me a caution in using too rigid a syllabus—instead using one which is 'rich' (Doll, 1993, ch. 7) in problematics. The power inherent in such richness is brought forth as students—individually or in groups—work on various texts which web together into a frame that combines closure with openness, *a modest rigidity with a structured flexibility*. As students work on these various texts, the aim is not for all to be on the same page at the same time but, contrarily, for groups within the web to be on different pages, in different texts, at the same time. Embracing complexity, the aim is for a process of cross-fertilization, pollination, catalyzation of ideas. Over time (an important ingredient for both Prigogine and Kauffman) a network of connections and interconnections becomes more and more webbed. Learning now occurs, not through direct transmission from expert to novice, or from teacher to student, but in a non-linear manner through all in a class exploring a situation/problem/issue together (and indeed from multiple perspectives). In Jardine *et al.*'s (2003) phrase, a community of learners is now 'living the world together'. The teacher's role in this community of learners becomes that of both 'planting a seed' and taking a lead (but not overly dominant) role in fertilizing the seed that it may grow (Dewey) to eventually pollinate and catalyze other ideas. In other words, the curriculum (with its expression in a syllabus) is now an emerging one within an ongoing process that actually catalyzes itself via interactions within the system or network. In Kauffman's terms, order now appears freely and naturally (indeed expectedly). Such order is not imposed, as has been the history of curriculum development from Ramus to Tyler to the present day. Order emerges from interactions having just the 'right amount' of tension or difference or imbalance among the elements interacting. Such a 'right amount' cannot be specified; it can only be felt or intuited, or to use Whitehead's (1929/1978) term 'prehended' (ch. 2 and *passim*).

In schooling situations (K–12), where rigid impositions are more common and more defined, other strategies are needed—strategies which can achieve the 'right amount' of interaction among students, teachers, ideas. Two classroom examples might help here. In one third grade classroom the teacher handed out a worksheet which had the following on it:

P I – – O W

The task of the students was to fill in the two blanks with the same letter. The students quickly choose L as the missing letter and the teacher was then prepared to move on to the next example. I asked her to stop a minute and let us explore (complexify) this example. Quite nervous, the teacher agreed—fearful I believe of losing control, especially to a university professor who had just dropped by to observe the two student interns he had placed in the class. I asked the students to find words they could 'see' within the word PILLOW. The class came alive; even the teacher entered. Along with the usual words seen (such as low, plow, pill, ill, po, pi, lip, will, I, pow, poll) we encountered the situation of determining whether WOP, a slang word for one of Italian descent, was allowed. My contribution of Po and PO sent us to the dictionary, which in turn raised the issue of P.O. and P.O.W. Already the learning (on which we had by now spent maybe three minutes) was raised to a new level—with all taking part quite wholeheartedly and even heatedly. To further complexify, I arranged the words chosen in a pattern—two letter words, three letter words, etc. along with those which proceeded in a linear fashion (low) and those which did not (will). New levels of organization arose spontaneously and immediately—my categorization was challenged (as it should have been) and seen as only one of a number of categorizations. Again, the 'time on task' here was no more than a total of five minutes; five minutes that led us into expanded vocabulary, word play, definitions, rules, categorizations. While I would not wish to draw a cause-effect relationship between studying complexity theory in my doctoral seminars and working with (third) grade students in the teacher-education program I direct, I would say that complexity theory (the study of self-organizing systems) has helped me to 'see' beyond the obvious, into that not-yet-seen.

Another example comes from a first grade classroom and has potential to be used in a recursive way through most of the elementary grades and to integrate art with mathematics, as well as to bring in the use of hand-held computers. In this grade (actually Kindergarten in May) the teacher wished the students to have a feel for whole digits that would add up to six: $4 + 2$, $1 + 5$, $3 + 3$, etc. She did this by having oblong disks, red on one side and white on the other. As the students, following her directions (little deviation allowed), would turn over the disks to see four red and two white she would then ask how many disks in all (six, of course). This went on for a while and (again) I asked if we might, as a class, play a bit with the disks. Although horrified (not just worried, but *horrified*) the teacher acquiesced. I asked the students to make whatever combinations they wished of the six disks in from of them. Some did Red, White, Red, White, Red, White (not all did six combinations but that was alright with me at this stage). Since I write poorly I asked if I could use an R for red and a W for white. There was quick agreement and soon we had such combinations as–:

R + R + R + W + W + W.
R + R + W + R + R + W.

With this last combination I asked how many R's and how many W's, and we agreed on:

4 R's + 2 W's.

With these students I (almost) left the exercise at this. I did, though, ask the class if anyone could find a combination if we had two of the six disks colored blue. One bright-eyed little girl said, 'Then we could have:

R + W + B + R + W + B'.

I gave the girl a hug and told the teacher, 'Now I am out of here'. I understand from others she talked of the brilliance of her class and what it was able to accomplish for a whole year after this.

It is obvious that much more than combinations and permutations sit within the six disk framework. One could easily arrange the combinations in a system form:

6 + 0
5 + 1
4 + 2
3 + 3
2 + 4
1 + 5
0 + 6

Starting at the bottom (0 + 6) and counting up the left column, one comes to 7 + ? The closed system (0 + 6 to 6 + 0, counting only whole digits) immediately is opened with the 7 + ?. Either subtraction or negative numbers emerge. Currently our intern students are working on this relationship with their first and second grade classrooms—on a number line, the numeral zero becomes important; it is not 'nothing'.

The six disk objects, of course, do not need to be arranged in a linear or boxed order. Transforming the oblong disks into circles one can arrange the six as is done in bowling:

0
0 0
0 0 0

The addition of another row gives one the 'ten-pins' of bowling as well as Pascal's triangle, which itself can be transformed into a, a^2, $a^2 + 2ab + b^2$, etc. The next line, that of the four circles (the last in the bowling sequence), is of course a trinomial.

If one wishes to go further with this pattern, the Fibonacci sequence can be found to exist within Pascal's triangle. Looking at the difference between the digits in the sequence (1, 1, 2, 3, 5, 8, etc.) one can find this difference attracting itself to .666 or 1.666 (depending on which numeral one wishes to call the denominator). This attraction is, as is well-known, the 'perfect form' which shows up in the architecture of the Parthenon or the proportions of medieval art.[39] Here mathematics in all its beauty and art/architecture in all its (western) beauty intertwine. (Asian and African 'beauty' have different forms.)

As I have said, I would not claim a cause-effect relation between studying complexity theory and teaching for 'that yet-to-be-seen'. I will, though, state my personal experience based on over a half-century of teaching—the study of complexity has opened my eyes to that which I did not see before (to a new and livelier sense of method, one based on seeing more and seeing from multiple perspectives). I now regularly ask myself when I enter a classroom (at any level), 'What can I learn today from this experience?' And I ask of those I am privileged to teach, 'Can you see another way to do/read/interpret what we have just done?' Combined with my personal metaphysical views, also developed while I have been studying complexity theory, I now begin to envision education as:

A fascinating imaginative realm,
Born of the echo of God's laughter,
Where no one owns the truth,
And everyone has the right to be understood. (Milan Kundera, 1988)

Notes

1. While the connection between Protestantism and capitalism has been explored well by Max Weber in his magnificent text, *Capitalism and the Spirit of Protestantism* (1930/1996), only recently has the connection between education and Protestantism been explored. David Hamilton (1989, 1990, 1992, 2003) has taken the lead in this research, which is now being carried on, most ably, by Stephen Triche and Douglas McKnight (2004).

2. I am indebted to Sean Buckreis for pointing out to me that C. Stephen Jaeger in his book, *The Envy of Angels*, dealing essentially with Cathedral schools in the 10th through 13th centuries, uses the word curriculum frequently (although there is no index reference of the word). Jaeger even gives a Latin phrase using the word curriculum: *Quod unicum curriculum pleraque veterum studia sibi vindicarunt.* Translating this phrase as 'Because most studies of the ancients claim for themselves a unique curriculum', it is possible, I believe (following Hamilton, as Triche & McKnight do), to see this use of curriculum as a collection of texts (usually influenced by Cicero), with each school and/or school master having his own unique approach. The notion of curriculum as a uniform and predetermined set of courses all students in the university would follow (for the purpose of acquiring basic mastery in a subject or field) did not come until the early 17th century when Leiden and Glasgow adopted Ramus' uniform *method*. (See Triche & McKnight, 2004.)

3. The Latin writings say:

   TABLE OF THE ARTS WHICH WE HAVE LISTED IN THIS VOLUME
   In the Philosophic Discipline of P. Ramus, Consider:
   (1) The idea of this discipline expressed in the Ciceronian corpus which by the example put into place by Cicero shows the pure way of well instituted learning and explores the many well-trodden faults of learning through public gymnasia and is a certain herald and extortion for the love of the liberal arts.
   (2) Curriculum and Philosophic work separated into:
   • Exoteric (suitable for the general public).
   • Esoteric (suitable only to an enlightened inner circle).

4. At this time, the candidate for the BA, always a male, one with a religious orientation, had to commence teaching before being fully accepted into the community of scholars. Hence our present term, commencement—or beginning of a teaching career. Those with a BA or MA or PhD were all expected to be teachers. Practitioners in the fields of law, medicine, even theology (or religious work) were not university trained.

5. One of Ramus' major contributions to pedagogy, or the study of teaching, was to place the knowledge to be taught into textbook form. Such methodizing is with us today. Virtually a century ago, the philosopher, mathematician, logician, educator, A. N. Whitehead, said of teaching and textbooks:

   In the schools of antiquity philosophers aspired to impart wisdom, in modern colleges our humbler aim is to teach subjects. The drop from divine wisdom ... to text-book knowledge of subjects ... marks an educational failure. (1929/1967, p. 29)

   David Hamilton (2003), commenting on textbooks, says, 'Textbooks contain a deep contradiction: They are *today's* mediation of *yesterday's* knowledge', all in the light of predicting *tomorrow's* future (p. 8). Triche and McKnight (2004) say, '[textbooks] privilege organization, memory and mimicry' (p. 48).

6. The best article I know on describing the relationship between schooling and Ramist methods is that by Stephen Triche and Douglas McKnight (2004). One of their arguments—that Ramus refined (and simplified for practical use), scholastic methods—takes an ironic twist in Kevin Gary's (2006) article. There, Gary points out that 'scholastics favored impersonal and systematic methods' (p. 127). Ramus did not alter this impersonalness; he just simplified the convolutions the scholastics used.

Method with its sense of impersonal objectivity as opposed to Spirit with its sense of personal Being is a dichotomy that goes back not only to Ramus but also to the scholastics who drew heavily on their (Ciceronian) interpretation of Aristotle.

7. Herbert Kliebard (1995) has done exemplary work in analyzing the Tyler rationale and its foundational assumptions. While he does not connect this rationale to either Ramus or Descartes, as I do, his comments about the personal and arbitrary nature of Tyler's goals fits in nicely with Ramus' notion of 'placing first that which is first'; and his comments about the linear ordering (and reductionism) of the rationale's sequence fit nicely with Descartes' 'long chains of reasoning'. For my own comments on the Tyler Rationale, see my essay in Doll & Gough, *Curriculum Visions* (2002).

8. It is interesting to note that in the Rationale—(1) goals chosen, (2) experiences expressing the goals, (3) organization of the experiences, (4) assessment—the assessment is of how well the experiences and their organization are ordered to fit the goals. The goals themselves are not questioned, in either Tyler's or Ramus' frame.

9. For a most interesting study about 'methods' and the nature of 'methods courses' in teacher-training, see Sarah Smitherman, 'Reflections on Teaching a Mathematics Education Course' (2006).

10. American pragmatist, Charles Sanders Peirce (1931), and later British/American anthropologist Gregory Bateson (1979), emphasize the importance of *abduction* in reasoned thought and in learning. Abduction, as an initial and playful phase of thought, arises from surprise or doubt, which itself arises from 'precepts'—pre-conscious senses of *experience*. Abduction, as it develops, leads to hypothesis formation and the pragmatic/scientific method. In itself, abduction is the imaginative, creative *play* of thought necessary for more formal methods of thought to develop (Peirce, 1931, VI, pp. 452–91; Bateson, 1979, pp. 140–55). For both Peirce and Bateson, abductive *play* is necessary for creativity, for learning—especially learning which has a sense of self in it.

11. The Puritan Protestants and the Wesleyan Methodists—rejecting the authority of King and Pope—were strong adherents to Method as 'the Way'—the one and only way.

12. The hero worship of the Colonial Puritans (again see Triche & McKnight, 2004) is really quite amazing. Not only were most theses done at Harvard College in the 1600s and 1700s filled with Ramus influences and citations, but as Perry Miller (1953) points out, it was Ramus to whom 'the Congregational theorist resorted', for every vexing question (Miller in Doll *et al.*, 2005, p. 27).

13. The story of Schmidt, a man 'strong as and dumb as an ox', and his exploitation by Taylor, as well as Taylor's rise and fall as the 'father of American efficiency', and his obsession with the moral implications of such efficiency, is well told by Robert Kanigel in his *The One Best Way: Frederick Winslow Taylor and the Enigma of Efficiency* (1997).

14. Again, I know of no better work than that of Triche and McKnight (2004) to help one understand the nature of Ramus' method and its connection to the 'textbookizing' of knowledge. For an understanding of conversation—its history, power, possibility, and subjugation to the written word—see Donna Trueit, 2005.

It is interesting to note that American pragmatism's 'scientific method', with its emphasis not only on an idea's practical results but also on the origins of an idea in an individual's day-to-day experience, including an accumulation of pre- and sub-conscious registers, sidesteps Ramus' knowledge/person dichotomy. (See Trueit, in preparation, 'Beyond Simple Order'.)

15. David Jardine, Patricia Clifford, and Sharon Friesen (2003) have done a fine job in calling into question just what is basic to teaching a curricular discipline. They assert that what is basic to teaching and learning is not merely the clear presentation nor 'understanding' of a subject's 'facts'—its 'bits and pieces'—but is rather an attitude and an activity. The attitude is one of opening oneself, as teacher or learner, to experiencing the situation at hand; the activity is immersing oneself in the situation fully enough for experiencing to happen (Introduction and *passim*). In such a view of teaching-learning,

the facts of a subject exist not in isolation, separate from one another, but acquire their validity through their contextual relationship with other facts, with the discipline in which they are embedded, and with their relation to those experiencing the facts. Such a hermeneutical view of teaching-learning, while not part of the new sciences of chaos and complexity, is allied with them in offering an alternative to the analytical-referential (Reiss, 1982) frame which has dominated our (educational) discourse since the advent of modernism.

16. Pierre Simon (Marquis) de LaPlace's 1776 statement, as quoted in Mullin (1993, p. 97) is:

> The present state of nature is evidently a consequence of what it was in the preceding moment, and if we conceive of an intelligence which at a given instant comprehends all of the relations of the entities of this universe, it could state the respected positions, motions, and general effects of all these entities at any time in the past or future.

17. The mechanistic system of Newton and others, that which dominated the early phases of the scientific revolution and which has left its metaphysical imprint on western thought since his time is really a simple form of dynamism—a push/pull form. As I have said, this metaphysical legacy is well detailed by Edwin Burtt (1932/1955). That which is commonly called dynamic today is really a complex dynamism, one coming from thermodynamics—dynamics built around heat and its transformative powers rather than a push/pull, reversible mechanism. It is an interesting aside that the potential (and transformative) power of fire/heat, when first developed by James Watt in the late 18th century, was quite an anomaly. The realization of its potential was slow in coming (Doll, 1993, p. 85, fn. 5) and it is only with Prigogine and his colleagues that a new metaphysics, one built around thermodynamics and its 'dissipative structure' has begun to emerge. (See particularly Prigogine, 1997.)

18. Ilya Prigogine (with his collaborative author, Isabelle Stengers) in his Postscript to Michel Serres' *Hermes* (1983) points out that the dynamics of classical systems such as that of Isaac Newton's atoms or Gottfried Wilhelm von Leibniz's monads is but one sort of dynamic system. As Prigogine says:

> Dynamics has discovered today that as soon as the dynamic system to be described is no longer completely simple, the *determinist description* cannot be realized ... . There are dynamic systems of different sorts (p. 150, emphasis added).

In this change, Prigogine and Serres realize that 'observation disappears in favor of relations'. This means that in 'Man's New Dialogue with Nature', to use the subtitle of Prigogine and Stengers' 1984 book, relations and their patterns replace observation and its data collection. This change, revolutionary in its import, educational thought has not yet assimilated.

19. It is interesting to speculate to what degree the second law of thermodynamics is actually based on classical, push-pull dynamics and not on thermodynamics, which may well have transformative powers built into its very structure.

20. Michel Serres, in a most fascinating article (1983, ch. 7), puts forth the proposition that the categorical distinction modernism makes between entropy/negentropy, order/disorder, closed/open, chaos/structure, noise/information, global/local is really one of levels of perception. What one sees at one level—the chaotic noise in a classroom (say)—is seen as structured information at another level. This 'ambiguity function' occurs at the boundaries of any system and has its own 'laws'. To adopt one level only is to place oneself inside a box (or bottle) from which extradition is most difficult. What is needed is a multi-perspectival view, one that moves beyond an either/or dichotomy to accept a both/and frame. Brent Davis considers, in some depth, this issue in his chapter in this collection.

21. The history and nature of chaos is well described by Tom Mullin, 1993 and by Edward Lorenz, 1995.

22. The difficulty Newton's equations of gravity have when a third body—say the moon—is introduced into the dyadic, gravitational relationship of the sun and the earth (or when the sun is introduced into the dyadic, gravitational relationship of the moon and the earth) was well known in Newton's day, indeed by Newton himself. The assumption though was that Newton's calculus (linear in nature) could indeed solve the three-body problem with a few more facts and maybe some equational adjustments. This assumption reinforced the then prevalent belief that the universe was stable, uniform, and simply ordered.

    In 1887 King Oscar II of Sweden asked if one could prove that indeed the universe was stable. Henri Poincaré worked on the problem and to his amazement found that not only could he not so prove, but also neither could anyone else with the mathematics of the day (linear). It would require non-linear mathematics to so prove, and then the proof would be that the universe was not 'simply' stable, but was stable only in a dynamic, non-predictable sense: *Prediction devient impossible.* There are too many works on the history of the 'three-body problem' for me to mention here. One I found most useful was Ian Stewart's *Does God Play Dice?* (1990). Here he not only talks of the 'three-body problem', but also of how, in working on it (early 20th century), Poincaré brought forth the 'whole towering edifice' of topology (p. 64 ff.).

23. David Holton and (Lord) Robert May in their 1993 article point out that back in 1903 Henri Poincaré stated, 'It may happen that small differences in initial conditions produce very great ones in the final phenomena' (p. 97). The power and usefulness of this point, though, lay rather dormant for the next seventy-five years, until mathematical pioneers Tien-Yien Li and James Yorke, Robert May, and Edward Lorenz began (with the use of computers) to see the possibilities inherent in adopting a nonlinear viewpoint.

    Expanding on the notion of the sensitivity of initial conditions, Poincaré in 1905 made a direct challenge to LaPlace's determinism:

    > Even if it were the case that the natural laws had no longer any secret for us we could still know the initial conditions only approximately ... (and since a) small error (in these conditions) will produce an enormous error (later on) prediction becomes impossible—*Prediction devient impossible.* (Poincaré in Doll *et al.*, 2005, p. 137)

24. This section on the life and thoughts of Ludwig von Bertalanffy is drawn mostly from Mark Davidson's *Uncommon Sense* (1983), written with the aid of Maria Bertalanffy. In addition to Bertalanffy's own writings, I have drawn on Erwin Laszlo's *The Systems View of the World* (1972).

25. Davidson (1983) has a nice *bon mot* from Bertalanffy regarding evolution: 'From the standpoint of general biology, the fundamental issue of evolution is not the origin of the species. It is the origin of organization' (p. 91).

    The concept of hierarchy, prominent in evolution as each specie's transformation brings along with it increased ability to interact with (and control) the environment in which we are all enmeshed, also has the unfortunate social connotation (social Darwinism) of one group—essentially white, European males—being 'better' than other groups. The social disasters this linear line of thinking has promulgated are too numerous to name. One chaos/complexity theorist to provide an alternative to this form of thinking is Michel Serres.

26. More on open and closed systems can be found in Doll (1993, Part II and *passim*). The nature of open (thermodynamic) systems underlies all the work Prigogine did in his lifetime, and for which he won the Nobel Prize in Chemistry in 1977.

27. While there are many books on these conferences, held in New York City from 1943–1954, the one I find most informative is N. Katherine Hayles' *How We Became Posthuman* (1999).

28. For Prigogine the long-term interactions of the system inevitably lead—by the very nature of their being long-term (inter)actions—away from equilibrium with its

universality, stability, even deadness, to states far-from-equilibrium where newness (birth) occurs, as time (with its arrow) takes on developmental and irreversible dimensions. Writing with Stengers (1983) and combining their voices with that of Michel Serres they state:

> Nature does not code the universal ... ; there is no code at the equilibrium point. Everything that exists, all the individual bodies that come into being, coded circumstances, tablets with their own law, do so by distancing themselves from the law without a memory of the law of ... the stable and infinite ... , [the law of] equilibrium, thus forgetting the specificity of initial states. (p. 155)

The new laws, those with a memory, arising from the process of equilibration or dissipation or imbalance—inherent in chaos and complexity theories—Prigogine brings forth in his final book, *The End of Certainty: Time, Chaos, and the New Laws of Nature* (1997). These new laws, dialogical and conversational, one's embracing ambiguity and uncertainty, have yet to be studied by educators. Chaos and complexity theories encourage such study.

29. A most interesting book describing this institute is George Johnson's *Fire in the Mind* (1996). Here the connection between the sacred and the complex begins to emerge.

30. Stephen Gould in his critique sees Kauffman 'following in the structuralist tradition' and believes that his '"order for free" is an outcome of sets of constraints'. Daniel Dennett in his critique worries that Kauffman comes close to seeing 'the divine hand of God in the workings of nature' (in Brockman, 1995, pp. 340–341).

31. By 'convergent [not divergent] flow', Kauffman means that what we see (on the surface) as random may well (under certain circumstances) have a deeper hidden order. Finding these certain circumstances (located, Kauffman believes, in open, far-from-equilibrium systems) is one of his main tasks.

32. I am suggesting here, really speculating, on the relation between these weekly hikes the two men took and the 'fitness landscapes', which play such an important role in Kauffman's notion of emergence in evolution, especially in co-evolution—'organisms adapt by genetic changes, [ever] seeking to improve their fitness'. But as we as organisms adapt, 'so do our competitors: [and] to remain fit, we must adapt to their adaptations. In coevolving systems, each partner clambers up its fitness landscape toward fitness peaks' (1995, p. 27). Those organisms/systems which seem most able to adapt and survive (reproduce and have influence) are the ones near (but not on) the 'edge of chaos'. Such far-from-equilibrium systems are the ones Prigogine also studied and called 'dissipative structures' (p. 53).

33. Kauffman sees chaos and complexity as different, with 'chaos as a subset of complexity' (in Brockman, p. 334).

34. It is, of course, this concept of a method having flexibility that distinguishes Kauffman's method from the rigid one of Ramus and Tyler. Flexibility is also the ingredient that keeps Kauffman's method in the looser teleological realm. For more on this realm, see Doll, 1993, p. 82.

35. Near the end of his (1995) book, Kauffman queries: 'Has not our Baconian tradition, which celebrates science as the power to predict and control, also brought us a secular loss of awe and respect?' He then goes on,

> If science lost us our Western paradise, our place at the center of the world, children of God, with the sun cycling overhead and the birds of the air, beasts of the field, and fish of the waters placed there for our bounty, if we have been left adrift near the edge of just another humdrum galaxy, perhaps it is time to take heartened stock of our situation.

> If the theories of emergence we have discussed here have merit, perhaps we are at home in the universe in ways we have not known ... . I do not know if the stories

of emergence we have discussed in this book will prove to be correct. But these stories are not evidently foolish. They are bits and pieces of a new arena of science, a science that will grow in the coming decades toward some new view of emergence and order in this far-from-equilibrium universe that is our home. (pp. 302–04)

36. I shall not in this chapter deal with Kauffman's speculations on the complexity of social systems other than to say that he believes democracy may be the best form of governmental organization possible, not for its perfections, but for its imperfections— ones which keep the system alive, dynamic, ever evolving.

37. This paraphrased comment is much akin to those Prigogine and Stengers (1983) make in commenting on Serres' *clinamen*: 'When trajectories become unstable [as do all laminar flows beyond a certain threshold of velocity] the world of the irreversible begins, the open world in which, through fluctuations and bifurcations, things are born, grow, die'. Here are 'the self-organizing processes that make up nature' (pp. 152 and 154).

38. Obviously a brilliant, even a good teacher, can deliver an outstanding lecture or lesson. Still in this model there is usually a certain passivity on the part of the student (the receiver of knowledge). The subject and object are still split and there is not, to use the phrase of Jardine *et al.*, a 'living of the world together'. Those wishing to embrace complexity (and not all will) will move toward Jardine's frame.

39. Mario Livio (2002) has a fascinating book on this intersection of mathematics and art, including our misreading (as he sees it) of that relationship.

References

Bak, P. (1996) *How Nature Works* (New York, Springer-Verlag).

Bateson, G. (1979) *Mind and Nature: A necessary unity* (New York, Bantam).

Bertalanffy, L. von (1968) *General System Theory* (New York, Braziller).

Bertalanffy, L. von (1981) *A Systems View of Man*, P. LaViolette, ed. (Boulder, CO, Westview Press).

Brockman, J. (1995) *The Third Culture* (New York, Simon & Schuster).

Bronowski, J. (1978) *The Common Sense of Science* (Cambridge, MA, Harvard University Press).

Burtt, E. A. (1932/1955) *The Metaphysical Foundations of Modern Physical Science* (New York, Doubleday).

Capra, F. (1996) *The Web of Life* (New York, Doubleday).

Davidson, M. (1983) *Uncommon Sense* (Los Angeles, Tarcher).

Davis, B. & Sumara, D. (2006) *Complexity and Education* (Mahweh, NJ, Erlbaum).

Dear, P. (1995) *Discipline and Experience* (Chicago, University of Chicago Press).

Doll, W. (1993) *A Post-Modern Perspective on Curriculum* (New York, Teachers College Press).

Doll, W. & Gough. N. (eds) (2002) *Curriculum Visions* (New York, Lang).

Doll, W., Fleener, M. J., Trueit, D. & St. Julien, J. (eds) (2005) *Chaos, Complexity, Curriculum and Culture* (New York, Lang).

Fleener, M. J. (2002) *Curriculum Dynamics: Recreating Heart* (New York, Lang).

Gary, K. (2006) Leisure, Freedom, and Liberal Education, *Educational Theory*, 56:2, pp. 121–136.

Gleick, J. (1987) *Chaos: Making a New Science* (New York, Viking).

Grafton, A. & Jardine, L. (1986) *From Humanism to the Humanities* (London, Duckworth).

Hamilton, D. (1989) *Towards a Theory of Schooling* (London, Falmer).

Hamilton, D. (1990) *Curriculum History* (Geelong, VIC, Deakin University Press).

Hamilton, D. (1992) Comenius and the New World Order, *Comenius*, 46, pp. 157–171.

Hamilton, D. (2003) Instruction in the Making: Peter Ramus and the beginnings of modern schooling. Paper presented at (2003) American Educational Research Association.

Hayles, N. K. (1990) *Chaos Bound* (Ithaca, NY, Cornell University Press).

Hayles, N. K. (1991) *Chaos and Order* (Ithaca, NY, Cornell University Press).

Hayles, N. K. (1999) *How We Became Posthuman* (Chicago, University of Chicago Press).

Holton, D. & May, R. (1993) Chaos and One-Dimensional Maps, in: T. Mullin (ed.), *The Nature of Chaos* (New York, Oxford University Press).

Jaeger, S. J. (1994) *The Envy of Angels* (Philadelphia, University of Pennsylvania Press).

Jardine, D., Clifford, P. & Friesen, S. (2003) *Back to the Basics of Teaching and Learning* (Mahweh, NJ, Erlbaum).

Jardine, D., Clifford, P. & Friesen, S. (2006) *Curriculum in Abundance* (Mahweh, NJ, Erlbaum).

Johnson, G. (1996) *Fire in the Mind* (New York, Vintage Books).

Kanigel, R. (1997) *The One Best Way: Frederick Winslow Taylor and the enigma of efficiency* (Harmondsworth, Penguin).

Kauffman, S. (1993) *The Origins of Order* (New York, Oxford University Press).

Kauffman, S. (1995) *At Home in the Universe* (New York, Oxford University Press).

Kauffman, S. (2000) *Investigations* (New York, Oxford University Press).

Kliebard, H. M. (1995) The Tyler Rationale Revisited, *Journal of Curriculum Studies*, 27:1, pp. 81–88.

Kundera, M. (1988) *The Art of the Novel*, L. Asher, trans. (New York, Grove Press).

Laszlo, E. (1972) *The Systems View of the World* (New York, Braziller).

Livio, M. (2002) *The Golden Ratio: The story of Phi, the world's most astonishing number* (New York, Broadway Books).

Lorenz, E. (1963) Deterministic Nonperiodic Flow, *Journal of the Atmospheric Sciences*, 20, pp. 130–141.

Lorenz, E. (1995) *The Essence of Chaos* (Seattle, University of Washington Press).

Mullin, T. (ed.) (1993) *The Nature of Chaos* (Oxford, Clarendon).

Ong, W. (1958/1983) *Ramus, Method, and the Decay of Dialogue* (Cambridge, MA, Harvard University Press).

Osberg, D. (2005) Emergent Knowledge: A Response to Jacques Daignault's 'Hacking the Future', *Proceedings of the Complexity Science and Educational Research Conference*, November 20–22, Loranger, LA, pp. 5–8, www.complexityandeducation.ca

Oxford English Dictionary (2005) OED Online: http://dictionary.oed.com.ezproxy.library.lsu

Peirce, C. S. (1931) *Collected Papers of Charles Sanders Peirce*, Vols. 1–VI, C. Hartshorne & P. Weiss, eds (Boston, Belknap).

Prigogine, I. (1961) *Introduction to the Thermodynamics of Irreversible Processes* (2nd rev. edn.) (New York, Wiley).

Prigogine, I. (1997) *The End of Certainty: Time, Chaos, and the New Laws of Nature* (New York, The Free Press).

Prigogine, I. & Stengers, I. (1983) Postface in: M. Serres, *Hermes* (Baltimore, Johns Hopkins University Press).

Prigogine, I. & Stengers, I. (1984) *Order Out of Chaos* (New York, Bantam).

Reiss, T. (1982) *The Discourse of Modernism* (Ithaca, NY Cornell University Press).

Serres, M. (1983) *Hermes: Literature, Science, Philosophy*, J. Harari & D. Bell, trans. (Baltimore, Johns Hopkins University Press).

Serres, M. & Latour, B. (1995) *Conversations on Science, Culture, and Time*, R. Lapidus, trans. (Ann Arbor, University of Michigan Press).

Smitherman, S. (2006) *Reflections on Teaching a Mathematics Education Course*. Louisiana State University Doctoral Dissertation.

Smolin, L. (2001) *Three Roads to Quantum Gravity* (New York, Basic Books).

Stanley, D. (2005) Paradigmatic Complexity, in W. Doll *et al.*, (eds) *Chaos, Complexity, Curriculum and Culture* (New York, Lang).

Stevens, W. (1982) Extracts on addresses to the academy of fine ideas, in: *Wallace Stevens: The collected poems* (New York, Vintage Books).

Stewart, I. (1990) *Does God Play Dice?* (Oxford, Blackwell).

Triche, S. & McKnight, D. (2004) The Quest for Method: The legacy of Peter Ramus, *History of Education*, 33:1, pp. 39–54.

Trueit, D. (2005) *Complexifying the Poetic: Toward a* poiesis *of curriculum*, Louisiana State University Doctoral Dissertation.

Trueit, D. (in preparation) Beyond Simple Order: Politically correct curriculum. Paper in preparation for presentation to AERA, Chicago, 2007.

Waddington, C. H. (1957) *The Strategy of the Genes: A discussion of some aspects of theoretical biology* (New York, Macmillan).

Weber, M. (1996) *The Protestant Ethic and the Spirit of Capitalism*, T. Parsons, trans. (Los Angeles, Roxbury).

Whitehead, A. N. (1929/1967) *The Aims of Education and Other Essays* (New York, Free Press).

Whitehead, A. N. (1929/1978) *Process and Reality: An essay concerning cosmology*, D. Griffin & D. Sherburne, eds (New York, Free Press).

14

From Representation to Emergence: Complexity's challenge to the epistemology of schooling

DEBORAH OSBERG,* GERT BIESTA** & PAUL CILLIERS***

*School of Education and Lifelong Learning, University of Exeter, United Kingdom
**Institute of Education, University of Stirling, United Kingdom
***Department of Philosophy, University of Stellenbosch, South Africa

Introduction

In modern, Western societies schooling is almost invariably organised as an epistemological practice. Educational institutions present knowledge about the world 'outside' and for that very reason they rely upon a representational epistemology. This is an epistemology which holds that our knowledge 'stands for' or represents a world that is separate from our knowledge itself. Since the object of knowledge is assumed to exist in a separate space from the knowledge itself, this epistemology can also be considered 'spatial.' In this chapter we show how 'complexity theory'[1] has challenged the spatial epistemology of representation and we explore possibilities for an alternative understanding of knowledge in its relationship to reality. Our alternative takes its inspiration from complexity, Deweyan 'transactional realism' and deconstruction. With complexity we suggest that 'knowledge' and 'the world' should not be understood as separate systems which somehow have to be brought into alignment with each other, but that they are part of the same evolving complex system. This not only introduces the notion of *time* into our understanding of the relationship between knowledge and reality, but also points to the importance of acknowledging the role of the *unrepresentable* or the 'radically non-relational.'

We should make clear, however, that in pointing out the incompatibility between complexity and representational epistemology, we do not mean to suggest that we can do without representations in schools. All we are suggesting is that we need to review the meaning of our representations in the educational sphere, and hence the representational character of schooling. Our interest is primarily in articulating an epistemology that helps us think about knowledge, representation, education and the world that does not result in, or seek, closure. To put it differently, we are trying to articulate a different ethic or 'way of being' in education, that is less concerned with representing the real than it is with living it out in different ways.

This is an argument more complicated than we will be able to develop in full in this chapter. Nevertheless, we have begun to approach this task firstly by providing a very brief account of education as a 're/presentational' practice, in order to make it clear what we are arguing against. Using perspectives from complexity we then show that all representations of complex phenomena ultimately betray their object (see Cilliers, 1998), and in doing this we address the question of what sort of epistemology is required if we would drop the conventional understanding of knowledge as reflecting or representing a pre-given world. We argue that complexity itself suggests an 'emergentist' alternative to representational epistemology. This alternative comes close to Dewey's transactional realism (see Biesta & Burbules, 2003). However it seems to lead to the more radical conclusion that because knowing is transactional, there will always necessarily be something that cannot make its appearance in the domain of representation. That however we order the world, there will always be more ordering yet to come. That there *cannot* be a notion of any final order. To conclude the chapter, we suggest that this alternative to representational epistemology—which could be called an 'emergentist' epistemology—could lead to a different way of understanding educational practice since we find education (becoming educated) is no longer about understanding a finished universe, or even about *participating* in a finished and stable universe. It is the *result*, rather, of participating in the creation of an *unfinished* universe.

Knowledge and Representation

Before discussing our 'emergentist' alternative to representational epistemology, we need to clarify briefly what we mean by representation, since this is an extremely broad concept with an extensive philosophical past. We want to talk about representation in a fairly restricted sense. Firstly, we want to talk about this concept as something external and 'public' (see Hacking, 1983, pp. 132–133). In this regard we are excluding internal mental representations or thoughts. Secondly, we are restricting the concept of representation to include only those forms of representation that claim to be likenesses of the things they represent. This is because external or public representations can include anything that can be examined or regarded, including art-works that aim to distort or challenge conventional understandings of reality. But we also want to stretch the concept a little, to include not only physical objects like drawings, photographs, maps, films, tape-recordings, and scientific or other *models* but also elegant *theories* about electrons, gravitational forces, language and so on. Although one could argue that there is a difference between models and theories, we are purposely conflating these two concepts, since both, in our understanding, are representations which intend to help us understand the world as it *really* is. The purpose of both is to enable our movement towards a knowledge/understanding of what the world is really like, once and for all. It is only when we use *truth* as a criterion to judge between alternative likenesses/representations (rather than, for example, usefulness), and when we understand truth to mean correspondence with reality, that we end up with an epistemology that can be called representational.

In contrast to this representational epistemology—which could also be called a 'spatial epistemology' since it depends on a correspondence between knowledge and reality—we propose that complexity suggests a *temporal* epistemology which implies that the quest for knowledge is not in order that we may develop more accurate understandings of a finished reality, *as it is*. Rather, the quest for knowledge is about finding more and more complex and creative ways of interacting with our reality. Through doing this—through intervening in our own realities—we find out how to create more complex realities with which we can interact in yet more complex and creative ways. The point is that, from a complex systems perspective, there are no final solutions, only ongoing interactions leading to increasingly more complex interactions (and 'solutions'). The key issue, for us, is that this is not how knowledge is commonly understood in Western educational institutions.

Education as a Re/Presentational Practice

Many if not most of our Western, modern educational practices and institutions seem to rely upon a representational epistemology (see Biesta & Osberg, 2007). What is significant here is, first of all, that they rely upon an *epistemology* rather than, say, a political, ethical or relational theory, and thus configure schooling in terms of the transmissions and acquisition of knowledge (there are, of course, some noticeable exceptions, particularly in the more radical forms of progressive education). Secondly, this epistemology is representational in that it is assumed that what is presented in education stands for something else: it stands for something in the world 'out there', and therefore is a representation.

One could argue that from a historical perspective educational practices were initially practices of *presentation* (see Mollenhauer, 1983). For long periods, new generations could learn through direct participation in existing ways of life, by mingling, competing and working with adults in the 'real' world (and in some cultures and settings this is still the way in which new generations learn). Mollenhauer argues, however, that in the sixteenth and seventeenth century the position of children in society changed. What disappeared was the situation in which children were direct participants in life. What emerged instead was a separate sphere or educational world especially for children, where they could be educated for later participation in real life (this first happened for the elites and only by the end of the nineteenth and the beginning of the twentieth century for the masses). Mollenhauer's claim is that it was only when a separate educational world was constructed, that the question of representation became a central educational question. After all, once we take children out of 'real life', but still want to prepare them for 'real life,' we need in some way to represent 'real life' within the confines of the world of the child. Since we obviously cannot get the whole world into the school, we have to select which forms of life to represent in the school. We must select what is valuable from what isn't, and we must then represent this selection in appropriate sequences and formats. It is in precisely this respect that we would say that the central rationale for education is in terms of a representational epistemology: what and how best to represent 'the world'?

There are, however, at least two sets of arguments that, in a sense, challenge the idea of schooling as representation. First, there are arguments from the point of view of learning. The main insight—relatively old, but for some reason education needs to be reminded of it from time to time—is that teaching does not determine learning. What students learn may have a link with what teachers teach, but the two are not necessarily identical. Through their participation in educational practices learners learn much more and much different things than that which they were supposed to learn. This poses a challenge to curriculum makers. The argument from progressive, participatory and 'situated' learning theories is that the only way in which young people can learn meaningfully is if they can participate in 'real world' practices (see, e.g. Lave & Wenger, 1991). Representational curricula, it is argued, are disconnected from the things they wish to represent and therefore devoid of any real, significant meaning. The solution is therefore to do away with the 're' and make educational institutions into places where the world itself is presented.

However, against this 'presentationalist' or 'participatory' position it has been argued, firstly from a conservative viewpoint, that a 'decent' education is not merely about practical work or apprenticeship, but one in which children get access to all the great works *of a particular cultural tradition*. In this regard, even Dewey argued that schools should present a purified selection of the world (Dewey, 1966). Secondly, from a radical viewpoint, it is argued that participatory or presentational forms of learning end up in socialisation and adaptation and make it difficult to create critical distance and therefore result in one-dimensional ways of learning. In this way 'representational' and 'presentational' pedagogies are somewhat (although not completely) opposed to each other—although both strategies are still the two main approaches to education, and perhaps becoming increasingly intertwined (see Biesta & Osberg, 2007).

But there is another argument that challenges the idea of representation. This argument challenges both presentation *and* representation and therefore opens the possibility of thinking about education in a way that gets away from the intertwined presentation/representation approach. This argument is supported by the work of Jacques Derrida—in particular his critique of 'the metaphysics of presence,' more familiarly known as 'deconstruction'—which can be substantiated by arguments from complexity theory (see Cilliers, 1998). According to this line of thinking, both presentational and representational pedagogies rely upon the idea of a world that is simply present and can simply be represented. Derrida would argue that both presentation and representation are examples of the 'metaphysics of presence'—the idea that there is a world 'out there' that is simply 'present' and to which all our understandings (meanings) are in relation. In contrast to this position, deconstruction resists being drawn into and subsumed by any relationship with presence. While deconstruction certainly offers some interesting perspectives on education (see Biesta & Egéa-Kuehne, 2001, for a general overview; and Ulmer, 1985, and Biesta, 2004, for a discussion about deconstruction and educational [re]presentation), we believe that by challenging both representation and presentation, complexity also offers a way out of the dilemmas in the representational approach to education.

Complexity's Challenge to Representation

Complexity's challenge to representation comes from the idea that models of complex systems appear *not* to be representations in the usual sense of the word. They cannot be understood to 'stand for' or depict reality as it really is. There is no isomorphism between the world and our descriptions of it. We would argue that this is also the case with scientific theories which attempt to reduce the world to a system of rules or laws. This challenge to representation, we believe, does not imply that we should attempt to do without representations, but that we need to rethink the status and the purpose of our representations.

The idea that complex models are not isomorphic with the complex systems they purport to represent has been defended in detail by Cilliers (1998, 2001). In a nutshell, the argument is that since we cannot understand something complex in all its complexity (as humans we have limited means and limited time), models, by definition, have to reduce complexity. It is exactly in this reduction that we generate understanding. A model must necessarily be simpler than the thing modelled. Complex systems, however, are by definition 'incompressible': they cannot be 'reduced' without losing something (Cilliers, 1998, pp. 7–10). This, in fact, is the criterion that can be used to distinguish complex systems from those that are merely 'complicated' (a distinction that, although useful, is not unproblematic: see Cilliers, 2000b). Complex systems cannot be reduced, because of the non-linear nature of their interconnections. The information they contain is not in the individual elements making up the system, but *distributed* in their pattern of interactions. This means that if we leave anything out of the system (which we have to do if we want to make a model) we disrupt the information contained in the system. What is more, the elements left out have non-linear relationships with the other elements, and we cannot therefore predict the magnitude of the effects this will have in a deterministic way.

This point can be expanded to general theories which aim at understanding the universe by reducing its processes to a system of rules or laws. Although our understanding is a result of a reduction (of a distributed set of relationships to a discrete set of rules), this reduction is by definition flawed, and therefore our understanding of complex phenomena is never perfect. We can have different models of the same system, but the understanding generated is always a function of the specific model chosen, and there is no meta-model that does this work for us. The choice of models is not arbitrary—some work better than others—but we cannot claim that they are chosen objectively. Understanding, and the model which generates that understanding, go hand in hand (see also Cilliers, 2000a).

We can therefore argue that models and theories that reduce the world to a system of rules or laws cannot be understood as pure representations of a universe that exists independently, but should rather be understood as valuable but provisional and temporary *tools* by means of which we constantly re-negotiate our understanding of and being in the world. We use the term re-negotiate (rather than the term negotiate) because we hold that the process of negotiating our world does not have an end: rather, it results in the creation of a new and different and sometimes more complex world. In this way our negotiations are always already re-negotiations; they are temporary by nature.

Rules and Boundaries in Complex Systems

To use models to get to the answer that our theories are not representations but re-negotiation tools, we first have to be clear about the fact that both models and theories about complex systems are well framed, receive specific inputs and produce specific outputs, and can therefore be considered as closed systems with well-defined boundaries. In contrast, the natural complex systems that we are interested in modelling—such as language, life, economic systems, ecosystems, education, consciousness, and so on—do *not* have clearly defined boundaries. This difference has an impact on the way in which rules operate in these systems.

What is of significance here is that from the fact that models of complex systems can be reduced to rules, it is sometimes inferred that natural complex systems can be reduced to rules (two examples of this kind of inference can be found in Holland, 1998 and Wolfram, 2002, but there are many other examples in the complexity literature). But in fact the only reason rules work in models is because models have well defined boundaries. For example, in a 'closed', non-linear system such as a cellular automaton, where all the initial conditions are very precisely known, and presuming the principle of causality holds, there is only a single trajectory which this system can follow, and the operating rules sharply determine this trajectory. The very same trajectory will be followed every time we have a particular set of initial conditions and rules. The system will produce the same effects time and again, and in this way we can say the output of the system can be accurately represented in terms of the operating rule plus the initial conditions of the system. Our point is that although this may be the case with closed systems (that is, our models and theories), the problem lies in extending such an understanding to natural complex systems, which are open systems, having boundaries that are not clearly defined.

In open systems that interact with their environment and that have interconnections which extend not only internally and between systems, but also across different hierarchical levels, complex behaviour is not so easily reduced to a system of rules. If we assume rules do indeed govern the behaviour of such systems, this would mean that different rules of operation would criss-cross in 'individual' complex systems. So the behaviour of any particular system is contingent on many *different* and overlapping sets of rules (which themselves are emergent products of other interacting complex systems). The problem therefore becomes one of how we can describe or represent or *theorise* a system like this in terms of a single or unified set of rules. The question is how we can represent the behaviour of the system in terms of a set of rules when its output is partially determined by sets of rules to which we have no access (see Cilliers, 2000b, 2001).

This is not to say we *cannot* model or theorise radically contingent systems by looking for their rules of operation. Obviously we can and do, and often successfully, although within limits (e.g. the weather). But we have to acknowledge that to model or theorise any interconnected system we first have to cut it off from the other regularities or systems with which it interacts. We cannot pretend this is not the case. We need boundaries around our regularities before we can model or theorise them, before we can find their rules of operation, because rules make sense only in terms of boundaries. The point is that the setting of the boundary creates the condition of possibility for a rule or a law to exist. When a boundary is not naturally given, as is the case with natural complex systems, the rules that we 'discover' also cannot be understood as naturally given. Rules and 'laws' are not 'real' features of the systems we theorise about. Theories that attempt to reduce complexity to a system of rules or laws, like our models which do precisely this, therefore cannot be understood as pictures of reality.

Representational versus Functional Correspondence

We still, however, have to get from this idea—that models and theories that reduce complexity to a handful of rules are not pure 'representations of reality'—to the idea that they are instead provisional, helpful tools by means of which we re-negotiate our world. We can start with the following question: if our models of complex systems do not reflect reality exactly, why does their behaviour appear to correspond with the behaviour of the system (reality) we are modelling? There are at least two perspectives from which this question can be answered.

First, we could take the traditional perspective that our model represents some real pattern or regularity (albeit a radically interconnected regularity) that actually exists and that all we have done is separate this regularity from 'reality at large.' If we look at the situation like this, we see that if we were to try and represent the behaviour of an isolated 'regularity' in terms of its rules of operation, we would find that the overlapping sets of rules that made the regularity behave in the way it did within the larger interconnected system are no longer accessible to us. If we want our model to behave in the way the interconnected regularity behaved, we have to find not only a new set of rules, but also a new set of initial conditions for these rules to operate upon. And because our model has a boundary, such new rules and initial conditions can be found/named. However, the rules and initial conditions that make our isolated model behave like the interconnected regularity cannot be understood to be isomorphic with the rules operating in the interconnected regularity. The rules of our model may produce the same effect as the interconnected regularity, but it is a completely different set of rules and initial conditions that creates this effect. In other words, regularities exist, we can detect them and even find rules that reliably describe their behaviour, but the rules we find are *pragmatic*, they are not real things, they are not pure reflections of reality. There is no isomorphic relationship between the rule in the model and the rule in the real system (if such 'real' rules even exist). While our models may imitate or simulate the behaviour of an observed regularity (at least for a while), and in this way appear to correspond to reality, we must acknowledge that this correspondence is not representational (or isomorphic) but functional or pragmatic. The ability to explain carries little warrant of truth. Our models are *tools*, not pictures of reality. For exactly the same reasons, theories which attempt to represent natural complex systems in terms of a few rules or laws can also not be understood to reflect the 'real' world. Like our models, these theories are pragmatic. They are tools. However, acknowledging that models and theories are tools rather than representations still doesn't get us to the point where we can say that models and theories are tools that *help us re-negotiate our world*. To do this we need to switch perspectives.

A different way of understanding knowledge—and here we draw on Hacking (1983)—is to say that we don't first 'see' the regularity and then try to describe it by means of a set of rules (which don't really exist) in order to understand it (which would be a rather futile operation, to say the least). Rather we *infer* the existence of a regularity from the nature of our interactions with our environment. For example, we can infer the existence of negatively charged electrons because we can do things with them. We can use them to find out something else.[2] However, the purpose of interacting with our environment is not simply to discover what the real world is like, but to find ways of manipulating our environment, so that we can live in it and change it. It is only through experimenting with our environment—interacting with our world—that knowledge emerges. We 'gain knowledge' not from passively observing, but from actively intervening, or, as Francis Bacon aptly put it, by 'twist[ing] the lion's tail' (quoted in Hacking, 1983, p. 246). From this perspective, knowledge is not about 'the world' as such, it is not about truth; rather, it is about what we can *do* in the world, how we can change it. The former understanding leads us to believe that 'the phenomena revealed in the laboratory are part of God's handiwork, waiting to be discovered' (Hacking, 1983, p. 225), and our models/ theories are reflections of this world. The latter, on the other hand, suggests that any phenomena that are 'revealed' are secondary *effects* of our transactions with our environment, and our models/theories are placeholders that allow us to develop more complex understandings, which in turn enable us to re-negotiate a reality that is becoming increasingly complex as a result of our interventions. We can never 'catch up' with this reality, for each time we make a move in this direction, we create a more complex situation for ourselves. One could say 'acquiring' knowledge does not 'solve' problems for us: it creates problems for us to solve. This represents a significant shift.

We are asked to shift from a spatial or representational understanding of knowledge to a *temporal* understanding of knowledge, where knowledge has to do with the relationship between our actions and their consequences. With the latter understanding there is a split in time rather than in space (that is, the split between mind and world) and so we could call this a *temporal* rather than a spatial epistemology (see Biesta & Burbules, 2003, for details about such a temporal understanding of knowledge and truth). This temporal understanding of knowledge meshes with the idea that our models and theories are not representations of the world as such, but functional or pragmatic *tools* which enable us to interact with the world in more complex ways. In other words, through experimenting with our world, we are led to certain realisations about it which enable us to interact with it differently. This in turn leads to more complex realisations about our world, which may replace those held previously, and so the cycle continues. Through this never ending process of experimenting and rethinking we are able to continuously re-negotiate our own theories, and thus we re-negotiate our position in the world.

Complexity's Challenge to Presentation

We have said that complexity asks us to make a shift from a spatial or re/presentational epistemology to a temporal epistemology. This shift, we believe, brings us to the issue of complexity's challenge to *presentation*. To make this clear we shall review the special way in which complexity understands temporality.

Linear versus Non-Linear Understandings of Temporality

Complexity's understanding of temporality and process contrasts with linear understandings which assume that processes (causal sequences of events) happen over time and so can be understood from *particular* temporal standpoints (with no temporal standpoint being privileged). With this understanding, time is just another variable or parameter that can be applied to the system from without. From a complex systems perspective, however, temporality is not a static variable but an *operator*—functioning from within, an integral part of the structure of the system itself. In other words, structure and process are inseparable. This is illustrated by the concept of emergence, where we find that first, we cannot talk about one set of structures being ontologically prior to and therefore simply 'giving rise to' another hierarchical level of structures, as is the case with a linear understanding of process. With emergence, if the higher (or emergent) level consists of units of the lower level, then they exist simultaneously (Emmeche *et al.*, 1997). Second, we find that emergent features *constrain* the space of possibilities simply by manifesting (ibid.): this is precisely *because* they exist simultaneously with lower level components. In this sense emergent effects must be understood as being imprinted on the lower level components. This sort of 'process' ensures that a complex system has an irreversible trajectory and, more than this, this directionality or historicity is part of the information contained in the very structure of the system itself. It cannot be taken out of the system without destroying the system, which is why structure and process are inseparable in complex systems. The question is, how does this 'emergentist' understanding of time/process affect our understanding of knowledge?

A Complexity Informed Understanding of Knowledge

Before articulating what knowledge could mean from a complex systems perspective, we first need to reiterate that conventional (that is, representational or spatial) understandings of knowledge create a divide between the mind and the world, or between the world and our knowledge of it. Again, we refer to it as a 'spatial' understanding because knowledge is assumed to be 'in the mind' while the object of this knowledge is assumed to be 'out there' in a different place. This understanding of knowledge, however, leaves us with the problem of needing some way of checking that our knowledge or representations of the world correspond to the real world. However, we find we can never be sure that our representations correspond to the real world because every test of our representations simply results in more representations. To attempt to argue for realism at the level of representation is to be locked into a world of representations.

Dewey solves this problem by understanding knowledge and learning in terms of action or, more accurately, transaction (Dewey & Bentley, 1949; Biesta & Burbules, 2003). Although this introduces the dimension of time into our conception of knowledge, it is important to be precise about the temporal character of Dewey's understanding of knowledge. Dewey's point is not simply that learning takes time and that we learn about 'the world' through the effects of our actions. If this were the case we could simply replace the idea of knowledge as a comparison between places (mind and world) with the idea of knowledge as a comparison between events (before and after). The key insight in Dewey's transactional theory of knowing is that the world that comes 'into focus' through our transactions is not a world that is simply 'out there' waiting to be discovered, since this would imply that there is an end to our knowing when the world is perfectly in focus. In fact transaction never stops and hence 'the world' never stops coming into focus. The continuing appearance of reality, in more and more complex guises, one could say, is an *effect* of our interacting in the world, not the starting point.

This situates Dewey's perspective very much within a complex systems framework. In the vocabulary of complexity we could say that knowledge *emerges* from our transactions with our environment and feeds back into this same environment, such that our environment becomes increasingly meaningful for us. This means we cannot have knowledge *of* our environment, once and for all—it is not something we can see, something to look at. Rather, it is something we have to actively feel our way around and through, unendingly. Why unendingly? Because in acting, we create knowledge, and in creating knowledge, we learn to act in different ways and in acting in different ways we bring about new knowledge which changes our world, which causes us to act differently, and so on, unendingly. There is no final truth of the matter, only increasingly diverse ways of interacting in a world that is becoming increasingly complex.

Although we don't have the space to develop this idea here, we believe that the way in which complexity understands the notion of knowledge is congruent with Dewey's transactional realism, and this helps put the observer back in the world as an interested participant rather than a disinterested observer. To put it differently: a 'complexity based' understanding of knowledge helps us towards an 'emergentist' epistemology in which 'the world' and our 'knowledge' of it are part of *the same complex system* (rather than being two separate complex systems, which we somehow need to get into alignment). But a similarity with Dewey's transactional realism is not the end of the story for the epistemology of complexity. There is a further aspect which needs unravelling, and this is complexity's relationship with the radically *non-relational*.

Knowledge and the Radically Non-relational

Dillon (2000) has suggested that both complexity and poststructuralism understand the world as 'radically relational', but that these two positions differ from each other in terms of their understanding of this 'radical relationality'. In his words:

> For complexity thinkers the anteriority of radical relationality is just that, the anteriority of radical relationality ... . For poststructuralists the anteriority of radical relationality is relationality with the radically non-relational. Here the radically non-relational is the utterly intractable, that which resists being drawn into and subsumed by relation, albeit [that] it transits all relationality as a disruptive movement that continuously prevents the full realisation or final closure of relationality, and thus the misfire that continuously precipitates new life and new meaning. There is no relational purchase to be had on the intractable. It resists relation. (Dillon, 2000, p. 5)

However, in contrast to Dillon, we believe that complexity is not oblivious to the 'radically non-relational'. Quite the contrary: 'relationality to the radically non-relational' could be considered *key* to the logic of complex systems.[3] This is evident in Prigogine (1997), who insists that although new order (emergence) results when a complex system explores and finds new ways of working with the initial conditions, and that these initial conditions are provided by the lower hierarchical level—and are 'causal' in this regard—the elements making up the lower level do not provide *everything* necessary for order of a particular kind to emerge at the higher level. In his words:

> The system 'chooses' one of the possible branches available when far from equilibrium. But *nothing in the macroscopic equations justifies the preference for any one solution.* (Prigogine, 1997, p. 68, italics added).

The single actualised version—the 'solution' that is 'chosen' by the system—is always one among a number of plausible alternatives *that happened not to occur.* This means that the 'solution' a system will finally 'settle on' is not a foregone conclusion, but always a matter of chance. To put this another way, the pattern (or organisation) that emerges at the higher level is not only a product of the system's relational past but also of 'something' that is *not present in the system at all.* The combination of the system's relational past with the totally intractable or unrepresentable to produce new emergent order that supervenes on lower levels *ad infinitum* ensures that the system is never in a state where it is fully actualised, is never fully 'present' at any point in time, because an integral part of it is that which is *not* part of it. It therefore remains always in the process of becoming without being (see Osberg & Biesta, 2007, for a more detailed account). This understanding of emergence comes close to key insights, developed by Derrida under the label of 'deconstruction'.

In describing the poststructuralist perspective, Dillon comments,

> for poststructuralist thinkers, not only is there more to life than meets the eye, that 'more' is never something that will ultimately make its appearance in the domain of representation. It is the intractable always already at work within but resistant to representation. Its presence-as-absence spoils the show for representation since it is always already subverting representation's productions. (Dillon, 2000, p. 15)

We believe this is also the case for complexity. Chance is always already at work in complex systems, thereby spoiling the show for representation.

Implications for Schooling

In this chapter we have explored issues of representation and presentation, using complexity theory, Deweyan transactional realism and deconstruction. We have shown how complexity theory challenges the idea and possibility of representation, partly through the idea of incompressibility and partly by showing the problem of attempting to represent open systems (reality) by closed systems (representations, models, theories). The upshot of this is not that we should no longer attempt to develop knowledge, models, or theories—but that we shouldn't think of them as 'copies' of the world 'out there'. Rather, we should understand knowledge, models and theories as tools that we use in engaging with 'the world'. This suggests an epistemology in which time has a central role to play—a temporal rather than a spatial epistemology. We have pushed this argument one step further by also problematising the idea and possibility of 'presentation' and 'presence.' The main step here was to see that time is not a static variable unaffected by systems, but rather an operator in the system itself. By using this line of thinking, and combining it with some insight from Dewey and deconstructive ideas, we suggested that complex systems can only be understood if we acknowledge the 'presence' of something that cannot be presented, that can never become 'present'. Here, as we suggested, our explorations came close to key insights developed by Derrida under the label of 'deconstruction'. Along these lines we have tried to show that complexity theory not only problematises conventional—i.e. representational—ways of thinking about knowledge in relation to reality. We have also tried to show that it is possible to develop an alternative 'epistemology' using key ideas from complexity. In this process we found it helpful to refer to the work of Dewey, whose temporal theory of knowledge and whose transactional ontology show a surprising affinity with ideas emerging from complexity theory and deconstruction. Rather, therefore, than thinking of knowledge as the representation of a world that is somewhere present in itself, our considerations suggest an 'emergentist' epistemology in which knowledge reaches us not as something we receive but as a response, which brings forth new worlds because it necessarily adds something (which was not present anywhere before it appeared) to what came before.

The challenge then is to see what this alternative 'emergentist' epistemology—which we may no longer even want to call an epistemology—would imply for the practice of schooling. What would schooling *actually* look like if we dropped the idea that its overall aim is to ensure the acquisition of knowledge of an already existing reality that is fully present? How might such a practice of schooling actually be 'performed'? Such questions, according to Ulmer (1985), open a search for a 'non-magisterial' style of teaching. When we consider the purpose of schooling in terms of an emergentist understanding of knowledge *and* reality, we must begin to imagine schooling as a practice which makes possible a dynamic, self-renewing and creative engagement with 'content' or 'curriculum' by means of which school-goers are able to respond, and hence bring forth new worlds. With this conception of knowledge, the purpose of the curriculum is no longer to facilitate the *acquisition* of knowledge *about* reality. Acquisition is no longer the name of the game (see

Biesta, 2006; Osberg & Biesta, forthcoming). This means questions about what to present in the curriculum and whether these things should be directly presented or should be represented (such that children may acquire knowledge of these things most efficiently or effectively) are no longer relevant as curricular questions. While content is important, the curriculum is less concerned with *what* content is presented and how, and more with the idea that content *is* engaged with and responded to (see Biesta, 2006). Here the content that is engaged is not pre-given, but emerges from the educative situation itself. With this conception of knowledge and the world, the curriculum becomes a tool for the emergence of new worlds rather than a tool for stabilisation and replication (Biesta, 2006; Osberg & Biesta, forthcoming).

An example of an approach which is supported by the emergentist framework that we have suggested in this chapter can be found in Davis and Sumara's 'enactivist' or 'complexivist' conception of teaching, which aims to 'expand the space of the possible' (Davis & Sumara, 1997). However, while Davis and Sumara have certainly not ignored epistemology in their pedagogical formulation, their theoretical framework (drawing strongly on recent developments in cognitive science, artificial intelligence and second order cybernetics) has oriented them towards a concern with *private* rather than with *public* knowledge. They focus primarily on questions about teaching and learning without questioning the (problematic) assumption that the knowledge taught and learned in schools stands for something more real than itself. By focussing on 'public knowledge' in this chapter, and (i) showing that the way in which public knowledge is thought about in schools aligns schooling with representational epistemology; (ii) offering an alternative 'emergentist' epistemology; and (iii) showing how public knowledge can be understood in terms of this alternative epistemology, we believe we have provided a framework that could serve as a platform from which to launch a series of fruitful discussions between educators and educational researchers who are attempting to articulate an educational ethic that operates some distance away from the representational epistemology of schooling that continues to structure classroom practice in many (Western) societies.

Notes

1. We use the popular term 'complexity theory' only for convenience. In fact ideas from complexity are too diverse to constitute a coherent theory.
2. Hacking (1983, pp. 22–23) gives the example of a super cooled niobium droplet, which, when 'sprayed' with electrons (there are standard emitters with which we can spray positrons and electrons) maintains an electric charge which can be kept going around the ball forever. This means the drop can be kept afloat in a magnetic field, and indeed driven back and forth by varying the field, and one can use a magnetometer to tell exactly where the drop is and how fast it is moving. Whatever 'electrons' are, they have real effects. It is from these effects that we infer their existence.
3. The difference of opinion here is largely a result of different understandings of the notion of 'emergence,' which can be understood in a 'weak' or deterministic sense as explicated, e.g. by Holland (1998) or in a 'strong,' non-deterministic, or Prigoginian sense (see Chalmers, 2006, Osberg & Biesta, 2007).

References

Biesta, G. (2004) Education after Deconstruction, in: J. Marshall (ed.) *Poststructuralism, Philosophy, Pedagogy* (Dordrecht/Boston, Kluwer Academic Press) pp. 27–42.

Biesta, G. (2006) *Beyond Learning. Democratic education for a human future* (Boulder, Co., Paradigm Publishers).

Biesta, G. & Burbules, N. (2003) *Pragmatism and Educational Research* (Rowman & Littlefield Publishers, Lanham, Maryland).

Biesta, G. & Egea-Kuehne, D. (eds) (2001) *Derrida & Education* (Routledge, London and New York).

Biesta, G. & Osberg, D. (2007) Beyond Re/Presentation: A case for updating the epistemology of schooling. *Interchange*, 38:1, pp. 5–29.

Chalmers, D. J. (2006) Strong and Weak Emergence, in: P. Clayton & P. Davies (eds), *The Re-emergence of Emergence* (Oxford, UK, Oxford University Press) pp. 244–256.

Cilliers, P. (1998) *Complexity and Postmodernism* (Routledge, London).

Cilliers, P. (2000a) Knowledge, Complexity and Understanding, *Emergence*, 2:4, pp. 7–13.

Cilliers, P. (2000b) Rules and Complex Systems, *Emergence*, 2:3, pp. 40–50.

Cilliers, P. (2001) Boundaries, Hierarchies and Networks in Complex Systems, *International Journal of Innovation Management*, 5:2, pp. 135–147.

Davis, B. & Sumara, D. J. (1997) Cognition, Complexity and Teacher Education, *Harvard Educational Review*, 67:1, pp. 105–125.

Dewey, J. (1966[1916]) *Democracy and Education* (Free Press, New York).

Dewey, J. & Bentley, A. F. (1949) *Knowing and the Known* (Boston, Beacon Press).

Dillon, M. (2000) Poststructuralism, Complexity and Poetics, *Theory, Culture and Society*, 17:5, pp. 1–26.

Emmeche, C., Koppe, S. & Stjernfelt, F. (1997) Explaining Emergence: Towards an ontology of levels, *Journal for General Philosophy of Science*, 28, pp. 83–119.

Hacking, I. (1983) *Representing and Intervening* (Cambridge, Cambridge University Press).

Holland, J. (1998) *Emergence: From Chaos to Order* (Massachusetts, Helix Books).

Lave, J. & Wenger, E. (1991) *Situated Learning: Legitimate Peripheral Participation* (New York, Cambridge Press).

Mollenhauer, K. (1983) *Vergessene Zusamenhange* (Weinheim, Juventa).

Osberg, D. & Biesta, G. (2007) Beyond Presence: Epistemological and pedagogical implications of 'strong' emergence, *Interchange*, 38:1, pp. 31–55.

Osberg, D. & Biesta, G. (forthcoming) The Emergent Curriculum: Navigating a complex course between unguided learning and planned enculturation, *Journal of Curriculum Studies*.

Prigogine, I. (1997) *The End of Certainty: Time, Chaos, and the New Laws of Nature* (London, The Free Press).

Ulmer, G. L. (1985) *Applied Grammatology: Post(e)-Pedagogy from Jacques Derrida to Joseph Beuys* (Baltimore, Johns Hopkins University Press).

Wolfram, S. (2002) *A New Kind of Science* (Wolfram Media Inc).

15
Educating Consciousness through Literary Experiences

DENNIS SUMARA,* REBECCA LUCE-KAPLER** &
TAMMY IFTODY***
*University of Alberta, Edmonton, Canada
**Queen's University, Ontario, Canada
***University of Alberta, Edmonton, Canada

Several decades ago when one published a literary book in Canada, promotion included flyers sent to prospective readers, reviews in newspapers and magazines, a book launch and, if the author was of sufficient stature among the literati, a cross-country tour and perhaps a nomination for a Governor-General's literary award. In today's digital world, an author will have a promotional campaign that resembles those earlier practices but includes much more. Writers now can expect to have a presence on web pages—their own and their publisher's. Their books might appear on a list of reading groups or on television talk shows; the range of awards and high profile attention has grown. Some of the more popular works now inevitably spin off into extra-textual connections such as film deals and toy franchises— *The DaVinci Code* and the Harry Potter books being two good examples of this phenomenon.

Such evidence points to the continued importance of print literature in Western culture, an importance that has continued to grow along with the number of readers. With the development of computer technology, text has expanded into the digital realm and new options such as literary hypertext or e-literature are gaining a presence. Since it is clear that our attachment to literature is not going to disappear any time soon, one might wonder what it is that secures the presence of this cultural practice.

Lodge (2002) argues that literary novels are an important form that authors have developed to represent the complexity of human consciousness. Referring to the rise of the classic realist novel pioneered by writers such as Henry James, James Joyce, and Virginia Woolf, Lodge describes the tendency of authors to centre the narrative in the consciousness of characters and to use that manifestation as a way to create and develop those characters. A reader of the novel, then, experiences the specific subjective experience, the qualia, of that character in the fictional world. Donald (2001) argues that literary novels are a prime opportunity to engage in 'mind-reading practices': that is, we learn to understand our sense of mind, our consciousness, by observing that others also have minds and that those minds are also aware of other minds. Therefore, in order to develop our self-awareness, we are dependent upon not only our own cognitive processes but also the social and cultural milieu that we inhabit.

The question arises of why educators, and in particular literacy educators, should care about consciousness. If we define consciousness as an emergent property of biology and culture, and if human beings develop self-awareness of their own minds by becoming cognisant of other minds, then we argue that literary experiences create productive mind-reading practices which contribute to the ongoing development and emergence of consciousness, and are as such important for education.

What is Consciousness and What Does it 'Feel Like'?

Contemporary cognitive science now recognises that most of what we would consider conscious thought is actually unconscious in origin (Lakoff & Johnson, 1999; Thompson & Varela, 1991). The knowledge gained through our interactions in the world is not limited to what is noticed by the 'conscious self', but also consists of vast amounts of information perceived by the biological body yet never brought to the level of explicit awareness. It is this embodied knowledge that gives human beings the ability to understand, through mere observation or interaction, how certain patterns are emerging without necessarily being able to explain how one knows. We experience a 'gut-feeling' that cannot be verbalised. Gladwell (2005) describes this form of rapid cognition as 'thin-slicing' (p. 23), a phrase that refers to our unconscious ability to extract patterns from our experiences with very little information.

Epstein (1994) similarly defines the cognitive unconscious as a fundamentally adaptive system that organises and influences behaviour automatically, effortlessly, and intuitively. Our body implicitly stores information from our environment and when a novel situation presents itself, emotional cues (or somatic markers) help us assess and address far more information than we could handle consciously (Damasio, 1999). We experience these neurobiological and neurochemical patterns of response in reactions like 'He's lying' or tacit mood assessments like 'Something doesn't feel right'.

It is important to note that what we are describing as the 'cognitive unconscious' differs from the Freudian conception of the unconscious as a repository for repressed knowledge. In this context, unconscious (implicit) cognition refers to an innate type of processing or mode of operation that is triggered by environmental conditions outside our conscious awareness. The result is neurobiological patterns of response that are much more efficient, and often more reliable, than the ones evoked by conscious thought (or reason) alone (Damasio, 1994; Epstein, 1994).

Damasio (1999) argues that a comprehensive theory of consciousness must address the level at which the 'movie-in-the-brain' (or primary consciousness) is generated as well as the level at which the brain generates the sense/appearance that there is an owner and observer for the 'movie-within-the-movie' (alternately called higher-order consciousness). He defines primary consciousness as a mental pattern, engendered by moment-to-moment experiences, that brings together the object and the self (Damasio, 1999). Edelman (1992) similarly defines primary consciousness in terms of the experiencing self involved in controlling the flow of mental events. Edelman (2004) coined the phrase the 'remembered present' to indicate this sense of true physical time that shapes our primary experience of consciousness. However, immediate experiential awareness fails to capture the uniquely human experience of extended consciousness (Damasio, 1999). This higher-order consciousness represents the integration of remembered, currently perceived, and imagined (projected) experiences. Edelman (2004) argues that this level of consciousness allows us to relate our experiences to a subjectively constructed, yet functionally emergent, experience of self. Although research strongly suggests that neurobiological patterns of response have already competed with one another outside our awareness to bring to the fore the sense of consciousness (self-awareness) we experience at any given moment, our consciousness continues to 'feel' as though it is most directly constructed and developed during moments of conscious senses of self-presence (Damasio, 1999; Dennett, 1996; Donald, 2001; Johnson, 2004, 2005). In other words, although there is now compelling evidence to suggest that consciousness is largely created through unconscious processes, as human beings we continue to be intrigued (and consoled) by the idea that we are largely 'in charge' of our own consciousness, and that we are able to change it at will.

Lodge (2002) argues that we use narrative forms of language to misrepresent the conscious self every time we try to describe it 'because we are trying to fix something that is always changing' (p. 90). However, he also argues that, in the end, we really have no alternative but to embrace the importance of these fictionalised narratives of self. As Fireman, McVeigh & Flanagan (2003) argue, 'The stories we tell to ourselves and others, for ourselves and others, are a central means by which we come to know ourselves and others, thereby enriching our conscious awareness' (p. 3). Yet these stories change as the contexts in which we tell them change. The challenge for human subjects is to try to maintain some sense of personal coherence amid this ongoing contextual/narrative flux. Moving away from the essentialist ideal of a pre-given self-contained 'eye' through which experience is filtered, the 'I' of consciousness emerges in complicity with culture, providing together the means for human beings to create and re-create the narratives that provide temporary coherence to their ongoing experiences.

In this sense, consciousness does not 'regulate' learning—as assumed when we strategise the processes of teaching and thinking—but rather serves to 'narrativise' it, rendering it useful in a social sense (Davis, 2004). From this perspective, consciousness does not merely emerge from the social context: consciousness co-emerges with an ever-evolving densely woven network of relationships. Or, as Donald (2001) argues, human consciousness is an emergent property of the creative collision between cognition and culture. This suggests, then, that a comprehensive definition of consciousness should not only address its physiological reality, but should also attempt a requisite understanding of the subjective experience of consciousness (Donald, 2001; Capra, 2002; Lodge, 2002; Johnson, 2004, 2005). The emergent field of neurophenomenology is developing a hybrid approach to studies in consciousness that attempts to combine non-linear dynamical understandings of neural circuitry with a rigorous analysis of lived experience (Capra, 1002; Damasio, 1994, 1999; Edelman, 1992, 1994; Stewart & Cohen, 1997). The following three themes associated with this 'enactivist' conception of consciousness approach (Capra, 2002; Davis, Sumara & Luce-Kapler, 2000; Thompson, 2001; Varela, Thompson & Rosch,

1991) represent a neurophenomenological understanding of consciousness that illuminates how literary experiences participate in the development of self and self understanding: consciousness is a process; consciousness is everywhere and nowhere; and, consciousness is an emergent phenomenon.

Consciousness is a Process

Abandoning essentialist conceptions of consciousness means rejecting the belief that consciousness objectively exists (Edelman, 1992, 2004; Damasio, 1994, 1999; Stewart & Cohen, 1997; Capra, 2002). This enactivist understanding suggests that consciousness emerges as a result of complex neurophysiological interactions occurring in the brain while also acknowledging that it cannot be explained as merely a product of those interactions. As Donald (2001) argues, the materialist claim that consciousness is 'epiphenomenal'—that is, a mere by-product of the brain's activity that plays no significant role in regulating our behaviour—is no longer adequate. From an enactivist perspective, both consciousness and cognition are distributed across the entire organism embedded in its environment. It has been further argued that the unified sense of self we rely on to control our actions, our consciousness, is an emergent property of both the brain's organisation and its enculturation (Donald, 2001). Simply put, as the culture becomes more complex, so do the neurological and social skills required to navigate it.

Consciousness is Everywhere and Nowhere

The processes that span brain–body–world connections are governed by emergent self-organisation. Although consciousness is experienced as unified and coherent, it is a global process involving the inter-penetrating activities of neuronal populations distributed throughout the brain (Edelman, 2004). Most scientists and philosophers now reject the notion of a 'Cartesian theatre'—that supposed place in the brain where objects are brought into the light of consciousness for a central observer (Damasio, 1999, 2001; Dennett, 1991, 1996, 2004; Stewart & Cohen, 1997). Yet, we continue to cling to mental images that evoke this sense of centrality in consciousness because that is what conscious thought feels like to us. This explanatory gap between the biological and phenomenological realities of consciousness represents the so-called 'hard problem' that plagues the field (Dennett, 1991). How can one theory explain the neural/biological processes that lead to consciousness and also account for the way consciousness is experienced by the individual?

The complexivist notion of 'complicity' allows us to theoretically bridge these two worlds. As developed by Stewart and Cohen (1997), the word 'complicity' represents the structural symbiosis that generates emergent phenomena. It is particularly useful in suggesting the mutuality that exists between neurobiological development and cultural experiences, which, as we have argued, is a relationship that ultimately gives shape to human consciousness. Consciousness is therefore not only organised by the independent human brain but, rather, it is a symbiotic by-product of the complex interweaving of the biological self with a surrounding cultural symbolic web.

Consciousness is an Emergent Phenomenon

From an enactivist perspective, both consciousness and cognition are distributed across the entire organism embedded in its environment. What Thompson (2001) adds to this conception is the idea that the 'higher-order' sense of self that permits reflection and enables us to formulate goals (what Capra [2002] calls 'reflective consciousness') ultimately depends on the 'other' for its emergence. That is, consciousness is not developed from the inside-out, but is instead an intersubjectively open phenomenon.

The open intersubjectivity of consciousness suggests that any act of perception presupposes other vantage points; that is, other possible perceptions that cannot be apprehended by the perceiving individual. As Thompson (2001) explains, 'the very meaning or sense of my perceptual experience refers to the perceptions of possible others' (p. 15). In this way, otherness is an intrinsic part of consciousness even though we may experience it as a unified and self-contained phenomenon. Consciousness does not emerge from the independent and isolated workings of individual brains, but rather is an elaborate process that evolves as the conscious self and the 'other' interweave and unfold in a complex choreography of co-determination.

One key stage in the development of human consciousness is what cognitive psychologists call the Theory of Mind—associated with which is the realisation that others have interpretations of the world that may be similar to or different from our own. Mind-reading is the innate ability to absorb and apply commonsense (folk-psychological) understandings about the minds of others in order to predict and explain behaviour. These patterns of feedback and response become part of a psychology of mind that influences the way we interact with others and the way we come to experience a sense of 'self' in those interactions. We are aware of the richness of our own consciousness by virtue of our ability to imagine the consciousness of others, not the other way around. As Johnson (2001) argues, 'Only when we begin to speculate on the mental life of others, do we discover that we have a mental life ourselves' (p. 202).

According to Donald (2001), the most demanding criterion of consciousness is a certain kind of social intelligence: that is, the ability to cultivate and remember individual relationships within a working social group. This cognitive skill relies on cues from the socio-cultural environment for its development. Successful navigation in social settings requires that we assess the mind-states of others very quickly, interpreting often subtle or ambiguous cues on-the-fly. Johnson (2005) further suggests that this intricate social mapping, like other cognitive capacities, is a product of the brain's inherent plasticity:

> By executing a certain cognitive function again and again, you recruit more neurons to participate in the task. Social intelligence works the same way: Spend more hours studying the intricacies of a social network, and your brain will grow more adept at tracking all those intersecting relationships. (Johnson, 2005, p. 108)

It may be argued that mind-reading is a neurobiological capacity that has evolved in symbiosis with a complex socio-cultural network. In this case, human consciousness need not be limited to the workings of individual brains, but rather, reaches its full potential in relation to and with others as part of a distributed social network (Donald, 2001). Consciousness is therefore an emergent property of an information-seeking human biology in complicity with a complex socio-cultural environment.

Literary Experience and the Creating of Consciousness

In this section, we offer descriptions of two literary texts in order to illustrate how these participate with other forms of culture and with human biology to produce experiences of self-conscious awareness. While we are describing two instances of engagement with texts—one print and the other digital—it is important to note that our understanding of what constitutes literary experience is not limited to engagements only with texts such as these. Instead, literary experience can include any imaginative engagement where individuals are required to engage in extended conversation-like practices. Or, put another way, literary experience can be created during creative processes of mind-reading where the cognising subject expands her or his own conscious awareness through thought experiments about how characters create and interpret their self-consciousness. Non-print media such as feature films, television dramas, situation comedies and so-called 'reality' television shows offer opportunities for this kind of engagement. With popular forms such as reality television, viewers' identifications are not limited to engagements with the television programming: they often supplement their experience with involvement in dedicated chat forums, web-logs and face-to-face conversations with other viewers. As argued by Kress (2003), these multimodal engagements do not so much centralise meaning but, instead, through a process of transduction, facilitate the movement of meaning across modes and genres and, at the same time, create a complex cultural/cognitive web of possible interaction. Emerging from these complex interactions is what one can identify as 'meaning' as well as an experience of 'self-consciousness'. From this perspective, consciousness is not 'caused' by either biology or engagement with the physical world, but rather emerges from human subjects' complex complicity with these bio-cultural hybrid networks.

Literature and the Phenomenology of Consciousness

Although consciousness emerges from the complex interactions of this bio-cultural network and cannot be pinpointed as existing at a particular location, we nevertheless continue to describe a cohesive feeling of consciousness as we develop the narrative that describes our existence. Describing the conscious self is a continual process of revision because it is a malleable 'nexus of meaning' rather than a stable referential core (Kerby, 1991, p. 34).

The first example of a literary experience illustrates this narrative shift in thinking about the self and consciousness by considering a moment in *Mrs. Dalloway*, Virginia Woolf's study of an individual consciousness. The reader lingers in the mind of Clarissa Dalloway during an entire and somewhat memorable day in her life. As she is preparing for a party that is to cap the day, Clarissa looks into the mirror and has a brief moment of insight:

> How many million times she had seen her face, and always with the same imperceptible contraction! She pursed her lips when she looked in the glass. It was to give her face point. That was her self—pointed; dartlike; definite. That was her self when some effort, some call on her to be her self, drew the parts together, she alone knew how different, how incompatible and composed so for the world only into one centre, one diamond, one woman who sat in her drawing-room and made a meeting-point ... . (Woolf, p. 179)

Just before this passage, Clarissa has had a moment of disquiet about turning fifty-two and comes to her dressing table to reassure herself and to 'collect the whole of her at one point'. As she gazes into the looking glass, the reconciliation of her self-awareness requires a sharpening or tightening of her efforts and appearance. Clarissa's sense of consciousness requires precision, composure, and centredness.

While Woolf's novel is a fascinating exploration of the fragmentation beneath the more collected narratives of self and an outward composure, Michael Cunningham's novel *The Hours* (1998) adds a level of imaginative intertextuality to Woolf's conception of consciousness. In this particular passage, Cunningham steps inside the mind of Virginia Woolf herself, creating the inner monologue as she prepares to write *Mrs. Dalloway*. He imagines the consciousness of the writer imagining the consciousness of a character.

> She can feel it inside her, an all but indescribable second self, or rather a parallel, purer self. If she were religious, she would call it the soul. It is more than the sum of her intellect and her emotions, more than the sum of her experiences, though it runs like the veins of brilliant metal through all three. It is an inner faculty that recognises the animating mysteries of the world because it is made up of the same substance, and when she is very fortunate she is able to write directly through that faculty. (Cunningham, 1998, pp. 34–35)

The result is a different depiction of consciousness from that of Clarissa Dalloway.

Through the persona of Virginia Woolf, Cunningham describes an experience of consciousness that also entails an impending sense of union, but it is not 'pointed' or 'dart-like' like Mrs. Dalloway's. Rather it flows, fractal-like and brilliant through all that she is. Much more than the sum of her parts, this 'inner faculty' is attuned to the 'animating mysteries of the world' seeking out the novelty in her experiences. This emergent sense of consciousness as more than the sum of its parts is oriented towards possibility rather than precision. Such a mindset reflects an emergent understanding of consciousness.

E-Literature and the Phenomenology of Consciousness

The second literary experience arises from a research study that one of the authors of this chapter conducted with adolescents, who read a literary hypertext, *Patchwork Girl* (Jackson, 1995), alongside their own e-literature creation using the software,

StorySpace. Luce-Kapler focussed the study on how the adolescents engaged with the fragmentation of the genre, their interpretations of character, and their engagement with fictional consciousness. For this paper, we describe the responses of one of the participants—a sixteen-year-old girl named Stevie—and how her reading of the hypertext became an opportunity to explore different facets of identity—a process that became more evident as she wrote her own story in response.

Patchwork Girl is a satirical feminist reading of *Frankenstein* that offers the possibility that the original disposal of the female monster off Orkney Island was a staged death. In the digital medium, Jackson is able to use text, picture and links to tell the story of a female monster who is created by Mary Shelley instead of Victor Frankenstein. The stitched-together monster becomes a metaphor for a patchwork story where a reader will find herself at times immersed in the consciousness of a monster pieced together from multiple characters. At other times, she will hear the monster's creator, Mary Shelley, and at still others the text itself as it discusses its creation. The hypertext, like the monster, is stitched together with ruptures plainly visible as it invites the reader to explore the mutability of identity.

As she began to read the hypertext, Stevie quickly noticed that she would have to take a different approach. In *Patchwork Girl*, a voice will be present in a textbox but when one clicks on a link, often it will be clear that another voice has appeared but without any introduction to the character, as in this example of two linked texts below:

> *I am buried here. You can resurrect me, but only piecemeal. If you want to see the whole, you will have to sew me together yourself. [graveyard]*

> *Burdened with body parts, your fingernails packed with mud and chips of bone, you slink out of the graveyard. A kind of resurrection has taken place. [out]*

One of the features that *Patchwork Girl* provides is an underlying view of the structure of the text, a feature Stevie relied on. She examined 'all the big parts' in the chart to organise her reading, using the colours of boxes, the names of sections, and the particular linkings. For instance, she focused first on the red boxes because she believed they had a certain importance regarding character and plot. She also quickly recognised that the font sometimes shifted in size according to which character was speaking.

Stevie noted that one of the features of the story she particularly appreciated were what she identified as 'afterthoughts.' In literary work, the writer often deletes those details or relegates them to a back page as she balances the demands of story with the minds of her characters. With hypertext, as Stevie pointed out, the author is able to signal that these are ideas that are part of the character's consciousness but are perhaps not necessarily critical to the story line. She explained:

> In *Patchwork Girl* there was one word 'Dream' and then you clicked on it and the whole thing was in brackets like one long continuing extension. So you can have the same experience reading it as the writer had writing it. It makes you feel closer to the story. That's what I'd really like people to do when they read mine.

In this observation, Stevie recognised that the writer is the one who imagines the consciousness of a character, drawing on the depths of his or her own experience to imagine and create the landscape of another mind.

Stevie searched to find language to describe the opportunities to experience the characters' consciousnesses through hypertext literature. Much of what she drew from were standard literary terms, but it became clear that she was finding them not entirely adequate to describe her experience with hypertext such as when she talked about how *Patchwork Girl* is mostly written from the first person viewpoint of several characters. Stevie commented that when reading first person, the reader thinks of that 'I' being almost like oneself, but with *Patchwork Girl,* there is an ever-shifting cast of first person opportunities that at times can be confusing. When Stevie finally gave an overall assessment of the story, however, she was able to point directly to the notion of how one experiences consciousness through literary engagement:

> I think it works because the whole story is [made up of] thoughts ... . I know that my thoughts bounce from one thing to another—so I think it's a stream-of-consciousness. It's almost like a written portrait of the human mind.

Shifting between the thoughts of three or more minds in the story, Stevie never felt immersed in the reading because the text demanded she attend to who was speaking and to be aware of the mind she was experiencing. She had to be more conscious of her response to the text and how consciousness was represented as, for example, dreams, asides and storytelling. Like a conversation with her friends, Stevie had to remain alert to what was unfolding with a level of awareness different to that which she generally used for reading novels. This attention meant that she also continued to monitor how the text related to her experience and her shifting sense of self-identity. Her understanding became more obvious as she wrote her own hypertext story using *StorySpace.*

StorySpace opens textboxes for the creator to insert text, image, or sound as she links them in whatever pattern she chooses. Stevie's story, titled *Fire,* jumps across time and features a narrator who has no name and a shifting gender, reminiscent of Virginia Woolf's novel, *Orlando.* As with much of Woolf's writing, *Orlando* is another experiment in representing consciousness where the main character is alternatively male and female as s/he moves through different eras. While Stevie was not familiar with the novel, her description of her own work bears real similarities:

> It sort of jumps ahead you know maybe several hundred years and it's the same character but it could be maybe a reincarnation of him or something ... . I was thinking about whether or not to make this in first person because I didn't even know if I wanted it to be a man or woman.

In one section that Stevie identified as being from the female perspective, a reader is introduced to the character and her friend Keziah, who are clearly being considered as slaves for purchase. The character describes herself as meek, serene and silent, and indeed the descriptions have a certain softness about them even though the character is afraid. In contrast, Stevie wrote about an earlier time in history in another section. The character this time is male, as is indicated in this description found in the textbox entitled, 'My Body.'

> I stand above the small stream running through cracks in the earth. It is almost dry now, and soon we'll have to move on. But there is enough water to see my blurred reflection in. Dark skin, hair and eyes glare back at me from the depths. The creature in the reflection has thick skin, a wide jaw, solemn lips. This is me, I think, and I am suddenly struck with a powerful awareness of my existence.

It seemed that Stevie was responding to the more fragmented sense of consciousness present in *Patchwork Girl* by writing her identity- and gender-shifting tale.

If, as Lodge claims, print novels such as those written by Virginia Woolf are our richest representation of human consciousness, how might we understand literary hypertexts? It is worthy of note that in the same essay Lodge characterises human consciousness as essentially narrative in its nature, but a narrative full of *lacunae*. As he puts it, 'We are conscious of existing in time, moving from a past that we recall very patchily, and into a future that is unknown and unknowable' (p. 31). Literary hypertext, through its many metonymies, interruptions and connections, is well suited to represent the sense of self-identity that each of us experiences. As an associative structure, it mimics the associative nature of the brain. In reading *Patchwork Girl*, for instance, Stevie compared the story to the way the mind works, suggesting that it is like a 'stream-of-consciousness' where connected ideas unfold in a type of loose narrative. Unlike streams-of-consciousness, however, hypertext must still have the enabling constraints of a planned structure so that a reader will not abandon the text as ultimately meaningless.

Consciousness, Literary Experience and Education

Human consciousness, defined both as perceptual awareness and the experience of knowing that one has awareness, is not caused by neuronal responses to the environment, and nor does the environment itself cause it. Instead, consciousness is an embodied experience that co-emerges with both the biological and the phenomenological. Following arguments made by Donald (2001), we have argued that one primary way that human beings develop self-awareness of their own minds is by becoming aware of other minds. These mind-reading abilities become fundamental to the continual adaptations that human beings must make in their daily lives. Cultural forms such as the novel and e-literature offer opportunities for readers and writers to practise their mind-reading skills. Engagement with literary imaginative forms, then, is not merely for personal pleasure or for the developing of aesthetic experience; one could argue that literary identifications create productive mind-reading practices that contribute to the ongoing development of the human sense of self-consciousness.

In order for these mind-reading opportunities to be maximised, however, readers need to become aware of their own mind-reading practices. In other words, the process by which their consciousness develops and evolves through literary identifications must become explicit. One way that this is done is for readers to notice how authors use textual forms to create the 'minds' of characters. Readers must become aware of the literary techniques authors use to invent consciousness for characters, and other literary devices they develop to create inter-character relationships within texts.

The now-common reflective response practices that are used in school contexts support a rather superficial attention to these concerns. However, deep understanding of how the imagined and the remembered aspects of human cognition are intimately entwined requires fine-grained critical reading practices, supported by informed dialogue and critical reflection (Sumara, 1996, 2002). While some students are intuitively aware of these relationships, most require careful guidance in learning how to notice the deeper structures of literary forms and how these contribute to the ongoing creation of consciousness awareness. It is through these critical close reading practices that readers develop a more sophisticated understanding of the complex ways consciousness emerges from the alliance between cultural forms, memory and currently experienced perceptual awareness. These insights suggest ways to improve how we might use literary experiences more productively in a classroom setting.

First, teachers need to interrupt the superficial reading practices of students that are now supported by school curricula and mandatory high-stakes testing regimes. Many students use the text to confirm rather than to question their own beliefs, including beliefs about their self-identity. Superficial readings need to be replaced with 'deep readings' that are supported by pedagogical attention to how the literary form is structured and, importantly, how readers become implicated in those forms. Further, readers need to notice how they also network the text with their own memories and imaginings and, in so doing, create new literary forms *and* new levels of self-consciousness.

One way to help readers to notice these complexly nested structures is to ask students to engage in practices of mimicking and copying the forms that they are studying. Good old-fashioned memorising of passages and transposing representations of personal experience onto existing literary plot structures help readers to develop a more fine-grained understanding of how the 'minds' of literary characters are created by authors. Experimenting with writing in different genres such as hypertext introduces readers to the techniques of representing consciousness. By engaging in these 'copying' practices, readers notice not only how form influences perception but also how perception influences form. Further, teachers must help students to understand that all reading requires a certain amount of 'writing' by readers (Luce-Kapler, 2004). Some texts demand more of this than others. In order to maximise the developing of self-consciousness, readers need to develop a body of skills that allow them to engage at many levels with a text and with a variety of different texts. In so doing, readers are not merely expanding what they know: they are also expanding and transforming their own sense of consciousness.

Finally, both researchers and teachers need to remember that access to seemingly unlimited amounts of information does not guarantee that understanding will occur, or that empathic engagement will develop. As Menzies (2005) argues, our wired world has not as promised reduced workload and work-related stress but, paradoxically, has increased it for most. Although we have access to a seemingly unlimited amount of information and are able to be available to communicate digitally at any time, there is a dramatic increase in reports of depression, stress-related physical ailments, detachment from the public world, apathy about politics and social problems, and a general reduction in empathy for others. Menzies suggests that deep understanding of one's own identity depends upon extended engagements with others within social contacts that include physical proximity and opportunities for dialogue.

She further suggests that sites of public education may be one of the last places left for such engagement since these are places where human bodies collect for purposes of communication and inquiry. Although Menzies does not make connections to the literature on human consciousness, it seems that what she is arguing would support the conditions needed for the development of the empathic understanding that is needed in social relationships. Further, it also seems that the importance of deep reading and opportunities for extended opportunities to critically inquire into one's 'imagined' identifications with characters and their situations might help to create not only educated citizens but also more empathic persons. Making time for deep literary engagement and critical dialogue with others around these engagements may be considered what Borgmann (1992) calls 'focal practices'—ways of centring oneself within a community supported by dialogue that has the potential to allow one to feel less fragmented. Creation of these communities requires that learners be able to limit access to information, to slow down, to make time for the difficulty of not knowing what might happen if one stays in one's place long enough to learn about it more deeply.

For educators, complexity science points to structural conditions that one can implement to help students become aware of how self-consciousness does not precede or follow pedagogical encounters: instead, consciousness emerges from the complex nested intertwinings of memory, imagination, and sensation. Like all complex forms, the experience of consciousness is the product of simple processes, ones that teachers can notice and nurture in the context of the classroom.[1]

Note

1. See Davis & Sumara (2006) *Complexity and Education: Inquiries into Learning, Teaching and Research* for a more elaborated discussion of implications of some of the ideas presented in this chapter. See also the 'Complexity and Education' website (www.complexityandeducation.ca) for a comprehensive listing of resources, including a link to the journal 'Complicity: An International Journal of Complexity and Education', a detailed glossary of terms, an annotated bibliography and webliography, educational resources for pre-service and practicing teachers, and an online discussion forum.

References

Borgmann, A. (1992) *Crossing the Postmodern Divide* (Illinois, The University of Chicago Press).

Capra, F. (2002) *The Hidden Connections: Integrating the Biological, Cognitive, and Social Dimensions of Life into a Science of Sustainability* (New York, Doubleday).

Cunningham, M. (1998) *The Hours* (New York, Picador).

Damasio, A. (1994) *Descartes' Error: Emotion, reason and the human brain* (New York, G.P. Putnam's Sons).

Damasio, A. (1999) *The Feeling of What Happens: Body and emotion in the making of consciousness* (San Diego, New York, and London, Harcourt Inc.).

Damasio, A. (2003) *Looking for Spinoza: Joy, sorrow, and the feeling brain* (New York, Harcourt Inc.).

Davis, B. (2004) *Inventions of Teaching: A genealogy* (Mahwah, NJ, Lawrence Erlbaum Associates).

Davis, B. & Sumara, D. (2006) *Complexity and Education: Inquiries into learning, teaching, and research* (Mahwah, NJ, Lawrence Erlbaum Associates).

Davis, B., Sumara, D. & Luce-Kapler, R. (2000) *Engaging Minds: Learning and teaching in a complex world* (Mahwah, NJ, Lawrence Erlbaum Associates).

Dennett, D. C. (1991) *Consciousness Explained* (Boston, New York and London, Little, Brown and Company).

Dennett, D. C. (1996) *Kinds of Minds: Toward an understanding of consciousness* (1st edn.) (New York, Basic Books).

Dennett, D. C. (2003) *Freedom Evolves* (New York, Viking Press).

Donald, M. (2001) *A Mind So Rare: The evolution of human consciousness* (New York and London, W.W. Norton and Co.).

Edelman, G. M. (1992) *Bright Air, Brilliant Fire: On the matter of the mind* (New York, Basic Books).

Edelman, G. (2004) *Wider than the Sky: The Phenomenal Gift of Consciousness* (New Haven, Yale University Press).

Fireman, G., McVeigh, T. & Flanagan, O. (eds) (2003) *Narrative and Consciousness: Literature, psychology and the brain* (New York, Oxford University Press).

Gladwell, M. (2005) *Blink: The power of thinking without thinking* (New York and Boston, Little, Brown and Company).

Jackson, S. (1995) *Patchwork Girl: A modern monster* [Hypertext software] (Massachusetts, Eastgate Systems).

Johnson, S. (2001) *Emergence: The connected lives of ants, brains, cities, and software* (New York, Touchstone).

Johnson, S. (2004) *Mind Wide Open: Your brain and the neuroscience of everyday life* (New York, Scribner).

Johnson, S. (2005) *Everything Bad for You is Good for You: How today's popular culture is actually making us smarter* (New York, Riverhead Books).

Kerby, A. (1991) *Narrative and the Self* (Bloomington, Indiana University).

Kress, G. (2003) *Literacy in the New Media Age* (London, Routledge).

Lakoff, G. & Johnson, M. (1999) *Philosophy in the Flesh* (New York, Basic Books).

Lodge, D. (2002) Consciousness and the Novel, in: D. Lodge, *Consciousness and the Novel* (New York and London, Penguin Books).

Luce-Kapler, R. (2004) *Writing With, Through, and Beyond the Text: An ecology of language* (Mahwah, NJ, Lawrence Erlbaum Associates).

Menzies, H. (2005) *No Time: Stress and the crisis of modern life* (Vancouver, Douglas & McIntyre).

Stewart, I. & Cohen, J. (1997) *Figments of Reality: The evolution of the curious mind* (Cambridge, Cambridge University Press).

Storyspace [Computer software] (Massachusetts: Eastgate Systems, http://www.eastgate.com)

Sumara, D. (1996) *Private Readings in Public: Schooling the literary imagination* (New York, Peter Lang Publishing).

Sumara, D. (2002) *Why Reading Literature in School Still Matters: Imagination, interpretation, insight* (Mahwah, NJ, Lawrence Erlbaum Associates).

Thompson, E. (2001) Editor's Introduction: Empathy and consciousness. *Journal of Consciousness Studies*, 8, pp. 5–7.

Thompson, E. & Varela, F. (2001) Radical Embodiment: Neural dynamics and consciousness. *Trends in Cognitive Science*, 5:10, pp. 418–425.

Varela, F., Thompson, E. & Rosch, E. (1991) *The Embodied Mind* (Cambridge MA, MIT Press).

Woolf, V. (1925/1994) *Mrs. Dalloway* (London, Chancellor Press).

Index